As one of the world's longest established and best-known travel brands, Thomas Cook are the experts in travel.

For more than 135 years our guidebooks have unlocked the secrets of destinations around the world, sharing with travellers a wealth of experience and a passion for travel.

Rely on Thomas Cook as your travelling companion on your next trip and benefit from our unique heritage.

Thomas Cook **language** guides

EUROPEAN PHRASEBOOK

BULGARIAN CZECH FRENCH GERMAN GREEK HUNGARIAN ITALIAN POLISH PORTUGUESE ROMANIAN SPANISH TURKISH

Published by Thomas Cook Publishing
A division of Thomas Cook Tour Operations Limited.
Company registration no. 3772199 England
The Thomas Cook Business Park, Unit 9, Coningsby Road,
Peterborough PE3 8SB, United Kingdom
Email: books@thomascook.com,
Tel: + 44 (0) 1733 416477
www.thomascookpublishing.com

ISBN: 978-1-84848-482-5

First published in 1995 as *The Thomas Cook European Travel Phrasebook*
Reprinted with revisions 1996, 2000, 2001, 2005
This edition 2011

Head of Travel Books: Lisa Bass
Production/DTP: Steven Collins
Original translation by UPS Translations, London, and Transtec, Stamford, Lincs
Original Editor: Giovanna Battiston
New translations for this edition by Atlas Translations, London
Text design and layout, editorial and project management by
183 Books, Peterborough

Cover picture:
(Spain,Andalucia,Feria of Sevilla,woman in traditional dress,man in cart) Bruno Morandi / Getty Images

Printed and bound in India by Replika Press Pvt. Ltd.

CONTENTS

CONTENTS

CONTENTS

CONTENTS

INTRODUCTION

This newly updated phrasebook from Thomas Cook Publishing contains a selection of essential and helpful vocabulary in twelve of the languages most commonly spoken in Europe. In general the English phrase is shown first, followed by the foreign-language translation and then a simple phonetic transcription, which will prove the most useful guide when trying to speak words and phrases if you are not familiar with the language. In cases where the phrase is most likely to be seen on a notice or sign, or spoken by a native language speaker to you, the foreign-language version is shown first, followed by its phonetic transcription and then the English meaning.

Where there is both a formal and informal way of speech, the formal one will be indicated so that no offence could inadvertently be caused.

Each chapter has been divided into themed sections with subheadings for quick reference. You will find shaded boxes which explain essential words that will help you at the station or airport, and while dining out, shopping and driving. Chapters begin with an introduction to the language and some practical details about the language's mother country or countries, and sometimes a few technical pointers on grammar and pronunciation.

Any attempt to speak a few words in the native tongue of these countries is always greatly appreciated by locals, and this phrasebook aims to enrich your travelling experience as well as help with day-to-day essentials.

Good luck!

MAP OF EUROPE

Czech Language(s) found in this book.

English Most useful second language.

RUSSIA
ESTONIA
LATVIA
LITHUANIA
RUSSIA
BELARUS
UKRAINE
MOLDOVA
NORWAY *English*
SWEDEN *English*
DENMARK *English*
UNITED KINGDOM
REPUBLIC OF IRELAND
NETHERLANDS *English*
BELGIUM French, *English*
LUXEMBOURG German, *French*
GERMANY German
POLAND Polish
CZECH REPUBLIC Czech
SLOVAKIA *Czech*
HUNGARY Hungarian
ROMANIA Romanian
AUSTRIA German
SWITZERLAND French, German, Italian
FRANCE French
SLOVENIA
CROATIA
BOSNIA-HERZEGOVINA
SERBIA-MONTENEGRO
BULGARIA Bulgarian
TURKEY Turkish
F.Y.R.O. MACEDONIA
ALBANIA
GREECE Greek
ITALY Italian
PORTUGAL Portuguese
SPAIN Spanish
MOROCCO *French, Spanish*
ALGERIA *French*
TUNISIA *French*

BULGARIAN

INTRODUCTION

Bulgarian is a Slavic language and like Russian, to which it is distantly related, it uses Cyrillic script, which is a development of the Greek alphabet. Russian itself is widely understood in Bulgaria; English and German may also be spoken to a degree in larger cities.

As with Greek, body language can be confusing if you are unaware that Bulgarians traditionally nod their heads up and down to signify no and shake them from side to side to mean yes. However, Bulgarians who are familiar with Western influences – younger people and those working in the main tourist resorts – often do the opposite, so be careful that you have understood correctly.

Addresses for Travel and Tourist Information

Australia: *Consulate-General,* 14 Carlotta Road, Double Bay, Sydney NSW 2028; tel: (02) 327 7592; fax: (02) 327 8067.

Canada: *Embassy,* 325 Steward Street, Ottawa, Ontario N1K 6K5; tel: (613) 789 3215; fax: (613) 789 3524.

South Africa: *Embassy,* Techno Plaza E., 305 Brooks St, Melo Park, Pretoria 0102; tel: (12) 342 3720; fax: (12) 324 3721.

UK: *Bulgarian Tourism Office,* 186–188 Queen's Gate, London SW7 5HL; tel: (020) 7589 8402; fax: (020) 7589 4875.

USA: *Bulgarian Tourist Information Center,* 41 E. 42nd St #508, New York, NY 10017; tel: (212) 573 5530.

Official tourism website: www.bulgariatravel.org.

Bulgaria Facts

CAPITAL: Sofia

CURRENCY: Leva (Lv.); 1 Lev = 100 stotinki, obtainable only in Bulgaria.

OPENING HOURS: Banks: Mon–Fri 0900–1600. Some exchange offices open weekends. Shops: Mon–Fri 0900–1900, Sat 0900–1300, closed 1200–1400 outside major towns. Museums: vary widely, but often 1000– 1730, closed 1 hour lunchtimes and sometimes one whole weekday.

TELEPHONES: To dial in, + 359. Outgoing, 00 and the country code. Police, 166. Fire, 160. Ambulance, 150.

PUBLIC HOLIDAYS: 1 Jan; 3 Mar; Orthodox Good Friday and Easter Sunday; 6, 24 May; 6, 22 Sept; 1 Nov; 25 Dec.

Technical Language Hints

- Adjectives always agree in gender and number with the noun. For example: "this beautiful house" – 'тази красива къща'
- There is no word for the indefinite article "a"; instead, you use "the" and add a special ending to the noun itself to indicate either one of the three genders (masculine, feminine or neuter) or plural. These are the endings you would apply:
- if the noun is masculine and singular: ending would be either '-а', '-ът' or '-ят', e.g. 'влакът' – 'the train'
- if the noun is feminine and singular, the ending would be '-та', e.g. 'къщата' – 'the house'
- if the noun is neuter and singular, the ending would be '-то', e.g. 'морето' – 'the sea'
- and if it is plural, the ending becomes either '-ите' or '-ете', for feminine and masculine, e.g. 'къщите', or '-ата' for neuter, e.g. 'моретата' – 'the seas'

ESSENTIALS

Alphabet and Pronunciation

	Name	Pronounced
А а	*ah*	long a as in father
Б б	*bah*	like English b
В в	*vah*	like English v
Г г	*gah*	like English g
Д д	*dah*	like English d
Е е	*eh*	short e as in bet
Ж ж	*zhe*	zh sound as in measure
З з	*ze*	like English z
И и	*ee*	short i as in bit
Й й	*iy*	y as in yet
К к	*kah*	like English k
Л л	*lah*	like English l
М м	*meh*	like English m
Н н	*neh*	like English n
О о	*o*	short o as in lock
П п	*pe*	like English p
Р р	*re*	like English r
С с	*ce*	hard s as in sit
Т т	*te*	like English t
У у	*ou*	u as in put
Ф ф	*fa*	like English f
Х х	*ha*	h as in hot
Ц ц	*tsa*	ts as in cats
Ч ч	*ch*	ch as in chair
Ш ш	*sh*	sh as in shoe
Щ щ	*sht*	sht as in ashtray
Ъ ъ	*eu*	er sound as in fur
Ь ь	*y*	y as in mayor
Ю ю	*yu*	yu sound as in tune
Я я	*ya*	ya sound as in yard

Basic Words and Phrases

Yes
Да
Dah

No
Не
Neh

Please
Моля
Molya

Thank you
Благодаря
Blagodarya

Hello
Здравейте
Zdraveiteh

Goodbye
Довиждане
Dovizhdaneh

Excuse me
Извинете
Izvinyavaite

Sorry
Съжалявам
Sazhalyavam

How
Как
Kak

When
Кога
Kogah

Why
Защо
Zashto

What
Какво
Kakvo

Who
Кой
Koy

That's O.K.
Няма проблеми
Nyama problemi

Perhaps
Може би
Mozhe bi

To
До
Doh

From
От
Ot

Here
Тук
Tuk

There
Там
Tam

I don't understand
Не разбирам
Neh razbiram

I don't speak Bulgarian
Не говоря български
Ne govoryah bulgarski

Do you speak English?
Говорите ли английски?
Govoriteh li angleeski?

Can you please write it down?
Може ли да го напишете?
Mozhe li da go napisheteh?

Please can you speak more slowly?
Моля, може ли да говорите по-бавно?
Molya, mozhe li dah govoriteh po-bavno?

Greetings

Good Morning/ Good Afternoon/ Good Evening/Good Night
Добро утро/Добър ден/ Добър вечер/Лека нощ/ Лека нощ
Dobro utro/Dobar den/Dobar vecher/Lekah nosht/Lekah nosht

Pleased to meet you
Приятно ми е да се запознаем
Priatno mi eh da se zapoznaem

How are you?
Как сте?
Kak steh?

I am well, thank you. And you?
Аз съм добе, благодаря. А Вие?
Az sam dobreh, blagodarya. A Vieh?

My name is ...
Казвам се ...
Kazvam se ...

This is my friend/boyfriend/ girlfriend/husband/wife/ brother/sister.
Това е моят приятел/моят приятел/моята приятелка/ моят съпруг/моята съпруга моят брат/моята сестра
Tova e moyat priyatel/moyat priyatel/moyata priyatelka/moyat saprug/moyata sapruga/moya brat/moyata sestra

Where are you travelling to?
За къде пътувате?
Za kadeh patuvateh?

I am/we are going to...
Аз отивам/ние отиваме в ...
Az otivam/nieh otivameh v ...

How long are you travelling for?
Колко дълго ще пътувате?
Kolko dalgo shteh patuvateh?

Where do you come from?
Откъде сте?
Otkadeh ste?

I am/we are from ... Australia/Britain/Canada/ America
Аз съм/ние сме от ... Австралия/Великобритания/ Канада/САЩ

ESSENTIALS

BULGARIAN

Az sam/nieh smeh ot … Avstralia/ Velikobritania/Kanada/Se-Ah-Sht

We are on holiday
Ние сме на почивка
Nieh smeh na pochivka

This is our first visit here
Тук сме за първи път
Tuk smeh za parvi pat

How old are you?
На колко години сте?
Na kolko godini steh?

I am … years old
Аз съм на ... години
Az sam nah … godini

I am a business person/ doctor/journalist/manual worker/administrator/ scientist/student/teacher
Аз съм бизнесмен/лекар/ журналист/равотник/служител /учен/студент/учител
Az sam biznesmen/lekar/ zhurnalist/rabotnik/sluzhitel/uchen/ student/uchitel

I am waiting for my husband/ wife/boyfriend/girlfriend
Чакам съпруга си/ съпругата си/приятеля си/приятелката си
Chakam sapruga si/saprugata si/priyatelya si/priyatelkata si

Would you like/may I have a cigarette?
Искате ли/имате ли цигара?
Iskateh li/imateh li tsigara?

Do you mind if I smoke?
Имате ли нещо против ако пуша?
Imateh li neshto protiv ako pusha?

Do you have a light?
Имате ли огънче?
Imateh li ogancheh?

Days

Monday
Понеделник
Ponedelnik

Tuesday
Вторник
Vtornik

Wednesday
Сряда
Sryada

Thursday
Четвъртък
Chetvartak

Friday
Петък
Petak

Saturday
Събота
Sabotah

Sunday
Неделя
Nedelya

Morning
Сутрин
Sutrin

Afternoon/Evening/Night
Следобед/Вечер/Нощ
Sledobed/Vecher/Nosht

Yesterday/Today/Tomorrow
Вчера/Днес/Утре
Vchera/Dnes/Utreh

Numbers

Zero
Нула
Nula

One
Едно
Edno

Two
Две
Dveh

Three
Три
Trih

Four
Четири
Chetiri

Five
Пет
Pet

Six
Шест
Shess

Seven
Седем
Sedem

Eight
Осем
Osem

Nine
Девет
Devet

Ten
Десет
Desset

Eleven
Единайсет
Edinaiset

Twelve
Дванайсет
Dvanaiset

Thirteen
Тринайсет
Trinaiset

Fourteen
Четиринайсет
Chetirinaiset

Fifteen
Петнайсет
Petnaiset

Sixteen
Шестнайсет
Shesnaiset

Seventeen
Седемнайсет
Sedemnaiset

Eighteen
Осемнайсет
Osemnaiset

Nineteen
Деветнайсет
Devetnaiset

Twenty
Двайсет
Dvaiset

Twenty-one
Двайсет и едно
Dvaiset ih edno

Twenty-Two
Двайсет и две
Dvaiset ih dveh

Thirty
Трийсет
Treeset

Forty
Четиридесет
Chetiridesset

Fifty
Петдесет
Petdesset

Sixty
Шейсет
Sheyset

Seventy
Седемдесет
Sedemdesset

Eighty
Осемдесет
Osemdesset

Ninety
Деветдесет
Devetdesset

One hundred
Сто
Stoh

Five hundred
Петстотин
Petstotin

One thousand
Хиляда
Hillyada

One million
Един милион
Edin million

Time

What time is it?
Колко е часът?
Kolko eh chasat?

It is .....
Часът е ...
Chasat eh ...

9.00
Девет
Devet

9.05
Девет и пет
Devet i pet

9.15
Девет и петнайсет
Devet I petnaiset

9.20
Девет и двайсет
Devet i dvaiset

9.30
Девет и половина
Devet i polovina

9.35
Десет без двайсет и пет
Desset bez dvaiset i pet

9.40
Десет без двайсет
Desset bez dvaiset

9.45
Десет без петнайсет
Desset bez petnaiset

9.50
Десет без десет
Desset bez desset

9.55
Десет без пет
Desset bez pet

12.00/Midday/Midnight
Дванайсет/Обед/Полунощ
Dvanaiset/Obed/Polunosht

Money

I would like to change these traveller's cheques/this currency
Искам да обменя тези пътнически чекове/тази валчта
Iskam da obmenya tezi patnicheski checkoveh/tazi valuta

How much commission do you charge? (What is the service charge?)
Колко ви е комисионната?
Kolko vi eh komisionnata?

Can I obtain money with my Mastercard?
Мога ли да изтегля пари с моята карта Mastercard?
Moga li da izteglya pari s moyata karta Mastercard?

Where is the nearest ATM?
Къде се намира най-близкият банкомат?
Kudeh se namira nay blizkiyat bankomat?

My name is ... Some money has been wired to here for me to collect
Казвам се ... Изпратили са ми пари, които трябва да получа тук
Kazvam se ... Ispratili sa mi parih, koito tryabva da polucha tuk

ARRIVING AND DEPARTING

Airport

Excuse me, where is the check-in desk for ... airline?
Извинявайте, къде е чекин за авиолиния ...?
Izvinyavaite, kadeh eh checkin za aviolinia ...?

What is the boarding gate for my flight?
Кой е изходът за моя полет?
Koy eh iz-hodat za moya polet?

What is the time for my flight?
В колко часа е моят полет?
V kolko chasa e moyat polet?

How long is the delay likely to be?
Колко ще е закъснението?
Kolko shte e zakasnenieto?

Where is the duty-free shop?
Къде е безмитният магазин?
Kadeh eh bezmitniyat magazin?

Which way is the luggage reclaim?
Откъде се взима багажът?
Otkadeh seh vzima bagazha?

I have lost my luggage. Please can you help?
Загубил съм си багажа. Можете ли да ми помогнете?
Zagubil sam si bagazha. Mozhete li da mi pomogneteh?

I am flying to ...
Пътувам за ...
Putuvam za ...

Where is the bus for the city centre?
Къде е автобусът за центъра на града?
Kadeh eh avtobussa za tsentara na grada?

Trains and Boats

Where is the ticket office/information desk?
Къде е гишето за билети/бюрото за информация?
Kadeh eh gisheto za bileti/byuroto za informatsiya?

Which platform does the train/speedboat/ferry to ... depart from?
От коя платформа тръгва влакът/корабът/фериботът до ...?
Ot koya platforma tragva vlaka/koraba/ferribota do ...?

Where is platform ...?
Къде е перон ...?
Kadeh eh peron ...?

When is the next train/boat to ...?
Кога е следващият влак/кораб до ...?
Koga eh sledvashtiya vlak/korab do ...?

Is there a later train/boat to ...?
Нма ли по-късен влак/кораб до ...?
Ima li po-kasen vlak/korab do ...?

Notices and Signs

Вагон-ресторант
Vagon-restorant
Buffet (dining) Car

Автобус
Avtobus
Bus

Питейна/непитейна вода
Piteyna/nepiteyna voda
Drinking/Non-drinking water

Вход
Vhod
Entrance

Изход
Iz-hod
Exit

Болница
Bolnitsa
Hospital

Информация
Informatsya
Information

Загубен багаж
Zaguben bagazh
Left Luggage (Baggage Claim)

Гардероб за багаж
Garderob za bagazh
Luggage Lockers

Поща
Poshta
Post Office

Перон
Peron
Platform

Ж. П. Гара
Zh. P. Gara
Railway (Railroad) Station

Летище/Аерогара
Letishteh/Aerogara
Airport

Полиция
Politsiya
Police Station

Пристанище
Pristanishteh
Port

Ресторант
Restaurant
Restaurant

Пушенето забранено/ Пушенето позволено
Pusheneto zabraneno/ Pusheneto pozvoleno
Smoking/Non Smoking

Телефон
Telefon
Telephone

Билетн
Bileti
Ticket Office

Чекин
Checkin
Check-in desk

Разписание
Razpisanieh
Timetable (Schedule)

Тоалетни
Toaletni
Toilets (Restroom)

Жени/Мъже
Zheni/Muzheh
Ladies/Gentlemen

Метро
Metro
Underground (Subway)

Чакалня
Chakalnya
Waiting Room

Buying a Ticket

I would like a first-class/ second-class/third-class single (one-way)/return (round-trip) ticket to ...
Бих искал първокласен/ второкласен/третокласен единичен билет/билет за отиване и връщане до ...
Bih iskal parvoklassen/vtoroklassen/ tretoklassen edinichen bilet/bilet za otivane i vrashtane do ...

Is it an express (fast) train/bus?
Този влак/автобус експресен ли е?
Tozi vlak/avtobus expressen li eh?

Is my rail pass valid on this train/ferry/bus?
Валиден ли е моят билет/пропуск за този влак/ ферибот/автобус?
Validen li eh moyat bilet/propusk za tozi vlak/ferribot/avtobus?

I would like an aisle/window seat
Бих желал място до пътеката/до прозореца
Bih zhelal myasto do puhtekata/do prozoretsa

No smoking/smoking please
За непушачи/За пушачи, моля
Za nepushachi/Za pushachi, molya

We would like to sit together
Искаме съседни места
Iskame sasedni mesta

I would like to make a seat reservation
Искам да запазя място
Iskam da zapazya myasto

I would like to reserve a couchette/sleeper for one person/two people/my family
Искам да запазя място в спален вагон за едно лице/ две лица/моето семейство
Iskam da zapazya myasto v spalen vagon za ednolitseh/dveh litsa/moeto semeistvo

I would like to reserve a cabin
Искам да запазя каюта
Iskam da zapazya kayuta

Timetables (Schedules)

Пристига
Pristiga
Arrive

Спира в ...
Spira v ...
Calls (Stops) at

С вагон-бюфет
S vagon byufet
Catering service

Смяна в ...
Smyana v ...
Change at

Връзка/през
Vrazka/prez
Connection/via

Ежедневно
Ezhednevno
Daily

На всеки 40 минути
Na vseki 40 minuti
Every 40 minutes

Първа класа
Parva klasa
First Class

На всеки час
Na vseki chas
Hourly

Препоръчва се местата да се резервират
Preporachva se mestata da se rezervirat
Seat reservations are recommended

Втора класа
Vtora klasa
Second Class

Допълнително заплащане
Dopalnitelno zaplashtaneh
Supplement payable

Luggage

How much will it cost to send (ship) my luggage in advance?
Колко ще струва да изпратя багажа си предварително?
Kolko shte struva da izpratya bagazha si predvaritelno?

Where is the left luggage (baggage claim) office?
Къде е службата за загубен баяаж?
Kadeh eh sluzhbata za zaguben bagazh?

What time do you open/close?
В колко часа отваряте/затваряте?
V kolko chasa otvaryateh/ zatvaryateh?

Where are the luggage trolleys (carts)?
Къде са количките за баяаж?
Kadeh sa kolichkiteh za bagazh?

Where are the lockers?
Къде е гардеробната?
Kadeh eh garderobnata?

I have lost my locker key
Изгубих си ключа за гардероба
Izgubih si klyucha za garderoba

On Board

Is this seat free?
Свободно ли е това място?
Svobodno li eh tova myasto?

Excuse me, you are sitting in my reserved seat
Извинете, вие седите на моето запазено място
Izvinete, vie sediteh na moeto zapazeno myasto

Which station is this?
Коя е тази гара?
Koya e tazi gara?

What time is this train/bus/ ferry/flight due to arrive/ depart?
В колко часа трябва да тръгне/пристигне този влак/автобус/ферибот/полет?
V kolko chasa tryabva da

tragne/pristigne tozi vlak/avtobus/ferribot/polet?

Travelling with Children

Do you have a high chair/ baby-sitting service/cot?
Имате ли висок стол/служба за гледане на деца/креватче?
Imateh li vissok stol/sluzhba za gledane na detsa/krevatcheh?

Where is the nursery/ playroom?
Къде е стаята за деца?
Kadeh e stayata za detsa?

Where can I warm the baby's bottle?
Къде мога да стопля шишето на бебето?
Kadeh moga da stoplya shisheto na bebeto?

Customs and Passports

Паспорти, моля!
Passporti, molya!
Passports please!

I have nothing/wine/spirits (alcohol)/tobacco to declare
Нямам нищо за деклариране /имам да декларирам вино/ спиртни напитки/тютюнени изделия
Nyamam nishto za deklarirane/ imam da deklarirm vino/spirtni napitki/tyutyuneni izdeliya

I will be staying for ... days/ weeks/months
Ще остана ... дни/седмици/ месеца
Shte ostana ... dni/sedmitsi/ messetsa

SIGHTSEEING

Asking the Way

Excuse me, do you speak English?
Извинете, говорите ли английски?
Izvinete, govorite li angleeski?

Excuse me, can you help me please?
Извинете, може ли да ми помогнете?
Izvinete, mozhe li da mi pomognete?

Where is the Tourist Information Office?
Къде се намира бюрото за туристическа информация?
Kadeh seh namira byuroto za turisticheska informatsiya?

Excuse me, is this the right way to...?
Извинете, това ли е пътят за ...?
Izvinete, tova li eh puhtyat za ...?

... the cathedral/the tourist office/the castle/the old town
... катедралата/ туристическото бюро/замъка/стария град
... katedralata/turisticheskoto byuro/zamuhka/stariya grad

SIGHTSEEING

BULGARIAN

Can you tell me the way to the railway station/ bus station/taxi rank/ city centre/beach?
Може ли да ми кажете как да стигна до ж.п. гарата/ автогарата/стоянката за таксита/центъра на града/ плажа?
Mozhe li da mi kazhete kak da stigna do zh.p. garata/avtogarata/ stoyankata za taksita/tsentara na grada/plazha?

Първата/втората наляво/надясно/направо
Parvata/vtorata nalyavo/nadyasno/ napravo
First/second/left/right/ straight ahead

На ъгъла/на светофара
Na ugala/na svetofara
At the corner/at the traffic lights

Where is the nearest police station/post office?
Къде е най-близкият/ близката полицейски участък/поща?
Kade e nai-blizkiyat/blizkata politseiski uchastak/poshta?

Is it near/far?
Близо/далече ли е?
Blizo/daleche li eh?

Do I need to take a taxi/catch a bus?
Трябва ли да взема такси/ автобус?
Tryabva li da vzema taxi/avtobus?

Do you have a map?
Имате ли карта?
Imate li karta?

Can you point to it on my map?
Може ли да ми покажете на моята карта?
Mozhe li da mi pokazhete na moyata karta?

Thank you for your help
Благодаря Ви за помощта Ви
Blagodarya Vi za pomoshta Vi

How do I reach the motorway/main road?
Как се стига до магистралата/главния път?
Kak se stiga do magistralata/glavniya pat?

I think I have taken the wrong turning
Мисля, че съм завил по погрешен път
Mislya, che sam zavil po pogreshen pat

I am looking for this address
Търся този адрес
Tarsya tozi adress

I am looking for the... hotel
Търся хотел ...
Tarsya hotel ...

How far is it to... from here?
Колко е далече оттук до ...?
Kolko e daleche ottuk do ...?

Продължете направо ... километра
Prodalzhete napravo... kilometra
Carry straight on for... kilometres

На следващата пресечка завийте надясно/наляво
Na sledvashtata presechka zaveeteh nadyasno/nalyavo
Take the next turning on the right/left

На следващата пресечка/светофар завийте надясно/наляво
Na sledvashtata presechka/svetofar zaveeteh nadyasno/nalyavo
Turn right/left at the next crossroads/traffic lights

Вие отивате в погрешна посока
Vieh otivateh v pogreshna posoka
You are going in the wrong direction

Where is the cathedral/church/museum/bank/pharmacy?
Къде се намира катедралата/църквата/музея/банката/аптеката?
Kade seh namira katedralata/tsarkvata/muzeya/bankata/aptekata?

How much is the admission/entrance charge?
Колко струва входът?
Kolko struva vhoda?

Is there a discount for children/students/senior citizens?
Има ли намаление за деца/студенти/възрастни хора?
Ima li namalenie za detsa/studenti/vazrastni hora?

What time does the next guided tour (in English) start?
В колко часа започва следващата обиколка с превод (на английски)?
V kolko chasa zapochva sledvashtata obikolka s prevod (na angleeski)?

One/two adults/children please
Един/два за възрастни/деца, моля
Edin/dvama za vazrastni/detsa, molya

May I take photographs here?
Мога ли да снимам тук?
Moga li da snimam tuk?

At the Tourist Office

Do you have a map of the town/area?
Имате ли карта на града/района?
Imate li karta na grada/raiona?

Do you have a list of accommodation?
Имате ли списък на Местата за Ношуване?
Imate li spisak na Mestata za Nozhuvane?

Can I reserve accommodation?
Мога ли да запазя квартира/хотел?
Moga li da zapazya kvartira/hotel?

ACCOMMODATION

Hotels

I have a reservation in the name of ...
Имам резервация на името на ...
Imam rezervatsiya na imeto na ...

I wrote to/faxed/telephoned you last month/last week
Писах ви/пуснах ви факс/телефонирах ви миналия месец/миналата седмица
Pisah vi/pusnah vi fax/telefonirah vi minalia mesets/minalata sedmitsa

Do you have any rooms free?
Имате ли свободни стаи?
Imate li svobodni stai?

I would like to reserve a single/double room with/without bath/shower
Искам да запазя единична/двойна стая с/без баня/душ
Iskam da zapazya edinichna/dvoina stay s/bez banya/dush

I would like bed/breakfast/(room and) full board
Бих искал легло/закуска/(стая и) пълен пансион
Bih iskal leglo/zakuska/(staya i) palen pansion

How much is it per night?
Колко струва на вечер?
Kolko struva na vecher?

Is breakfast included?
Закуската включва ли се?
Zakuskata vklyuchva li seh?

Do you have any cheaper rooms?
Имате ли по-евтини стаи?
Imate li po-evtini stai?

I would like to see/take the room
Искам да видя/взема стаята
Iskam da vidya/vzema stayata

I would like to stay for ... nights
Искам да остана за ... нощи
Iskam da ostana za ... noshti

The shower/light/tap/hot water doesn't work
Душът/лампата/мивката/топлата вода не работи
Dushat/lampata/mivkata/toplata voda neh raboti

At what time/where is breakfast served?
В колко часа/къде се сервира закуската?
V kolko chasa/kadeh se servira zakuskata?

What time do I have to check out?
В колко часа трябва да напусна?
V kolko chasa tryabva da napusna?

Can I have the key to room number ...?
Може ли да дадете ключа за стая номер ...?
Mozhe li da mi dadete klyucha za staya nomer ...?

My room number is ...
Номерът на стаята ми е ...
Nomerat na stayata mi eh ...

My room is not satisfactory/not clean enough/too noisy. Please can I change rooms?
Стаята не ми харесва/не е достатъчно чиста/е твърде шумна. Мога ли да взема друга стая, моля?
Stayata ne mi haresva/neh eh dostatchno chista/eh tvrdeh shumna. Moga li da vzema druga staya, molya?

Where is the bathroom?
Къде е банята?
Kadeh e banyata?

Do you have a safe for valuables?
Имате ли сейф за ценни вещи?
Imateh li seif za tsenni veshti?

Is there a laundry/do you wash clothes?
Имате ли пералня/перете ли дрехи?
Imate li peralnya/pereteh li drehi?

I would like an air - conditioned room
Искам стая с климатична инсталация
Iskam staya s klimatichna instalatsia

Do you accept traveller's cheques/credit cards?
Приемате ли пътнически чекове/кредитни карти?
Priemate li patnicheski checkove/kreditni karti?

May I have the bill please?
Сметката, моля?
Smetkata, molya?

Excuse me, I think there may be a mistake in this bill
Извинете, мисля че в тази сметка има грешка
Izvinete, mislya, che v tazi smetka ima greshka

Youth Hostels

How much is a dormitory bed per night?
Колко струва едно легло на нощ?
Kolko struva edno leglo na nosht?

I am/am not an HI member
Аз не съм член на HI
Az ne sam chlen na HI

May I use my own sleeping bag?
Мога ли да използвам собствен спален чувал?
Moga li da izpolzvam sobstven spalen chuval?

What time do you lock the doors at night?
В колко часа заключвате вратите нощем?
V kolko chasa zaklyuchvate vratite noshtem?

Camping

May I camp for the night/two nights?
Мога ли да престоя една нощ/две нощи?
Moga li da prestoya edna nosht/dve noshti?

Where can I pitch my tent?
Къде мога да си опъна палатката?
Kadeh moga da si opuhna palatkata?

How much does it cost for one night/week?
Колко струва за една нощ/седмица?
Kolko struva za edna nosht/sedmitsi?

Where are the washing facilities?
Къде са умивалните/душовете?
Kadeh sa umivalnite/dushovete?

Is there a restaurant/supermarket/swimming pool on site/nearby?
Има ли ресторант/супермаркет/плувен басейн в къмпинга/наблизо?
Ima li restaurant/supermarket/pluven basein v kampinga/nablizo?

Do you have a safety deposit box?
Имате ли сейф за ценни вещи?
Imate li seif za tsenni veshti?

EATING AND DRINKING

Cafés and Bars

I would like a cup of/two cups of/another coffee/tea
Искам чаша/две чаши/още една чаша кафе/чай
Iskam chasha/dve chashi/oshteh edna chasha kafeh/chai

With/without milk/sugar
С/без мляко/захар
S/bez mlyako/zahar

I would like a bottle/glass/two glasses of mineral water/red wine/white wine, please
Бих искал бутилка/чаша/две чаши минерална вода/червено/бяло вино, моля
Bih iskal butilka/chasha/dve chashi mineralna voda/cherveno/byalo vino, molya

I would like a beer/two beers, please
Бих искал една бира/две бири, моля
Bih iskal edna bira/dve biri, molya

Please may I have some ice?
Извинете, може ли да ми донесете малко лед?
Izvinete, mozhe li da mi donesete malko led?

Do you have any matches/cigarettes/cigars?
Имате ли кибрит/цигари/пури?
Imate li kibrit/tsigari/puri?

Restaurants

Can you recommend a good/cheap restaurant in this area?
Може ли да препоръчате добър/евтин ресторант наоколо?
Mozhe li da preporachateh dobar/evtin restaurant naokolo?

I would like a table for ... people
Бих искал маса за ... души
Bih iskal masa za ... dushi

Do you have a non-smoking area?
Имате ли маси за непушачи?
Imate li masi za nepushachi?

Waiter/waitress!
Келнер!
Kelner!

Excuse me, please may we order?
Извинете, може ли да поръчаме?
Izvinete, mozhe li da porachame?

Do you have a set menu/ children's menu/wine list .../ in English?
Имате ли фиксирано меню/детско меню/списък на вината ...
на английски?
Imate li fixirano menyu/detsko menyu/spisak na vinata ... na angleeski?

Do you have any vegetarian dishes?
Имате ли нещо вегетарианско?
Imate li neshto vegetaryansko?

Do you have any local specialities?
Имате ли местни специалитети?
Imateh li mestni spetsialiteti?

Are vegetables included?
Включени ли са зеленчуци?
Vklyucheni li sah zelenchutsi?

Could I have it well-cooked/ medium rare please?
Може ли да го приготвите добре опечено/средно опечено, моля?
Mozhe li da go prigotvite dobre opecheno/sredno opecheno, molya?

What does this dish consist of?
От какво се състои това ястие?
Ot kakvo se sastoi tova yastieh?

I am a vegetarian. Does this contain meat?
Аз съм вегетарианец.
Има ли месо тук?
Az sm vegetarianets.
Ima li mesoh tuk?

I do not eat nuts/dairy products/meat/fish.
Аз не ям ядки/млечни продукти/месо/риба
Az ne yam yadki/mlechni produkti/meso/riba

Not (very) spicy please
Без (много) подправки, моля
Bez (mnogo) podpravki, molya

I would like the set menu please
Искам да видя фиксираното меню, моля
Iskam da vidia fixiranoto menu, molya

We have not been served yet
Още не са ни сервирали
Oshte ne sa ni servirali

Please bring a plate/knife/ fork
Моля, донесете чиния/нож/ вилица
Molya, donesete chiniya/nozh/vilitsa

Excuse me, this is not what I ordered
Извинете, но аз не съм поръчвал това
Izvinete, no az ne sam porachval tova

May I have some/more bread/water/coffee/tea?
Може ли да ми донесете малко/още хляб/вода/кафе/чай?
Mozhe li da mi doneseteh malko/oshteh hlyab/voda/kafeh, chai?

May I have the bill please?
Сметката, моля?
Smetkata, molya?

Does this bill include service?
Сметката включва ли обслужване?
Smetkata vklyuchva li obsluzhvane?

Do you accept traveller's cheques/Mastercard/US dollars?
Приемате ли пътнически чекове/Mastercard/щатски долари?
Priemate li patnecheski checkoveh/Mastercard/shtatski dollari?

Can I have a receipt please?
Може ли касовата бележка, моля?
Mozhe li kasovata belezhka, molya?

Where is the toilet (restroom) please?
Къде е тоалетната, моля?
Kadeh eh toaletnata, molya?

On the Menu

Закуска/Обяд/Вечеря
Zakuska/Obyad/Vecherya
Breakfast/Lunch/Dinner

Ордьоври
Ordeuvri
First Courses

Супи
Supi
Soups

Предястия
Predyastia
Main Courses

Рибни ястия
Ribni yastia
Fish Dishes

Месни ястия
Mesni yastia
Meat Dishes

Говеждо месо
Govezhdo mesoh
Beef

Пържола
Parzhola
Steak

Свинско месо
Svinsko mesoh
Pork

Телешко месо
Teleshko mesoh
Veal

Пилешко месо
Pileshko mesoh
Chicken

Агнешко месо
Agneshko mesoh
Lamb

Шунка
Shunka
Ham

Вегетариански ястия
Vegetarianski yastia
Vegetarian Dishes

Зеленчуци
Zelenchutsi
Vegetables

Пържени картофи
Purzheni kartofi
Chips (french fries)

Варени картофи/задушени картофи (соте)/картофено пюре
Vareni kartofi/zadusheni kartofi (sote)/kartofeno pyure
Boiled/sauté/mashed potatoes

Ориз
Oriz
Rice

Сирене
Sireheh
Cheese

Десерти
Desserti
Desserts

Сладолед
Sladoled
Ice cream

Торти
Torti
Cakes

Сладкиши
Sladkishi
Pastries

Плодове
Plodovi
Fruit

Хляб
Hlyab
Bread

Кифли
Kifli
Rolls

Препечени филийки
Prepechenih filiyki
Toast

Масло
Maslo
Butter

Сол/пипер
Sol/piper
Salt/pepper

Захар
Zahar
Sugar

Специалитети
Spetsialiteti
Specialities

Местни специалитети
Mestni spetsialiteti
Local specialities

Фиксирано меню
Fiksirano menyu
Set Menu

Винена листа
Vinena lista
Wine list

Червени вина
Cherveni vina
Red wines

Бели вина
Beli vina
White wines

Розови вина (розе)
Rozovi vina (roze)
Rosé wines

Шампанско (шумящи вина)
Shampansko (shumyashti vina)
Sparkling wines

Бира
Bira
Beer

Бутилирана бира/Наливна бира
Butilirana bira/nalivna bira
Bottled beer/ Draught (draft) beer

Безалкохолни напитки
Bezalkoholni napitki
Non-alcoholic drinks

Минерална вода
Mineralna voda
Mineral water

Плодови сокове
Plodovi sokoveh
Fruit juices

Портокалов сок
Portokalov sok
Orange juice

Лимонада
Limonada
Lemonade

Лед
Led
Ice

Кафе с мляко/черно кафе/еспресо
Kafeh s mlyako/cherno kafeh/espreso
White coffee/black coffee/espresso coffee

Чай с мляко/с лимон
Chai s mlyako/s limon
Tea with milk/with lemon

Шоколад (питие)
Shokolad (pitiye)
Chocolate (drink)

Мляко
Mlyako
Milk

Закуски/леки ястия
Zakuski/Leki yastiya
Snacks/Light meals

Салати
Salati
Salads

Сандвичи
Sandvichi
Sandwiches

Яйца
Yayitsa
Eggs

Наденица, салам
Nadenitsa, salam
Sausage

Варени/пържени/бъркани яйца
Vareni/purzheni/burkani yayitsa
Boiled/fried/scrambled eggs

Typical Local Dishes

Таратор
Tarator
Cold yoghurt and cucumber soup

Сарми
Sarmi
Stuffed vine leaves

Баница
Banitsa
Pie

Кюфтета
Kyufteta
Meatballs

Мешана скара
Meshana skara
Mixed grill

GETTING AROUND

Public Transport

Where is the bus stop/coach stop/nearest metro (subway) station?
Къде е най-близката автобусна спирка/станция на метрото?
Kadeh e nai-blizkata avtobusna spirka/stantsia na metroto?

When is the next/last bus to ...?
Кога е следващият/последният автобус до ...?
Koga e sledvashtia/poslednia avtobus do ...?

How much is the fare to the city centre (downtown)/railway (railroad) station/airport?
Колко струва билетът до центъра на града/ж.п. гарата/летището?
Kolko struva bileta do tsentara na grada/zh.p. garata/letishteto?

Will you tell me when to get off?
Може ли да кажете кога трябва да сляза?
Mozhe li da mi kazhete koga tryabva da slyaza?

Does this bus go to ...?
Този автобус отива ли до ...?
Tozi avtobus otiva li do ...?

Which number bus goes to ...?
Кой номер автобус отива до ...?
Koi nomer avtobus otiva do ...?

May I have a single (one way)/return (round trip)/day ticket/book of tickets?
Бих искал единичен билет/билет за отиване и връщане/дневна карта/талон?
Bih iskal edinichen bilet/bilet za otivane i vrashtane/dnevna karta/talon?

Taxis (Таксита)

I would like to go to ... How much will it cost?
Бих искал да отида до... Колко ще струва?
Bih iskal da otida do ... Kolko shteh struva?

Please may I stop here?
Може ли да спрете тук?
Mozhe li da sprete tuk?

I would like to order a taxi today/tomorrow at 2pm to go from ... to ...
Бих искал да поръчам такси за днес/утре за 2 ч., тръгване от ... за ...
Bih iskal da poracham taxi za dnes/utre za 2 chasa, tragvanreh ot ... za ...

Entertainment

Can you recommend a good bar/nightclub?
Може ли да препоръчате добър бар/нощен клуб?
Mozhe li da preporachate dobar bar/noshten klub?

Do you know what is on at the cinema (playing at the movies)/theatre at the moment?
Знаете ли кои филми прожектират в киното/какви пиеси играят в театъра в момента?
Znaete li koi filmi prozhektirat v kinoto/kakvi piesi igrayat v teatara v momenta?

I would like to book (purchase) ... tickets for the matinee/evening performance on Monday
Бих искал да резервирам (купя) ... билета за сутрешното/вечерното представление в понеделник
Bih iskal da rezerviram (kupia) ... bileta za sutreshnoto/bechernoto predstavlenie v ponedelnik

What time does the film/performance start?
В колко часа започва филмът/представлението?
V kolko chasa zapochva filmal/predstavlenieto?

COMMUNICATIONS

Post

How much will it cost to send a letter/postcard/this package to Britain/Ireland/ America/Canada/Australia/ New Zealand?
Колко струва да изпратя писмо/картичка/този пакет до Великобритания/ Ирландия/САЩ/Канада/ Австралия/Нова Зеландия?
Kolko struva da izpratya pismo/ kartichka/tozi paket do Velikobritania/Irlandia/Se-Ah-Sht/ Kanada/Avstralia/Nova Zelandia?

I would like one stamp/two stamps
Бих искал една марка/две марки
Bih iskal edna marka/dve marki

I'd like ... stamps for postcards to send abroad, please
Бих искал ... марки за картички за чужбина, моля
Bih iskal ... marki za kartichki za chuzhbina, molya

Phones

I would like to make a telephone call/reverse the charges to (make a collect call to) ...
Бих искал да се обадя/да се обадя за тяхна сметка до...
Bih iskal da seh obadyah do/da se obadyah za tyahna smetka do...

Which coins do I need for the telephone?
Какви монети ми трябват за телефона?
Kakvi moneti mi tryabvat za telefona?

The line is engaged (busy)
Линията е заета
Liniyhata eh zaeta

The number is...
Номерът е ...
Nomerat eh ...

Hello, this is ...
Ало, обажда се ...
Alo, obazhda seh ...

Please may I speak to..?
Може ли да говоря с ..., моля?
Mozhe li da govorya s ..., molya?

He/she is not in at the moment. Please can you call back?
Той/тя не е тук в момента. Може ли да се обадите по-късно?
Toi/tya neh eh tuk v momenta. Mozheh li da se obaditeh po-kasno?

SHOPPING

Shops

Книжарница
Knizharnitsa
Bookshop/Stationery

Бижутерия/подаръци
Bizhuteria/Podaratsi
Jeweller/Gifts

Обувки
Obuvki
Shoes

Железария
Zhelezaria
Hardware

Бръснаро-фризьорски салон
Brasnaro-frizyorski salon
Hairdresser

Хлебарница
Hlebarnitsa
Baker

Супермаркет
Supermarket
Supermarket

Фото
Foto
Photo shop

Туристическа агенция
Touristicheska agentsia
Travel Agent

Аптека
Apteka
Pharmacy

In the Shops

What time do the shops open/close?
В колко часа отварят/затварят магазините?
V kolko chasa otvaryat/zatvaryat magazinite?

Where is the nearest market?
Къде е най-близкият пазар?
Kadeh eh nai-blizkiat pazar?

Can you show me the one in the window/this one?
Може ли да ми покажете онзи на витрината/този тук?
Mozhe li da mi pokazhete onzi na vitrinata/tozi tuk?

Can I try this on?
Може ли да го пробвам?
Mozhe li da go probvam?

What size is this?
Кой размер е това?
Koi razmer e tova?

This is too large/too small/too expensive. Do you have any others?
Това е много голямо/малко/скъпо. Имате ли други?
Tova eh mnogo golyamo/malko/skapo. Imateh li drugi?

My size is...
Моят размер е ...
Moyat razmer eh ...

Where is the changing room/children's/cosmetic/ladieswear/menswear/food department?

Къде е пробната/детските стоки/козметиката/дамското облекло/мъжкото облекло/хранителните стоки?
Kadeh sa probnata/detskite stoki/kozmetikata/damskoto obleklo/mazhkoto obleklo/hranitelniteh stoki?

I would like ... a quarter of a kilo/half a kilo/a kilo of bread/butter/ham/this fruit
Бих искал ... четвърт кило/половин кило/кило хляб/масло/шунка/от тези плодове
Bih iskal ... chetvart kilo/polovin kilo/kilo hlyab/maslo/shunka/ot tezi plodove

How much is this?
Колко струва това?
Kolko struva tova?

I'll take this one, thank you
Ще взема този, благодаря
Shte vzema tozi, blagodarya

Do you have a carrier (shopping) bag?
Имате ли торба?
Imateh li torba?

Do you have anything cheaper/larger/smaller/ of better quality?
Имате ли нещо по-евтино/по-голямо/по-малко/по-качествено?
Imateh li neshto po-evtino/po-golyamo/po-malko/po-kachestveno?

I would like a film/to develop this film for this camera
Бих искал филм/да промия филма от този апарат
Bih iskal film/da promia filma ot tozi aparat

I would like some batteries, the same size as this old one
Бих искал няколко батерии същия размер като тази
Bih iskal nyakolko baterii, sashtia razmer kato tazi

Would you mind wrapping this for me, please?
Може ли да ми опаковате това, моля?
Mozhe li da mi opakovate tova, molya?

Sorry, but you seem to have given me the wrong change
Извинявайте, но изглежда не сте ми върнали точното ресто
Izvinyavaite, no izglezhda neh steh mi varnali tochnoto resto

MOTORING

Car Hire (Rental)

I have ordered (rented) a car in the name of ...
Поръчал съм (взел съм под наем) кола на името на ...
Porachal sam (vzel sam pod naem) kola na imeto na ...

How much does it cost to hire (rent) a car for one day/ two days/a week?
Колко струва да се наеме кола за един ден/два дни/седмица?
Kolko struva da se naemeh kola za edin den/dva din/sedmitsa?

Is the tank already full of petrol (gas)?
Резервоарът пълен ли е с бензин?
Reservoarat palen li eh s benzin?

Is insurance and tax included? How much is the deposit?
Включени ли са застраховка и данъци? Колко е депозитът?
Vklyucheni li sa zastrahovka i danatsi? Kolko eh depozita?

By what time must I return the car?
Кога най-късно трябва да върна колата?
Koga nai-kasno tryabva da varna kolata?

I would like a small/large/family/sports car with a radio/cassette
Бих искал малка/голяма/семейна/спортна кола с радио/касетофон
Bih iskal malka/golyama/semeina/sportna kola s radio/kasetofon

Do you have a road map?
Имате ли пътна карта?
Imateh li patna karta?

Parking

How long can I park here?
Колко време мога да паркирам тук?
Kolko vremeh moga da parkiram tuk?

Is there a car park near here?
Има ли паркинг наблизо?
Ima li parking nablizo?

At what time does this car park close?
В колко часа затваря паркингът?
V kolko chasa zatvarya parkinga?

Signs and Notices

Еднопосочна улица
Ednoposochna ulitsa
One way

Влизането забранено
Vlizaneto zabraneno
No entry

Паркирането забранено
Parkiraneto zabraneno
No parking

Отклонение
Otklonenieh
Detour (Diversion)

Стоп
Stop
Stop

Път/улица с предимство
Pat/ulitsa s predimstvo
Give way (Yield)

Хлъзгав път
Hlazgav pat
Slippery road

Изпреварването забранено
Izprevarvaneto zabraneno
No overtaking

Опасност
Opasnost
Danger

At the Filling Station (На бензиностанцията)

Unleaded (lead free)/ standard/premium/diesel
Безоловен/обикновен/ супер/дизел
Bezoloven/obiknoven/ super/deezel

Fill the tank please
Напълнете резервоара, моля
Napalneteh rezervoara, molya

Do you have a road map?
Имате ли пътна карта?
Imateh li patna karta?

How much is the car wash?
Колко струва измиването на кола?
Kolko struva izmivaneto na kola?

Breakdowns

I've had a breakdown at ...
Колата ми се повреди в ...
Kolata mi seh povredi v ...

I am a member of the ... [motoring organisation]
Аз съм член на ...
Az sm chlen na ...

I am on the road from ... to ...
Аз съм на пътя от ... до ...
Az sam na patya ot ... do ...

I can't move the car. Can you send a tow-truck?
Не мога да помръдна колата. Можете ли да изпратите аварийна кола?
Ne moga da pomradna kolata. Mozheteh li da izpratiteh avariyina kola?

I have a flat tyre
Спука ми се гума
Spuka mi se guma

The windscreen (windshield) has smashed/cracked
Предното стъкло е счупено/ спукано
Prednoto staklo eh schupeno/spukano

There is something wrong with the engine/brakes/ lights/steering/gearbox/ clutch/exhaust
Имам повреда в двигателя/ спирачките/светлините/ волана/скоростната кутия/ амбреажа/ауспуха
Imam povreda v dvigatelya/ spirachkiteh/svetliniteh/volana/ skorostnata kutia/ambreazha/ auspuha

It's overheating
Прегрява
Pregriava

It won't start
Не пали
Ne pali

Where can I get it repaired?
Къде може да се ремонтира?
Kadeh mozhe da seh remontira?

Can you take me there?
Може ли да ме закарате там?
Mozhe li da me zakarateh tam?

Will it take long to fix?
Дълго време ли ще отнеме да се ремонтира?
Dalgo vremeh li shteh otnemeh da seh remontirah?

How much will it cost?
Колко ще струва?
Kolko shteh struva?

Please can you pick me up/ give me a lift?
Може ли да ме докарате/ закарате?
Mozhe li da meh dokarateh/ zakarateh?

Accidents and Traffic Offences (Violations)

Can you help me? There has been an accident
Може ли да ми помогнете? Стана катастрофа
Mozhe li da mi pomognete? Stana katastrofa

Please call the police/an ambulance
Моля повикайте полиция/линейка
Molya, povikayte politsiya/lineyka

Is anyone hurt?
Има ли ранени?
Ima li raneni?

I'm sorry, I didn't see the sign
Съжалявам, не видях знака
Sazhaliavam, ne vidiah znaka

Must I pay a fine? How much?
Трябва ли да платя глоба? Колко?
Tryabva li da platya globa? Kolko?

Покажете ми документите си
Pokazhete mi dokumentite si
Show me your documents

HEALTH

Pharmacy (Аптека)

Do you have anything for a stomach ache/headache/sore throat/toothache?
Имате ли нещо за стомашни болки/главоболие/болно гърло/зъбобол
Imateh li neshto za stomashni bolki/glavobolie/bolno garlo/zabobol

I need something for diarrhoea/constipation/ a cold/a cough/insect bites/ sunburn/travel (motion) sickness
Трябва ми нещо за диария/ запек/настинка/кашлица/ ужилвания/изгаряне/гадене
Triabva mi neshto za diaria/zapek/ nastinka/kashlitsa/uzhilvania/ izgariane/gadeneh

How much/how many do I take?
Колко трябва да взимам?
Kolko tryabva da vzimam?

I am taking anti-malaria tablets/these pills
Аз взимам таблетки срещу малария/тези хапчета
Az vzimam tabletki sreshtu malaria/tezi hapcheta

How often do I take it/them?
Колко често трябва да го/ги взимам?
Kolko cheshto tryabva da go/gi vzimam?

I am/he is/she is taking this medication
Аз взимам/той/тя взима това лекарство
Az vzemam/toi/tya vzima tova lekarstvo

How much does it cost?
Колко струва?
Kolko struva?

Can you recommend a good doctor/dentist?
Може ли да ми препоръчате добър лекар/зъболекар?
Mozhe li da mi preporachate dobar lekar/zabolekar?

Is it suitable for children?
Може ли да се взима от деца?
Mozhe li da se vzima ot detsa?

Doctor (Доктор/Лекар)

I have a pain here/in my arm/leg/chest/stomach
Боли ме тук/ръката/кракът/гърдите/стомахът
Boli me tuk/rakata/kraka/gardite/stomaha

Please call a doctor, this is an emergency
Моля повикайте лекар, това е спешен случай
Molya povikaite lekar, tova e speshen sluchai

I would like to make an appointment to see the doctor
Искам да си определя час за преглед при лекаря
Iskam da si opredelya chas za pregled pri lekaria

I am diabetic/pregnant
Аз имам диабет/Аз съм бременна
Az imam diabet/Az sam bremenna

I need a prescription for ...
Трябва ми рецепта за ...
Triabva mi retsepta za ...

Can you give me something to ease the pain?
Може ли да ми дадете нещо за болката?
Mozhe li da mi dadeteh neshto za bolkata?

I am/he is/she is/allergic to penicillin
Аз имам/той/тя има алергия към пеницилин
Az imam/toi/tya ima alergia kam penitsilin

Това боли ли?
Tova boli li?
Does this hurt?

Трябва да отидете/отиде в болницата
Tryabva da otideteh/otideh v bolnitsata
You must/he must/she must go to hospital

Вземайте ги веднъж/два пъти/три пъти на ден
Vzimaite gi vednazh/dva pati/tri pati na den
Take these once/twice/three times a day

I am/he is/she is taking this medication
Аз взимам/той/тя взима това лекарство
Az vzemam/toi/tya vzima tova lekarstvo

I have medical insurance
Аз имам здравна застраховка
Az imam zdravna zastrahovka

Dentist (Зъболекар)

I have toothache/my filling has come out
Боли ме зъб/паднала ми е пломбата
Boli me zab/padma mi plombata

I do/do not want to have an injection first
Искам/не искам първо инжекция
Iskam/ne iskam parvo inzhektsia

EMERGENCIES

Help!
Помощ!
Pomosht!

Fire!
Пожар!
Pozhar!

Stop!
Стоп!/Спри!
Stop!/Spri!

Call an ambulance/a doctor/ the police/the fire brigade!
Извикайте линейка/лекар/ полицията/пожарната!
Izvikaite lineika/lekar/politsiata/ pozharnata!

Please may I use a telephone?
Може ли използвам телефона, моля?
Mozhe li da izpolzvam telefona, molya?

I have had my traveller's cheques/credit cards/ handbag/rucksack/luggage/ wallet/passport/mobile phone stolen
Откраднаха ми пътническите чекове/кредитните карти/ чантата/раницата/багажа/ портфейла/паспорта/ мобилния телефон
Otkradnaha mi patnicheskite chekoveh/kreditniteh karti/ chantata/ranitsata/bagazha/ portfeila/pasporta/mobilniya telefon

May I please have a copy of the report for my insurance claim?
Може ли да ми дадете копие на полицейския протокол, необходим за застрахователния иск?
Mozhe li da mi dadete kopie na politseyskiya protocol, neobhodim za zastrahovatlniya isk?

Can you help me, I have lost my daughter/son/my companion(s)?
Може ли да ми помогнете, загубих дъщеря си/сина си/ приятеля/приятелите си?
Mozhe li da mi pomogneteh, zagubih dashteria si/sina si/ priatelya si?

BULGARIAN

Please go away/leave me alone
Идете си/оставете ме намира, моля
Idete si/ostaveteh meh namira, molya

I'm sorry
Съжалявам
Sazhalyavam

I want to contact the British/ American/Canadian/Irish/ Australian/New Zealand/ South African Consulate
Искам да се свържа с консулството на Великобритания/САЩ/ Канада/Ирландия/Австралия /Нова Зеландия/Южна Африка
Iskam da seh svarzha s konsultstvoto na Velikobritania/ Ess-Ah-Sht/Kanada/Irlandia/ Avstralia/Nova Zelandia/ Yuzhna Afrika

I'm/we're/he is/she is/they are/ill/lost/injured
Аз съм/ние сме/той е/тя е/ те са болен (болни)/ изгубен(изгубени)/ранен(и)
Az sam/nieh smeh/toy eh/tya eh/the sa bolen (bolni)/izguben (izgubeni)/ ranen(i)

CZECH

INTRODUCTION

Czech is the official language of the Czech Republic. The language spoken in neighbouring Slovakia is Slovak, but the two are so closely related that speakers of one can easily understand the other. Both belong to the Slavic family of languages that includes Russian and Polish. In larger cities, particularly in the Czech Republic, English is spoken, and German is often a second language for many Czechs. Russian is also widely understood, but not popular.

Addresses for Travel and Tourist Information

Except where stated, addresses are tourist authorities for both the Czech Republic and Slovakia.

Australia: *Czech Embassy,* 8 Culgoa Circuit, O'Malley, Canberra, ACT 2606; tel: (02) 6290 1386; fax: (02) 6290 0006. *Slovakian Embassy,* 47 Culgoa Circuit, O'Malley, Canberra, ACT 2606; tel: (02) 6290 1516; fax: (02) 6290 1755.

Canada: *Czech Tourist Authority,* 401 Bay Street, Suite #1510, Toronto, Ontario M5H 2Y4; tel:(416) 363 9928; fax:(416) 363 0239.

South Africa: *Czech Embassy,* 936 Pretorius Street, Arcadia, Pretoria; tel: (12) 342 3477. *Slovak Embassy,* 930 Arcadia Street, Arcadia, Pretoria; tel: (12) 342 2051.

UK: *Czech Tourist Authority,* Suite 29–31, 2nd Floor, Morley House, 320 Regent St, London W1B 3BG; tel: (020) 7631 0427; fax: (020) 7631 0419.

USA: *CzechTourism USA,* 1109 Madison Ave, New York, NY 10028; tel: (212) 288 0830, ext. 101, 105; fax: (212) 288 0971.

Official tourism website: www.czechtourism.com.

Czech Facts

CAPITAL: Prague (Praha, pronounced Prahah)

CURRENCY: Czech Koruna (Korroonah) or Crown (KČ);
1 Koruna = 100 Haliřú (Hallers).

OPENING HOURS: Banks: Mon–Fri 0800–1800. Shops: Mon–Fri 0900–1800, Sat 0900–1200 (longer in Prague Sat and Sun). Museums: Tues–Sun 1000–1800. Castles closed Nov–Mar.

TELEPHONES: To dial in, +420. Outgoing, 00 plus the country code. Police, Fire, Ambulance, 155.

PUBLIC HOLIDAYS: 1 Jan; Easter Monday; 1, 8 May; 5–6 July; 28 Sept; 28 Oct; 17 Nov; 24–26 Dec.

ESSENTIALS

Alphabet and Pronunciation

A few hints

- Stress the first syllable.
- T, P and K are pronounced quickly (without a drawn out 'ay' or 'ee' sound).
- Pronounce each part of the word, and pay particular attention to pronouncing vowels.

	Name	Pronounced
A a	*ah*	**short neutral sound as in sun**
Á á		**long a as in father**
B b	*beh*	**like English b**
C c	*tsey s*	**sound like the c in censor**
Č č	*ch*	**as in cheap**
D d	*dey*	**like English d**
Ď ď	*dy*	**sound like the d in the British pronunciation of dew**
E e	*ey*	**short e as in get**
É é		**long e as in hey**
Ě ě		**ye sound as in yet**
F f	*ef*	**like English f**
G g	*gey*	**hard g as in goose**
H h	*hah*	**h as in hurry**
Ch ch	*khah*	**kh sound as in Scottish loch**
I i	ee	**short i as in tip**
Í í		**ee sound like the i in machine**
J j	*yeh*	**y sound as in yard**
K k	*kah*	**like English k**
L l	*el*	**like English l**
M m	*em*	**like English m**
N n	*en*	**like English n**
Ň ň	*ny*	**like the n in the British pronunciation of new**
O o	*oh*	**short o as in hot**
Ó ó		**long aw sound as in shore**
P p	*pey*	**like English p**

R r	*yer*	**like English r**
Ř ř		**rzh sound as in French argent**
S s	*es*	**like English s**
Š š	*sh*	**as in sheet**
T t	*tey*	**like English t**
Ť ť	*ty*	**like the t in the British pronunciation of Tuesday**
U u	*oo*	**short u as in put**
Ú ů		**long u sound as in cool**
V v	*veh*	**w as in wine**
W w	*dvoyiteh veh*	**not a native Czech letter, pronounced as English w**
X x	*iks*	**not a native Czech letter, pronounced as English x**
Y y	*oopsilon ee*	**as in meet**
Ý ý		**as in meet**
Z z	*tset*	**like English z**
Ž ž		**soft zh sound like the s in measure**

Basic Words and Phrases

Yes Ano *Annoh*	**No** Ne *Neh*
Please Prosím *Prosseem*	**Thank you** Děkuji *Dekooyee*
Hello Ahoj *Ahoy*	**Goodbye** Nashledanou *Nazhlehdano*
Excuse Me Promiňte *Prohminyteh*	**Sorry** Pardon *Pardohn*
How Jak *Yack*	**When** Kdy *Gdyh*
Why Proč *Proch*	**What** Co *Tsoh*
Who Kdo *Gdoh*	
That's O.K. Prima *Preemmah*	**Perhaps** Možná *Mozhnah*
To Do *Doh*	**From** Od *Ohd*
Here Tady *Taddee*	**There** Tam *Tamm*

I don't understand
Nerozumím
Nerozumeem

I don't speak Czech
Neumím česky
Neumeem cheskee

Do you speak English?
Umíte anglicky?
Oomeeteh anglitskee?

Can you please write it down?
Můžete mi to napsat, prosím?
Moozhehteh mee toh napsat, prosseem?

Please can you speak more slowly?
Můžete mluvit pomaleji prosím?
Moozhehteh mloovit pomaleyi proseem?

Greetings

Good Morning/Good Afternoon/Good Evening/ Good Night
Dobrý den/Dobré odpoledne/ Dobrý večer/Dobrou noc
Dobree den/Dobreh odpoledneh/ Dobree vecher/Dobrow nots

Pleased to meet you
Těší mě
Tyeshee mnye

How are you?
Jak se máte?
Yak seh mahte?

I am well, thank you. And you?
Děkuji, dobře. A vy?
Dekooyi, dobrzeh. Ah vyh?

My name is ...
Jmenuji se ...
Menooyi sch ...

This is my friend/boyfriend/ girlfriend/husband/wife/ brother/sister
To je můj známý/přítel/ přítelkyně/manžel/manželka/ bratr/sestra
Toh yeh mooy znahmyh/przeetehl/ przeetelkynye/manzhel/manzhelkah/ bratr/sestrah

Where are you travelling to?
Kam jedete?
Kamm yedeteh?

I am/we are going to ...
Jedu/Jedeme do ...
Yedoo/Yedemeh doh ...

How long are you travelling for?
Jak dlouho cestujete?
Yack dlowhoh tsestuyeteh?

Where do you come from?
Odkud jste?
Odkood ysteh?

I am/we are from... Australia/Britain/Canada/ America
Jsem/Jsme z ... Austrálie/ Británie/Kanady/Ameriky
Ysem/Ysmeh z ... Austrahliye/ Britahniye/Ehvropyh/Ahmerikyh

We are on holiday
Jsme na dovolené
Ysmeh nah dovoleneh

ESSENTIALS

This is our first visit here
Jsme zde poprvé
Ysmeh zdeh poprveh

How old are you?
Kolik je vám let?
Kollick yeh vahm lett?

I am ... years old.
Jsem ... let starý/stará
Ysem ... lett staree/starah

I am a business person/doctor/journalist/manual worker/administrator/scientist/student/teacher
Jsem podnikatel/doktor/novinář/dělník/úředník/vědec/student/učitel
Ysem podnyikatel/doktor/novinahrz/dyelneek/oorzedneek/vyedets/stoodent/oochitel

I am waiting for my husband/wife/boyfriend/girlfriend
Čekám na manžela/manželku/přítele/přítelkyni
Chekahm nah manzhella/manzhelkoo/przeetelleh/przeetelkeenee

Would you like/may I have a cigarette?
Chcete cigaretu/můžu si zapálit?
Khtsete tsigaretoo? Moozoo see zappahleet?

Do you mind if I smoke?
Vadí vám když kouřím?
Vadyee vahm kdeezh kowrzeem?

Do you have a light?
Máte oheň?
Mahte ohenye?

Days

Monday Pondělí *Pondyelee*	**Tuesday** Úterý *Ootehree*
Wednesday Středa *Strzehda*	**Thursday** Čtvrtek *Chtvrtek*
Friday Pátek *Pahtek*	**Saturday** Sobota *Sobotah*
Sunday Neděle *Nedyele*	**Morning** Ráno *Rahno*

Afternoon/Evening/Night
Odpoledne/Večer/Noc
Odpoledneh/Vecher/Nots

Yesterday/Today/Tomorrow
Včera/Dnes/Zítra
Vcherah/Dnehs/Zeetrah

Numbers

Zero Nula *Noola*	**One** Jedna *Yednah*
Two Dvě *Dvyeh*	**Three** Tři *Trzhee*
Four Čtyři *Chteerzee*	**Five** Pět *Pyet*
Six Šest *Shest*	**Seven** Sedm *Sehdoom*

Eight
Osm
Ohsoom

Nine
Devět
Devyet

Ten
Deset
Dessett

Eleven
Jedenáct
Yeddenahtst

Twelve
Dvanáct
Dvannahtsts

Thirteen
Třináct
Trzeenahtst

Fourteen
Čtrnáct
Chrtnahtst

Fifteen
Patnáct
Patnahtst

Sixteen
Šestnáct
Shestnahtst

Seventeen
Sedmnáct
Sedoomnahtst

Eighteen
Osmnáct
Osoomnahtst

Nineteen
Devatenáct
Devattenahtst

Twenty
Dvacet
Dvatseht

Twenty-one
Jednadvacet
Yednadvatseht

Twenty-two
Dvádvacet
Dvahdvatseht

Thirty
Třicet
Trzheetseht

Forty
Čtyřicet
Chtyrzheetseht

Fifty
Padesát
Padehsaht

Sixty
Šedesát
Shedesaht

Seventy
Sedmdesát
Sedoomdesaht

Eighty
Osmdesát
Osoomdesaht

Ninety
Devadesát
Devahdesáht

One hundred
Sto
Stoh

Five hundred
Pět set
Pyet sett

One thousand
Tisíc
Tyiseets

One million
Milión
Milioh

Time

What time is it?
Kolik je hodin?
Kollick yeh hodyin?

It is ...
Je ...
Yeh ...

9.00
devět
devyet

9.05
je devět hodin a pět minut
yeh devyet hodyin ah pyet meenoot

9.15
je čtvrt na deset
yeh chtvert nah dessett

9.20
je devět hodin dvacet minut
yeh devyet hodyin a dvatsett meenoot

9.30
je půl desáté
yeh pool desahteh

9.35
je devět třicet pět
yeh devyet trzitsett pyet

9.40
je za dvacet minut deset
yeh za dvatsett meenoot dessett

9.45
je třičtvrtě na deset
yeh trzichtrvtye nah dessett

9.50
je za deset minut deset
yeh zah desset meenoot dessett

9.55
je za pět minut deset
yeh za pyet meenoot dessett

12.00/Midday/Midnight
dvanáct hodin/poledne/půlnoc
dvanahtst hodyin/polledneh/poolnots

Money

I would like to change these traveller's cheques/this currency
Rád/Ráda bych vyměnil/vyměnila tyto cestovní šeky/tuto měnu
Rahd/Rahdah bykh veemnyeneel /veemnyeneela teetoh tsestovnee shekyh/tutoh mnyenoo

How much commission do you charge? (What is the service charge?)
Kolik účtujete jako komisi?
Kollick oochtuyete yacko commeesee?

Can I obtain money with my Mastercard?
Můžu dostat peníze s Mastercard?
Moozhoo dostatt peneezeh s Mastercard?

Where is the nearest ATM?
Kde je nejbližší bankomat?
Gdeh yeh neyblishee bahnkomaht?

My name is ... Some money has been wired to here for me to collect
Jmenuji se ... Byly mi sem zaslány nějaké peníze na vyzvednutí
Ymenooyee seh ... Beelee mee sem zahsslahnee nyeyahkeh penyeezeh na veezvednootyee

ARRIVING AND DEPARTING

Airport

Excuse me, where is the check-in desk for ... airline?
Prosím vás, kde je přepážka pro odbavování zavazadel?
Proseem vahs, gdeh yeh przepazhkah proh odbavovahnee zavazzadell?

What is the boarding gate for my flight?
Kterým východem mám jít k mému letadlu?
Gderzhim weekhodem maam yeet k mehmu lettadlu?

What is the time of my flight?
Kdy letí moje letadlo?
Gdee letyee moye lettadloh?

How long is the delay likely to be?
Jak dlouho bude asi zpoždění trvat?
Yack dlowhoh boodeh assee zpozhdyenee trvatt?

Where is the duty-free shop?
Kde je prodejna bezcelného zboží?
Gdeh yeh proddeynah beztselnehoh zbozhee?

Which way is the luggage reclaim?
Kde se vyzvedávají zavazadla?
Gdeh seh vyzvedahvayee zahvazzadlah?

I have lost my luggage. Please can you help?
Ztratil/ztratila jsem zavazadla. Můžete mi, prosím, pomoci?
Ztrattill/ztrattillah ysemm zavazzadlah. Moozheteh mee, proseem, pomotsee?

I am flying to ...
Letím do ...
Letteem doh ...

Where is the bus for the city centre?
Odkud jede autobus do středu města?
Odkood yedeh awtoboos doh strzeddoo myestah?

Trains and Boats

Where is the ticket office?/Where is the information desk?
Kde je pokladna?/Kde jsou informace?
Gdeh yeh pockladnah?/Gdeh ysow informatse?

Which platform does the train/speedboat/ferry to ... depart from?
Z kterého nástupiště odjíždí vlak/motorový člun/převozní loď do ...?
Z kterehhoh nahstupishtye odyeezhdee vlack/mottorovee chloon/przevoznee lodye doh ...?

Where is platform ...?
Kde je nástupiště ...?
Gdeh yeh nahstupishtye ...?

When is the next train/boat to...?
Kdy jede další vlak/lod'do ...?
Gdee yedeh dalshee vlack/lod doh ...?

Is there a later train/boat to...?
Jede nějaký vlak/nějaká loď později?
Yedeh nyeyakee vlack/nyeyakah lodye pozdyeyee?

Notices and Signs

Jídelní vůz
Yeedelnee vooz
Buffet (Dining) Car

Autobus
Awtoboos
Bus

Pitná voda/Nepitná voda
Peetnah voddah/Neppeetnah voddah
Drinking/Non-drinking water

Vstup
Vstoop
Entrance

Východ
Veekhod
Exit

Nemocnice
Nemmotsnitse
Hospital

Informace
Informatse
Information

Úschovna zavazadel
Ooskhovnah zavazzaddel
Left Luggage (Baggage Claim)

Skřínka na zavazadla
Skrzeenkah nah zavazzadlah
Luggage Lockers

Poštovní úřad
Poshtovnee oorzadd
Post Office

Nástupiště
Nahstupishtye
Platform

Železniční stanice
Zheleznichnee stanyeetseh
Railway (Railroad) Station

Letiště
Letishtye
Airport

Policejní stanice
Politseynee stanitseh
Police Station

Přístav
Przeestav
Port

Restaurace
Restawratse
Restaurant

Kuřáci/Nekuřáci
Koorzahtsi/Nekoorzahtsi
Smoking/Non Smoking

Telefón
Telefohn
Telephone

Pokladna
Pokladnah
Ticket Office

Přepážka
Przepahzhkah
Check-in desk

Cestovní řád
Tsestovnee rzahd
Timetable (Schedule)

Záchody
Zahkhodee
Toilets (Restroom)

Dámy/Páni
Dahmee/Pahnee
Ladies/Gentlemen

Podzemní dráha
Podzemnee drahhah
Underground (Subway)

Čekárna
Checkahrnah
Waiting Room

Buying a Ticket

I would like a first-class/second-class/third-class single (one-way)/return (round-trip) ticket to....
Prosím jízenku první třídy/druhé třídy/třetí třídy pouze tam/zpáteční (okružní) do ...
Prosseem yeezdenkoo prvnee trzeedee/drooheh trzeedee/trzetee trzeedee powzeh tamm/zpahtechne (ockroozhnee) doh ...

Is it an express (fast) train/bus?
Je to rychlín/rychlíkový autobus?
Yeh toh reekhleen/reekhleekovy awtoboos?

Is my rail pass valid on this train/ferry/bus?
Platí moje jízdenka na vlak pro tento vlak/přepravní loď/autobus?
Platee moyeh yeezdenkah nah vlack proh tentoh vlack/przepravnee lodye/awtoboos?

I would like an aisle/window seat
Přeji si sedadlo u chodbičky/u okna
Przeyee see seddahdloh u chodbichtse/oo ocknah

No smoking/smoking please
V kuřáckém/nekuřáckém oddělení prosím
V koorzahtsem/neckoorzahtsem oddelenee proseem

We would like to sit together
Přejeme si místa vedle sebe
Przeyeme see meestenkoo vedleh sebbeh

I would like to make a seat reservation
Přeji si rezervovat místenku
Przeyee see rezzervovatt meestenkoo

I would like to reserve a couchette/sleeper for one person/two people/my family
Přeji si rezervovat lehátko/místo v lehátkovém voze pro jednu osobu/dvě osoby/pro rodinu
Przeyee see rezzervovatt lehahtkoh/meestoh v lehahtkovehm vozzeh proh yednoo ossobboo /dvye ossobbee/proh rodyeenoo

I would like to reserve a cabin
Přeji si rezervovat kabinu
Przeyee see rezzervovatt kabeenoo

Timetables (Schedules)

Příjezd
Przeeyezd
Arrival

Zastavuje
Zastavooyeh
Calls (Stops)

Jídelní služby
Yeedelnee sloozhbee
Catering Service

Přesednout v
Przessednowt v
Change at

CZECH

Spojení/přes
Spoyenee/przezz
Connection/via

Denně
Dennye
Daily

Každých čtyřicet minut
Kazdeekh chteerzitset meenoot
Every 40 minutes

První třída
Prvnee trzeedah
First Class

Každou hodinu
Kazdnow hodyinoo
Hourly

Doporučuje Vám obstarat si místenku
Doporoochooye Vam obstaratt see meestenkoo
Seat Reservations are recommended

Druhá třída
Droohah trzeedah
Second Class

Příplatek
Przeeplateck
Supplement Payable

Luggage

How much will it cost to send (ship) my luggage in advance?
Kolik stojí poslat dopředu zavazadla?
Kollick stoyee poslatt doprzedoo zavazzadlah?

Where is the left luggage (baggage claim) office?
Kde je úschovna zavazadel?
Gdeh yeh ooskhovnah zavazzadell?

What time do you open/close?
Kdy je otvíráte/zavíráte?
Gdee yeh otveerahte/zaveerahte?

Where are the luggage trolleys (carts)?
Kde jsou vozíky na zavazadla?
Gdeh ysow vozeekee nah zavazzadlah?

Where are the lockers?
Kde jsou skříňky?
Gdeh ysow skrzeenkee?

I have lost my locker key
Ztratil/ztratila jsem klíč od skřínky
Ztrattill/ztrattillah ysemm kleech ohd skrzeenkee

On Board

Is this seat free?
Je toto místo volné?
Yeh tottoh meestoh volneh?

Excuse me, you are sitting in my reserved seat
Promiňte, ale sedíte na místě

které jsem si rezervoval
Promminyteh, alleh sedeeteh nah meestye ktehreh ysehm see rezzervovall

Which station is this?
Jak se jmenuje tato zastávka?
Yak se ymenuyhe tattoh zastahvkah?

What time is this train/bus/ferry/flight due to arrive/depart?
V kolik hodin tenhle vlak/tenhle autobus/tahle loď/tohle letadlo přijiždí/odjíždí?
Fkollick hodyin tenhleh vluck/tenhleh aootohbuhs/tahhleh lodye/tohhleh lehtadloh przhiyeezhdyee/odyeezhdyee?

Travelling with Children

Do you have a high chair/baby-sitting service/cot?
Máte vysokou židli pro děti/služby baby-sitting/dětskou postýlku?
Mahteh veesockow zhidlee proh dyetee/sloozhbee baby-sitting/dyetskow posteelkoo?

Where is the nursery/playroom?
Kde jsou jesle/dětská klubovna?
Gdeh ysow yesleh/dyetskah kloobovnah?

Where can I warm the baby's bottle?
Kde mohu ohřát lahvičku pro miminko?
Gdeh mohoo ohrzaht lahvichkoo proh meemeenkoh?

Customs and Passports

Pasy, prosím!
Passee, prosseem!
Passports please!

I have nothing/wine/spirits (alcohol)/tobacco to declare
Nemám nic k procelní/víno/lihoviny/cigarety
Nemmahm nits k protslenee/veenoh/leehohveenee/tsigarettee

I will be staying for ... days/weeks/months.
Zůstanu zde ... dnů/týdnů/měsíců
Zoostanoo zdeh … dnoo/teednoo/myeseetsoo

SIGHTSEEING

Asking the Way

Excuse me, do you speak English?
Promiňte, mluvíte anglicky?
Prommeenyteh, mlooveeteh anglitskee?

Excuse me, can you help me please?
Promiňte, potřebuji poradit?
Promminyteh, potrzebujee porradyit?

Where is the Tourist Information Office?
Kde je turistická informační kancelář?
Gdeh yeh tooristitskah informachnee kantselarz?

Excuse me, is this the right way to ...?
Promiňte, jedu/jdu správně do ...?
Prommeenyteh, yeddoo/ydoo sprahvnye doh …?

... the cathedral/the tourist office/the castle/the old town
... katedrála/turistická kancelář/hrad/staré město
... katteddrahlah/tooristitskah kantselahrz/hradd/starreh myestoh

Can you tell me the way to the railway station/bus station/taxi rank/ city centre/beach?
Můžete mi, prosím, ukázat kudy se jede/jde na železniční nadraží/autobusové nádraží/ kde jsou taxíky/střed města/ na pláž?
Moozheteh mee, proseem, ookahzatt koodee seh yeddeh nah zhelezneechnee nahdrazhee/awto-boosoveh nahdrazhee/gdeh ysow taxeekee/strzedd myestah/nah plazh?

První/druhá/do leva/do prava/ přímo
Prvnee/droohah/doh levah/ doh pravah/przeemoh
First/second/left/right/ straight ahead

Na rohu/u dopravních světel
Nah rohhoo/oo dopravneekh svyetell
At the corner/at the traffic lights

Where is the nearest police station/post office?
Kde je nejbližší policejní stanice/poštovní úřad?
Gdeh yeh neybleezhshee poleetseynee staneetseh/ poshtovnee oorzadd?

Is it near/far?
Je to blízko/daleko?
Yeh toh bleezkoh/dalekoh?

Do I need to take a taxi/catch a bus?
Musím jet taxíkem/ autobusem?
Mooseem yet taxeekemm/ awtoboosemm?

Do you have a map?
Máte mapu?
Mahteh mappoo?

Can you point to it on my map?
Můžete mi to ukázat na mapě?
Moozheteh mee toh ookahzatt nah mappye?

Thank you for your help
Děkuji za vaši ochotu
Dyekooyi zah vashee okhotoo

How do I reach the motorway/main road?
Jak se dostanu na dálnici/ na hlavní silnici?
Yack seh dostanoo nah dahlneetsee/nah hlavnee silnitsee?

I think I have taken the wrong turning
Myslím, že jsem špatně zahnul
Meesleem, zheh ysemm shpatne zahnul

I am looking for this address
Hledám tuto adresu
Hledahm tootoh adressoo

CZECH

I am looking for the ... hotel
Hledám hotel ...
Hledahm hottell ...

How far is it to ... from here?
Jak je to odtud daleko do ...?
Yack yeh toh odtood dalleckoh doh ...?

Jeďte přímo rovně ... kilometrů
Yedyteh przeemoh rovnye ... kilometroo
Carry straight on for ... kilometres

Na první křižovatce zabočte do prava/do leva
Nah prvnee krzeezhovattse zabochteh doh pravvah/doh levvah
Take the next turning on the right/left

Na příští křižovatce/u dopravních světel zabočte do prava/do leva
Nah przeeshtee krzeezhovvatse/oo dopravneekh svyetell zabochteh doh pravvah/doh levvah.
Turn right/left at the next crossroads/traffic lights

Jedete/Jdete špatně
Yedetteh/Ydetteh shpatnye
You are going in the wrong direction

Where is the cathedral/church/museum/ pharmacy?
Kde je katedrála/kostel/ museum/lékárna?
Gdeh yeh kattedrahlah/kostell/ mooseum/lehkahrna?

How much is the admission/ entrance charge?
Kolik stojí lístky/vstupné?
Kollick stoyee leestkyh/vstoopneh?

Is there a discount for children/students/senior citizens?
Je sleva pro děti/studenty/ dříve narozené?
Yeh slevah proh dyetee/ stoodenteeh/drzeeveh narozeneh?

What time does the next guided tour (in English) start?
Kdy půjde příští skupina s průvodcem (mluvícím anglicky)?
Gdee poojdeh przeeshtee skoopeenah s proovodtsem (mlooveetseem anglitskee)?

One/two adults/children please.
Jeden/dva dospělí/děti prosím
Yeddenn/dvah dospyelee/dyetee proseem

May I take photographs here?
Smím tady fotografovat?
Smeem taddee phottographovatt?

At the Tourist Office

Do you have a map of the town/area?
Máte mapu města?
Mahteh mappoo myestah?

Do you have a list of accommodation?
Máte seznam ubytování?
Mahteh seznamm oobeetovahnee?

Can I reserve accommodation?
Mohu si rezerovat ubytování?
Mohoo see rezzervovatt oobeetovahnee?

ACCOMMODATION

Hotels

I have a reservation in the name of ...
Mám rezervaci na jméno
Mahm rezervatsi nah ymehnoh ...

I wrote to/faxed/telephoned you last month/last week
Poslal/poslala jsem dopis/fax/ telefonoval/telefonovala jsem minulý měsíc/minulý týden
Poslall/poslallah ysemm doppees/ fahx/telephonnovall/telephonnovallah ysemm meenoolee myeseets/ meenoolee teedenn

Do you have any rooms free?
Máte volné pokoje?
Mahteh volneh pockoyeh?

I would like to reserve a single/double room with/ without bath/shower
Rád/Ráda bych si rezervoval/ rezervovala jednolůžkový/ dvoulůžkový pokoj s/bez koupelny/sprchy
Rahd/Rahdah beekh see rezzervo-vall/rezzervoalla yednolloozhkovee/ dvowloozhkovee pockoy s/bez kowpelnee/sprkhee

I would like bed/breakfast/ (room and) full board
Přeji si lůžko se snídaní/ (pokoj) s plnou penzí
Przeyee see loozhkoh seh sneeda-nee/(pockoy) s plnow penzee

How much is it per night?
Koliks tojí pokoj na den?
Kollick stoyee pockoy nah denn?

Is breakfast included?
Zahrnuje to snídani?
Zahrnooye toh sneedanye?

Do you have any cheaper rooms?
Máte nějaké lacinější pokoje?
Mahteh nyeyakeh latsinyeyshee pockoyeh?

I would like to see/take the room
Rád/Ráda bych se na pokoj podívala
Rahd/Rahdah beekh seh nah pockoy podeevallah

I would like to stay for ... nights
Zůstanu ... dnů
Zoostanoo ... dnoo

The shower/light/tap/hot water doesn't work
Sprcha/světlo/voda/horká voda nefunguje
Sperkha/svyetloh/voddah nephoongooye

At what time/where is breakfast served?
Kdy/kde se podává snídaně?
Gdee/gdeh seh podahvah sneedanye?

What time do I have to check out?
Kdy musím pokoj uvolnit?
Gdee mooseem pockoy oovolneet?

Can I have the key to room number ... ?
Přeji si klíč pokoje číslo ...?
Przeyee see kleech pockoyeh cheesloh ...?

My room number is ...
Můj pokoj má číslo ...
Mooy pockoy mah cheesloh ...

My room is not satisfactory/ not clean enough/too noisy. Please can I change rooms?
Nejsem spokojený/spokojená s Pokojem, není dost čistý/je slyšet hluk. Je možné změnit pokoj?
Neysemm spockoyenee/spockoyenah s pockoyemm, nennee dostyi cheesteh/je sleeshet hluk. Yeh mozhneh zmnyeneet pockoy?

Where is the bathroom?
Kde je koupelna?
Gdeh yeh kowpelnah?

Do you have a safe for valuables?
Máte trezor pro cennosti?
Mahteh trezohr proh tsenostee?

Is there a laundry/do you wash clothes?
Je tady prádelna/perete prádlo?
Yeh tadee prahdelnah/pereteh prahdloh?

I would like an air-conditioned room
Přeji si pokoj s klimatizací
Przeyee see pockoy s climatizatsee

Do you accept traveller's cheques/credit cards?
Berete cestovní šeky/ kreditní karty?
Berretteh tsestovnee checkee/ creditnee cartee?

May I have the bill please?
Můžu platit, prosím?
Moozhoo plateet, proseem?

Excuse me, I think there may be a mistake in this bill
Promiňte, myslím že v účtu je chyba
Prommeenyteh, meesleem zhe oochtu yeh khybah

Youth Hostels

How much is a dormitory bed per night?
Kolik stojí postel ve společné noclehárně na jednu noc?
Kollick stoyee postell veh spollechneh notslehahrnye nah yednoo nots?

I am/am not an HI member.
Jsem/Nejsem členem HI
Ysemm/Neysemm chlenemm Hah Ee

May I use my own sleeping bag?
Mohu použít vlastní spací pytel?
Mohoo powzheet vlastnee spatsee peetell?

What time do you lock the doors at night?
Kdy v noci zamykáte?
Gdee v notsee zammeekahteh?

CZECH

Camping

May I camp for the night/two nights?
Můžu tady kampovat jednu noc/dvě noci?
Moozhoo tadee kampovatt yednoo nots/dveh notsee?

Where can I pitch my tent?
Kde si můžu postavit stan?
Gdeh see moozhoo postavitt stann?

How much does it cost for one night/week?
Kolik to stojí na jednu noc/ na jeden týden?
Kollick toh stoyee nah yednoo nots/nah yedenn teedenn?

Where are the washing facilities?
Kde je umývárna?
Gdeh yeh oomeevahrnah?

Is there a restaurant/ supermarket/swimming pool on site/nearby?
Je tady/nebo blízko restaurace /supermarket/plovárna?
Yeh taddee/neboh bleezkoh restawratse/suppermarkett/ plowahrnah?

Do you have a safety deposit box?
Máte skřínku na úschovu cenin?
Mahteh skrzeenkoo nah ooskhovoo tseneen?

EATING AND DRINKING

Cafés and Bars

I would like a cup of/two cups of/another coffee/tea
Přeji si šálek/dva šálky/ještě jednu kávu/ještě jeden čaj
Przeyee see shahleck/dvah shalckee/yeshtye yednoo kahvoo/ yeshtye yedenn chay

With/without milk/sugar
S/bez mléka/cukru
S/bezz mlehkah/tsoocroo.

I would like a bottle/glass/two glasses of mineral water/red wine/white wine, please.
Přeji si láhev/sklenici/dvě sklenice minerální vody/ červeného vína/bílého vína, prosím
Przeyee see lahhev/sclenitsee/dvye sclenitseh minerahlnee vodee/ chervenehhoh veenah/beelehhoh veenah, prosseem

I would like a beer/two beers, please
Přeji si pivo/dvě piva, prosím
Przeyee see peevoh/dvyeh peevah, prosseem

Please may I have some ice?
Mohu dostat prosím led?
Mohhoo dostatt prosseem ledd?

Do you have any matches/ cigarettes/cigars?
Máte zápalky/cigarety/ doutníky?
Mahteh zahpalkee/tsigaretee/ dowtneekee?

Restaurants

Can you recommend a good/ cheap restaurant in this area?
Můžete doporučit dobrou/ lacinou restauraci v okolí?
Moozheteh dopporoocheet dobrow /latsinow restawratsee v ockolee?

I would like a table for ... people
Přeji si stůl pro ... osob.
Przheyee see stool proh ... ossobb

Do you have a non-smoking area?
Máte místnost pro nekuřáky?
Mahte meestnost proh nekoorzahkee?

Waiter/waitress!
Čisniku/čisnice!
Cheeshneekoo/cheeshnitse!

Excuse me, please may we order?
Promiňte, přejeme si objednat?
Promminyteh, przeyemmeh see obyednatt?

Do you have a set menu/ children's menu/wine list in English?
Máte menu dne/dětské menu/vinný lístek v angličtině?
Mahteh menoo dneh/dyetskeh menuh/veenee leesteck v anglichtinye?

Do you have any vegetarian dishes?
Máte vegetariánská jídla?
Mahteh vegetahriahnskah yeedlah?

Do you have any local specialities?
Máte nějaké místní speciality?
Mahteh nyeyakeh meestnee spetsialeetee?

Are vegetables included?
Zahrnuje to zeleninu?
Zahrnooye toh zelleneenoo?

Could I have it well-cooked/ medium/rare, please?
Přeji si to dobře propečené/ středně/jen lehce propečené, prosím
Przeyee see toh dobrzeh proppecheneh/strzednyeh/yen lehtseh proppecheneh, prosseem

What does this dish consist of?
Co je v tomto pokrmu?
Tsoh yeh v tomtoh pokrmoo?

I am a vegetarian. Does this contain meat?
Jsem vegetarián. Není v tom maso?
Ysem vegetahreeahn. Nenyee ftom mahsoh?

I do not eat nuts/dairy products meat/fish
Nejím ořechy/mléčné výrobky/ maso/ryby
Neyeem orzekhee/mlehchneh veerobkee/massoh/reebee

Not (very) spicy please
Ne (příliš) ostré, prosím
Neh (przeelish) ostreh, prosseem

I would like the set menu please
Přeji si menu dne, prosím
Przeyee see menoo dneh, prosseem

We have not been served yet
Jeste jsme nebyli obslouženi
Yeshtye smeh nehbyhli obslowzhenih

Please bring a plate/knife/ fork
Přineste mi, prosím talíř/nůž/ vidličku
Przeenesteh mee proseem tahleerz/noozh/veedleetchkoo

Excuse me, this is not what I ordered
Promiňte, toto jsem si neobjednal/neobjednala
Promminyteh, tottoh ysemm see neobyednall/neobyednallah

May I have some/more bread/water/coffee/tea?
Mohu dostat chleba/vodu/ kávu/čaj?
Mohoo dostatt khlebah/voddoo/ kahvoo/chay?

May I have the bill please?
Přeji si platit, prosím?
Przeyee see platteet, prosseem?

Does this bill include service?
Zahrnuje účet spropitné?
Zahrnooye oochet spropitneh?

Do you accept traveller's cheques/Mastercard/ US dollars?
Berete cestovní šeky/ Mastercard/americké dolary?
Berreteh tsestovnee shekee/ Mastercard/amerritskeh dollaree?

Can I have a receipt please?
Můžete mě dát stvrzenku, prosím vás?
Moozheteh mnye daht stverzenkoo, prosseem vahs?

Where is the toilet (restroom) please?
Kde je záchod, prosím vás?
Gdeh yeh zakhod, prosseem vahs?

On the Menu

Snídaně/Oběd/Večeře
Snyeedahnyeh/Obyed/Vetchehrzeh
Breakfast/Lunch/Dinner

První chod *Prvnee khodd* **First Courses**	Polévky *Polehvkee* **Soups**
Hlavní chod *Hlavnee khodd* **Main Courses**	Rybí jídla *Reebee yeedlah* **Fish Dishes**
Chod s masem *Khodd s massemm* **Meat Dishes**	Hovězí *Hovyehzee* **Beef**
Steak *Steak* **Steak**	Vepřové *Veprzoveh* **Pork**
Telecí *Teletsee* **Veal**	Kuře *Koorzeh* **Chicken**
Jehněčí *Yehnyetchee* **Lamb**	Šunka *Shoonka* **Ham**

Jídla pro vegetariány
Yeedlah proh vegetariyahnee
Vegetarian Dishes

Zelenina *Zelenyeena* **Vegetables**	Hranolky *Hrahnolkee* **Chips (french fries)**

Vařené/opékané brambory/ bramborová kaše
Varzeneh/opehkahneh brahmboree/brahmborovah kahsheh
Boiled/sauté/mashed potatoes

Rýže
Reezheh
Rice

Sýry
Seeri
Cheese

Zákusky
Zackooskee
Desserts

Zmrzlina
Zmrzleena
Ice cream

Cukrovinky
Tsookroveenkee
Pastries

Ovoce
Ovotseh
Fruit

Chléb
Khleb
Bread

Rohlíky
Rolleekee
Rolls

Toast
Toast
Toast

Máslo
Mahsloh
Butter

Sůl/pepř
Sooll/peprz
Salt/pepper

Cukr
Tsookrr
Sugar

Speciality
Spetsialitee
Specialities

Místní speciality
Meestnyee spetseeyahleetee
Local specialities

Jídelní lístek
Yeedelnyee leesteck
Set Menu

Vinný lístek
Veeny leesteck
Wine list

Červená vína
Chehrvenah veena
Red wines

Bílá vína
Beelah veena
White wines

Růžová vína
Roozhovah veena
Rosé wines

Šumivá vína
Shoomeevah veena
Sparkling wines

Pivo
Peevoh
Beer

Lahvové pivo/točené pivo
Lahvoveh peevoh/totcheneh peevoh
Bottled beer/draught (draft) beer

Nealkoholické nápoje
Nehalcoholeetskeh nahpoyeh
Non-alcoholic drinks

Minerální voda
Meenerahlnyee vohda
Mineral water

Ovocné džusy
Ovotsneh joosee
Fruit juices

Pomerančový džus
Pomehrahntchovee joos
Orange juice

Limonáda
Leemonahda
Lemonade

Led
Led
Ice

Bílá káva/černá káva/espreso
Beelah kahva/chehrnah kahva/espresso
White coffee/black coffee/espresso coffee

Čaj s mlékem/s citrónem
Chy smlehkem/stseetronem
Tea with milk/with lemon

Čokoláda
Chocolahda
Chocolate (drink)

Mléko
Mlehkoh
Milk

Občerstvení/Lehká jídla
Obchehrstvenyee/Lehhkah yeedla
Snacks/Light meals

Saláty
Sahlahtee
Salads

Sendviče
Sendvicheh
Sandwiches

Vejce
Veytseh
Eggs

Klobása
Klohbahsa
Sausage

Vařená/smažená/ míchaná vejce
Vahrzenah/smahzenah/ meekhahnah veytseh
Boiled /fried/ scrambled eggs

Typical Local Dishes

Knedlíky
Knedleekee
Dumplings

Vepřová pečeně
Veprzovah pechenye
Roast pork

Kyselé zelí
Keeseleh zellee
Sauerkraut (Pickled cabbage)

Svíčková na smetaně
Sveechkovah nah smettanye
Beef in soured cream

Řízky
Rzheezkee
Escalopes

Bramborový salát
Bramborovee salaht
Potato salad

Dort
Dort
Gateaux

Koblihy
Kobleehee
Doughnuts

Ovocné knedlíky
Ovotsneh knedleekee
Fruit dumplings

Chlebíčky
Khlebeechkee
Open sandwiches

GETTING AROUND

Public Transport

Where is the bus stop/coach stop/nearest metro (subway) station?
Kde je autobusová/autokarová zastávka/nejbližší stanice metra?
Gdeh yeh awtoboosovah/ awtocarovah zastahvkah/ neyblizhshee stannitse metrah?

When is the next/last bus to ...?
Kdy jede příští/poslední autobus do ...?
Gdee yedeh przheeshtee/poslednee awtoboos doh ...?

How much is the fare to the city centre (downtown)/ railway station/airport?
Kolik stojí jízdenka do středu města/na železniční nádraží/na letiště?
Kollick stoyee yeezdenkah doh strzedoo myestah/nah zhelleznich-nee nahdrazhee/nah letishtye?

Will you tell me when to get off?
Řeknete mně kde mám vytoupit?
Rzeknyeteh mnye gdeh mahm veestowpeet?

Does this bus go to ...?
Jede tento autobus do ...?
Yedeh tentoh awtoboos doh ...?

Which number bus goes to ...?
Které číslo autobusu jede do ...?
Ktereh cheesloh awtoboosoo yeddeh doh ...?

May I have a single (one-way)/return (round-trip)/day ticket/book of tickets?
Prosím jízdenku jen tam/ zpáteční/jízdenku na celý den/ blok jízdenek?
Prosseem yeezdenkoo yenn tamm/ zpahtechnee/yeezdenkoo nah tselee denn/blohkh yeezdeneck?

Taxis (Taxíky)

I would like to go to ... How much will it cost?
Rád bych jel/jela do ... Kolik to bude stát?
Rahd beekh yell/yellah doh ... Kollick toh boodeh staht?

Please may I stop here?
Zastavíte mi zde, prosím?
Zastaveeteh mee zdeh, prosseem?

I would like to order a taxi today/tomorrow at 2pm to go from ... to ...
Rád bych/Ráda bych si objednala taxíka na dnes/na zitra ve dvě hodiny odpoledne na cestu z ... do ...
Rahd beekh/Rahdah beekh see obyednallah taxeekah nah dness/nah zeetrah veh dvye hoddee-nee odpoledneh nah tsestoo z ... doh ...

Entertainment

Can you recommend a good bar/nightclub?
Můžete doporučit dobrý bar/ nightclub?
Moozheteh dopporroochit dobree bar/nightclub?

Do you know what is on at the cinema (playing at the movies)/on at the theatre at the moment?
Víte co zrovna dávají v kině/divadle?
Veeteh tsoh zrovnah dahvayee v kinye/dyivadleh?

I would like to book (purchase) ... tickets for the matinee/evening performance on Monday
Rád/Ráda bych si zamluvil/zamluvila ... lístků na odpolední/večerní představení v pondělí
Rahd/Rahdah beekh see zamlooveel/zamlooveellah ... leestkoo nah odpolednee/vechernee przedstavenee v pondyelee

What time does the film/performance start?
Kdy začíná film/představení?
Gdee zacheenah film/przeds tavenee?

COMMUNICATIONS

Post

How much will it cost to send a letter/postcard/this package to Britain/Ireland/America/Canada/Australia/New Zealand?
Kolik stojí poslat dopis/pohlednici/tento balík do Británie/do Irska/do Ameriky/do Kanady/do Austrálie/na Nový Zealand?
Kollick stoyee posllatt doppees/pohlednitsee/tentoh baleeck doh Britahniye/doh Irskah/doh Americee/do Canadee/nah Novee Zehland?

I would like one stamp/two stamps
Prosím jednu známku/dvě známky.
Prosseem yednoo znahmkoo/dvye znahmkee

I'd like ... stamps for post-cards to send abroad, please.
Prosím ... známky pro pohlednice do zahraničí.
Prosseem ... znahmkee proh pohled-nitseh doh zahraneechee.

Phones

I would like to make a telephone call/reverse the charges to (make a collect call to) ...
Rád/Ráda bych zatelefonoval/zatelefonovala na účet volaného do ...
Rahd/Rahdah beekh zattelephonno-vall/zattelephonnovallah nah oochett vollannehoh do ...

Which coins do I need for the telephone?
Jaké mince na telefon potřebuji?
Yackeh meentseh nah telephonn potrzebooyee?

The line is engaged (busy)
Linka je obsazená
Linkah yeh obsazenah

The number is ...
To číslo je ...
Toh cheesloh yeh ...

Hello, this is ...
Haló, tady je ...
Halloh, taddee yeh ...

Please may I speak to ...?
Mohu, prosím, mluvit s ...?
Mohhoo prosseem, mlooveet s ...?

He/she is not in at the moment. Please can you call back?
Momentálně tady není. Můžete zavolat později, prosím vás?
Mommentalnye taddee nenee. Moozhetteh zavollat pozdyeyee, prosseem vahs?

SHOPPING

Shops

Knihkupectví/Papírnické zboží
Knyihkoopetstvee/papeernitskeh zbozhee
Bookshop/Stationery

Klenotnictví/Dárky
Klenottnitstvee/Dahrkee
Jeweller/Gifts

Obuv
Obboof
Shoes

Železářské zboží
Zhelezahrzskeh zbozhee
Hardware

Kadeřník
Kaderzhneek
Hairdresser

Pekárna
Peckahrnah
Baker

Supermarket
Suppermarkett
Supermarket

Fotografický obchod
Photographitskee obkhod
Photo Shop

Cestovní kancelář
Tsestovnee kantselarz
Travel Agent

Drogerie
Droggerriye
Pharmacy

In the Shops

What time do the shops open/close?
Kdy obchody otevírají/zavírají?
Gdee obkhodee ohteveerahyee/ zavveerayee?

Where is the nearest market?
Kde je nejbližší trh?
Gdeh yeh neyblizhshee terh?

Can you show me the one in the window/this one?
Můžete mi ukázat to ve výkladě/tento?
Moozheteh mee oocahzatt toh veh veekladye/tentoh?

Can I try this on?
Můžu si to vyzkoušet?
Moozhoo see toh veezkowshett?

SHOPPING

C Z E C H

What size is this?
Jaká je to velikost?
Yackah yeh toh velleeckost?

This is too large/too small/too expensive. Do you have any others?
To je příliš velké/příliš malé/příliš drahé. Máte jiné?
Toh yeh przeeleesh velckeh/przeelish malleh/przeellish draheh. Mahteh yeeneh?

My size is ...
Moje velikost je ...
Moye vellickost yeh ...

Where is the changing room/children's/cosmetic/ladieswear/menswear/food department?
Kde jsou převlékárny/dětské/kosmetika/dámské/pánské/potravinářské oddělení?
Gdeh ysow przevlehkahrnee/dyetskeh/cosmetitskeh/dahmskeh/potraveenarzskeh oddyelenee?

I would like ... a quarter of a kilo/half a kilo/a kilo of bread/butter/ham/this fruit
Prosím| čtvrt kila/půl kila/kilo chleba/másla/šunky/tohoto ovoce ...
Prosseem ... chtvert killah/pool killah/killoh khlebah/mahslah/shoonkee/tohotoh ovotse ...

Do you have a carrier (shopping) bag?
Máte sáček?
Mateh sahcheck?

How much is this?
Kolik je to?
Kollick yeh toh?

I'll take this one, thank you
Koupím toto, děkuji pěkně
Kowpeem totoh, dekujee pyeknye

Do you have anything cheaper/larger/smaller/of better quality?
Máte něco lacinějšího/většího/menšího/nebo lepší kvality?
Mahteh nyetso latsinyejsheehoh/vyetsheehoh/mensheehoh/neboh lepshee kvalitee?

I would like a film/to develop this film for this camera
Přeji si film/vyvolt film z této kamery
Przeyee see film/veevolt film z tehto kameree

I would like some batteries, the same size as this old one
Potřebuji baterie, stejné velikosti jako je tato stará
Potrzebuyee batteriye, steyneh velickostyee yackoh yeh tatoh starah

Would you mind wrapping this for me, please?
Mužete mi to, prosím vás, zabalit?
Moozhete mee toh, prosseem vahs, zabbaleet?

Sorry, but you seem to have given me the wrong change
Promiňte, ale vrátil jste mně peníze špatně
Promminyteh, aleh vrahtil ysteh mnye penneezeh shpatnye

MOTORING

Car Hire (Rental)

I have ordered (rented) a car in the name of ...
Objednal jsem si (najal) auto na jméno ...
Obyednall ysemm see (nayall) awtoh nah ymehnoh ...

How much does it cost to hire (rent) a car for one day/ two days/a week?
Kolik stojí pronajmutí auta na jeden den/na dva dny/na týden?
Kollick stoyee pronnaymootee awtah nah yeddenn denn/dvah dnee/na teedenn?

Is the tank already full of petrol (gas)?
Je nádrž plná benzínu?
Yeh nahdrzh plnah benzeenoo?

Is insurance and tax included? How much is the deposit?
Zahrnuje to pojištění a daně? Kolik je záloha?
Zahrnooyeh toh poyeeshtyenee ah danye? Kollick yeh zahlohah?

By what time must I return the car?
Kdy musím auto vrátit?
Gdee mooseem awtoh vrahtyit?

I would like a small/large/ family/sports car with a radio/cassette
Přeji si menší/větší/rodinné/ sportovní auto s radiem/ kazetou
Przeyee see menshee/vyetshee/ roddeeneh(sportovnee awtoh s raddiyem/cazzettow.

Do you have a road map?
Máte silniční mapu?
Mahteh seelnichnee mappoo?

Parking

How long can I park here?
Jak dlouho tady můžu parkovat?
Yack dlowhoh taddee moozhoo parkovatt?

Is there a car park near here?
Je tady blízko parkoviště?
Yeh taddee bleezckoh parcovishtye?

At what time does this car park close?
Kdy se toto parkoviště zavírá?
Gdee seh tottoh parcovishtyeh zaveerah?

Signs and Notices

Jednosměrka
Yednosmnyerkah
One way

Zákaz vjezdu
Zahkaz vyezdoo
No entry

Zákaz parkování
Zahkaz parckovahnee
No Parking

Objížďka
Obyeezhdykah
Detour (Diversion)

Stop
Stop
Stop

Dejte přednost
Deyteh przednost
Give Way (Yield)

Kluzká vozovka
Kloozkah vozzovkah
Slippery Road

Zákaz předjíždění
Zahkaz przedyeezhdyenee
No overtaking

Nebezpečí !
Nebbezpechee !
Danger!

At the FIlling Station (U Benzínové Pumpy)

Unleaded (lead free)/ standard/ premium/diesel
Metylizovaný benzín (bezolovnatý)/standardní/ premium/diesel
Meteelizovannee benzeen (bezzollovnatee)/standardnee/ deezl)

Fill the tank please
Naplňte nádrž, prosím
Naplnyteh nahdrzh, prosseem

Do you have a road map?
Máte silniční mapu?
Mahteh seelnichnee mappoo?

How much is the car wash?
Koliks tojí umytí auta?
Kollick stoyee oomeetyee awtah?

Breakdowns

I've had a breakdown at ...
Porouchalo se mi auto u ...
Porrowkhaloh seh mee awtoh oo ...

I am a member of the ... [motoring organisation]
Jsem členem ...
Ysem chlenem ...

I am on the road from ... to ...
Jsem na silnici od ... do ...
Ysemm nah seelnitsee odd ... doh ...

I can't move the car. Can you send a tow-truck?
Auto je nepojizdné. Můžete poslat vlečný vůz?
Awtoh yeh nepoyeezdneh. Moozheteh poslatt vlechnee vooz?

I have a flat tyre
Pneumatika je splasklá
Pneoomaticah yeh splasklah

The windscreen (windshield) has smashed/cracked
Čelní sklo je rozbité/prasklé
Chelnee skloh yeh rozbeeteh/ praskleh

There is something wrong with the engine/brakes/ lights/steering/gearbox/ clutch/exhaust
Je porouchaný motor/jsou porouchané brzdy/světla/ řízení/převodovka/spojka/ výfuk
Yeh porrowkhanee mottor/ysow poroukhaneh brzdee/svyetlah/ rzeezenee/przevodovkah/spoyckah/ veefook

It's overheating
Je přehřátý
Yeh przehrzahtee

It won't start
Nemohu nastartovat
Nemmohoo nastartovatt

Where can I get it repaired?
Kde to mohu nechat opravit?
Gdeh toh mohhoo nekhat opraveet?

Can you take me there?
Můžete mě tam vzít?
Moozhetteh mnye tamm vzeet?

Will it take long to fix?
Bude oprava trvat dlouho?
Boodeh opravah trvatt dlowhoh?

How much will it cost?
Kolik to bude stát?
Kollick toh boodeh staht?

Please can you pick me up/ give me a lift?
Prosím vás, můžete mě vyzvednout? Vzít sebou?
Prosseem vahs, moozhetteh mnye veezvednowt? Vzeet sebow?

Accidents and Traffic Offences (Violations)

Can you help me? There has been an accident.
Můžete mi pomoct? Stala se nehoda
Moozheteh me pomotst? Stahlah seh nahodah

Please call the police/an ambulance
Zavolejte, prosím, policii/záchranku
Zahvohlehyteh, prohseem, pohlitssiyi/zahhrankooh.

Is anyone hurt?
Je někdo zraněný?
Jeh nyekdoh zranyehnee?

I'm sorry, I didn't see the sign
Omlouvám se, neviděl jsem značku
Omlowvahm seh, neveedyel ysemm znachkoo

Must I pay a fine? How much?
Musím zaplatit pokutu? Kolik je to?
Mooseem zaplatteet pockootoo? Kollick yeh toh?

Ukažte mi dokumenty
Ookazhteh mee docoomentee
Show me your documents

HEALTH

Pharmacy (Farmacie)

Do you have anything for a stomach ache/headache/sore throat/toothache?
Máte něco na bolení žaludku/ bolení hlavy/bolení v krku/ bolení zubů?
Mahteh nyetsoh nah bollenee zhaloodkoo/bollenee hlavee/bolenee v kerkoo/bollenee zooboo?

I need something for diarrhoea/constipation/a cold/a cough/insect bites/ sunburn/travel (motion) sickness
Potřebuji něco proti průjmu/

proti zácpě/proti rýmě/proti kašli/na pokousání hmyzem/na spálení sluncem/na nevolnost při cestování
Potrzebooyee nyetso prottee prooymoo/prottee zatspye/prottee reemnye/prottee kashlee/nah pockowsahnee hmeezemm/nah spahlenee sloontsemm/nah nevolnost przee tsestovahnee

How much/how many do I take?
Jaké množství/kolik jich mám brát?
Yakeh mnozhstvee/kollick yeekh mahm braht?

I am taking anti-malaria tablets/these pills
Beru tablety proti malárii/tyto tablety
Beroo tabletee prottee malahriyee/teetoh tabletee

How often do I take it/them?
Jak často to mám brát?
Yack chastoh toh mahm braht?

I am/he is/she is taking this medication
Já beru/on bere/ona bere tento lék
Yah berroo/onn berreh/onnah berreh tentoh lehk

How much does it cost?
Kolik to stojí?
Kollick toh stoyee?

Can you recommend a good doctor/dentist?
Můžete doporučit dobrého doktora/zubaře?
Moozheteh dopporoochit dobrehoh doktorah/zoobarze?

Is it suitable for children?
Je to vhodné pro děti?
Yeh toh vhodneh proh dyetee?

Doctor (Doktor)

I have a pain here/in my arm/leg/chest/stomach
Tady mě to bolí/bolí mě ruka/noha/na prsou/žaludek
Taddee mnye toh bollee/bollee mnye roockah/nohah/nah prsow/zhaloodeck

Please call a doctor, this is an emergency
Prosím zavolejte doktora, je to náhlý případ
Prosseem zavoleyteh doctorrah, yeh toh nahlee przeepadd

I would like to make an appointment to see the doctor.
Rád/Ráda bych se objednala u doktora
Rahd/Rahdah beekh seh obyednall /obyednallah oo doctorrah

I am diabetic/pregnant
Jsem diabetik/jsem těhotná
Ysemm deeyabeteeck/ysemm tyehotnah

I need a prescription for ...
Potřebuji lékařský předpis na ...
Potoeboojee lehkarzskee przedpees nah ...

Can you give me something to ease the pain?
Můžete mi dát něco aby se mi ulevilo?
Moozheteh mee daht nyetso abee seh mee ooleveeloh?

I am/he is/she is/allergic to penicillin
Jsem/on je/ona je/alergický/alergická na penicilín
Ysemm/onn yeh/onnah yeh/alerghitskee/alergitskah nah pennitsileen

Bolí toto?
Bollee tottoh?
Does this hurt?

Musíte/on musí/ona musí do nemocnice
Mooseeteh/onn moosee/ohnah moosee doh nemmotsnitseh
You must/he must/she must go to hospital

Berte tyto jednou/dvakrát/třikrát denně
Berteh teetoh yednow/dvakraht/trzeekraht dennye
Take these once/twice/three times a day

I am/he is/she is taking this medication
Já beru/on bere/ona bere tento lék
Yah berroo/onn berreh/onnah berreh tentoh lehk

I have medical insurance
Mám zdravotní pojištění
Mahm zdrahvotnee poyeeshtyenee

Dentist (Zubař)

I have toothache/my filling has come out
Bolí mě zub/vypadla mi plomba
Bollee mnye zoob/veepadlah mee plombah

I do/do not want to have an injection first
Přeji si/nepřeji si nejdříve injekci
Przeyee see/neprzeyee see neydrzeeveh inyektsee

EMERGENCIES

Help!
Pomoc!
Pommots!

Fire!
Hoří!
Horzee!

Stop!
Stop!
Stop!

Call an ambulance/a doctor/the police/the fire brigade!
Zavolejte sanitku/doktora/policii/požárníky!
Zavoleyteh sanitkoo/doktorah/politsiyee/pozhahrneeckee!

Please may I use a telephone?
Mohu prosím Vás použít telefon?
Mohu prohseem Vahs powzheet tehlehfohn?

I have had my traveller's cheques/credit cards/handbag/rucksack/luggage/wallet/passport/mobile phone stolen
Byly mi ukradeny cestovní šeky/kreditní karty/kabelka/ruksak/zavazadla/peněženka/pas/mobilní telefon
Beelee mee oockradenee tsestovnee

chekee/creditnee cartee/kabbelkah/ rooksuck/zavazzadlah/ pennyezhenkah/pahss/mobeelnyee telefon

May I please have a copy of the report for my insurance claim?
Mohl bych dostat kopii protokolu pro svou pojišťovnu?
Mohl beekh dostaht kopeeyee protokoloo proh swoe poyeeshtyovnoo?

Can you help me, I have lost my daughter/son/my companion(s)?
Prosím vas, pomozte mi, ztratila se mi dcera/syn/společník/ společníci?
Prosseem vahs, pommozteh mee, ztrattilah seh mee tserah/seen/ spollechneeck/spollechneetseh?

Please go away/leave me alone
Běžte pryč/nechte mně být
Byezhteh preech/nekhteh mnye beet

I'm sorry
Promiňte
Prommeenyteh

I want to contact the British/ American/Canadian/Irish/ Australian/New Zealand/ South African Consulate
Rád/Ráda bych se spojil/ spojila s Britským/Americkým/ Kanadským/Irským/ Australským/Novozelandským/ Jihoafrickým Konzulátem
Rahd/Rahdah beekh seh spoyeel/ spoyeelah s Britskeem/ Ameritskeem/Kanadskeem/ Eerskeem/Novvozehlandskeem/ Yeehoafritskeem Konzullahtem

I'm/we're/he is/she is/they are/ill/lost/injured
Jsem/jsme/on je/ona je/oni jsou/nemocní/ztracení/ poraněni
Ysemm/ysmeh/onn yeh/onnah yeh/onnee ysow/nemmotsnee/ ztratsenee/porannyenee

FRENCH

INTRODUCTION

French is spoken not only in France but also in Monaco, in south and west Belgium and Brussels, in western Switzerland and as a second language in Luxembourg. English may also be spoken, but it will pay dividends to at least attempt some French.

Addresses for Travel and Tourist Information

For Luxembourg, see p.108.

Australia: *French Tourist Bureau,* 25 Bligh Street, Level 22, Sydney, NSW 2000; tel: (02) 9231 5244; fax: (02) 9221 8682.

Canada: *Maison de la France,* 1981 Ave McGill College, Suite 490, Montreal, Quebec H3A 2W9; tel: (514) 288 4264; fax: (514) 845 4868.

New Zealand: *Embassy,* 34–42 Manners Street, 13th Floor, PO Box 11–281, Wellington; tel: (04) 802 7779; fax: (04) 384 2578.

South Africa: *Maison de la France,* PO Box 41022, Craighall, Johannesburg 2024; tel: (11) 880 8062; fax: (11) 770 1666.

UK: *Maison de la France,* 178 Piccadilly, 3rd Floor, London W1J 9AL; tel: 09068 244123; fax: (020) 7493 6594. *Belgian Tourist Office Brussels–Wallonia* (French-speaking areas only), 217 Marsh Wall, London E14 9FJ; tel: 0800 954 5245; fax: (020) 7531 0393. *Switzerland Tourism,* 30 Bedford St, London WC2E 9ED; tel: (020) 7845 7680; fax: (020) 7845 7699.

USA: *French Government Tourist Office,* 444 Madison Ave, New York, NY 10022; tel: (212) 838 7800 (Tourist Information Line 900 990 0040 – calls charged). *Belgian Tourist Office,* 780 Third Ave, #1501, New York, NY 10017; tel: (212) 758 8130. *Swiss National Tourist Office,* 608 Fifth Ave, New York, NY 10020; tel: (212) 757 5944; fax: (212) 262 6116.

Official tourism websites: www.franceguide.com; www.monaco-tourisme.com; www.belgiumtheplaceto.be; www.MySwitzerland.com.

France Facts

CAPITAL: Paris (pronounced Paree)
CURRENCY: Euro (€, pronounced er-oh).€1 = 100 cents.
OPENING HOURS: Banks: Mon–Fri 0900–1600/1700. Shops: Mon–Sat 0800–1800 but often a 2-hour closing during lunch hours, except for big city shops. Museums: as for shops, but often closed on Mon.
TELEPHONES: To dial in, +33. Outgoing, 00 plus the country code. Police, 17. Fire, 18. Ambulance, 15.
PUBLIC HOLIDAYS: 1 Jan; Easter Sunday and Monday; Ascension Day (forty days after Easter); Pentecost (Monday following seventh Sunday after Easter); 1, 8 May; 14 Jul; 15 Aug; 1, 11 Nov; 25 Dec.

Belgium Facts

CAPITAL: Bruxelles (pronounced Broozell)
CURRENCY: Euro (€, pronounced er-oh). €1 = 100 cents.
OPENING HOURS: Banks: Mon–Fri 0900–1600. Shops: Mon–Sat 0900–1700/1800. Museums: Tues–Sat 1000–1700.
TELEPHONES: To dial in, +32. Outgoing, 00 plus the country code. Police, 101. Fire, Ambulance, 100.
PUBLIC HOLIDAYS: 1 Jan; Easter Monday; 1 May; Ascension Day (forty days after Easter); 21 Jul; 15 Aug; 1,11 Nov; 25 Dec.

Switzerland Facts

CAPITAL: Berne/Bern (pronounced Bairn)
CURRENCY: Swiss franc (Sfr, pronounced Frawng). Sfr 1 = 100 centimes/Rappen.
OPENING HOURS: Banks: Mon–Fri 0830–1630. Shops: Mon–Fri 0900–1200 and 1400–1830, Sat 0830–1200 (1600 in cities). Museums: Tues–Sun, hours approx. as for shops.
TELEPHONES: To dial in, +41. Outgoing, 00 plus the country code. Police, 117. Fire, 118. Ambulance, 144.
PUBLIC HOLIDAYS: 1 Jan; Good Friday and Easter Monday; Ascension Day (forty days after Easter); Pentecost (Monday following seventh Sunday after Easter); 1 Aug; 25, 26 Dec. In addition there are local public holidays.

FRENCH

ESSENTIALS

Alphabet and Pronunciation

	Name	Pronounced
A a à	*ah*	ah, like the vowel sound in barn; ai is pronounced like the a in late
B b	*beh*	like English b
C c	*seh*	hard c, as in cut, except before e or i, when it is an s sound as in sea
Ç ç		always an s sound as in sea
ch		always an sh sound, like the ch in machine
D d	*deh*	like English d
E e Ê ê È è	*e*	short e sound, as in fed; but en is pronounced more like a nasal long a, ahng; eu is like the vowel sound in fur
É é		long eh sound, like the vowel in hay
F f	*eff*	like English f
G g	*ge*	hard g before most letters, as in girl; before e and i it is a soft zh sound, like the s of pleasure; gn is pronounced ny, like the sound in onion
H h	*ash*	not pronounced in French
I i Î î	*ee*	a short i, as in hit, or more often a long ee sound like the i in machine
J j	*zhi*	always a soft zh sound, like the s of pleasure
K k	*ka*	like English k; not much used in French words
L l	*ell*	like English l; ll in the middle of a word is often pronounced like the y in layer
M m	*em*	like English m
N n	*en*	at the start of a word like the English n; a single n in the middle or at the end of a word is not pronounced but gives a nasal sound to the preceding vowel, like the effect of ng in thing and song
O o Ô ô	*oh*	either a short o as in cot or a long o sounding almost like the vowel sound in store; oe is like the vowel sound in fur; ou is pronounced oo, like the sound in zoo
P p	*pe*	like English p
Q q	*ku*	always together with u, making a k sound
R r	*her*	a more 'throaty' sound than English r
S s	*ess*	at the start of a word, a hard s as in sea; in the mid-

		dle of a word, a z sound as in prison; at the end of a word, not usually pronounced
T t	*te*	**like English t**
U u	*ew*	**like the vowel sound in hewn but without the preceding y sound; un by itself or before a consonant is a short nasal sound approximately like the sound in hung**
V v	*ve*	**like English v**
W w	*doobler ve*	**only in a few words in French, can be pronounced as a v or a w depending on the word**
X x	*iks*	**always a soft gz sound, like the x in exam**
Y y	*ee grek*	**an ee sound, like the y in party**
Z z	*zed*	**like English z**

Basic Words and Phrases

Yes
Oui
Wee

No
Non
Nawng

Please
S'il vous plaît
Seel voo pleh

Thank you
Merci
Mehrsee

Hello
Bonjour
Bawngzhoor

Goodbye
Au revoir
Aw revwahr

Excuse me
Excusez-moi
Ekskeweh mwah

Sorry
Désolé(e)
Dehzoleh

How
Comment
Kommahng

When
Quand
Kahng

Why
Pourquoi
Poorkwah

What
Quel
Kehl

Who
Qui
Kee

That's O.K.
Ça va
Sahr vahr

Perhaps
Peut-être
Purtehtr

To
À
Ah

From
De
Der

Here
Ici
Eesee

There
Là
lah

I don't understand
Je ne comprends pas
Zher ner kawngprahng pah

I don't speak French
Je ne parle pas français
Zher ner pahrl pah frahngsay

Do you speak English?
Vous parlez anglais?
Voopahrlay ahnglay?

Can you please write it down?
Pouvez-vous l'écrire s'il vous plaît?
Poovehvoo laycreer seelvooplay?

Please can you speak more slowly?
Pouvez-vous parler plus lentement s'il vous plaît?
Poovehvoo pahrlay plew lahntermahng seelvooplay?

Greetings

Good morning/good afternoon/good evening/ goodnight
Bonjour/bonjour/bonsoir/bonne nuit
Bawng-zhoor/bawng-zhoor/bawng-swahr/bun nwee

Pleased to meet you
Enchanté de faire votre connaissance
Ahngsahngteh der fair votr konehssahngss

How are you?
Comment allez-vous?
Komahng ahlehvoo?

Well, thank you. And you?
Bien merci. Et vous?
Beeang mehrsee. Eh voo?

My name is ...
Je m'appelle...
Zher mahpehl ...

This is my friend/boyfriend/ girlfriend/husband/wife/ brother/sister
C'est un ami/c'est mon ami/mon amie/mon mari/ma femme/mon frère/ma soeur
Saytangnahmee/say mawngnamee/ mawngnahmee/mawng mahree/ mah fahm/mawng frayr/mah surr

Where are you travelling to?
Où partez-vous en voyage?
Oo pahrtehvoo ahng vwahahzh?

I am/we are going to ...
Je vais/nous allons à ...
Zher vay/noozahlawng ah ...

How long are you travelling for?
Combien de temps partez-vous?
Kawngbeeang der tahng pahrtehvoo?

Where do you come from?
D'où venez-vous?
Doo vernehvoo?

I am/we are from Australia/Britain/Canada/ America
Je suis/nous sommes d'Australie/ de Grande-Bretagne/du Canada/ d'Amérique
Zher swee/noo soam dohstrahlee/der grahng brertahnyer/ dew canadah/dahmehreek

We are on holiday
Nous sommes en vacances
Noo som ahng vahkahngss

This is our first visit here
C'est la première fois que nous venons ici
Seh lah prermiair fwah ker noo vernon eeesee

How old are you?
Quel âge avez-vous?
Kehl ahzh aveh voo?

I am ... years old
J'ai ... ans
Zheh ... ahng

I am a businessman/business woman/doctor/journalist/ manual worker/ administrator/scientist/ student/teacher
Je suis homme d'affaires/femme d'affaires/médecin/journaliste/ouvrier (ouvrière **fem.**)/employé administratif (employée administrative **fem.**)/un(e) scientifique/étudiant(e)/ professeur
Zher swee om dafehr/fam dafehr/medisang/zhoornaleest/ oovrieh (oovriehr)/ahngplwahyeh administrateef (ahngplwahyeh administrateeve)/ang (ewn) seeanhgtifeek/ehtewdiangh (ehtewdianght)/professer

Would you like/may I have a cigarette?
Voulez-vous/puis-je avoir une cigarette?
Voolehvoo/pweezhahvwahr ewn seegahrett?

Do you mind if I smoke?
Est-ce que cela vous ennuie si je fume?
Ehsker cerlah vooz ahngnewee see zher fewm?

Do you have a light?
Avez-vous du feu?
Ahveh-voo dew fur?

I am waiting for my husband/ wife/boyfriend/girlfriend
J'attends mon mari/ma femme/mon ami/mon amie
Zhatahng mawng mahree/mah fahm/mawngnahmee/ mawngnahmee

Days

Monday
Lundi
Langdee

Tuesday
Mardi
Mahrdee

Wednesday
Mercredi
Mehrkrerdee

Thursday
Jeudi
Zhurdee

Friday
Vendredi
Vahndrerdee

Saturday
Samedi
Sahmdee

Sunday
Dimanche
Deemahngsh

Morning
Le matin
Ler mahtang

Afternoon
L'après-midi
Lahpreh meedee

Evening
Le soir
Ler swahr

Night
La nuit
Lah nwee

Yesterday/Today/Tomorrow
Hier/Aujourd'hui/Demain
Yehr/Ojoordewee/Dermang

Numbers

Zero
Zéro
Zayroa

One
Un/Une
Ang/Ewn

Two
Deux
Dur

Three
Trois
Trwah

Four
Quatre
Kahtr

Five
Cinq
Sangk

Six
Six
Seess

Seven
Sept
Seht

Eight
Huit
Weet

Nine
Neuf
Nurf

Ten
Dix
Deess

Eleven
Onze
Awngz

Twelve
Douze
Dooz

Thirteen
Treize
Trehz

Fourteen
Quatorze
Kahtorz

Fifteen
Quinze
Kangz

Sixteen
Seize
Sehz

Seventeen
Dix-sept
Deess seht

Eighteen
Dix-huit
Deez weet

Nineteen
Dix-neuf
Deez nurf

Twenty
Vingt
Vang

Twenty-one
Vingt et un
Vang tay ang

Twenty-two
Vingt-deux
Vangt dur

Thirty
Trente
Trahngt

Forty
Quarante
Kahrahngt

Fifty
Cinquante
Sangkahnt

Sixty
Soixante
Swahssahngt

Seventy
Soixante-dix
Swassahngt deess

Eighty
Quatre-vingts
Kahtrer vang

Ninety
Quatre-vingt-dix
Kahtrer vang deess

One hundred
Cent
Sahng

Five hundred
Cinq cents
Sang sahng

One thousand
Mille
Meel

One million
Un million
Ang meelyawng

Time

What time is it?
Quelle heure est-il?
Kel urr ehteel?

It is ...
Il est...
Eel eh ...

9.00
Neuf heures
Nurv urr

9.05
Neuf heures cinq
Nurv urr sangk

9.15
Neuf heures et quart
Nurv urr eh kahr

9.20
Neuf heures vingt
Nurv urr vang

9.30
Neuf heures et demie
Nurv urr eh dermee

9.35
Dix heures moins vingt-cinq
Dee zurr mwang vang sangk

9.40
Dix heures moins vingt
Dee zurr mwang vang

9.45
Dix heures moins le quart
Dee zurr mwang le kahr

9.50
Dix heures moins dix
Dee zurr mwang deess

9.55
Dix heures moins cinq
Dee zurr mwang sangk

12.00/Midday/Midnight
Douze heures/Midi/Minuit
Doowz urr/meedee/meenurhee

Money

I would like to change these traveller's cheques/this currency
J'aimerais changer ces chèques de voyage/ces devises
Zhaymray shahngzheh seh shek der vwahahzh/seh derveez

How much commission do you charge? (What is the service charge?)
Quelle commission prenez-vous?
Kehl komyssyawng prernehvoo?

Can I obtain money with my Mastercard?
Puis-je avoir de l'argent avec ma Mastercard?
Pweezh ahvwahr der largaang ahvek mah mastercard?

Where is the nearest ATM?
Où se trouve le distributeur de billets le plus proche?
Oo ser troov ler distribewter der beeyeh ler plew prosh?

My name is ... Some money has been wired to here for me to collect
Je m'appelle ... De l'argent m'a été envoyé ici
Zher mappell ... Der larzhahng ma etteh ahngvwahyeh eesee

ARRIVING AND DEPARTING

Airport

Excuse me, where is the check-in desk for ... airline?
Excusez-moi, où est le comptoir d'enregistrement de ...?
Ekskewsehmwah, oo eh ler kongtwahr dahngrehzheestreh mahng der ...?

What is the boarding gate/time for my flight?
Quelle est la porte d'embarquement/l'heure d'embarquement de mon vol?
Kehl eh lah pohrt dahng-bahrkehmahng/lurr dahng-bahrkehmahng der mawng vohl?

How long is the delay likely to be?
Le retard est de combien?
Ler rurtahr eh der kawngbyang?

Where is the duty-free shop?
Où est la boutique hors-taxe?
Oo eh lah booteek ohrtahks?

Which way is the baggage reclaim?
Où se trouve l'aire de réception des bagages?
Oo ser troov lair der rehsseh-psseeawng deh bahgahzh?

I have lost my luggage. Please can you help?
J'ai perdu mes bagages. Pouvez-vous m'aider?
Zheh pehrdew meh bagahzh. Pooveh voo mehdeh?

I am flying to ...
Je me rends à ...
Zher mer ranhg ah...

Where can I get the bus to the city centre?
Où puis-je prendre le bus pour le centre-ville?
Oo pweezh prahngdr ler bews poor ler sahngtr veel?

Trains and Boats

Where is the ticket office/ information desk?
Où se trouve le guichet/le bureau de renseignements?
Oo ser troov ler geesheh/ler bewroa der rahngsehniehmahng?

Which platform does the train/speedboat/ferry to ... depart from?
De quel quai part le train/bateau/ferry pour ...?
Der kehl kay pahr ler trang/batoh/ferry poor ...?

Where is platform ...?
Où se trouve le quai ...?
Oo ser troov ler kay ...?

When is the next train/boat to ...?
A quelle heure est le prochain train/bateau pour ...?
Ah kehl er eh ler proshang trang/batoh poor ...?

Is there a later train/boat to ...?
Y a-t-il un train/bateau plus tard pour ...?
Ee ahteel ang trang/batoh plew tahr poor ...?

Notices and Signs

Voiture-restaurant
Vwature restorahn
Buffet (Dining) car

Autobus
Otoebewss
Bus

Eau potable/Eau non potable
Oa poatahbl/Oa nawng poatahbl
Drinking/Non-drinking water

Entrée
Ahngtray
Entrance

Sortie
Soartee
Exit

Hôpital
Oppitahl
Hospital

Renseignements
Rahngsehnyermahng
Information

Consigne
Kawngsseenyer
Left luggage (Baggage claim)

Consigne automatique
Kawngsseenyer oatomahtick
Luggage lockers

Poste
Posst
Post office

Quai
Kay
Platform

Gare
Gahr
Railway (Railroad) station

Aéroport
Ahehrohpohr
Airport

Poste de police
Posst der poleess
Police station

Port
Pohr
Port

Restaurant
Rehstoarahng
Restaurant

Fumeurs/non fumeurs
Fewmurh/nawng fewmurh
Smoking/Non-smoking

Téléphone
Taylayphone
Telephone

Guichet
Geechay
Ticket office

Enregistrement des bagages
Ahngrehzheestrehmahng day bahgahzh
Check-in desk

Horaires
Oarayrh
Timetables (Schedules)

Toilettes
Twahlayt
Toilets (Restrooms)

Femmes/Hommes
Fam/Ommh
Ladies'/Gentlemen

Métro
Maytroa
Underground (Subway)

Salle d'attente
Sahldahtahngth
Waiting room

ARRIVING AND DEPARTING

FRENCH

Buying a Ticket

I would like a first-class/ second-class single (one-way)/return (round-trip) ticket to ...
Je voudrais un billet de première classe/deuxième classe aller/ aller-retour pour ...
Zher voodray ang beeyeh der prermyehr/durzyehm klahss ahlay/ahlay rertoor poor ...

Is it an express (fast) train/bus?
Est-ce que c'est un train/car express?
Essker seh ang trang/cahr express?

Is my rail pass valid on this train/ferry/bus?
Est-ce que ma carte ferroviaire est valable pour ce train/ce ferry/ce bus?
Ehss ker mah kahrt fehrohveealr eh vahlahblh dahng ser trang/ser ferry/ser bewss?

I would like an aisle/window seat
Je voudrais être près de l'allée/la fenêtre
Zher voodray aytr pray der lahlaeh/lah fernaytr

No smoking/smoking, please
Non fumeur/fumeur
Nawng fewmur/fewmur

We would like to sit together
Nous aimerions être assis ensemble
Noo aymerreeawng ehtr ahssee ahngsahngbl

I would like to make a seat reservation
Je voudrais réserver une place
Zher voodray rehzehrveh ewn plahss

I would like to reserve a couchette/sleeper for one person/two people/ my family
Je voudrais réserver une couchette/place de voiture-lit pour une personne/deux personnes/pour ma famille
Zher voodray rehzehrveh ewn kooshayt/plahss der vwature-lee poor ewn pehrson/dur perhson/poor mah fahmeeye

I would like to reserve a cabin
Je voudrais réserver une cabine
Zher voodray rehzehrveh ewn kahbeen

Timetables (Schedules)

Arrive
Ahrivh
Arrive

S'arrête à ...
Sahrayth ah...
Calls (Stops) at ...

Restauration
Restoarahsseeawng
Catering service

Changez à
Chahngzay ah ...
Change at ...

Correspondance
Koarespawngdahngss
Connection/Via

Tous les jours
Too ley joorh
Daily

Toutes les quarante minutes
Tooth lay kahrahngt menewt
Every 40 minutes

Première classe
Prermeeayrh class
First class

Toutes les heures
Toot lay zur
Hourly

Il est recommandé de réserver sa place
Eel eh rekomahngday der rayzayrvay sa plahs
Seat reservations are recommended

Deuxième classe
Derziem class
Second class

Supplément à payer
Sewplaymahng ah payay
Supplement payable

Luggage

How much will it cost to send (ship) my luggage in advance?
Quel est le prix pour envoyer mes bagages en avance?
Kehl eh ler pree poor ahngwahllay meh bahgahz ahng ahvahngss?

Where is the left luggage (baggage claim) office?
Où se trouve la consigne?
Oo ser troov lah kawngseen?

What time do you open/close?
A quelle heure ouvrez-vous/fermez-vous?
Ah kehl ur oovrayvoo/fairmehvoo?

Where are the luggage trolleys (carts)?
Où se trouve les chariots à bagages?
Oo ser troov leh shahryo ah bahgahzh?

Where are the lockers?
Où se trouve la consigne automatique?
Oo ser troov lah kawngseen awtoematique?

I have lost my locker key
J'ai perdu la clé de mon casier
Zhay payrdew lah kleh der mawng kahzeeay

On Board

Is this seat free?
Est-ce que cette place est libre?
Essker set plahss eh leebre?

Excuse me, you are sitting in my reserved seat
Excusez-moi, vous occupez la place que j'ai réservée
Ehskewzaymwah voo okewpeh lah plahss ker zay rehzehrveh

Which station is this?
Quelle est cette gare?
Kehl eh sayt gahr?

What time is this train/bus/ ferry/flight due to arrive/ depart?
A quelle heure arrive/part le train/le bus/le ferry?
Ah kehlur ahrivh/pahr ler trang/ ler bewss/ler ferry?

Travelling with Children

Do you have a high chair/ babysitting service/cot?
Avez-vous une chaise pour bébé/un service de garde pour enfants/un berceau?
Ahvehvoo ewn shehz poor behbeh/ang sehrvees der gahrd poor ahngfahng/ang behrso?

Where is the nursery/ playroom?
Où se trouve la chambre d'enfants/la salle de jeux?
Ooser troov lah shahngbr dahngfahng/lah sall der zhur?

Where can I warm the baby's bottle?
Où puis-je faire réchauffer le biberon?
Oo pweezh fair rehshoffeh ler beebrawng?

Customs and Passports

Les passeports, s'il vous plaît!
Leh pahsspor, seelvooplay!
Passports, please!

I have nothing/wine/spirits (alcohol)/tobacco to declare
Je n'ai rien à déclarer/J'ai du vin/ de l'alcool/du tabac à déclarer
Zher neh reeang ah dehklahreh/zhay dew yang/der lahlkol/dew tahbah ah dehklahreh

I will be staying for ... days/weeks/months
Je vais rester ... jours/semaines/mois
Zhe veh resteh ... zoor/sermehn/mwah

SIGHTSEEING

Asking the Way

Excuse me, do you speak English?
Excusez-moi, parlez-vous anglais?
Ekskewsehmwah, pahrlehvoo ahnglay?

Excuse me, can you help me please?
Excusez-moi, pouvez-vous m'aider s'il vous plaît?
Ekskeweh mwah, pooveh voo mehdeh seel voo pleh?

Where is the Tourist Information Office?
Où se trouve l'office de tourisme?
Oo ser troov loffyss de toorism?

Excuse me, is this the right way to ...?
Excusez-moi, c'est la bonne direction pour ...?
Ekskewzaymwah, seh lah bon deerekseeawng poor ...?

... the cathedral/the tourist information office/the castle/ the old town
... la cathédrale/l'office de tourisme/le château/la vieille ville

.. *lah kahtehdrahl/lohfeece de tooreezm/ler chateau/lah veeay veel*

Can you tell me the way to the railway (railroad) station/bus station/taxi rank (stand)/city centre (downtown)/beach?
Pour aller à la gare/gare routière/station de taxis/ au centre-ville/à la plage, s'il vous plaît?
Poor ahleh ah lah gahr/gahr rootyair/stahssion der taxi/oh sahngtr veel/ah lah plahzh, sylvooplay?

Première/deuxième à gauche/à droite/tout droit
Prermeyair/derzeaim ah goash/ah drwaht/too drwah
First/second left/right/ straight ahead

Au croisement/aux feux
Oh crwahzmahng/oh fer
At the corner/at the traffic lights

Where is the nearest police station/post office?
Où se trouve le poste de police/le bureau de poste le plus près?
Oo ser troov ler post der poliss/ler bewro der post ler plew pray?

Is it near/far?
Est-ce que c'est près/loin d'ici?
Esskerseh preh/lwang deesee?

Do I need to take a taxi/catch a bus?
Faut-il prendre un taxi/un autobus?
Foteel prahngdr ewn taxi/ewn otobewss?

Do you have a map?
Avez-vous un plan de la ville?
Aveh voo ang plahng der lah veel?

Can you point to it on my map?
Pouvez-vous me le montrer sur la carte?
Poovehvoo mer ler mawngtreh sewr lah kart?

Thank you for your help
Merci pour votre aide
Mehrsee poor votrayd

How do I reach the motorway/main road?
Pour aller jusqu'à l'autoroute/la route principale?
Poor ahleh zhewskah lowtohroot/lah root prahngsipahl?

I think I have taken the wrong turning
Je crois que je me suis trompé de chemin
Zher krawh ker zhay mer trompay der sheman

I am looking for this address
Je cherche cette adresse
Zher shaersh set adress

I am looking for the ... hotel
Je cherche l'hôtel ...
Zher shaersh lohtel ...

How far is it to ... from here?
... c'est loin d'ici?
... say looahng deesee?

Continuez tout droit pendant ... kilomètres
Kohnteeneway too drooah pahngdahng ... kilomehtr
Carry straight on for ... kilometres

Prenez la prochaine rue/route à droite/à gauche
Prernay lah proshen rew/root ah drwaht/ah goash
Take the next turning on the right/left

Tournez à droite/à gauche au prochain croisement/aux feux
Toornay ah drwaht/ah goash oh prohshahng krowzmahng/oh phyer
Turn right/left at the next crossroads/traffic lights

Vous allez dans la mauvaise direction
Vooz ahleh dahng lah mowvehz deerekseeawng
You are going in the wrong direction

Where is the cathedral/ church/museum/pharmacy?
Où se trouve la cathédrale/l'église/le musée/la pharmacie?
Oo ser troov lah catehdrahl/ lehgleez/ler mewzeh/lah fahrmah-see?

How much is the admission/entrance charge?
Quel est le prix d'entrée?
Khel eh ler pree delahngtreh?

Is there a discount for children/students/senior citizens?
Y a-t-il une réduction pour les enfants/les étudiants/les personnes du troisième âge?
Eeahteel ewn rehdewkssyawng poor lehzahngfahng/lehzehtewdyahng/leh pehrson dew trwahzyehm ahzh?

What time does the next guided tour (in English) start?
A quelle heure commence la prochaine visite guidée (en anglais)?
Ah kehlur komahngs lah proshain vysyt gueedeh (ahngn ahngleh)?

One/two adults/children, please
Un/deux adulte(s)/enfant(s), s'il vous plaît
Ewn/durzahdewlt/ahngfahng, seel voo play

May I take photographs here?
Je peux prendre des photos ici?
Zher per prangdr deh phowtoh eessee?

At the Tourist Office

Do you have a map of the town/area?
Avez-vous une carte de la ville/région?
Ahveh-voo ewn cart der lah veel/rehjyawng?

Do you have a list of accommodation?
Vous avez une liste de logements?
Voozahveh ewn leesst der lozhmahng?

Can I reserve accommodation?
Puis-je réserver un logement?
Peweezh rehzehrveh ang lozhmahng?

ACCOMMODATION

Hotels

I have a reservation in the name of ...
J'ai fait une réservation au nom de ...
Zheh feh ewn rehsehrvahssyawng o nawng der ...

I wrote to/faxed/telephoned you last month/last week
Je vous ai écrit/faxé/téléphoné le mois dernier/la semaine dernière
Zher voozeh ehkree/faxeh/ tehlehfoneh ler mwah dehrnyeh/lah sermayn dehrnyair

Do you have any rooms free?
Vous avez des chambres disponibles?
Voozahveh deh shahngbr deesspohneebl?

I would like to reserve a single/double room with/ without bath/shower
Je voudrais réserver une chambre pour une personne/ pour deux personnes avec/sans salle de bain/douche
Zhe voodray rehsehrveh ewn shahngbr poor ewn pehrson/poor dur pehrson avek/sawns sal der bang/doosh

I would like bed and breakfast/(room and) full board
Je voudrais le petit-déjeuner/la pension complète
Zher voodray ler pewtee-dehjew-neh/lah pahngsyawng kawngplait

How much is it per night?
Quel est le prix pour une nuit?
Khel eh ler pree poor ewn nuwy?

Is breakfast included?
Est-ce que le petit-déjeuner est compris?
Ehsker ler pertee dehjerneh eh kawngpree?

Do you have any cheaper rooms?
Avez-vous des chambres moins chères?
Ahvehvoo deh shahngbr mooang shayr?

I would like to see/take the room
Je voudrais voir/prendre la chambre
Zher voodreh vwahr/prahngdrer lah shahngbrer

I would like to stay for ... nights
Je voudrais rester ... nuits
Zhe voodray resteh ... newyh

The shower/light/tap/hot water doesn't work
La douche/la lumière/le robinet/ l'eau chaud ne marche pas
Lah doosh/lah luhmiair/ler rohbeenay/loh shoh ner marsh pah

At what time/where is breakfast served?
A quelle heure/où servez-vous le petit-déjeuner?
Ah khel ur/ooh serveh-voo ler perteedehjerneh?

FRENCH

What time do I have to check out?
A quelle heure dois-je laisser la chambre?
Ah khel ur dwahz lehseh lah shahngbr?

Can I have the key to room number ... ?
Je voudrais la clé de la chambre ...
Zher voodray lah klay der lah shahngbr ...

My room number is ...
Le numéro de ma chambre est ...
Ler newmehro der mah shahngbr eh ...

My room is not satisfactory/ not clean enough/too noisy. Please can I change rooms?
La chambre n'est pas agréable/ pas assez propre/trop bruyante. Je voudrais changer de chambre s'il vous plaît?
Lah shahngbrer neh pahz agrehah-bler/pahz asseh propreritroh bre-weeyahngt. Zher voodreh shahnzheh der shahngbrer, seel voo pleh?

Where is the bathroom?
Où se trouve la salle de bain?
Oo ser troov lah sall der bang?

Do you have a safe for valuables?
Avez-vous un coffre pour les objets précieux?
Aveh vooz ang coffrer poor lehz ohzheh prehsyer?

Is there a laundry/do you wash clothes?
Avez-vous un service de blanchisserie?
Aveh vooz ang sehrvees der blahngsheeseree?

I would like an air-conditioned room
Je voudrais une chambre avec l'air conditionné
Zher voodreh ewn shahngbrer avek lehr condeesioneh

Do you accept traveller's cheques/credit cards?
Vous acceptez les chèques de voyage/les cartes de crédit?
Voos aksepteh leh sheck der vwoyazh/leh kart der krehdee?

May I have the bill please?
Pouvez-vous me donner la note, s'il vous plaît?
Poovehvoo mer doneh lah nott seelvooplay?

Excuse me, I think there may be a mistake in this bill
Excusez-moi, mais je crois qu'il y a une erreur dans la note
Ehskewzaymwah, zhe kwaw ke eel ee ah oon errer don la not

Youth Hostels

How much is a dormitory bed per night?
Quel est le prix d'un lit en dortoir par nuit?
Kehl eh ler pree dang lee ahng dortwarr pahr newy?

I am/am not an HI member
Je suis/Je ne suis pas membre d'une Auberge de Jeunesse
Zhe sewy/zhe ner sewy pah mahngbr dewn obehrz der jurnehss

May I use my own sleeping bag?
Est-ce que je peux me servir de mon propre sac de couchage?
Ehsker zhe pur mer sairvyr der mawng proprer sahk der kooshahz?

What time do you lock the doors at night?
A quelle heure fermez-vous la porte le soir?
Ah kehlur fehrmehvoo lah port ler swahr?

Camping

May I camp for the night/two nights?
Puis-je camper pour la nuit/deux nuits?
Pweehze kahngpeh poor lah newy/dur newy?

Where can I pitch my tent?
Où puis-je dresser ma tente?
Oo pweehze dresseh mah tahngt?

How much does it cost for one night/week?
Quel est le prix par nuit/par semaine?
Kehl eh ler pree pahr newy/pahr sermayn?

Where are the washing facilities?
Où se trouve le bloc sanitaire?
Oo ser troov ler block sanitaire?

Is there a restaurant/ supermarket/swimming pool on site/nearby?
Y a-t-il un restaurant/ supermarché/une piscine sur place/ près d'ici?
Yahteel ang restorahng/ supermahrsheh/ewn peassinn sewr plahss/pray deessee?

Do you have a safety deposit box?
Avez-vous un coffre-fort?
Ahvehvoo ang koffr-for

EATING AND DRINKING

Cafés and Bars

I would like a cup of/two cups of/another coffee/tea
Je voudrais une tasse de/deux tasses de/encore une tasse de café/thé
Zher voodray ewn tahss der/der tahss der/oncaw ewn tahss der kafeh/teh

With/without milk/sugar
Avec/sans lait/sucre
Ahvek/sahng lay/sewkr

I would like a bottle/glass/ two glasses of mineral water/ red wine/white wine, please
Je voudrais une bouteille/un verre/deux verres d'eau minérale/de vin rouge/de vin blanc, s'il vous plaît
Zhe voodray ewn bootayy/ang vair/der vair doa mynehral/der vang roozh/der vang blahng, sylvooplay

I would like a beer/two beers, please
Je voudrais une bière/deux bières, s'il vous plaît
Zhe voodray ewn byair/der byair, sylvooplay

Please may I have some ice?
Puis-je avoir de la glace s'il vous plaît?
Pweezh ahvoar der lah glass seel vous pleh?

Do you have any matches/ cigarettes/cigars?
Avez-vous des allumettes/des cigarettes/des cigares?
Ahveh-voo dehzahlewmaitt/deh cigaraytt/deh ssigar?

Restaurants

Can you recommend a good/ cheap restaurant in this area?
Pouvez-vous recommander un bon restaurant/un restaurant bon marché dans les environs?
Pooveh-voo rekomahngdeh ewn bawng restorahng/ewn restorahng bawng mahrcheh dahng lehzah-ngvyrawng?

I would like a table for ... people
Je voudrais une table pour ... personnes
Zher voodray ewn tabl poor ... pehrson

Do you have a non-smoking area?
Vous avez une zone non-fumeurs?
Voozahvah ewn zohn nong fewmur?

Waiter/Waitress!
Monsieur/Mademoiselle, s'il vous plaît!
M'sewr/madmwahzel, sylvooplay!

Excuse me, please may we order?
Pardon, nous pouvons commander, s'il vous plaît?
Pahrdawng, noo poovawng commahngdeh sylvooplay?

Do you have a set menu/ children's menu/wine list?
Avez-vous un menu fixe/un menu pour enfants/la carte des vins?
Ahvehvoo ewn menew feex/ewn menew poor ahngfahng/lah list deh vang?

Do you have any vegetarian dishes?
Avez-vous des plats végétariens?
Ahvehvoo der plah vehgehtahryang?

Do you have any local specialities?
Y a-t-il des spécialités locales?
Eeahteel deh spayseeahleeteh locahl?

Are vegetables included?
Est-ce que les légumes sont compris?
Essker leh lehgewm sawng kohngpree?

Could I have it well-cooked/ medium/rare please?
Je le voudrais bien cuit/à point/ saignant
Zher ler voodray beeang kwee/ah pwang/saynyang

What does this dish consist of?
En quoi consiste ce plat?
Ahng koah kawngsist ser plah?

I am a vegetarian. Does this contain meat?
Je suis végétarien (végétarienne). Est-ce que ce plat contient de la viande?
Zher swee vehzhehtarianhg (vehzhehtarien). Essker ser plah kontyang der lah veeahngd?

I do not eat nuts/dairy products/meat/fish
Je ne mange pas de noix ni de noisettes/produits laitiers/viande/poisson
Zher ner mahngzh pah der nwah nee der nwahzett/prodwee lehtieh/veeahngd/pwasong

Not (very) spicy, please
Pas (trop) épicé, s'il vous plaît
Pah (troh) ehpeeseh, seel voo pleh

I would like the set menu, please
Je voudrais le menu du jour, s'il vous plaît
Zher voodray ler mernew dew zhoor, seelvooplay

We are still waiting to be served
Nous n'avons pas été encore servis
Noo nahvawng pahzehteh ahngkor sehrvee

Please bring a plate/knife/fork
Pouvez-vous me donner une assiette/un couteau/une fourchette, s'il vous plaît
Pooveh voos mer donneh ewn assiett/ang cootoh/ewn foorshett, seel voo pleh

Excuse me, this is not what I ordered
Excusez-moi, ce n'est pas ce que j'ai commandé
Ekskewzaymwah, ser nay pah ser ker zheh komandeh

May I have some/some more bread/water/coffee/tea?
Puis-je avoir du pain/encore du pain/de l'eau/du café/du thé?
Pweezh ahvoar dew pang/ahngkor dew pang/der lo/dew kafeh/dew teh?

May I have the bill, please?
L'addition, s'il vous plaît!
Laddyssyawng, sylvooplay!

Does this bill include service?
Est-ce que le service est compris?
Ehsk ler sehrveess eh kawngpree?

Do you accept traveller's cheques/MasterCard/US dollars?
Prenez-vous les chèques de voyage/la Mastercard/les dollars américains?
Prernehvoo leh cheque der vwahahzh/lah Mastercard/leh dolar ahmehrykang?

Can I have a receipt, please?
Je pourrais avoir un reçu s'il vous plaît?
Zher pooray avwahr ahng rerssew seelvooplay?

Where is the toilet (restroom), please?
Où sont les toilettes, s'il vous plaît?
Oo sawng leh twahlaitt, sylvooplay?

On the Menu

Petit-déjeuner/Déjeuner/Dîner
Pertee dehzherneh/dehzherneh/deeneh
Breakfast/Lunch/Dinner

Entrées *Ahngtray* **First courses**	Soupes *Soup* **Soups**

Plats principaux
Plah prangseepo
Main courses

Poissons *Pooahsong* **Fish dishes**	Viandes *Veeanhd* **Meat dishes**
Bœuf *Berf* **Beef**	Steak *Steak* **Steak**
Porc *Por* **Pork**	Veau *Voh* **Veal**
Poulet *Pooleh* **Chicken**	Agneau *Ahnyoh* **Lamb**

Jambon
Zhahmbong
Ham

Plats végétariens
Plah vehzhehtahryang
Vegetarian dishes

Légumes
Lehgewm
Vegetables

Frites
Freet
Chips (french fries)

Pommes de terre à l'eau/sautées/purée de pommes de terre
Pom der tehr ah loh/sohteh/pewreh der pom de tehr
Boiled/sauté/mashed potatoes

Riz *Ree* **Rice**	Fromages *Frohmahzh* **Cheese**

Desserts
Dehser
Desserts

Glace *Glass* **Ice cream**	Gâteaux *Gattoh* **Cakes**
Pâtisseries *Pateeseree* **Pastries**	Fruits *Frwee* **Fruit**
Pain *Pang* **Bread**	Petits pains *Pertee pang* **Rolls**

Toast
Toast
Toast

Beurre *Ber* **Butter**	Sel/Poivre *Sel/pwahvrer* **Salt/pepper**

Sucre
Sewkrer
Sugar

Spécialités
Spehsseeahleeteh
Specialities

Spécialités locales
Spehseealiteh lokahl
Local specialities

Menu fixe/du jour
Mernew fix/dew zhoor
Set Menu

Liste des vins
Leest deh vang
Wine list

Vins rouges
Vang roozh
Red wines

Vins blancs
Vang blahng
White wines

Vins rosés
Vang rohzeh
Rosé wines

Vins pétillants
Vang pehteeyahng
Sparkling wines

Bière
Beeyehr
Beer

Bière en bouteille/Bière (à la) pression
Beeyehr ahng booteh/Beeyehr (a lah) pressyong
Bottled beer/Draught (draft) beer

Boissons non alcoolisées/sans alcool
Bwahsong nong alco-olizeh/sahngz alco-ol
Non-alcoholic drinks

Eau minérale
Oh minerahl
Mineral water

Jus de fruits
Zhew der frwee
Fruit juices

Jus d'orange
Zhew dorahngzh
Orange juice

Limonade
Limonahd
Lemonade

Glaçons
Glassong
Ice

Café au lait/Café noir/Espresso
Kaffeh oh leh/Kaffeh nwahr/Espressoh
White coffee/black coffee/espresso coffee

Thé au lait/Thé citron
Teh oh leh/Teh seetrong
Tea with milk/with lemon

Chocolat chaud
Shokolah shoh
Chocolate (drink)

Lait
Leh
Milk

En-cas/Repas légers
Ahngkah/Rerpah lehzheh
Snacks/Light meals

Salades
Salahd
Salads

Sandwiches
Sahngweezh
Sandwiches

Œufs
Erf
Eggs

FRENCH

Œufs durs/Œufs au plat/
Œufs brouillés
Erf dewr/Erf zoh plah/Erf brooeeyeh
Boiled/fried/scrambled eggs

Saucisse
Sohseess
Sausage

Typical local dishes

Salade niçoise
Sahlahd neeswahze
Salad with eggs, anchovy, olives and tuna

Marmite dieppoise
Marmeet dee-eppwahz
Fish casserole with cream, white wine and mushrooms

Choucroute
Shookroot
Pickled cabbage with boiled potatoes, sausages and smoked meat

Bœuf bourguignon
Berf boorgeenyonng
Rich beef stew with onions and red wine

Gigot à la Bretonne
Zheegoh ah lah Brettonn
Lamb cooked with haricot beans

Crêpes Suzette
Krepp soozett
Pancakes soaked in orange juice and liqueurs and then flamed

GETTING AROUND

Public Transport

Where is the bus stop/coach stop/nearest metro (subway) station?
Où se trouve l'arrêt d'autobus le plus proche/la gare routière/la station de métro la plus proche?
Oo ser troov lahreh dotobewss la plew prosh/lah gahr rootyair/lah stassion der mehtro lah plew prosh?

When is the next/last bus to ...?
À quelle heure est le prochain/dernier autobus pour ...?
Ahkehlur eh ler prochang/dehrneeyeh otobewss poor ...?

How much is the fare to the city centre (downtown)/railway station/airport?
Quel est le prix du billet pour le centre-ville/la gare/l'aéroport?
Kehl eh ler pree dew beeyeh poor ler sahngtr-veel/lah gahr/lahehropor?

Will you tell me when to get off?
Pouvez-vous me dire quand je devrai descendre?
Poovehvoo mer deer kahng zher deuvreh dehssahngdr?

Does this bus go to ... ?
Est-ce que cet autobus va à ... ?
Ehsk sayt otobewss vah ah ... ?

Which number bus goes to ... ?
Quel est le numéro de l'autobus qui va à ... ?
Khel eh ler newmehro de lotobewss kee vah ah ... ?

May I have a single (one-way)/return (round-trip)/day ticket/book of tickets?
Puis-je avoir un aller/un aller-retour/un ticket pour la journée/un carnet de tickets?
Pweezh ahvwahr ewn ahleh/ewn ahleh-retoor/ewn tickeh poor lah joorneh/ewn kahrneh der tickeh?

Taxis (Taxi)

I would like to go to ... How much will it cost?
Je voudrais aller à ... Quel est le prix?
Zhe voodray ahleh ah ... kehl eh ler pree?

Please may I stop here?
Arrêtez ici, s'il vous plaît
Ahrehteh yssy, sylvooplay

I would like to order a taxi today/tomorrow/at 2pm to go from ... to ...
Je voudrais réserver un taxi aujourd'hui/demain/à deux heures pour aller de ... à ...
Zher voodray rehzehrveh ewn taxi ojoordewee/dermang/ah derzur poor ahleh der ... ah ...

Entertainment

Can you recommend a good bar/nightclub?
Pouvez-vous me recommander un bar/une boîte de nuit?
Poovehvoo mer rerkomahngdeh ang bahr/ewn boaht der newee?

Do you know what is on at the cinema (playing at the movies)/theatre at the moment?
Savez-vous ce qu'il y a au cinéma/théâtre en ce moment?
Sahvehvoo ser keelyah o cinema/tehahtr ahng ser momahng?

I would like to book (purchase) ... tickets for the matinée/evening performance on Monday
Je voudrais réserver ... places pour la séance en matinée/soirée lundi
Zher voodray rehzehrveh ... plass poor lah sehahngss ahng mahteeneh/swoiray lerndi

What time does the film/ performance start?
A quelle heure commence la séance/la représentation?
Ah kehlur komahngss lah sehahngs/ lah rerprehzahngtahssyawng?

COMMUNICATIONS

Post

How much will it cost to send a letter/postcard/this package to Britain/Ireland/ America/Canada/Australia/ New Zealand?
Quel est le tarif pour envoyer une lettre/carte postale/ce paquet en Grande-Bretagne/Irlande/ Amérique/au Canada/Australie/ Nouvelle-Zélande?
Kehl eh ler tariff poor ahngvwahyeh ewn lettr/kahrt postahl/ser pahkeh ahng grahngdbrertahnya/irland/ amehrick/oh kahnahdah/ostrahlee/ noovelzehland?

I would like one stamp/two stamps
Je voudrais un timbre/deux timbres
Zher voodray ang tangbr/der tangbr

I'd like ... stamps for postcards to send abroad, please
Je voudrais ... timbres pour envoyer des cartes postales à l'étranger sil vous plaît
Zher voodray ... tangbr poor ahngvwahyeh deh kahrt postahl ah lehtrahngzhai seelvooplay

Phones

I would like to make a telephone call/reverse the charges to (make a collect call to) ...
Je voudrais téléphoner/ téléphoner en PCV à ...
Zher voodray telephoneh/telephoneh ahng PehCehVeh ah ...

Which coins do I need for the telephone?
Quelles pièces me faut-il pour téléphoner?
Kehl peaehss mer foteel poor tehlehphoneh?

The line is engaged (busy)
La ligne est occupée
Lah leenyer eht okewpeh

The number is ...
Le numéro est ...
Ler newmehro eh ...

Hello, this is ...
Bonjour, c'est ... à l'appareil
Bawngzhoor, seh ... ahlahparay

Please may I speak to ...?
Je voudrais parler à ... s'il vous plaît?
Zher voodray pahrlay ah ... seelvooplay?

He/she is not in at the moment. Can you call back?
Il/elle n'est pas là. Pouvez-vous rappeler?
Eel/ehl nay pah lah. Poovey-voo rahperlay?

SHOPPING

Shops

Librairie/Papeterie
Leebrayree/pahpaytehree
Bookshop/Stationery

Bijoutier/Cadeaux
Beezhootehree/Kahdow
Jeweller/Gifts

Chaussures
Showsewr
Shoes

Quincaillerie
Kahngkahyeree
Hardware

Coiffeur (hommes)/(femmes)
Cwafferr (om)/(fam)
Hairdresser (men's)/(women's)

Boulangerie
Boolahngzheree
Baker

Supermarché
Sewpermahrshay
Supermarket

Photographe
Phohtowgraf
Photo-Shop

Bureau de voyages
Bureoh der vwoyazh
Travel agent

Pharmacie
Fahrmahsee
Pharmacy

In the Shops

What time do the shops open/close?
A quelle heure ouvrent/ferment les magasins?
Ah kehlur oovr/fehrm leh mahgazhang?

Where is the nearest market?
Où est le marché le plus proche?
Oo eh ler mahrshay ler plew prosh?

Can you show me the one in the window/this one?
Pouvez-vous me montrer celui/celle dans la vitrine/ celui-ci/celle-ci?
Poovayvoo mer mohntray serlwee/sel dahng lah veetreen/serlweesi/selsi?

Can I try this on?
Puis-je essayer ceci?
Pweezh ehssayeh cerssee?

What size is this?
Quelle est cette taille?
Kehleh saytt tahye?

This is too large/too small/ too expensive. Do you have any others?
C'est trop grand/trop petit/trop cher. Vous en avez d'autres?
Say trohw grahng/trohw pertee/trohw share. Voozahngnahvay doatr?

My size is ...
Ma taille (clothes)/ma pointure (shoes) est ...
Mah tie/mah pooahngtewr ay ...

Where is the changing room/ children's/cosmetic/ ladieswear/menswear/food department?
Où se trouve le salon d'essayage/ le rayon enfants/le rayon produits de beauté/le rayon femmes/le rayon hommes/ l'alimentation?
Oo ser troov ler sahlawng dehsayahzh/ler rehyawng ahngfahng/ ler rehyawng prodewee der boteh/ler rehyawng fahm/ler rehyawng ohm/lahleemahng-tahsyawng?

I would like ... a quarter of a kilo/half a kilo/a kilo of bread/butter/cheese/ham/ this fruit
Je voudrais ... deux cent cinquante grammes (250g)/un demi-kilo/un kilo de pain/ beurre/fromage/jambon/ce fruit
Zher voodray ... dur sahng sang-kahngt gram/ahng dermeekilo/ang kilo der pang/burr/frohmahzh/ zhahngbawng/ser frewee

FRENCH

How much is this?
C'est combien?
Cey combyahng?

I'll take this one, thank you
Je prends celui-ci/celle-ci merci
Zher prahng serlweesi/sehlsee mehrsee

Do you have a carrier (shopping) bag?
Avez-vous un sac?
Ahvehvoo ang sahk?

Do you have anything cheaper/larger/smaller/ of better quality?
Avez-vous quelque chose de moins cher/plus grand/plus petit/de meilleure qualité?
Ahvehvoo kehlkershos der moang shehr/plew grohnd/plew pertee/ der mehyur kaleeteh?

I would like a film/to develop this film for this camera
Je voudrais une pellicule/donner cette pellicule à développer pour cet appareil photo
Zher voodray ewn pehleekewl/donneh set pehleekewl ah dehveloppeh poor sayt ahpahrehye foto

I would like some batteries, the same size as this old one
Je voudrais des piles, comme celle-ci
Zher voodray deh peel, kom cehlsee

Would you mind wrapping this for me, please?
Pourriez-vous m'envelopper ceci, s'il vous plaît?
Pooreeehvoo mahngverloppeh cersee, seelvooplay?

Sorry, but you seem to have given me the wrong change
Excusez-moi, mais je crois que vous ne m'avez pas rendu le compte
Excewsehmwah meh zher krwah ker voo ner mahveh pah rahngdew ler kawngt

MOTORING

Car Hire (Rental)

I have ordered (rented) a car in the name of ...
J'ai réservé une voiture au nom de ...
Zhay rehzehrveh ewn vwahtewr o nawng der ...

How much does it cost to hire (rent) a car for one day/ two days/a week?
Quel est le prix de location d'une voiture pour un jour/deux jours/une semaine?
Kehl eh ler pree der lokahsyawng d'ewn vwahtewr poor ang zoor/der zoor/ewn sermen?

Is the tank already full of petrol (gas)?
Le plein est-il fait?
Ler plang ehtylfeh?

Is insurance and tax included? How much is the deposit?
Est-ce que l'assurance et les taxes sont comprises? Combien faut-il donner de caution?
Ehss ker lahsewrahngss eh leh tax sawng kawngpreezh? Kawngbyabg foteel doneh der kossyawng?

By what time must I return the car?
A quelle heure dois-je ramener la voiture?
Ah kehlur dwahzh rahmerneh lah vwahtewr?

I would like a small/large/ family/sports car with a radio/cassette player
Je voudrais une petite/grande voiture/une voiture familiale/un coupé avec radio/lecteur de cassettes
Zher voodray ewn perteet/ grahngd vwahtewr/ewn vwahtewr fameeliahl/ang koopeh ahvehk rahdio/lecturr der kassaytt

Do you have a road map?
Avez-vous une carte routière?
Aveh vooz ewn kahrt rootiiehr?

Parking

How long can I park here?
Combien de temps est-ce que je peux rester garé ici?
Kawngbeeang der tahng essker zher per restay gahray eessce?

Is there a car park near here?
Y a-t-il un parking près d'ici?
Eeyahteel ahng parking preh deessee?

At what time does this car park close?
A quelle heure est-ce que le parking ferme?
Ah kehl urr essker ler parking fehrm?

Signs and Notices

Sens unique
Sahns uhneek
One way

Sens interdit
Sahns ahngterdee
No entry

Stationnement interdit
Stassionmahng ahngterdee
No parking

Déviation
Dehvccasseeawng
Detour (diversion)

Stop
Stop
Stop

Cédez la passage
Sehdeh lah passahzh
Give way (yield)

Chaussée glissante
Showsay gleesahnt
Slippery road

Dépassement interdit
Daypassmahng ahngterdee
No overtaking

Danger!
Dahngzheh!
Danger!

At the Filling Station (Station Essence)

Unleaded (lead-free)/ standard/premium/diesel
Sans plomb/normal/super/ gazole (diesel)
Sahng plong/normall/sewpehr/ gahzohl (deezerl)

Fill the tank please
Le plein s'il vous plaît
Ler plahng seelvooplay

Do you have a road map?
Avez-vous une carte routière?
Aveh vooz ewn kahrt rootiiehr?

How much is the car wash?
Le lavage automatique coûte combien?
Ler lahvahzh automateek koot kawngbeeang?

Breakdowns

I've had a breakdown at ...
Je suis tombé(e) en panne à ...
Zher sewee tombay ahng pan ah ...

I am a member of the [motoring organisation]
Je suis membre de [motoring organisation]
Zher swee mahngbrer der

I am on the road from . . to . .
Je suis sur la route de ... à ...
Zher sewee sewr lah root der ... ah ...

I can't move the car. Can you send a tow-truck?
Je ne peux pas déplacer la voiture. Vous pouvez envoyer une dépanneuse?
Zher ner purr pah dehplahsay lah vwahtewr. Voo poovay ahngvwahyeh ewn daypahnurze?

I have a flat tyre
J'ai un pneu crevé
Zhai ang punerr krervay

The windscreen (windshield) has smashed/cracked
Le pare-brise est cassé/fendu
Ler pahrbreez ay kahseh/fahngdew

There is something wrong with the engine/brakes/ lights/steering/gearbox/ clutch/exhaust
Il y a un problème avec le moteur/les freins/les feux/la direction/la boîte à vitesses/ l'embrayage/le pot d'échappement
Eeleeyah ang problairm ahvek ler mowturr/leh frahng/leh fur/lah deerehkseeawng/lah bwahtahveet-ess/lahngbrayyazh/ler poh dehshah-pmahng

It's overheating
Le moteur chauffe
Ler mohturr showf

It won't start
La voiture ne démarre pas
Lah vwahtewr ner dehmahr pah

Where can I get it repaired?
Où est-ce que je peux le/la faire réparer?
Oo essker zher purr ler/lah fair reh-pahray?

Can you take me there?
Vous pouvez m'y emmener?
Voo poovay mee ahngmernay?

Will it take long to fix?
La réparation prendra longtemps?
Lah rehpahrasseeawng prahngdrah lohngtahng?

How much will it cost?
Ça coûtera combien?
Sah kootrah kawngbeeang?

Please can you pick me up/give me a lift?
Pouvez-vous me prendre/conduire?
Pooveh voo mer prahngdrer/condweer?

Accidents and Traffic Offences (Violations)

Can you help me? There has been an accident
Vous pouvez m'aider? Il y a eu un accident
Voo poovay mayday? Eelyaew ang akseedahng

Please call the police/an ambulance
Vous pouvez appeler la police/une ambulance s'il vous plaît
Voo poovay ahperleh lah poleess/ewn ahngbewlahngss seelvooplay

Is anyone hurt?
Y a-t-il des blessés?
Eeahteel deh blaysay?

I'm sorry, I didn't see the sign
Je suis désolé(e), je n'ai pas vu le panneau
Zher sewee dehzoleh, zher nay pah vew ler panow

Must I pay a fine? How much?
Est-ce que je dois payer une amende? Combien?
Ehsker zher dwah payeh ewn amahnd? Kawngbeeang?

Show me your documents
Vos papiers s'il vous plaît
Vow pahpyeh seelvooplay

HEALTH

Pharmacy (Pharmacie)

Do you have anything for a stomach ache/headache/sore throat/toothache?
Avez-vous quelque chose contre le mal à l'estomac/les maux de tête/le mal de gorge/le mal de dents?
Ahveh-voo kelhkshoz kawngtr ler mal ah lestoma/leh mo der teht/ler mal der gorzh/ler mal der dahng?

I need something for diarrhoea/constipation/ a cold/a cough/ insect bites/sunburn/travel (motion) sickness
J'ai besoin de quelque chose contre la diarrhée/la constipation/le rhume/la toux/les piqûres d'insectes/les coups de soleil/le mal de la route **(car)**/de l'air **(plane)**/de mer **(boat)**
Zhai berzwoang der kehlkshoz kawngtr lah diarrhae/ler rhoom/lah tou/lers peakewr dangsect/leh coo der soleye/ler mal der lah root/der l'air/der mair

How much/how many do I take?
Combien dois-je en prendre?
Kawngbeeang dwahzh ahng prahngdr?

How often do I take it/them?
Combien de fois dois-je en prendre?
Kawngbeeang der fwah dwahzh ahng prahngdr?

I am/he is/she is taking this medication
Je prends/il prend/elle prend ces médicaments
Zher prahng/eel prahng/ehl prahng say medeekahmahng

How much does it cost?
Quel est le prix?
Khel eh ler pree?

Can you recommend a good doctor/dentist?
Pouvez-vous me recommander un bon médecin/dentiste?
Pooveh-voo mer rerkomahngdeh ang bawng medeesang/dahngtist?

Is it suitable for children?
Est-ce qu'on peut le donner aux enfants?
Esskawng pew ler doneh ozahnfahn?

Doctor (Médecin)

I have a pain here/in my arm/leg/chest/stomach
J'ai mal ici/au bras/à la jambe/à la poitrine/à l'estomac
Zhai mal eessee/o brah/ah lah zhahngb/ah lah pwahtryn/ah lestomah

Please call a doctor, this is an emergency
Appelez un médecin, s'il vous plaît, c'est urgent
Ahperleh ewn medeesang, seel voo play, sehtewrzhahng

I would like to make an appointment to see the doctor
Je voudrais prendre rendez-vous chez le médecin
Zher voodray prahngdr rahngdehvoo sheh ler medeesang

I am diabetic/pregnant
Je suis diabétique/enceinte
Zher sewee diabetic/ahngsang

I need a prescription for ...
J'ai besoin d'une ordonnance pour ...
Zhai berzooang dewnordonahngss poor ...

Can you give me something to ease the pain?
Pouvez-vous me donner quelque chose contre la douleur?
Poovayvoo mer doneh kehlkshoz kawngtr lah doolur?

I am/he is/she is allergic to penicillin
Je suis/il est/elle est allergique à la pénicilline
Zher sewee/eel ay/ehl ay allerzheek ah lah pehneeseeleen

Ça fait mal?
Sah fay mahl?
Does this hurt?

Vous devez/il doit/elle doit aller à l'hôpital
Voo dervay/eel dwah/ehl dwah ahleh ah lopeetahl
You must/he must/she must go to hospital

Prenez ces médicaments une fois/deux fois/trois fois par jour
Prernay say medeekahmahng ewn fwah/dur fwah/trwah fwah pahr zhoor
Take these once/twice/three times a day

I am/he is/she is taking this medication
Je prends/il prend/elle prend ces médicaments
Zher prahng/eel prahng/ehl prahng say medeekahmahng

I have medical insurance
J'ai une assurance médicale
Zhay ewn assurans mehdeekahl

Dentist (Dentiste)

I have toothache
J'ai mal aux dents
Zhai mahl o dahng

My filling has come out
Mon plombage est tombé
Mawng plawngbahz eh tawngbeh

I do/do not want to have an injection first
Je veux/je ne veux pas qu'on me donne une piqûre avant
Zher vur/zher nur vur pah ke orn mer don oon peakewr ahvehn

EMERGENCIES

Help!
Au secours!
Ossercoor!

Fire!
Au feu!
Oh fur!

Stop!
Stop!
Stop!

Call an ambulance/a doctor/ the police/the fire brigade!
Appelez une ambulance/un médecin/la police/les pompiers!
Ahperleh ewnahngbewlahngss/ang medesang/lah poleess/leh pompeeyeh!

Please may I use a telephone?
Je peux utiliser le téléphone s'il vous plaît?
Zher perz ewteeleezeh ler tehlehfonn seel voo pleh?

I have had my traveller's cheques/credit cards/hand-bag/rucksack/(knapsack)/ luggage/wallet/passport/ mobile phone stolen
On m'a volé mes chèques de voyage/mes cartes de crédit/mon sac à main/mon sac à dos/mes bagages/mon porte-feuille/mon passeport/ mon téléphone portable
Awng mah voleh meh cheque der vwahahzh/meh carte der crehdite/ mawng sackamahn/mawng sacka-doe/meh bahgagzh/mawng portfur-ye/mong pahsspor/mong tehlehfonn portahbler

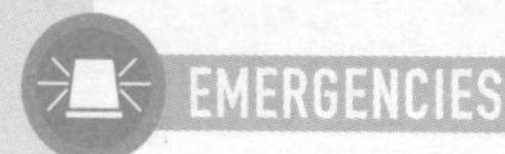

May I please have a copy of the report for my insurance claim?
Je peux avoir une copie du rapport pour ma compagnie d'assurançe, s'il vous plaît?
Zher perz avwahr ewn coppee dew rappor poor mah compahnyee dassewrahngss, seel voo pleh?

Can you help me? I have lost my daughter/my son/my companion(s)
Pouvez-vous m'aider? J'ai perdu ma fille/mon fils/mon ami(e)/mes amis (amies)
Pooveh voo mehdeh? Zheh pehrdew mah fee/mong feess/mon ammee/mehz ammee

Please go away/leave me alone
Allez-vous en/laissez-moi tranquille
Ahlehvoozahng/lehssehmwah trahngkeel

I'm sorry
Je suis désolé(e)
Zher swee dehzohleh

I want to contact the British/ American/Canadian/Irish/ Australian/New Zealand/ South African consulate
Je veux contacter le consulat britannique/américain/canadien/ irlandais/australien/ néo-zélandais/sud-africain
Zher vurr kontaktay ler kohnsewlah breetahneek/ahmehreekahng/ kahnahdyahng/eerlahnday/ austrahleeahng/nayozaylahngday/ sewdafreekahng

I'm/we're/he is/she is ill/lost/injured. They are ill/lost/injured.
Je suis/nous sommes/il est/elle est malade(s)/perdu(e)(s)/ blessé(e)(s). Ils/Elles sont malades/perdu(e)s/blessé(e)s
Zher swee/noo somm/eel eh/ell/malahd/pairdew/blesseh. Eel/Ell sawng malahd/pairdew/ blesseh

GERMAN

INTRODUCTION

German is the official language of both Germany and Austria, and is also spoken in regions of Switzerland, in the East Cantons area of Belgium, some areas of northern Italy and in Luxembourg. It is also used as a second language in Central European countries, such as Hungary and the Czech Republic. Considerable regional variation exists in accent, vocabulary and sometimes spelling.

Note that all nouns in German begin with a capital letter, even in the middle of a sentence.

Addresses for Travel and Tourist Information

For Switzerland, see p.74.

Australia: *German National Tourist Office,* PO Box 1461, Sydney, NSW 2001; tel: (02) 8296 0488; fax: (02) 8296 0487.

Canada: *German National Tourist Office,* 480 University Ave, Suite 1410, Toronto, Ontario M5G 1V2; tel: (416) 968 1685; fax: (416) 968 0562.

South Africa: *German National Tourist Office,* c/o Lufthansa German Airlines, PO Box 412246, Craighall, Johannesburg 2024; tel: (11) 325 1927; fax: (11) 325 0867.

UK: *German National Tourist Office,* PO Box 2695, London W1A 3TN; tel: (020) 7317 0908; fax: (020) 7317 0917. *Austrian National Tourist Office,* 9–11 Richmond Buildings, off Dean St, London W1D 3HF; tel: (020) 7440 3830. *Luxembourg Tourist Office,* 122 Regent St, London W1B 5SA; tel: (020) 7434 2800; fax: (020) 7734 1205.

USA: *German National Tourist Office,* 122 E. 42nd St, 52nd Floor, New York, NY 10168; tel: (212) 661 7200. *Austrian National Tourist Office,* PO Box 1142, New York, NY 10108; tel: (212) 944 6880. *Luxembourg National Tourist Office,* 17 Beekman Place, New York, NY 10022; tel: (212) 935 8888.

Official tourism websites: www.germany-tourism.co.uk (UK); www.cometogermany.com (USA); www.austria.info; www.MySwitzerland.com; www.luxembourg.co.uk.

Germany Facts

CAPITAL: Berlin (pronounced Bear-lin)
CURRENCY: Euro (€, pronounced oy-roh). €1 = 100 cents.
OPENING HOURS: Banks Mon–Fri 0830–1300,1400–1600 (Thur 1730). Shops: Mon–Fri 0800–1800/2000, Sat 0800–1600. Museums: Tues–Sun 0900–1800.
TELEPHONES: To dial in, +49. Outgoing, 00 plus the country code. Police, 110. Fire, Ambulance, 112.
PUBLIC HOLIDAYS: 1 Jan; Good Friday and Easter Monday; 1 May; Ascension Day (forty days after Easter); Pentecost (Monday following seventh Sunday after Easter); 3 Oct; 25, 26 Dec. Other dates in the Church calendar are public holidays in some states.

Austria Facts

CAPITAL: Vienna, Wien (pronounced Veen)
CURRENCY: Euro (€, pronounced oy-roh). €1 = 100 cents.
OPENING HOURS: Banks: Mon–Fri 0800–1230, 1330–1500. Shops: Mon–Fri 0900–1830, Sat 0900–1200 (some till 1700). Museums: Tues–Sat 1000–1700.
TELEPHONES: To dial in, +43. Outgoing, 00 plus the country code. Police, 133. Fire, 122. Ambulance, 144. Mountain Rescue, 140.
PUBLIC HOLIDAYS: 1, 6 Jan; Easter Monday; 1 May; Ascension Day (forty days after Easter); Pentecost (Monday following seventh Sunday after Easter); Corpus Christi (May/Jun); 15 Aug; 26 Oct; 1 Nov; 8, 25, 26 Dec.

Luxembourg Facts

CAPITAL: Luxembourg
CURRENCY: Euro (€, pronounced oy-roh). €1 = 100 cents.
OPENING HOURS: Banks: 0830–1630. Shops: Mon–Sat 0900–1800/1900. Museums: Tues–Sun, 1000–1600/1700.
TELEPHONES: To dial in, +352. Outgoing, 00 plus the country code. Police, 113. Fire, Ambulance, 112.
PUBLIC HOLIDAYS: 1 Jan; Easter Monday; 1 May; Ascension Day (forty days after Easter); Pentecost (Monday following seventh Sunday after Easter); 23 Jun; 15 Aug; 1 Nov; 25, 26 Dec.

ESSENTIALS

Alphabet and Pronunciation

	Name	Pronounced
A a	*ah*	**long a, as in father, or short sound like the u in hut; au is pronounced ow as in how**
Ä ä	*ah oomlowt*	**long ey sound, as in gain; äu is an oi sound, as in hoist**
B b	*bey*	**like English b, except more like p at the end of a word**
C c	*tsey*	**ts, as in hats; ch is pronounced before or after an a or o like a kh, as in Scottish loch, or before or after other vowels more like sh in shift**
D d	*dey*	**like English d except at the end of words, when is is like English t**
E e	*ey*	**long ey sound, as in gain, or short e as in hen; at the end of a word a neutral uh sound; ei is like the sound in eye; eu is an oi sound, as in hoist; eh is pronounced ey**
F f	*ef*	**like English f**
G g	*gey*	**hard g as in get; at the end of words a kh sound, like the ch of Scottish loch**
H h	*hah*	**like English h, or silent after long vowels**
I i	*ee*	**long ee sound like the i in machine, or short i sound as in sit; ie is also pronounced ee, as in yield**
J j	*yot*	**normally a y sound as in yes; in some words of foreign origin as zh, like the s in measure**
K k	*kah*	**like English k**
L l	*el*	**open l sound as in left, never like the closed l in hold**
M m	*em*	**like English m**
N n	*en*	**like English n**
O o	*oh*	**long aw shound as in shore, or short o as in hot**
Ö ö	*oh oomlowt*	**er sound, approximately like the vowel in fur**
P p	*pey*	**like English p**
Q q	*koo*	**qu is pronounced as kv**

R r	*eyr*	**'throaty' r sound, like French r**
S s	*ess*	**single s is pronounced as a z, as in zoo at the beginning or in the middle of a word; at the end of a word it is always a hard s as in see; doubles is always hard. At the beginning of words (only), sp is pronounced as shp, st as sht; sch is always pronounced as sh.**
ß	*ess-tsett*	**represents a double s**
T t	*tey*	**like English t**
U u	*oo*	**long or short oo sound, approximately as in zoom or put**
Ü ü	*oo oomlowt*	**ew sound, approximately like vowel in hewn but with no preceding y sound**
V v	*fow*	**at the beginning of a word like f in foot, otherwise like English v**
W w	*vey*	**like English v as in haven**
X x	*iks*	**like English x**
Y y	*oopsilon*	**rarely found in German words**
Z z	*tsett*	**ts, as in hats**

Basic Words & Phrases

Yes
Ja
Yah

No
Nein
Nine

Please
Bitte
Bitter

Thank you
Danke
Danke

Hello
Hallo
Hallo

Goodbye
Auf Wiedersehen.
Owf Veederzeyhen.

Excuse me
Entschuldigen Sie
Entshooldigen zee

Sorry
Entschuldigung
Entshooldigoong

How
Wie
Vee

When
Wann
Ven

What
Was
Vas

Why
Warum
Varum

Who
Wer
Vair

That's O.K.
Das stimmt
Das shtimt

Perhaps
Vielleicht
Feellykht

To
Nach
Nakh

From
Von
Fon

Here
Hier
Here

There
Dort
Dort

ESSENTIALS

GERMAN

I don't understand
Ich verstehe Sie nicht
Ikh ferhstayher zee nikht

I don't speak German
Ich spreche kein Deutsch
Ikh shprekher kine doitsh

Do you speak English?
Sprechen Sie Englisch?
Shprekhen zee eng-lish?

Can you please write it down?
Könnten Sie das bitte aufschreiben?
Kernten zee das bitter owfshryben?

Can you please speak more slowly?
Könnten Sie bitte langsamer sprechen?
Kernten zee bitter langzamer shprekhen?

Greetings

Good morning/good afternoon/good evening/ goodnight
Guten Morgen/guten Tag/guten Abend/gute Nacht
Gooten morgen/gooten targ/gooten arbent/goote nakht

Pleased to meet you
Es freut mich Sie kennenzulernen
Es froyt mikh zee kennen-tsoo-ler-nen

How are you?
Wie geht es Ihnen?
Vee gayht es eehnen?

I am well thank you. And you?
Gut danke, und Ihnen?
Goot, danker, oond eenen?

My name is . . .
Mein Name ist . . .
Mine naamer ist . . .

This is my friend/boyfriend/ girlfriend/husband/wife/ brother/sister
Dies ist mein Freund/mein Freund/meine Freundin/mein Mann/meine Frau/mein Bruder/meine Schwester
Dees ist mine froynd/mine froynd/miner froindeen/mine man/miner frow/mine brooder/miner shvester

Where are you travelling to?
Wohin reisen Sie?
Voheen ryzen zee?

I am/we are going to . . .
Ich fahre/wir fahren nach . . .
Ikh faare/weer faaren nakh . . .

How long are you travelling for?
Wie lange reisen Sie?
Vee lange ryzen zee?

Where do you come from?
Woher kommen Sie?
Vohair kommen zee?

I am/we are from ... Australia/Britain/Canada/ America?
Ich komme/wir kommen aus ... Australien/Großbritannien/ Kanada/Amerika?
Ikh kommer/veer kommen aus ... Owstralee-en/Grohssbritannien/ Canada/ America

We are on holiday
Wir machen Urlaub
Veer makhen oorlowb

This is our first visit here
Wir sind zum ersten Mal hier
Veer zint tsum airsten marl here

I am waiting for my husband/wife/boyfriend/girlfriend
Ich warte auf meinen Mann/meine Frau/meinen Freund/meine Freundin
Ikh varter owf minen mann/miner frow/minen froind/miner froindin

How old are you?
Wie alt sind Sie?
Vee alt zint zee?

I am ... years old
Ich bin ... Jahre alt
Ish bin ... yaarer alt

I am a business person/doctor/journalist/manual worker/administrator/scientist/student/teacher
Male: Ich bin Geschäftsmann/Arzt/Journalist/Arbeiter/Verwaltungskraft/Wissenschaftler/Student/Lehrer
Ish bin gershefts-man/artst/zhoor-nalist/arbiter/fervaltoongs-kraft/vis-senshaftler/shtoodent/leyrer
Female: Ich bin Geschäftsfrau/Ärztin/Journalistin/Arbeiterin/Verwaltungskraft/Wissenschaftlerin/Studentin/Lehrerin
Ish bin gershefts-frow/artstin/zhoor-nalistin/arbiterin/fervaltoongs-kraft/vissenshaftlerin/shtoodentin/leyrerin

Would you like/may I have a cigarette?
Möchten Sie/Kann ich bitte eine Zigarette haben?
Merkhten zee/Can ikh bitter iner tsigaretter haaben?

Do you mind if I smoke?
Darf ich rauchen?
Darf ikh raukhen?

Do you have a light?
Haben Sie Feuer bitte?
Haaben see foyer bitter?

Days

Monday
Montag
Mohntagh

Tuesday
Dienstag
Deenstagh

Wednesday
Mittwoch
Mitvokh

Thursday
Donnerstag
Donnerstagh

Friday
Freitag
Frytagh

Saturday
Samstag
Samstagh

Sunday
Sonntag
Sontagh

Morning
Morgen
Morgen

Afternoon
Nachmittag
Naakhmittag

Evening
Abend
Aabend

Night
Nacht
Naakht

Yesterday/Today/Tomorrow
Gestern/Heute/Morgen
Gess-tern/Hoyter/Morgen

Numbers

Zero
Null
Nool

One
Eins
Ines

Two
Zwei
Tsvy

Three
Drei
Dry

Four
Vier
Feer

Five
Fünf
Foonf

Six
Sechs
Zex

Seven
Sieben
Zeeben

Eight
Acht
Akht

Nine
Neun
Noyn

Ten
Zehn
Tseyn

Eleven
Elf
Elf

Twelve
Zwölf
Tsverlf

Thirteen
Dreizehn
Drytseyn

Fourteen
Vierzehn
Feertseyn

Fifteen
Fünfzehn
Foonftseyn

Sixteen
Sechzehn
Zekhtseyn

Seventeen
Siebzehn
Zeeptseyn

Eighteen
Achtzehn
Akhttseyn

Nineteen
Neunzehn
Noinetseyn

Twenty
Zwanzig
Tvantsikh

Twenty-one
Einundzwanzig
Ine-oont-tsvantsikh

Twenty-two
Zweiundzwanzig
Tsvy-oont-vsvantsikh

Thirty
Dreißig
Drysikh

Forty
Vierzig
Feertsikh

Fifty
Fünfzig
Foonftsikh

Sixty
Sechzig
Zekhtsikh

Seventy
Siebzig
Zeebtsikh

Eighty
Achtzig
Akhtsikh

Ninety
Neunzig
Noyntsikh

One hundred
Hundert
Hoondert

Five hundred
Fünfhundert
Foonfhoondert

One thousand
Eintausend
Inetowsend

One million
Eine Million
Iner millyohn

Time

What time is it?
Wie spät ist es?
Vee shpeyt is es?

It is . . .
Es ist . . .
Es ist . . .

9.00
Neun Uhr
Noyn oor

9.05
Neun Uhr fünf
Noyn oor foonf

9.15
Neun Uhr fünfzehn
Noyn oor foonftseyn

9.20
Neun Uhr zwanzig
Noyn oor vsvantsikh

9.30
Neun Uhr dreißig
Noyn oor drytsig

9.35
Neun Uhr fünfunddreißig
Noyn oor foonf-oont-drysikh

9.40
Neun Uhr vierzig
Noyn oor feertsikh

9.45
Neun Uhr fünfundfvierzig
Noyn oor foonf-oont-feertsikh

9.50
Neun Uhr fünfzig
Noyn oor foonftsikh

9.55
Neun Uhr fünfundfünfzig
Noyn oor foonf-oont-foonftsikh

Midday/Midnight
Mittag/Mitternacht
Mittagh/mitternakht

Money

I would like to change these traveller's cheques/this currency
Ich möchte gerne diese Reiseschecks/dieses Geld/ wechseln.
Ikh merkhter gairner deezer ryzersheks/deezes gelt/vexseln.

How much commission do you charge? (What is the service charge?)
Wie hoch ist Ihre Provision?
Vee hokh ist eere provizion?

Can I obtain money with my Mastercard?
Kann ich mit meiner Mastercard Geld bekommen?
Can ikh meet miner Mastercard gelt bekommen?

Where is the nearest ATM?
Wo ist der nächste Geldautomat?
Voh ist dair nexter geld-owtomaat?

My name is ... Some money has been wired to here for me to collect
Mein Name ist ... Es wurde Geld für mich hierher überwiesen
Mine naamer ist ... Ess voorder gelt fewr mish heerhair ewberveezen

ARRIVING AND DEPARTING

Airport

Excuse me, where is the check-in desk for . . . airline?
Entschuldigung, wo ist der Abfertigungsschalter für . . ?
Entshuldeegen, vo ist dair abfairti-goongs-shalter foor . . ?

What is the boarding gate for my flight?
Von welchem Flugsteig geht mein Flug ab?
Fon velchem floogstyge geyht mine floog ab?/Vann moos ikh eynstygen?

What is the time for my flight?
Wann muß ich einsteigen?
Vann moos ikh eynstygen?

How long is the delay likely to be?
Wieviel Verspätung hat mein Flug?
Veefeel fershpeytung hat mine floog?

Where is the duty-free shop?
Wo ist der zollfreie Laden?
Vo ist dair tsollfryer larden?

Which way is the luggage reclaim?
Wo ist die Gepäckausgabe?
Vo ist dee gepekowsgarber?

I have lost my luggage. Please can you help?
Ich habe mein Gepäck verloren. Können Sie mir bitte helfen?
Ish hahber mine gerpeck verlawren. Kernen zee meer bitter helfen?

I am flying to...
Ich fliege nach...
Ish fleeger nahkh...

Where is the bus for the city centre?
Wo fährt der Bus ins Stadtzentrum ab?
Vo fairt dair boos ins shtat-tsentrum ab?

Trains and Boats

Where is the ticket office/ information desk?
Wo ist der Fahrkartenschalter/ das Informationszentrum?
Voh ist der faarkartenshalter/das informatsion tsentroom?

Which platform does the train to ... depart from?
Von welchem Bahnsteig fährt der Zug nach ... ab?
Fon velshem bahnshteikh fairt dair tsook nakh . . . ap?

Which platform does the speedboat/ferry to ... depart from?
Von welchem Kai fährt das Schnellboot/die Fähre nach ... ab?
Fon velkhem baanshtykh fairt dass shnellbawt/dee fairer nakh . . . ap?

Where is platform . . ?
Wo ist Bahnsteig . . ?
Voh ist baanshtykh . . ?

When is the next train/boat to ...?
Wann fährt der nächste Zug/das nächste Schiff nach ...?
Van fairt dair nexter tsook/dass nexter shiff nakh ...?

Is there a later train/boat to ...?
Gibt es einen späteren Zug/ein späteres Schiff nach ...?
Gipt ess inen shpeyteren tsook/ine shpeyteress shiff nakh ...?

Notices and Signs

Speisewagen
Shpyzevaagen
Buffet (Dining) car

Bus
Bus
Bus

Trinkwasser/kein Trinkwasser
Treenkvasser/kine treenkvasser
Drinking/non-drinking water

Eingang
Ine-gang
Entrance

Ausgang
Ows-gang
Exit

Krankenhaus
Krankenhowss
Hospital

Information
Eenformatsion
Information

Gepäckaufbewahrung
Gepeckowfbevaarung
Left luggage (Baggage reclaim)

Schließfächer
Schleessfekher
Luggage lockers

Postamt
Postamt
Post office

Bahnsteig
Baanshtykh
Platform

Bahnhof
Baanhof
Railway (Railroad)station

Flughafen
Flooghorfen
Airport

Polizeistation
Politseye-shtatsiohn
Police station

Hafen
Harfen
Port

Restaurant
Restohrong
Restaurant

Raucher/Nichtraucher
Raukher/nikhtraukher
Smoking/non-smoking

Telefon
Taylefohn
Telephone

Fahrkartenschalter
Faarkartenshalter
Ticket office

Abfertigungsschalter
Abfairtigoongs-shalter
Check-in desk

Fahrplan
Faarplaan
Timetable (Schedule)

Toiletten
Toletten
Toilets (Restrooms)

Damen/Herren
Daamen/Herren
Ladies/Gentlemen

Die U-Bahn
Dee Oo-baan
Underground (Subway)

Warteraum
Varterowm
Waiting room

Buying a Ticket

I would like a first-class/second-class/single (one-way)/return (round-trip) ticket to . . .
Ich möchte bitte eine einfache Fahrkarte/Rückfahrkarte erster Klasse/zweiter Klasse nach . . .
Ikh merkhter bitter iner inefakhe faarkaarte/rookfaarkaarte airster classer/tsvyter classer nakh . . .

Is it an express (fast) train/bus?
Ist es ein Schnellzug/Schnellbus?
Ist ess ine shnelltsook/shnellboos?

Is my rail pass valid on this train/ferry/bus?
Gilt mein Rail Pass für diesen Zug/diese Fähre/diesen Bus?
Gilt mine rail pass foor deesen zook/deese fairer/deesen boos?

I would like an aisle/window seat
Bitte einen Sitzplatz am Durchgang/Fenster
Bitter inen zitsplats am doorshgang/fenster

No smoking/smoking please
Raucher/Nichtraucher
Raukher/nikhtraukher

We would like to sit together
Wir möchten gerne zusammen sitzen
Veer merkhten gairner tsoozammen zitsen

I would like to make a seat reservation
Ich möchte gern einen Platz reservieren
Ikh merkhter gairn inen plats resairveeren

I would like to reserve a couchette/sleeper for one person/two people/my family
Ich möchte eine Schlafwagen-/Liegewagenreservierung für eine Person/zwei Personen/meine Familie
Ikh merkhter ine shlaafvaagen-/leegevaagen-reserveerung foor iner pairzohn/tsvy pairzohnen/miner fameelyer

I would like to reserve a cabin
Ich möchte gern eine Kabine reservieren
Ikh merkhther gairn iner cabeener resairveeren

Timetables (Schedules)

Ankunft
Ankunft
Arrive

Hält in . . . an
Helt in . . . an
Calls (Stops) at

Mini bar
Minibar
Catering service

In . . . umsteigen
In . . . oomshtygen
Change at . . .

Anschluss/über
Aanshluss/Oober
Connection/Via

Täglich
Tayglikh
Daily

Alle 40 Minuten
Aller 40 minooten
Every 40 minutes

Erste Klasse
Airster classer
First class

Stündlich
Shtundlikh
Hourly

Sitzplatzreservierung empfohlen
Zitsplats-reserveerung empfohlen
Seat reservations are recommended

Zweite Klasse
Tsvyte classe
Second class

Zuschlagspflichtig
Tsooshlaags-pfleechteeg
Supplement payable

Luggage

How much will it cost to send (ship) my luggage in advance?
Wieviel kostet es mein Gepäck vorauszuschicken?
Veefeel kostet es mine gepeck forowss-tsoosheeken?

Where is the left luggage (baggage claim) office?
Wo ist die Gepäckaufbewahrung?
Voo ist dee gepeck-owfbevaarung?

What time do you open/close?
Um wieviel Uhr machen Sie auf/zu?
Oom veefeel oor makhen zee owf/tsoo?

Where are the luggage trolleys (carts)?
Wo finde ich die Gepäckwagen?
Voo feende ikh dee gepeckvaagen?

Where are the lockers?
Wo sind die Schließfächer?
Vo seent dee shlees-fekher?

I have lost my locker key
Ich habe den Schlüssel für mein Schließfach verloren
Ikh haaber den shloossel foor mine shleesfakh ferlooren

On Board

Is this seat free?
Ist dieser Platz frei?
Ist deezer plats fry?

Excuse me, you are sitting in my reserved seat
Entschuldigen Sie bitte, aber Sie sitzen auf meinem reservierten Platz
Entshuldigen zee bitter, aber zee zitsen owf minem rezerveerten plats

Which station is this?
Wie heißt dieser Bahnhof?
Vee hysst deezer baanhof?

What time is this train/bus/ferry/flight due to arrive/depart?
Wann kommt dieser Zug/dieser Bus/diese Fähre/dieser Flug an?/ Wann geht dieser Zug/dieser Bus/diese Fähre/dieser Flug?
Van kommt deeser tsug/deeser boos/deeser fairer/deeser floog an?/Van geyt deeser tsug/deeser boos/deeser fairer/deeser floog?

Travelling with Children

Do you have a high chair/babysitting service/cot?
Haben Sie einen Kinderstuhl/Babysitter/ein Kinderbett?
Haaben zee inen kindershtool/Babysittier/ine kinderbet?

Where is the nursery/playroom?
Wo ist das Kinderzimmer/Spielzimmer?
Voh ist das kindertsimmer/speeltsimmer?

Where can I warm the baby's bottle?
Wo kann ich die Milchflasche für das Baby aufwärmen?
Voh can ikh die Milkflasher foor das Baby owf-vairme

Customs and Passports

Ihren Reisepass bitte!
Eeren ryzerpass, bitter!
Passports, please!

I have nothing/wine/spirits (alcohol)/tobacco to declare
Ich habe nichts/ Wein/ Schnaps/ Tabak zu verzollen
Ikh haabe neekhst/kinen vine/kinen shnapps/kinen tabak tsoo fertsollen

I will be staying for . . . days/weeks/months.
Ich werde für . . .
Tage/Wochen/Monate bleiben.
Ikh verder foor . . .
tager/wokhen/mohnate blyben.

SIGHTSEEING

Asking the Way

Excuse me, do you speak English?
Entschuldigen Sie, sprechen Sie Englisch?
Entshuldigen zee, shprekhen zee english?

Excuse me, can you help me please?
Entschuldigen Sie bitte, können Sie mir helfen?
Entshooldigen zee bitter, kernen zee meer helfen?

Where is the Tourist Information Office?
Wo ist das Touristeninformationsbüro?
Voo ist das touristen-informatisons-booro?

Excuse me, is this the right way to ...?
Entschuldigung, geht es hier ...?
Entshuldeegoong, gayt es here ...?

... the cathedral/the tourist information office/the castle/ the old town
... zum Dom/zur Touristeninformation/zum Schloss/zur Altstadt
... tsoom dorm, tsoor tooristen-informatsion/tsoom shloss/tsoor altshtat

Can you tell me the way to the railway station/bus station/taxi rank/city centre/beach?
Können Sie mir bitte sagen, wie ich zum Bahnhof/zum Busbahnhof/zum Taxistand/zur Stadtmitte/zum Strand komme?
Kernen zee meer bitter zaagen, vee ikh tsoom baanhof/tsoom busbaanhof/tsoom taxishtand/tsoor shtatmitter/tsoom shtrant kommer?

Die erste Straße links/rechts/ geradeaus
Dee airste shtraasser leenks/rekhts/geraader-ows
First/second left/right/ straight ahead

An der Ecke/An der Ampel
An dair ekker/An dair ampell
At the corner/At the traffic lights

Where is the nearest police station/post office?
Wo ist die nächste Polizeiwache/das nächste Postamt?
Voo ist dee nexter politsywakhe/das nexter postamt?

Is it near/far?
Ist es weit?
Ist es vyte?

Do I need to take a taxi catch a bus?
Muss ich ein Taxi/einen Bus nehmen?
Moos ikh ine taxi/inen bus nayhmen?

Can you point to it on my map?
Können Sie es mir bitte auf der Karte zeigen?
Kernen see es meer bitter owf der kaarte tsygen?

Thank you for your help
Vielen Dank für Ihre Hilfe
Feelen dank foor eehrer heelfe

How do I reach the motorway/main road?
Wie komme ich zur Autobahn/zur Hauptstraße?
Vee kommer ikh tsur owtobarn/tsur howpt-shtrarser?

I think I have taken the wrong turning
Ich glaube, ich bin falsch abgebogen
Ikh glowber, ikh bin falsh abgeborgen

I am looking for this address
Ich suche diese Adresse
Ikh sookher deeser ardresse

I am looking for the ... hotel.
Ich suche das ... Hotel.
Ikh sookher das ... hotel.

How far is it to . . . from here?
Wie weit ist es bis . . . von hier?
Vee vite ist es bees . . . fon here?

Fahren Sie . . . Kilometer geradeaus.
Faren zee . . . keelometer gerarde ows.
Carry straight on for . . . kilometres.

Biegen Sie die nächste Straße rechts/links ab
Beegen zee dee nekste shtrarser rekhts/links ab
Take the next turning on the right/left

Biegen Sie an der nächsten Kreuzung/Ampel rechts/links ab
Beegen zee un dair neksten kroit-sung/ampel rekhts/links ab
Turn right/left at the next crossroads/traffic lights

Sie fahren in die falsche Richtung
Zee faren in dee falsher richtung
You are going in the wrong direction

Where is the cathedral/ church/museum/pharmacy?
Wo ist der Dom/die Kirche/das Museum/die Apotheke?
Voh ist der dohm/dee keerkhe/das moozeyum/dee Apoteyker?

How much is the admission entrance charge?
Was kostet der Eintritt?
Vas kostet der inetreet?

Is there a reduction for children/students/senior citizens?
Gibt es eine Ermäßigung für Kinder/Studenten/Rentner?
Geebt es iner ermeyssigung foor kinder/shtudenten/rentner?

What time does the next guided tour in English start?
Um wieviel Uhr ist die nächste Führung auf Englisch?
Oom veefeel oor ist dee nexter foohrung owf Eng-lish?

One/two adults/children, please.
Ein Erwachsener/Kind zwei Erwachsene/Kinder, bitte.
Ine ervaxener/kint tsvy ervaxener/kinder, bitter.

May I take photographs here?
Darf man hier fotografieren?
Darf man here fotografeeren?

At the Tourist Office

Do you have a map of the town/area?
Haben Sie eine Stadtkarte/Landkarte?
Haaben zee iner shtatkaarter/ landkaarter?

Do you have a list of accommodation?
Haben Sie ein Unterkunftsverzeichnis?
Haben see ine unterkunfts-fertsychnis?

Can I reserve accommodation here?

Kann ich hier eine Unterkunft reservieren?
Can ikh here iner oonterkoonft reserveeren?

ACCOMMODATION

Hotels

I have a reservation in the name of . . .
Ich habe eine Reservierung für . . .
Ikh haabe iner reserveerung foor . . .

I wrote to/faxed/telephoned you last month/last week
Ich habe Ihnen letzten Monat/die letzte Woche geschrieben/ein Fax geschickt/ angerufen
Ikh haber eenen letsten mohnat/dee letste wokhe geshreeben/ine fax gesheekt/angeroofen

Do you have any rooms free?
Haben Sie Zimmer frei?
Haben zee tsimmer fry?

I would like to reserve a single/double room with/ without a bath/shower
Ich möchte ein Einzelzimmer/ Doppelzimmer mit/ohne Bad/Dusche reservieren
Ikh merkhter ine inetsel-tsimmer/doppel-tsimmer meet/ oohner baad/doosher reserveeren

I would like bed/breakfast/ (room and) full board
Ich möchte Übernachtung mit Frühstück/Vollpension
Ikh merkhter oobernakhtung meet frooshtook/follpensiohn

How much is it per night?
Wieviel kostet das pro Nacht?
Veefeel kostet das pro nakht?

Is breakfast included?
Einschließlich Frühstück?
Ineshleesslykh frooshtook?

Do you have any cheaper rooms?
Haben Sie billigere Zimmer?
Haaben see beeligerer tsimmer?

I would like to see/take the room
Ich möchte das Zimmer sehen/nehmen
Ish mershter dass tsimmer zeyen/neymen

I would like to stay for ... nights
Ich möchte für ... Nächte bleiben
Ikh merkhter foor ... nekhte blyben

The shower/light/tap/hot water doesn't work
Die Dusche/das Licht/der Wasserhahn/das heiße Wasser funktioniert nicht
Dee doosher/das licht/dair vasseharn/ dass hyser vasser foonktsioneert nikht

At what time/where is breakfast served?
Um wieviel Uhr/wo wird Frühstück serviert?
Omm veefeel oor/vo veerd frooshtook serveert?

What time do I have to check out?
Um wieviel Uhr müssen wir das Zimmer verlassen?
Oom veefeel oor moossen veer das tsimmer ferlassen?

GERMAN

Can I have the key to room number . . ?
Könnten Sie mir bitte den Schlüssel für Zimmer Nummer. . . geben?
Kernten zee mere bitter dayn shloosel foor tsimmer noomer . . . geyben?

My room number is . . .
Meine Zimmernummer ist . . .
Miner tsimmer-noomer ist . . .

My room is not satisfactory/ not clean enough/too noisy. Please can I change rooms?
Mein Zimmer ist nicht zufriedenstellend/nicht sauber genug/zu laut. Kann ich bitte ein anderes Zimmer haben?
Mine tsimmer ist nisht tsoofreeden-shtellent/nisht zowber genook/tsoo lowt. Kan ish bitter ine anderess tsimmer haaben?

Where is the bathroom?
Wo ist das Badezimmer?
Voh ist dass baader-tsimmer?

Do you have a safe for valuables?
Haben Sie einen Safe für Wertsachen?
Haaben zee inen safe fewr vairt-zakhen?

Is there a laundry/do you wash clothes?
Gibt es einen Waschraum/einen Waschservice?
Gipt ess inen vashrowm/ inen vashsairvees?

I would like an air-conditioned room.
Ich möchte ein Zimmer mit Klimaanlage.
Ish mershte ine tsimmer mit kleema-anlaager.

Do you accept traveller's cheques/credit cards?
Nehmen Sie Reiseschecks/Kreditkarten an?
Neymen zee ryzersheks/credeet-carten an?

May I have the bill please?
Die Rechnung, bitte?
Dee rekhnung, bitter?

Excuse me, I think there may be mistake in this bill
Entschuldigung, ich glaube auf dieser Rechnung ist ein Fehler
Entshuldeegoong, ikh glowbe owf deeser rekhnoong ist ine feyler

Youth Hostels

How much is a dormitory bed per night?
Wieviel kostet ein Bett im Schlafsaal pro Nacht, bitte?
Veefeel kostet ine bet eem shlaafza-al pro nakht, bitter?

I am/am not an HI member
Ich bin ein/kein Mitglied des internationalen Jugendherbergsverbands
Ikh been ine/kine meetgleed des internatsionaalen yoogent-hairbairgs-ferbands

May I use my own sleeping bag?
Kann ich meinen eigenen Schlafsack benutzen?
Can ikh minen ygenen shlaafzack benootsen?

What time do you lock the doors at night?
Um wieviel Uhr wird abends abgeschlossen?
Oom veefeel oor weerd abends abgeshlossen?

Do you have a safety deposit box?
Haben Sie ein Tresorfach?
Haaben see ine traysorfakh?

Camping

May I camp for the night/two nights?
Kann ich für eine Nacht/zwei Nächte hier campen?
Can ikh foor ine/tsvy nekhte here campen?

Where can I pitch my tent?
Wo kann ich mein Zelt aufstellen?
Voo can ikh mine tselt owfshtellen?

How much does it cost for one night/week?
Wieviel kostet es für eine Nacht/Woche?
Veefeel kostet es foor iner nakht/wokhe?

Where are the washing facilities?
Wo sind die Waschräume?
Voh zint dee vashroyme?

Is there a restaurant/supermarket/swimming pool on site/nearby?
Gibt ein Restaurant/einen Supermarkt/ein Schwimmbad in der Nähe dieses Campingplatzes?
Geebt es ine restohrong/inen zoopermarkt/ine shvimmbad in der neyher deezes campingplatses?

EATING AND DRINKING

Cafes and Bars

I would like a cup of/two cups of/another coffee/tea
Eine Tasse/Zwei Tassen/noch eine Tasse Kaffee/Tee, bitte
Ikh merkhter iner tasser/tsvy tassen kafey/tey, bitter

With/without milk/sugar
Mit/ohne Milch/Zucker
Meet/ohner milkh/tsukker

I would like a bottle/glass/two glasses of mineral water/red wine/white wine, please
Ich möchte eine Flasche/ein Glas/zwei Gläser Mineralwasser/Rotwein/Weißwein, bitte
Ikh merkhter iner flasher/ine glas/tsvy glayzer mineraalvasser/rohtvine/vice-vine, bitter

I would like a beer/two beers, please
Ein Bier/Zwei Biere, bitte
Ine beer/tsvy beerer, bitter

Please may I have some ice?
Kann ich etwas Eis haben, bitte?
Can ikh etvas ice haaben, bitter?

GERMAN

Do you have any matches/ cigarettes/cigars?
Haben Sie Streichhölzer/ Zigaretten/Zigarren?
Haaben see shtrykhherltser/ tseegaretten/tseegarren?

Restaurants

Can you recommend a good/ cheap restaurant in this area?
Können Sie ein gutes/nicht zu teueres Restaurant in dieser Gegend empfehlen?
Kernen zee ine gootes/nikht tsoo toyeress restohrong in deezer gey-gent empfeylen?

I would like a table for . . . people
Ein Tisch für . . . Personen, bitte
Ine teesh foor . . . perzohnen, bitter

Do you have a non-smoking area?
Haben Sie einen Bereich für Nichtraucher?
Haben zee inen berykh foor nikhtrowkher?

Waiter/Waitress!
Herr Ober/Fräulein, bitte!
Hair ohber/froyline, bitter!

Excuse me, please may we order?
Bitte, dürfen wir bestellen?
Bitter, dewrfen veer bershtellen?

Do you have a set menu/ children's menu/wine list?
Haben Sie eine Tageskarte/Kinderspeisekarte/ Weinkarte?
Haaben zee iner tahgeskaarter/ keender-shpyzekaarter/vinekaarter?

Do you have any vegetarian dishes?
Gibt es bei Ihnen vegetarische Gerichte, bitte?
Geebt es by eehnen veggetareesher gereekhter, bitter?

Do you have any local specialities?
Gibt es örtliche Spezialitäten?
Geebt es ortlikhe specialitayten?

Are vegetables included?
Ist Gemüse dabei?
Ist gemoose darbye?

Could I have it well-cooked/ medium/rare please?
Ich möchte es bitte durch/halb durch/englisch gebraten?
Ikh merkhter es bitter doorkh/halb doorkh/eng-lish gebrarten?

What does this dish consist of?
Was für ein Gericht ist es?
Vas foor ine gereekht ist es?

I am a vegetarian. Does this contain meat?
Ich bin Vegetarier (Vegetarierin fem.). Enthält das hier Fleisch?
Ish bin veggetaareer (veggetaa-reerin). Enthelt dass heer flyshe?

I do not eat nuts/dairy products/meat/fish
Ich esse keine Nüsse/keine Molkereiprodukte/kein Fleisch/keinen Fisch
Ish esser kiner newsser/kiner molk-erey-produkter/kine flyshe/kinen fish

Not (very) spicy, please
Nicht (sehr) scharf, bitte
Nisht (zair) sharf, bitter

I would like the set menu, please
Die Tageskarte, bitte
Dee tahgeskaarte, bitter

We are still waiting to be served
Wir warten noch auf Bedienung
Veer varten nokh owf bedeenung

Please bring a plate/knife/fork
Bitte bringen Sie einen Teller/ein Messer/eine Gabel
Bitter bring-en zee inen teller/ine messer/iner gaabel

Excuse me, this is not what I ordered
Entschuldigung, das habe ich nicht bestellt
Entshuldeegoong, das haber ikh nikht beshtelt

May I have some (more) bread/water/coffee/tea?
Kann ich (noch) etwas Brot, Wasser/Kaffee/Tee haben?
Can ikh etvas (nokh) etvas broht/vasser/kaffey/tey haaben?

May I have the bill, please?
Die Rechnung, bitte?
Dee rekhnung, bitter?

Does this bill include service?
Ist diese Rechnung einschließlich Bedienung?
Ist deeze rekhnung ine-shleessleekh bedeenung?

Do you accept traveller's cheques/Mastercard/US dollars?
Nehmen sie Reiseschecks /Mastercard/US Dollars?
Naymen zee Ryzersheks/Mastercard/US Dollars?

Can I have a receipt, please?
Könnte ich bitte eine Quittung haben?
Kernter ikh bitter ine kwitoong harben?

Where is the toilet (restroom), please?
Wo sind die Toiletten, bitte?
Voo zeent dee toletten, bitter?

On the Menu

Frühstück/Mittagessen/ Abendbrot
Frewshtewk/Mittaag-essen/ Aabend-broht
Breakfast/Lunch/Dinner

Vorspeisen
Fore-shpysen
First courses

Suppen
Sooppen
Soups

Hauptgerichte
Howpt-gerikhte
Main courses

Fischgerichte
Fish-gerikhte
Fish dishes

GERMAN

GERMAN

Fleischgerichte
Flyesh-gerikhte
Meat dishes

Rindfleisch
Rint-flyshe
Beef

Steak
Steak
Steak

Schweinefleisch
Shvyner-flyshe
Pork

Kalbfleisch
Kalp-flyshe
Veal

Hähnchenfleisch
Heynshen-flyshe
Chicken

Lamm
Lamm
Lamb

Schinken
Shinken
Ham

Vegetarische Gerichte
Veggetairishe gerikhte
Vegetarian dishes

Gemüse
Gemewzer
Vegetables

Pommes frites
Pomm freet
Chips (french fries)

Salzkartoffeln/Bratkartoffeln/Kartoffelpüree
Zalts-kartoffeln/Braat-kartoffeln/Kartoffelpewrey
Boiled/sauté/mashed potatoes

Reis
Rice
Rice

Käse
Keyse
Cheese

Desserts
Desayrs
Desserts

Eiskrem
Ice-kreym
Ice cream

Kuchen
Kookhen
Cakes

Gebäck
Gerbeck
Pastries

Obst
Obst
Fruit

Brot
Broht
Bread

Brötchen
Brert-shen
Rolls

Toast
Toast
Toast

Butter
Booter
Butter

Salz/Pfeffer
Zalts/Pfeffer
Salt/pepper

Zucker
Tsooker
Sugar

Spezialitäten
Specialitayten
Specialities

Lokale Spezialitäten
Lokaaler Shpetsialiteyten
Local specialities

Menü
Mernew
Set menu

Weinliste
Vinelister
Wine list

Rotweine
Roht-viner
Red wines

Weißweine / Rosé-Weine
Vice-viner / *Rohzey-viner*
White wines / **Rosé wines**

Sekt
Zekt
Sparkling wines

Bier
Beer
Beer

Flaschenbier/Bier vom Fass
Flashenbeer/Beer fom fass
Bottled beer/Draught (draft) beer

Alkoholfreie Getränke
Alkoholfryer gertrenker
Non-alcoholic drinks

Mineralwasser
Mineraal-vasser
Mineral water

Obstsäfte / Orangensaft
Obst-zefter / *Oranzhen-zaft*
Fruit juices / **Orange juice**

Limonade / Eis
Limonaader / *Ice*
Lemonade / **Ice**

Kaffee mit Milch/Schwarzer Kaffee/Espresso
Kaffey mit milsh/shvartser kaffey/espresso
White coffee/black coffee/espresso coffee

Tee mit Milch/mit Zitrone
Tey mit milsh/mit tsitrohner
Tea with milk/with lemon

Schokolade
Shockohlaader
Chocolate (drink)

Milch
Milsh
Milk

Snacks/Leichte Gerichte
Snacks/Lyshter gerlshter
Snacks/Light meals

Salate / Sandwiches
Zalaater / *Zentvitch*
Salads / **Sandwiches**

Eier
Eye-er
Eggs

Gekochte Eier/Spiegeleier/Rühreier
Gekokhter eye-er/speegel-eye-er/Rewr-eye-er
Boiled/fried/scrambled eggs

Würstchen
Vewrst-shen
Sausage

Typical local dishes

Schweinehaxe
Shvynerhaxer
Crisp-grilled pork knuckle

Bratwurst/Bockwurst
Brahtwoorst/Bokwoorst
Grilled/boiled pork sausages

Himmel und Erde
Himmel oont airder
'Heaven and earth' - puréed salad of apple and potato

Zigeunerschnitzel
Tsigoyner-shnitsel
'Gipsy escalope' - veal or pork cutlet in a pepper and tomato sauce

Tafelspitz **(Austria)**
Taafelshpits
Sliced boiled beef with apple and horseradish sauce

Kaiserschmarren **(Austria)**
Kyzer-shmarren
Shredded pancake with raisins and syrup

GETTING AROUND

Public Transport

Where is the bus stop/coach stop/nearest metro station?
Wo ist die Bushaltestelle/der Busbahnhof/die nächste U-Bahnhaltestelle, bitte?
Voo ist die nexterbushaltersteller/der nexter busbaanhof/dee nexter Oo-baahn-halter-shteller?

When is the next/last bus to ..?
Wann fährt der nächste/letzte Bus nach ..?
Vann fairt der nexter/letster bus nakh ..?

How much is the fare to the city centre (downtown)/ railway station/airport?
Wieviel kostet es zur Stadtmitte/zum Bahnhof/zum Flughafen?
Veefeel kostet es tsoor shtatmitte/tsoom baanhof/tsoom flooghaafen?

Will you tell me when to get off?
Sagen Sie mir bitte, wann ich aussteigen muss?
Zaagen zee meer bitter vann ikh ows-shtygen muss?

Does this bus go to ..?
Fährt dieser Bus nach ..?
Fairt deezer bus nakh ..?

Which number bus goes to ..?
Welcher Bus fährt nach ..?
Velkher bus fairt nakh ..?

May I have a single (one-way)/return (round-trip)/ day ticket/book of tickets?
Ich möchte eine einfache Fahrkarte/Rückfahrkarte/ Rundfahrkarte/Tageskarte/ ein Fahrkartenheft?
Ikh merkhter iner inefakher faarkaarter/ruekfaarkaarter/tagh-eskaarter/iner faarkaartenheft?

Taxis (Taxi)

I would like to go to ... How much will it cost?
Ich möchte nach ... fahren, wieviel kostet das?
Ikh merkhter nakh ... faaren, veefeel kostet das?

Please may I stop here
Bitte hier anhalten
Bitter here anhalten

I would like to order a taxi today/tomorrow/at 2pm to go from . . . to . . .
Ich möchte gerne ein Taxi für heute/morgen/zwei Uhr bestellen um von . . . nach . . . zu fahren
Ikh merkhter gairner ine Taxi foor hoyter/morgen/tsvy oor bestellen oom fon . . . nakh . . . zu faaren

Entertainment

Can you recommend a good bar/nightclub?
Können Sie eine gute Bar/einen guten Nachtklub empfehlen?
Kernen zee iner gooter bar/inen gooten nakhtklub empfehlen?

Do you know what is on at the cinema (playing at the movies)/ theatre at the moment?
Was spielt im Augenblick im Kino/Theater?
Vass shpeelt im augenbleek im keeno/teyaater?

I would like to book (purchase) . . . tickets for the matinee/evening performance on Monday
Ich möchte gerne Eintrittskarten für die Frühvorstellung/Abendvorstellung am Montag bestellen
Ikh merkhter gairner inetreet-skaarten foor dee frooforshtellung/ahbendforshtellung am mohntagh beshtellen

What time does the film/performance start?
Um wieviel Uhr fängt der Film/die Vorstellung an?
Oom veefeel oor fengt der film/dee forshtellung an?

COMMUNICATIONS

Post

How much will it cost to send a letter/postcard/this package to Britain/Ireland/America/Canada/Australia/New Zealand?
Wieviel kostet ein Brief/eine Postkarte/dieses Paket nach Großbritannien/Irland/Amerika/Kanada/Australien/Neuseeland?
Veefeel kostet ine breef/iner postkaarter/deezes pakayt nakh Grohssbritannien/Eerland/America/Canada/Owstralee-en/Noyzeyland?

I would like one stamp/two stamps
Ich möchte eine/zwei Briefmarke(n)
Ikh merkhter iner/tsvy breefmarke(n)

I'd like . . . stamps for postcards to send abroad, please
Ich möchte . . . Briefmarken für Postkarten ins Ausland bitte
Ikh merkhter . . . breefmarken foor postkarten ins owslund bitter

Phones

I would like to make a telephone call/reverse the charges to (make a collect call to) ...
Ich möchte einen Anruf/ein R-Gespräch nach ... machen
Ikh merkhter inen aanroof/ine eyr-geshprekh nakh ... makhen

Which coins do I need for the telephone?
Welche Münzen brauche ich für dieses Telefon?
Velkhe moontsen browkhe ikh foor deezes teylefohn?

The line is engaged (busy)
Die Nummer ist besetzt
Dee noommer ist bezetst

The number is ...
Die Nummer ist ...
Dee noommer ist ...

Hello, this is ...
Hallo, hier spricht ...
Hallo, here shprikht ...

Please may I speak to ...?
Kann ich bitte mit ... sprechen?
Can ikh bitter mit ... shprekhen?

He/she is not in at the moment. Please can you call back?
Er/sie ist im Moment nicht da. Könnten Sie später noch einmal anrufen?
Air/Zee ist im morment nikht dar. Kernten zee shpeter nokh inemarl anroofen?

SHOPPING

Shops

Buchgeschäft/Schreibwaren
Bookhgesheft/Shribevahren
Bookshop/Stationery

Schmuckgeschäft/Geschenke
Shmookgesheft/Geshenker
Jeweller/Gifts

Schuhe
Shooher
Shoes

Eisenwaren
Eyesenvahren
Hardware

Friseur (Herren)/(Damen)
Freesoor (hairren)/(darmen)
Hairdresser (men's)/(women's)

Bäckerei
Bekkereye
Baker

Supermarkt
Soopermarkt
Supermarket

Fotogeschäft
Fotogesheft
Photo shop

Reisebüro
Ryesebewro
Travel agent

Apotheke
Appoteyker
Pharmacy

In the Shops

What time do the shops open/close?
Um wieviel Uhr öffnen/schließen die Geschäfte?
Oom veefeel oor erffnen/shleessen dee geshefter?

Where is the nearest market?
Wo ist der nächste Markt?
Vo ist dair nekster markt?

Can you show me the one in the window/this one?
Zeigen Sie mir bitte das im Fenster/dieses da?
Tsyegen zee mere bitter dass im fenster/deezess dar?

Can I try this on?
Kann ich das anprobieren?
Can ikh das anprobeeren?

What size is this?
Welche Größe ist dieses Stück?
Velkhe grersser ist deezes shtook?

This is too large/too small/too expensive
Es ist zu groß/zu klein/zu teuer
Es ist tsu gross/tsu kline/tsu toyer

Do you have any others?
Haben Sie noch andere?
Haben zee nokh anderer?

My size is . . .
Ich habe Größe . . .
Ikh haber grerser . . .

Where is the changing room/children's/cosmetic/ladieswear/menswear/food department?
Wo ist der Umkleideraum/die Kinder- /Damen- /Herrenkleidungs-/ Lebensmittel-Abteilung?
Voh ist der oomklyderowm/dee kinder/daamen/herenklydungs/ ley-bensmittel abtylung?

I would like . . . a quarter of a kilo/half a kilo/a kilo of bread/butter/this fruit/ham
Ich möchte gerne . . . ein viertel Kilo/halbes Kilo/ein Kilo Brot/Butter/dieses Obst/Schinken
Ikh merkhter gairner . . . ine feertel keelo/halbes keelo/ine keelo broht/bootter/deezess obst/sheenken

How much is this?
Wieviel kostet das?
Veefeel kostet das?

I'll take this one, thank you
Ich nehme das, danke schön
Ikh neymer das, danker shern

Do you have a carrier (shopping) bag?
Haben Sie eine Tragetasche?
Haaben zee iner traager-tasher?

Do you have anything cheaper/larger/smaller/of better quality?
Haben Sie etwas Billigeres/ Größeres/Kleineres/Haben Sie eine bessere Qualität?
Haaben zee etvas billigeress/ grersseress/klineress/Haaben zee iner bessere qualitaet?

I would like a film to develop this film/this for my camera
Ich möchte einen Film/diesen Film entwickeln lassen für meinen Fotoapparat
Ikh merkhter inen film deezen film entvickeln lassen foor minen fotoaparat

I would like some batteries, the same size as this old one
Ich möchte einige Batterien, die gleiche Größe wie die alten
Ikh merkhter iyniger batteree-en, dee glykhe grersser vee dee alten

Would you mind wrapping this for me, please?
Können Sie es bitte einpacken?
Kernen zee es bitter ine-pakken?

Sorry, but you seem to have given me the wrong change
Entschuldigung, aber Sie scheinen einen Fehler mit dem Wechselgeld gemacht zu haben
Entshuldigung, aber zee shinern inen fayler mit dem vekhselgeld gemahkt tsoo haaben

MOTORING

Car Hire (Rental)

I have ordered (rented) a car in the name of . . .
Ich habe einen Wagen für . . . bestellt
Ikh haaber inen vaagen foor . . . beshtellt

How much does it cost to hire (rent) a car for one day/ two days/one week?
Was kostet es einen Wagen für einen Tag/zwei Tage/eine Woche zu mieten?
Vas kostet es inen vaagen foor inen taagh/tsvy taager/iner wokher tsoo meeten?

Is the tank already full of petrol (gas)?
Ist der Tank voll?
Ist der tank foll?

Is insurance and tax included? How much is the deposit?
Ist die Versicherung und Steuer inbegriffen? Wieviel muss man anzahlen?
Ist dee ferzeekherung oont shtoyer inbegreeffen? Veefeel muss man aantsahlen?

By what time must I return the car?
Um wieviel Uhr muss ich den Wagen zurückbringen?
Oom veefeel oor muss ikh den vaagen tsoo-rookh bringen?

I would like a small/large/ family/sports car with a radio/cassette player
Ich möchte einen kleinen/einen großen Wagen/einen Familienwagen/einen Sportwagen mit Radio/ Kassettenspieler
ikh merkhter inen klinen/inen grohssen vahgen/inen fameelyen vahgen/ inen shportvahgen mit rah-dioh/cassetten-shpeeler

Do you have a road map?
Haben Sie eine Straßenkarte?
Haben zee iner shtrasen-karte?

Parking

How long can I park here?
Wie lange darf man hier parken?
Vee langer darf man here parken?

Is there a car park near here?
Gibt es einen Parkplatz in der Nähe?
Geebt es inen parkplats in dair neher?

At what time does this car park close?
Wann schließt dieser Parkplatz?
Van shleest deeser parkplats?

Signs and Notices

Einbahnstraße
Ine-barn-shtraser
One way

Zutritt/Einfahrt verboten
Tsutreet/Inefart ferbohten
No entry

Parkverbot
Park-ferboht
No parking

Umleitung
Oomlytung
Detour (diversion)

Halt
Halt
Stop

Vorfahrt beachten
Forfart beakhten
Give way (yield)

Straßenglätte
Shtrasen-gletter
Slippery road

Überholen verboten
Ooberhohlen ferbohten
No overtaking

Gefahr!
Gerfaar!
Danger!

At the Filling Station
(An der Tankstelle)

Unleaded (lead-free)/ standard/premium/diesel
Bleifrei/Normal/Super/Diesel
Blye-frye/normahl/super/deezel

Fill the tank please
Volltanken, bitte
Foll-tanken, bitter

Do you have a road map?
Haben Sie eine Straßenkarte?
Haben zee iner shtrasen-karte?

How much is the car wash?
Was kostet die Autowäsche?
Vas kostet dee owtowesher?

Breakdowns

I've had a breakdown at . . .
Ich habe eine Panne bei . . .
Ikh haber ine panner bye . . .

I am a member of the . . . [motoring organisation]
Ich bin Mitglied von . . .
Ish bin mitgleet fon . . .

I am on the road from ... to ...
Ich bin auf der Straße von ... nach ...
Ikh bin owf dair shtrase fon ... nakh ...

I can't move the car. Can you send a tow-truck?
Mein Auto ist kaputt. Können Sie einen Abschleppwagen schicken?
Mine owto ist kapoot. Kernnen zee inen Abshlep-vagen shiken?

I have a flat tyre
Mein Reifen ist platt
Mine ryefen ist platt

The windscreen (windshield) has smashed/cracked
Die Windschutzscheibe ist kaputt/gesprungen
Dee vindshoots-shyeber ist kapoot/geshprungen

There is something wrong with the engine/brakes/ lights/steering/gearbox/ clutch/exhaust
Ich habe Probleme mit dem Motor/der Bremse/dem Licht/der Steuerung/dem Getriebe/der Kupplung/dem Auspuff
Ikh haber probleyme mit dem motor/dair bremser/dem licht/dair shtoyerung/dem getreeber/dair koopploong/dem owspooff

It's overheating
Der Motor ist überhitzt
Dair motor ist ooberhitst

It won't start
Es springt nicht an
Es shpringt nikht an

Where can I get it repaired?
Wo kann ich es reparieren lassen?
Vo can ikh es repareeren lassen?

Can you take me there?
Können Sie mich dort hinbringen?
Kernen zee mikh dort hinbringen?

Will it take long to fix?
Dauert die Reparatur lange?
Dowert dee reparatoor languer?

How much will it cost?
Was wird es kosten?
Vas veerd es kosten?

Please can you pick me up/give me a lift?
Können Sie mich bitte abschleppen/mitnehmen?
Kernen zee mish bitter abshleppen/mitneymen?

Accidents and Traffic Offences (Violations)

Can you help me? There has been an accident
Können Sie mir helfen? Es ist ein Unfall passiert
Kernen zee mere helfen? Es ist ine oonfal paseert

Please call the police/an ambulance
Bitte rufen Sie die Polizei/einen Krankenwagen
Bitter roofen zee dee politsye/inen krankenvagen

Is anyone hurt?
Ist jemand verletzt?
Ist yemant fairletst?

I'm sorry, I didn't see the sign
Tut mir leid, ich habe das Schild nicht gesehen
Toot mere lyed, ikh haber das shilt nikht gesayhen

Must I pay a fine? How much?
Gibt das einen Strafzettel? Wieviel?
Geebt das inen shtraf-tsettel? Veefeel?

Show me your documents
Zeigen Sie mir Ihre Papiere
Tsyegen zee mere eere papeerer

HEALTH

Pharmacy (Apotheke)

Do you have anything for a stomach ache/headache/sore throat/toothache?
Haben Sie etwas für Magenschmerzen/Kopfschmerzen/Halsschmerzen/Zahnschmerzen?
Haaben zee etvas foor maagensh-mertsen/kopfshmertsen/hals-shmert-sen/tsahnschmertsen?

I need something for diarrhoea/constipation/ a cold/a cough/insect bites/ sunburn/travel (motion) sickness
Ich benötige etwas für Durchfall/Verstopfung/eine Erkältung/einen Husten/Insektenstiche/Sonnenbrand/Reisekrankheit
Ikh benertiger etvas foor doorkhfall/fershtopfung/iner erkel-tung/inen hoosten/insektensh-teekhe/zonnenbrand/ryzerkrankhite

How much/how many do I take?
Wieviel/wieviele soll ich nehmen?
Veefeel/veefeeler soll ikh neymen?

How often do I take it/them?
Wie oft soll ich es/sie nehmen?
Vee oft soll ikh es/zee neymen?

How much does it cost?
Wieviel kostet das?
Veefeel kostet das?

Can you recommend a good doctor/dentist?
Können Sie einen guten Arzt/Zahnarzt empfehlen?
Kernen see meer inen gooten artst/tsaanartst empfehlen?

Is it suitable for children?
Ist es gut für Kinder?
Ist es goot fewr kinnder?

Doctor (Arzt)

I have a pain here/in my arm/ leg/chest/stomach
Ich habe hier Schmerzen/an meinem Arm/Bein/an meiner Brust/an meinem Magen
Ikh haaber shmertsen here/an minem arm/bine/an miner broost/an minem maagen

Please call a doctor, this is an emergency
Rufen Sie bitte einen Arzt, es ist ein Notfall
Roofen zee bitter inen artst, es ist ine nohtfall

HEALTH

G E R M A N

I would like to make an appointment to see a doctor
Ich möchte einen Arzttermin vereinbaren
Ikh merkhter inen artst-termeen fer-inebaaren

I am diabetic/pregnant
Ich bin Diabetiker/ich bin schwanger
Ikh been deeabetiker/ikh been shvanger

I need a prescription for ...
Ich benötige ein Rezept für ...
Ikh benertiger ine retsept fewr ...

Can you give me something to ease the pain?
Können Sie mir etwas gegen die Schmerzen geben?
Kernen zee meer etvas geygen dee shmertsen geyben?

I am/he is/she is allergic to penicillin
Ich bin/er ist/sie ist allergisch auf Penizillin
Ikh bin/air ist/zee ist allergish owf penitsileen

Tut das weh?
Toot das way?
Does this hurt?

Sie müssen/er muss/sie muss ins Krankenhaus
Zee moossen/air muss/zee muss ins krankenhouse
You must/he must/she must go to hospital

Nehmen Sie diese einmal/zweimal/dreimal täglich
Naymen zee deeser inemal/tsvyemal/drymal teyglikh
Take these once/twice /three times a day

I am/he is/she is taking this medication
Ich nehme/er nimmt/sie nimmt diese Medikamente
Ikh naymer/air nimmt/zee nimmt deeser medikamenter

I have medical insurance
Ich habe eine Krankenversicherung
Ikh haber ine kranken-fersikheroong

Dentist (Zahnarzt)

I have toothache
Ich habe Zahnschmerzen
Ikh haabe tsahn-shmertsen

My filling has come out
Eine Füllung ist herausgefallen
Iner fooloong ist herowsgefallen

I do/do not want to have an injection first
Ich will eine/keine Spritze haben
Ikh vill iner/kiner shpreetse haaben

EMERGENCIES

Help!
Hilfe!
Heelfe!

Fire!
Feuer!
Foyer!

Stop!
Halt!
Halt!

Call an ambulance/a doctor/ the police/the fire brigade!
Rufen Sie bitte einen Krankenwagen/einen Arzt/die Polizei/die Feuerwehr!
Roofen zee bitter inen krankenvaagen/inen artst/dee politsye/dee foyervair!

Please may I use a telephone?
Darf ich bitte das Telefon benutzen?
Darf ish bitter dass teylefon benootsen?

I have had my traveller's cheques/credit cards/ handbag/rucksack/luggage/ wallet/ passport/mobile phone stolen
Man hat mir meine Reiseschecks/ Kreditkarten//meine Handtasche/ meinen Rucksack/ Gepäck/meine Brieftasche/meinen Reisepass/ mein Handy gestohlen
Man hat meer miner ryzersheks/creditkaarten/miner handtasher/minen ruckzack/ gepeck/miner breeftasher/minen rizerpass/mine hendy geshtohlen

May I please have a copy of the report for my insurance claim?
Darf ich für meine Versicherung eine Kopie des Berichts haben?
Darf ish fewr miner fairzisheroong iner koppier dess berishts haaben?

Can you help me, I have lost my daughter/son/my companion(s)?
Können Sie mir bitte helfen, ich habe meine Tochter/meinen Sohn/ meine Begleitung verloren?
Kernen zee meer bitter helfen, ikh haabe miner tokhter/minen zohn ferloren/miner beglytoong ferlohren?

Please go away/leave me alone
Lassen Sie mich bitte in Ruhe
Lassen see meekh bitter in roohe

I'm sorry
Es tut mir Leid
Ess toot meer lite

I want to contact the British/ American/Canadian/Irish/ Australian/New Zealand/ South African consulate
Ich möchte mich mit dem Britischen/Amerikanischen/ Kanadischen/Irischen/ Australischen/Neuseeländischen/ Südafrikanischen Konsulat in Verbindung setzen
Ikh merkhter mikh mit dem Britishen/Amerikanishen/ Karnardishen/Eereeshen/ Owstralishen/Noysaylendishen/ Soodafrikanishen Konsoolat in ferbeendoong setsen

I am ill/injured. I am lost
Ich bin krank/verletzt. Ich habe mich verirrt
Ish bin krank/fairletst. Ish haaber mish faireert

We're ill/injured. We are lost
Wir sind krank/verletzt. Wir haben uns verirrt
Veer zint krank/fairletst. Veer haaben oonss faireert

He/she is ill/injured. He/she is lost
Er/sie ist krank/verletzt. Er/sie hat sich verirrt.
Air/zee ist krank/fairletst. Air/zee hat zish faireert

They are ill/injured. They are lost
Sie sind krank/verletzt. Sie haben sich verirrt
Zee zint krank/fairletst. Zie haaben zish faireert

GREEK

INTRODUCTION

Greek, the language of Greece and the Republic of Cyprus, has a 3000-year history, and modern written Greek would be readable, and probably to a large degree comprehensible, to an ancient Athenian.

The spoken language has fewer pitfalls, although beware that the word for 'yes' sounds like English 'nay', whereas a Greek who nods his head up and down is probably saying 'no', this being the equivalent of shaking the head. English is widely spoken in tourist areas, and French is a second language, but be prepared to speak Greek when off the beaten track.

Addresses for Travel and Tourist Information

Australia: *Greek National Tourist Organisation,* 37–49 Pitt Street, Sydney, NSW 2000; tel: (02) 9241 1663/4/5; fax: (02) 9241 2499.

Canada: *Hellenic Tourism Organisation,* 91 Scollard Street, 2nd Floor, Toronto, Ontario M5R 1G4; tel: (416) 968 2220; fax: (416) 968 6533.

UK: *Greek National Tourism Organisation,* 4 Conduit St, London W1S 2DJ; tel: (020) 7495 9300; fax: (020) 7287 1369.

USA: *Greek National Tourist Office,* 645 Fifth Ave, New York, NY 10022; tel: (212) 421 5777. *Greek National Tourist Organisation,* 611 W. Sixth St, #2198, Los Angeles, CA 90017; tel: (213) 626 6696.

Official tourism website: www.gnto.gr.

Greece Facts

CAPITAL: Athens.

CURRENCY: Euro (€). €1 = 100 cents.

OPENING HOURS: Banks: Mon–Thur 0830–1400, Fri 0830–1330. Shops: Mon–Fri 0900–1430 and Tues, Thur, Fri 1730–2030; Sat 0900–1500. Museums: Variable, but usually not open Mondays.

TELEPHONES: To dial in, +30. Outgoing, 00 plus the country code. Police, 100. Tourist Police, 171. Fire, 199. Ambulance, 178.

PUBLIC HOLIDAYS: 1, 6 Jan; 14, 25 Mar; Orthodox Easter Monday (Apr/May); 4 Jun; 15 Aug; 28 Oct; 25, 26 Dec.

Technical Language Hints

The non-Roman script is the most difficult aspect of the language for the visitor, although many street signs and notices have both the Greek characters and a transliteration into the Roman alphabet. This is in itself a source of potential confusion, however, as there is no one accepted way of writing a Greek word in Roman script, so any Greek text can have a variety of spellings in the Roman alphabet. The question mark in Greek is represented by a semi-colon, ; .

ESSENTIALS

Alphabet and Pronunciation

	Name	Pronounced
Α, α	*alfa*	**like 'a' in father**
αι		**like 'e' in pet**
αυ		**like 'af' in after or like 'av' in avalanche**
Β, β	*vita*	**like 'v' in vase**
Γ, γ	*gamma*	**like 'y' in yard, or like 'w' in want**
Δ, δ	*delta*	**like 'th' in then**
Ε, ε	*epsilon*	**like 'e' in egg**
ει		**like 'i' in pill**
ευ		**like 'ef' in left or like 'ev' in ever**
Ζ, ζ	*zeeta*	**like 'z' in zebra**
Η, η	*eeta*	**like 'i' in pill**
Θ, θ	*theeta*	**like 'th' in thermometer**
Ι, ι	*iota*	**like 'i' in pill**
Κ, κ	*kappa*	**like 'k' in keep**
Λ, λ	*lamda*	**like 'l' in lamp, or like 'll' in brilliant**
Μ, μ	*mi*	**like 'm' in monster or like 'my' in miaow**
Ν, ν	*ni*	**like 'n' in no**
Ξ, ξ	*xi*	**like 'cks' in lacks**
Ο, ο	*omikron*	**like 'o' in top**
οι		**like 'i' in pill**
ου		**like 'u' in pull**
Π, π	*pi*	**like 'p' in part or like 'py' in piano**
Ρ, ρ	*ro*	**rolled, like 'r' in Scottish dialects or like 'rj' in are you**
Σ,σ, ς	*sigma*	**like 's' in stop**
Τ, τ	*taf*	**like 't' in table or 'ty' in get you**
Υ, υ	*ipsilon*	**like 'i' in pill**
υι		**like 'i' in pill**
Φ, φ	*fi*	**like 'f' in fly**
Χ, χ	*hi*	**like 'h' in holiday, or like 'ch' in Scottish loch**
Ψ, ψ	*psi*	**like 'ps' in taps**
Ω, ω	*omega*	**like 'o' in hot**

ESSENTIALS

GREEK

Basic Words and Phrases

Yes
Ναι
Ne

No
Οχι
Ohi

Please
Παρακαλώ
Parakalo

Thank you
Ευχαριστώ
Efharisto

Hello
Γειά σας
Ya sas

Goodbye
Χαίρετε
Herete

Excuse me
Με συγχωρείτε
Me sinhorite

Sorry
Συγγνώμη
Signomi

How
Πώς
Pos

When
Πότε
Pote

Why
Πού
Pu

What
Τι
Ti

Who
Ποιος/Ποια/Ποιο
Pios/Pia/Pio

That's O.K.
Εντάξει
Entaxi

Perhaps
Ισως
Isos

To
Προς
Pros

From
Από
Apo

Here
Εδώ
Edo

There
Εκεί
Eki

I don't understand
Δεν καταλαβαίνω
Den katalaveno

I don't speak Greek
Δεν μιλώ Ελληνικά
Den milo Ellinika

Do you speak English?
Μιλάτε Αγγλικά;
Milate Anglika?

Please can you write it down?
Μπορείτε σας παρακαλώ να το γράψετε;
Borite sas parakalo na to grapsete?

Can you please speak more slowly?
Μπορείτε σας παρακαλώ να μιλάτε πιο αργά;
Borite sas parakalo na milate pio arga?

Greetings

Good morning/good afternoon/good evening/goodnight
Καλημέρα/χαίρετε/καλησπέρα/καληνύχτα
Kalimera/herete/kalispera/kalinihta

Pleased to meet you
Χαίρω πολύ
Hero poli

How are you?
Τι κάνετε;
Ti kanete?

I am well, thank you. And you?
Πολύ καλά, ευχαριστώ. Κι εσείς;
Poli kala, efharisto. Ki esis?

My name is ...
Ονομάζομαι ...
Onomazome ...

This is my friend/boyfriend/girlfriend/husband/wife/brother/sister
Σας συστήνω το φίλο μου/το φίλο μου/τη φίλη μου/το σύζυγό μου/τη σύζυγό μου/τον αδελφό μου/την αδελφή μου
Sas sistino to filo mu/to filo mu/ti fili mu/to sizigo mu/ti sizigo mu/ton adelfo mu/tin adelfi mu

Where are you travelling to?
Για πού ταξιδεύετε;
Ya pu taxidevete?

I am/we are going to ...
Πάω/πάμε στο ...
Pao/pame sto ...

How long are you travelling for?
Για πόσο καιρό θα ταξιδέψετε;
Ya poso kero tha taxidepsete?

Where do you come from?
Από πού είστε;
Apo pu iste?

I am/we are from ... Australia/Britain/Canada/America
Είμαι/είμαστε από Αυστραλία/Βρετανία/Καναδά/Αμερική/Νέα Ζηλανδία
Ime/imaste apo Avstralia/Bretania/Canada/Ameriki/Nea Zilandia

We are on holiday
Είμαστε σε διακοπές
Imaste se diakopes

This is our first visit here
Είναι η πρώτη μας επίσκεψη εδώ
Ine i proti mas episkepsi edo

How old are you?
Πόσο χρονών είστε;
Poso hronon iste?

I am ... years old
Είμαι ... χρονών
Ime ... hronon

I am a business person/doctor/journalist/manual worker/administrator/scientist/student/teacher
Είμαι επιχειρηματίας/γιατρός/δημοσιογράφος/εργάτης/υπάλληλος/επιστήμονας/φοιτητής (φοιτήτρια fem.)/δάσκαλος (δασκάλα fem.)
Ime epihirimatias/yatros/dimosioyrafos/eryatis/ipalilos/epistimonas/fititis (fititria)/daskalos (daskala)

I am waiting for my husband/wife/boyfriend/girlfriend
Περιμένω τον/την/το/τη άντρα/γυναίκα/φίλο/φίλη μου
Perimeno ton/tin/to/ti/antra/gineka/filo/fili mu

Would you like/may I have a cigarette?
Θα θέλατε/Μπορώ να έχω ένα τσιγάρο;
Tha thelate/Boro na eho ena tsigaro?

Do you mind if I smoke?
Θα σας πείραζε να καπνισω;
Tha sas piraze na kapniso?

Do you have a light?
Μήπως έχετε φωτιά;
Mipos ehete fotia?

Days

Monday
Δευτέρα
Deftera

Tuesday
Τρίτη
Triti

Wednesday
Τετάρτη
Tetarti

Thursday
Πέμπτη
Pembti

Friday
Παρασκευή
Paraskevi

Saturday
Σάββατο
Savvato

Sunday
Κυριακή
Kiriaki

Morning
Πρωί
Proi

Afternoon/Evening/Night
Απόγευμα/Βράδυ/Νύχτα
Apoyevma/Vradi/Nihta

Yesterday/Today/Tomorrow
Χτες/Σήμερα/Αύριο
Htes/Simera/Avrio

Numbers

Zero
Μηδέν
Miden

One
Ενα
Ena

Two
Δύο
Dio

Three
Τρία
Tria

Four
Τέσσερα
Tessera

Five
Πέντε
Pente

Six
Εξι
Exi

Seven
Επτά
Epta

Eight
Οκτώ
Okto

Nine
Εννέα
Ennea

Ten
Δέκα
Deka

Eleven
Εντεκα
Endeka

Twelve
Δώδεκα
Dodeka

Thirteen
Δεκατρία
Dekatria

Fourteen
Δεκατέσσερα
Dekatessera

Fifteen
Δεκαπέντε
Dekapente

Sixteen
Δεκαέξι
Dekaexi

Seventeen
Δεκαεπτά
Dekaepta

Eighteen
Δεκαοχτώ
Dekaokto

Nineteen
Δεκαεννέα
Dekaennea

Twenty
Είκοσι
Ikosi

Twenty-one
Είκοσι ένα
Ikosi ena

Twenty-two
Είκοσιδύο
Ikosi dio

Thirty
Τριάντα
Trianta

Forty
Σαράντα
Saranta

Fifty
Πενήντα
Peninta

Sixty
Εξήντα
Exinta

Seventy
Εβδομήντα
Evdominta

Eighty
Ογδόντα
Ogdonta

Ninety
Ενενήντα
Eneninta

One hundred
Εκατό
Ekato

Five hundred
Πεντακόσια
Pentakosia

One thousand
Χιλια
Hilia

One million
Ενα εκατομμύριο
Ena ekatommirio

Time

What time is it?
Τί ώρα είναι;
Ti ora ine?

It is ...
Είναι ...
Ine ...

9.00
Εννέα
Ennea

9.05
Εννέα και πέντε
Ennea ke pente

9.15
Εννέα και τέταρτο
Ennea ke tetarto

9.20
Εννέα και είκοσι
Ennea ke ikosi

9.30
Εννέα και μισή
Ennea ke misi

9.35
Δέκα πάρα είκοσι πέντε
Deka para ikosi pente

9.40
Δέκα πάρα είκοσι
Deka para ikosi

9.45
Δέκα πάρα τέταρτο
Deka para tetarto

9.50
Δέκα πάρα δέκα
Deka para deka

9.55
Δέκα πάρα πέντε
Deka para pente

12.00/Midday/Midnight
Δώδεκα/Μεσημέρι/Μεσάνυχτα
Dodeka/Mesimeri/Mesanihta

Money

I would like to change these traveller's cheques/this currency
Θα ήθελα να εξαργυρώσω αυτές τις ταξιδιωτικές επιταγές/αυτό το συνάλλαγμα
Tha ithela na exaryiroso aftes tis taxidiotikes epitayes/afto to sinallagma

How much commission do you charge? (What is the service charge?)
Τί προμήθεια επιβάλλετε;
Ti promithia epivallete?

Can I obtain money with my Mastercard?
Μπορώ να τραβήξω λεφτά με την Μάστερκαρτ μου;
Boro na travixo lefta me tin Mastercard mu?

ARRIVING AND DEPARTING

Airport

Excuse me, where is the check-in desk for ... airline?
Με συγχωρείτε πού είναι ο έλεγχος αποσκευών και εισιτηρίων για την αερογραμμή ...;
Me sinhorite, pu ine o elenhos aposkevon kai isitirion ya tin aerogrammi ...?

What is the boarding gate/time for my flight?
Ποια είναι η θύρα/ώρα επιβίβασης για την πτήση μου;
Pia ine i thira/ora epivivasis ya tin ptisi mu?

How long is the delay likely to be?
Πόσο προβλέπεται να διαρκέσει η καθυστέρηση;
Poso provlepete na diarkesi i kathisterisi?

Where is the duty-free shop?
Πού είναι το κατάστημα αφορολόγητων;
Pu ine to katastima aforoloyiton?

Which way is the baggage reclaim?
Πού είναι η αίθουσα αποσκευών;
Pu ine i ethusa aposkevon?

I have lost my luggage. Please can you help?
Έχω χάσει τις αποσκευές μου. Παρακαλώ μπορείτε να βοηθήσετε;
Eho hasi tis aposkeves mu. Parakalo borite na voithisete?

I am flying to ...
Πετάω για ...
Petao ya ...

Where is the bus for the city centre?
Από πού μπορώ να πάρω το λεωφορείο για το κέντρο της πόλης;
Apo pu boro na paro to leoforio ya to kentro tis polis?

Trains and Boats

Where is the ticket office/information desk?
Πού είναι το γραφείο εισιτηρίων/το γραφείο πληροφοριών;
Pu ine to grafio isitirion/to grafio pliroforion?

Which platform does the train/speedboat/ferry to ... depart from?
Από ποια αποβάθρα αναχωρεί το τρένο/το ταχύπλοο/το φέριμποτ για ...;
Apo pja apovathra anahori to treno/to tahiploo/to feribot ya ...?

Where is platform . . ?
Πού είναι η πλατφόρμα ...;
Pu ine i platforma ...?

When is the next train/boat to ...?
Πότε είναι το επόμενο τρένο/πλοίο για ...;
Pote ine to epomeno treno/plio ya ...?

Is there a later train/boat to ...?
Έχει αργότερα τρένο/πλοίο για ...;
Ehi argotera treno/plio ya ...?

Notices and Signs

Αμαξοστοιχία με μπουφέ
Amaxostihia me Buffet
Buffet (Dining) Car

Λεωφορείο
Leoforio
Bus

Πόσιμο/μη πόσιμο νερό
Posimo/mi posimo nero
Drinking/Non-drinking water

Είσοδος
Isodos
Entrance

Εξοδος
Exodos
Exit

Νοσοκομείο
Nosokomio
Hospital

Πληροφορίες
Plirofories
Information

Χώρος Αποσκευών
Horos Aposkevon
Left Luggage (Baggage Claim)

Θυρίδες Αποσκευών
Thirides Aposkevon
Luggage Lockers

Ταχυδρομείο
Tahidromio
Post Office

Πλατφόρμα/Εξέδρα
Platforma/Exedra
Platform

Σιδηροδρομικός Σταθμός
Sidirodromikos Stathmos
Railway (Railroad) Station

Αεροδρόμιο
Aerodromio
Airport

Αστυνομικό τμήμα
Astinomiko tmima
Police station

Λιμάνι
Limani
Port

Εστιατόριο
Estiatorio
Restaurant

Για Καπνιστές/Για μη καπνιστές
Ya kapnistes/ya mi kapnistes
Smoking/Non-smoking

Τηλέφωνο
Tilephono
Telephone

Γραφείο Εισιτηρίων
Grafio Isitirion
Ticket Office

GREEK

Ελεγχος Αποσκευών και Εισιτηρίων
Elenhos Aposkevon ke Isitirion
Check-in Desk

Δρομολόγιο
Dromologio
Timetable (Schedule)

Αποχωρητήρια
Apohoritiria
Toilets (Restrooms)

Γυναικών/Ανδρών
Yinekon/Andron
Ladies/Gentlemen

Υπόγειος Σιδηρόδρομος
Ipoyios Sidirodromos
Underground (Subway)

Αίθουσα Αναμονής
Ethusa Anamonis
Waiting Room

Buying a Ticket

I would like a first-class/second-class/single (one-way)/return (round-trip) ticket to ...
Θα ήθελα πρώτη θέση/δεύτερη θέση/απλό/μετ' επιστροφής εισιτήριο για ...
Tha ithela proti thesi/defteri thesi/aplo/met epistrofis isitirio ya ...

Is it an express (fast) train/bus?
Είναι εξπρές τρένο/λεωφορείο;
Ine express treno/leoforio?

Is my rail pass valid on this train/ferry/bus?
Το σιδηροδρομικό εισιτήριο που έχω ισχύει για αυτό το τρενο/φέρρυ/λεωφορείο;
To sidirodromiko isitirio pu eho ishii ya afto to treno/ferry/leoforio?

I would like an aisle/window seat
Θα ήθελα μια θέση δίπλα στο διάδρομο/παράθυρο
Tha ithela mia thesi dipla sto diadromo/parathiro

No smoking/smoking, please
Απαγορεύεται το κάπνισμα/επιτρέπεται το κάπνισμα παρακαλώ
Apagorevete to kapnisma/epitrepete to kapnisma, parakalo

We would like to sit together
Θα θέλαμε να καθίσουμε μαζί
Tha thelame na kathisoume mazi

I would like to make a seat reservation
Θα ήθελα να κλείσω μια θέση
Tha ithela na kliso mia thesi

I would like to reserve a couchette/sleeper for one person/two people/my family
Θα ήθελα να κλείσω κουκέτα/κλινάμαξα για ένα άτομο/δύο άτομα/την οικογένειά μου
Tha ithela na kliso kuketa/klinamaxa ya ena atomo/dio atoma/tin ikoyenia mu

I would like to reserve a cabin
Θα ήθελα να κλείσω μία καμπίνα
Tha ithela na kliso mia kabina

Timetables (Schedules)

Αφίξεις
Afixis
Arrive

Σταματά στο
Stamata sto
Calls (Stops) at

Υπηρεσία Εστίασης
Ipiresia estiasis
Catering Service

Αλλάζει στο
Allazi sto
Change at

Σύνδεση/Μέσω
Sindesi/Meso
Connection/Via

Καθημερινά
Kathimerina
Daily

Κάθε σαράντα (40) λεπτά
Kathe saranta (40) lepta
Every 40 minutes

Πρώτης θέσεως
Protis Theseos
First class

Κάθε ώρα
Kathe ora
Hourly

Συστήνονται κρατήσεις θέσεων
Sistinonte kratisis theseon
Seat reservations are recommended

Δευτέρας Θέσεως
Defteras Theseos
Second class

Συμπληρωματικό Ποσό
Simpliromatiko Poso
Supplement Payable

Luggage

How much will it cost to send (ship) my luggage in advance?
Πόσο θα μου στοιχίσει να στείλω εκ των προτέρων τις αποσκευές μου;
Poso tha mu stihisi na stilo ek ton proteron tis aposkeves mu?

Where is the left luggage (baggage claim) office?
Πού είναι το γραφείο αποσκευών;
Pu ine to grafio aposkevon?

What time do you open/close?
Τί ώρα ανοίγετε/κλείνετε;
Ti ora aniyete/klinete?

Where are the luggage trolleys (carts)?
Πού είναι τα τρόλλε των αποσκευών;
Pu ine ta trolley ton aposkevon?

Where are the lockers?
Πού είναι οι θυρίδες;
Pu ine i thirides?

I have lost my locker key
Εχασα το κλειδί της θυρίδας μου
Ehasa to klidi tis thiridas mu

On Board

Is this seat free?
Μήπως αυτή ή θέση είναι ελεύθερη;
Mipos afti i thesi ine eleftheri?

Excuse me, you are sitting in my reserved seat
Με συγχωρείτε, αλλά κάθεστε στην κρατημένη μου θέση
Me sinhorite, alla katheste stin kratimeni mu thesi

Which station is this?
Ποιος σταθμός είναι αυτός;
Pios stathmos ine aftos?

What time is this train/bus/ferry/flight due to arrive/depart?
Τι ώρα αναμένεται να φθάσει/αναχωρήσει το τραίνο/λεωφορείο/φέρρυ/ πτήση;
Ti ora anamenete na fthasi/anahorisi to treno/leoforio/ferry/ptisi?

Travelling with Children

Do you have a high chair/babysitting service/cot?
Μήπως έχετε καρέκλα μωρού/υπηρεσία μπέιμπυ σίττιγκ/παιδικό κρεβάτι;
Mipos ehete karekla moru/ipiresia babysitting/pediko krevati?

Where is the nursery/playroom?
Πού είναι το νηπιαγωγείο/η αίθουσα παιχνιδιών;
Pu ine to nipiagoyio/i ethusa pehnidion?

Where can I warm the baby's bottle?
Πού μπορώ να ζεστάνω το μπιμπερό του μωρού;
Pu boro na zestano to biberio tu moru?

Customs and Passports

Τα διαβατήριά σας, παρακαλώ!
Ta diavatiria sas, parakalo!
Passports, please!

I have nothing/wine/spirits (alcohol)/tobacco to declare
Δεν έχω τιποτα να δηλώσω/κρασί/οινοπνευματώδη/καπνό
Den eho tipoto na diloso/krasi/inopnevmatodi/kapno

I shall be staying for ... days/weeks/months
Θα μείνω για ... ημέρες/εβδομάδες/μήνες
Tha mino ya ... imeres/evdomades/mines

SIGHTSEEING

Asking the Way

Excuse me, do you speak English?
Με συγχωρείτε, μήπως μιλάτε Αγγλικά;
Me sinhorite, mipos milate Anglika?

Excuse me, can you help me please?
Συγγνώμη, μπορείτε να με βοηθήσετε παρακαλώ;
Siwnomi, borite na me voithisete parakalo?

Where is the Tourist Information Office?
Πού είναι το Γραφείο Τουρισμού;
Pu ine to grafio Turismu?

Excuse me, is this the right way to ...?
Με συγχωρείτε μπορείτε να μου πείτε πώς θα πάω στο/στη ...;
Me sinhorite, borite na mu pite pos tha pao sto/sti ...?

... the cathedral/the tourist office/the castle/the old town
... καθεδρικό ναό/τουριστικό γραφείο πληροφοριών/κάστρο/παλιά πόλη
... kathedriko nao/turistiko grafio pliroforion/kastro/palia poli

Can you tell me the way to the railway (railroad) station/bus station/taxi rank (stand)/city centre (downtown)/beach?
Μπορείτε να μου πείτε το δρόμο προς τον σιδηροδρομικό σταθμό/σταθμό λεωφορείων/στάση ταξί το κέντρο της πόλεως/την παραλία;
Borite na mu pite ton dromo pros ton sidirodromiko stathmo/stathmo leoforion/stasi taxi/to kentro tis poleos/tin paralia?

Πρώτη/δεύτερη στροφή/αριστερά/δεξιά/ευθεία
Proti/defteri strofi/aristera/dexia/efthia
First/second/left/right/straight ahead

Στη γωνία/στα φανάρια
Sti wonia/sta fanarja
At the corner/at the traffic lights

Where is the nearest police station/post office?
Πού είναι ο πλησιέστερος αστυνομικός σταθμός/το ταχυδρομείο;
Pu ine o plisiesteros astinomikos stathmos/to tahidromio?

Is it near/far?
Είναι κοντά/μακριά;
Ine konda/makria?

Do I need to take a taxi/catch a bus?
Χρειάζομαι να πάρω ταξί/λεωφορείο;
Hriazome na paro taxi/leoforio?

Do you have a map?
Έχετε χάρτη;
Ehete harti?

Can you point to it on my map?
Μπορείτε να μου το υποδείξετε στο χάρτη;
Borite na mu to ipodixete sto harti?

Thank you for your help
Σας ευχαριστώ για τη βοήθειά σας
Sas efharisto ya ti voithia sas

How do I reach the motorway/main road?
Από πού μπορώ να πάω στον αυτοκινητόδρομο/κύριο δρόμο;
Apo pu boro na pao ston aftokinito-dromo/kirio dromo?

I think I have taken the wrong turning
Νομίζω πως πήρα λάθος στροφή
Nomizo pos pira lathos strofi

I am looking for this address
Ψάχνω για αυτή τη διεύθυνση
Psachno ya afti ti diefthinsi

I am looking for the ... hotel
Ψάχνω για το ξενοδοχείο ...
Psahno ya to xenodohio ...

How far is it to ... from here?
Πόσο μακριά είναι από εδώ το ...
Poso makria ine apo edo to ...

Προχωρήστε ευθεία για ... χιλιόμετρα
Prohoriste efthia ya ... hiliometra
Carry straight on for ... kilometres

Στρίψετε στην επόμενη στροφή δεξιά/αριστερά
Stripsete stin epomeni strofi dexia/aristera
Take the next turning on the right/left

Στρίψετε δεξιά/αριστερά στο(α) επόμενο(α) σταυροδρόμι/φανάρια
Stripsete dexia/aristera sto(a) epomeno(a) stavrodromi/fanaria
Turn right/left at the next crossroads/traffic lights

Εχετε πάρει την αντίθετη κατεύθυνση
Ehete pari tin antitheti katefthinsi
You are going in the wrong direction

Where is the cathedral/church/museum/pharmacy?
Πού είναι η μητρόπολη/εκκλησία/το μουσείο/φαρμακειο;
Pu ine i mitropoli/ekklisia/to musio/farmakio?

How much is the admission/entrance charge?
Πόσο κάνει η είσοδος;
Poso kani i isodos?

Is there a reduction for children/students/senior citizens?
Μήπως υπάρχει έκπτωση για παιδιά/φοιτητές/ηλικιωμένους;
Mipos iparhi ekptosi ya pedia/fitites/ilikiomenus?

What time does the next guided tour (in English) start?
Τί ώρα αρχίζει η επόμενη ξενάγηση στα αγγλικά;
Ti ora arhizi i epomeni ksenagisi sta anglika?

One/two adults/children, please
Ενα/δυό ενήλικες/παιδιά, παρακαλώ
Ena/dio enilikes/pedia, parakalo

May I take photographs here?
Επιτρέπεται η λήψη φωτογραφιών εδώ;
Epitrepete i lipsi photographion edo?

At the Tourist Office

Do you have a map of the town/area?
Μήπως έχετε χάρτη της πόλης/περιοχής;
Mipos ehete harti tis polis/periohis?

Do you have a list of accommodation?
Εχετε κάποια λίστα δωματίων που νοικιάζονται;
Ehete kapia lista domation pu nikiazonte?

Can I reserve accommodation here?
Μπορώ να κρατήσω δωμάτια εδώ;
Boro na kratiso domatia edo?

ACCOMMODATION

Hotels

I have a reservation in the name of ...
Εχω κρατήση στο όνομα ...
Eho kratisi sto onoma ...

I wrote to/faxed/telephoned you last month/last week in ...
Σας έγραψα/έστειλα φαξ/τηλεφώνησα τον/την περασμένο(η) μήνα/ εβδομάδα ...
Sas egrapsa/estila fax/tilephonisa ton/tin perasmeno(i) mina/evdoma-da ...

Do you have any rooms free?
Εχετε ελεύθερα δωμάτια;
Ehete elefthera domatia?

I would like to reserve a single/double room with/ without a bath/shower
Θα ήθελα να κρατήσω ένα μονό/διπλό δωμάτιο με/ χωρίς μπάνιο/ντους
Tha ithela na kratiso ena mono/ diplo domatio me/horis banio/dush

I would like bed/breakfast/ (room and) full board
Θα ήθελα διατροφή δωμάτιο με πρόγευμα/δωμάτιο με διατρωθέ
Tha ethela diatrofi domatio me proyevma/domatio me diatrofi

How much is it per night?
Πόσο στοιχίζει τη μέρα;
Poso stihizi ti mera?

GREEK

Is breakfast included?
Περιλαμβάνει και πρωινό;
Perilamvani ke proino?

Do you have any cheaper rooms?
Μήπως έχετε φτηνότερα δωμάτια;
Mipos ehete ftinotera domatia?

I would like to see/take the room
Θέλω να δω/να πάρω το δωμάτιο
Thelo na do/na paro to domatio

I would like to stay for ... nights
Θα ήθελα να μείνω για ... νύχτες
Tha ithela na mino ya ... nihtes

The shower/light/tap doesn't work
Το ντούς/ηλεκτρικό/βρύση δεν λειτουργεί
To dush/ilektriko/vrisi den lituryi

At what time/where is breakfast served?
Τι ώρα/πού σερβίρεται το πρωινό;
Ti ora/pu servirete to proino?

What time do I have to check out?
Τι ώρα πρέπει να αδειάσω το δωμάτιο;
Ti ora prepi na adiaso to domatio?

Can I have the key to room number ...?
Μπορείτε να μου δώσετε το κλειδί για το δωμάτιο αριθμός ...;
Borite na mu dosete to klidi ya to domatio arithmos ... ?

My room number is ...
Ο αριθμός του δωματίου μου είναι ...
O arithmos tu domatiu mu ine ...

My room is not satisfactory/ not clean enough/too noisy. Please can I change rooms?
Το δωμάτιό μου δεν είναι ικανοποιητικό/δεν είναι αρκετά καθαρό/έχει πολύ θόρυβο. Παρακαλώ μπορώ να αλλάξω δωμάτιο;
To domatio mu den ine ikanopiitiko/den ine arketa katharo/ehi poli thorivo. Parakalo boro na alakso domatio?

Where is the bathroom?
Που είναι το μπάνιο;
Pu ine to banio?

Do you have a safe for valuables?
Έχετε θυρίδα για πολύτιμα αντικείμενα;
Ehete thirida ya politima andikimena?

Is there a laundry/do you wash clothes?
Υπάρχει πλυντήριο/πλένετε ρούχα;
Iparhi plindirio/plenete ruha?

I would like an air-conditioned room
Θέλω δωμάτιο με κλιματισμό
Thelo domatio me klimatismo

Do you accept traveller's cheques/credit cards?
Δέχεστε ταξιδιωτικές επιταγές/πιστωτικές;
Deheste taxidiotikes epitayes/ pistotikes kartes?

May I have the bill, please?
Μπορώ να έχω το λογαριασμό, παρακαλώ;
Boro na eho to logariasmo, parakalo?

Excuse me, I think there may be a mistake in this bill
Με συγχωρείτε, νομίζω πως υπάρχει κάποιο λάθος στο λογαριασμό
Me sinhorite, nomizo pos iparhi kapio lathos sto logariasmo

Youth Hostels

How much is a dormitory bed per night?
Πόσο κάνει ένα κρεβάτι κοιτώνα τη μέρα;
Poso kani ena krevati kitona ti mera?

I am/am not an HI member
Είμαι/δεν είμαι μέλος της HI
Ime/den ime melos tis HI

May I use my own sleeping bag?
Μπορώ να χρησιμοποιήσω το δικό μου σλήπιγκ μπαγκ;
Boro na hrisimopiiso to diko mu sleeping bag?

What time do you lock the doors at night?
Τί ώρα κλείνετε τις πόρτες τα βράδια;
Ti ora klinete tis portes ta vradia?

Camping

May I camp for the night/two nights?
Μπορώ να κάνω κάμπιγκ εδώ για τη νύχτα/δύο νύχτες;
Boro na kano camping edo ya ti nihta/dio nihtes?

Where can I pitch my tent?
Πού μπορώ να στήσω τήν σκηνή μου;
Pu boro na stiso tin skini mu?

How much does it cost for one night/one week?
Πόσο στοιχίζει για μία νύχτα/μία εβδομάδα;
Poso stihizi ya mia nihta/mia evdomada?

Where are the washing facilities?
Πού είναι τα πλυντήρια;
Pu ine ta plintiria?

Is there a restaurant/ supermarket/swimming pool on site/nearby?
Υπάπχει μήπως εστιατόριο/ σουπερμάρκετ/πισίνα εδώ/ εδώ κοντά;
Iparhi mipos stiatorio/isupermarket/ pisina edo/edo konta?

Do you have a safety deposit box?
Μήπως έχετε χρηματοκιβώτιο;
Mipos ehete hrimatokivotio?

EATING AND DRINKING

Cafés and Bars

I would like a cup of/two cups of/another coffee/tea
Θα ήθελα ένα φλιτζάνι/δύο φλιτζάνια/ακόμη ένα καφέ/τσάι
Tha ithela ena flitzani/dio flitzania/akomi ena kafe/tsai

With/without milk/sugar
Με/χωρίς γάλα/ζάχαρη
Me/horis gala/zahari

I would like a bottle/glass/two glasses of mineral water/red wine/white wine, please
Θα ήθελα ένα μπουκάλι/ποτήρι/δύο ποτήρια μεταλλικό νερό/κόκκινο κρασί/άσπρο κρασί, παρακαλώ
Tha ithela ena bukali/potiri/dio potiria metalliko nero/kokkino krasi/aspro krasi, parakalo

I would like a beer/two beers, please
Θα ήθελα μια μπύρα/δύο μπύρες, παρακαλώ
Tha ithela mia bira/dio bires, parakalo

May I have some ice?
Μπορώ να έχω λίγο πάγο;
Boro na eho ligo pago?

Do you have any matches/cigarettes/cigars?
Μήπως έχετε σπίρτα/τσιγάρα/πούρα;
Mipos ehete spirta/tsigara/pura?

Restaurants

Can you recommend a good/cheap restaurant in this area?
Μπορείτε να μου συστήσετε ένα καλό/φτηνό εστιατόριο σε αυτή τήν περιοχή;
Borite na mu sistisete ena kalo/ftino estiatorio se afti tin periohi?

I would like a table for ... people
Θα ήθελα ένα τραπέζι για ... άτομα
Tha ithela ena trapezi gia ... atoma

Do you have a non-smoking area?
Εχετε χώρο μη καπνιζόντων;
Ehete horo mi kapnizonton?

Waiter/Waitress!
Γκαρσόν/Σερβιτόρα!
Garson/Servitora!

Excuse me, please may we order?
Με συγχωρείτε, μπορώ παραγγείλω, παρακαλω;
Me sinhorite, boro parangilo, parakalo?

Do you have a set menu/children's menu/wine list ... (in English)?
Εχετε μενού/παιδικό μενού/κατάλογο κρασιών (Αγγλικά);
Ehete menu/pediko menu/katalogo krasion (Anglika)?

Do you have any vegetarian dishes?
Μήπως έχετε πιάτα για χορτοφάγους, παρακαλώ;
Mipos ehete piata ya hortofagous, parakalo

Do you have any local specialities?
Εχετε τοπικές σπεσιαλίτέ;
Ehete topikes spesialite?

Are vegetables included?
Χορταρικά και λαχανικά συμπεριλαμβάνονται;
Hortarika ke lahanika simperilamvanonte?

Could I have it well-cooked/ medium/rare please?
Μπορώ να το έχω καλά/μέτρια/ελάχιστα ψημένο, παρακαλώ;
Boro na to eho kala/metria/elahista psimeno, parakalo?

What does this dish consist of?
Από τι αποτελείται αυτό το πιάτο;
Apo ti apotelite afto to piato?

I am a vegetarian. Does this contain meat?
Είμαι χορτοφάγος. Περιέχει κρέας αυτό;
Ime hortofawos. Periehi kreas afto?

I do not eat nuts/dairy products/meat/fish
Δεν τρώω ξηρούς καρπούς/ προϊόντα γάλακτος/κρέας/ψάρι
Den troo ksirus karpus/proionda walaktos/kreas/psari

Not (very) spicy, please
Όχι (πολύ) πικάντικο, παρακαλώ
Ohi (poli) pikandiko, parakalo

I would like the set menu, please
Θα ήθελα το μενού, παρακαλώ
Tha ithela to menu, parakalo

We are still waiting to be served
Δεν σερβιριστήκαμέ ακόμη
Den serviristikame akomi

Please bring a plate/knife/ fork
Παρακαλώ φέρτε ένα πιάτο/ μαχαίρι/πιρούνι
Parakalo ferte ena pjato/maheri/ piruni

Excuse me, this is not what I ordered
Με συγχωρείτε, δεν είναι αυτό που παράγγειλα
Me sinhorite, den ine afto pu paragila

May I have some/more bread/water/coffee/tea?
Μπορώ να έχω λίγο/ακόμη λίγο ψωμί/νερό/καφέ/τσάι;
Boro na eho ligo/akomi ligo psomi/nero/kafe/tsai?

May I have the bill, please?
Μπορώ να έχω το λογαριασμό, παρακαλώ;
Boro na eho to logariasmo, parakalo?

Does this bill include service?
Ο λογαριασμός περιλαμβάνει και σέρβις;
O logariasmos perilamvani ke service?

Do you accept traveller's cheques)/Mastercard/ US dollars?
Μήπως παίρνετε ταξιδιωτικές επιταγές/Μάστερκαρτ/ Αμερικανικά Δολλάρια;
Mipos pernete taxidiotikes epitayes/Mastercard/Amerikanika dollaria?

Can I have a receipt, please?
Μπορώ να έχω την απόδειξη, παρακαλώ;
Boro na eho tin apodixi, parakalo?

Where is the toilet (restroom), please?
Πού είναι η τουαλέτα, παρακαλώ;
Pu ine i tualeta, parakalo?

On the Menu

Πρωϊνό/Μεσημεριανό/Δείπνο
Proino/Mesimeriano/Dipno
Breakfast/Lunch/Dinner

Πρώτα φαγητά *Prota fayita* **First courses**	Σούπες *Supes* **Soups**

Κυρίως πιάτα
Kirios piata
Main courses

Φαγητά με ψάρι
Fayita me psari
Fish dishes

Φαγητά με κρέας *Fayita me kreas* **Meat dishes**	Μοσχάρι *Moshari* **Beef**
Μπριζόλα *Brizola* **Steak**	Χοιρινό *Hirino* **Pork**
Μοσχαράκι *Mosharaki* **Veal**	Κοτόπουλο *Kotopulo* **Chicken**
Αρνί *Arni* **Lamb**	Ζαμπόν *Zambon* **Ham**

Πιάτα για χορτοφάγους
Piata ya hortophagous
Vegetarian dishes

Λαχανικά
Lahanika
Vegetables

Τηγανητές πατάτες
Tiganites patates
Chips (french fries)

Βραστές πατάτες/σοταρισμένες πατάτες/πουρές
Vrastes patates/sotarismenes patates/pures
Boiled/sauté/mashed potatoes

Ρύζι *Rizi* **Rice**	Τυριά *Tiria* **Cheese**

Γλυκά
Glyka
Desserts

Παγωτό *Pawoto* **Ice cream**	Πάστες *Pastes* **Cakes**

Γλυκά
Wlika
Pastries

Φρούτα
Fruta
Fruit

Ψωμί
Psomi
Bread

Καρβελάκια
Karvelakia
Rolls

Τόστ
Tost
Toast

Βούτυρο
Vutiro
Butter

Αλάτι/ πιπέρι
Alati/Piperi
Salt/ pepper

Ζάχαρη
Zahari
Sugar

Πιάτο της ημέρας
Piato tis imeras
Specialities

Τοπικές σπεσιαλιτέ
Topikes spesialite
Local specialities

Ορισμένο Μενού
Orismeno Menu
Set Menu

Κατάλογος κρασιών
Katalowos krasion
Wine list

Κόκκινα κρασιά
Kokina krasia
Red wines

Λευκά κρασιά
Lefka krasia
White wines

Ροζέ κρασιά
Roze krasia
Rosé wines

Αφρώδη κρασιά
Afrodi krasia
Sparkling wines

Μπύρα
Bira
Beer

Μπύρα σε μπουκάλι/
βαρελίσια μπυρα
Bira se bukali/varelisia bira
Bottled beer/ draught (draft) beer

Μη οινοπνευματώδη ποτά
Mi inopnevmatodi pota
Non-alcoholic drinks

Μεταλλικό νερό
Metaliko nero
Mineral water

Φρουτοχυμοί
Frutohimi
Fruit juices

Πορτοκαλάδα
Portokalada
Orange juice

Λεμονάδα
Lemonada
Lemonade

Παγάκια
Pawakia
Ice

Καφές με γάλα/Καφές χωρίς γάλα/καφές εσπρέσο
Kafes me wala/Kafes xoris wala/kafes espresso
White coffee/black coffee/espresso coffee

Τσάι με γάλα/με λεμόνι
Tsai me wala/me lemoni
Tea with milk/with lemon

Σοκολάτα (ρόφημα)
Sokolata (rofima)
Chocolate (drink)

Γάλα
Wala
Milk

Σνακ/Ελαφρά γεύματα
Snak/Elafra yevmata
Snacks/Light meals

Σαλάτες
Salates
Salads

Σάντουιτς
Sanduits
Sandwiches

Αυγά
Avga
Eggs

Βραστά αυγά/τηγανητά αυγά/αυγά ομελέτα
Vrasta avga/tiwanita avga/avga omeleta
Boiled /fried/scrambled eggs

Λουκάνικο
Lukaniko
Sausage

Typical Local dishes

Ταραμοσαλάτα
Taramosalata
Appetiser of fish roe puréed with lemon juice

Τυρόπιτα
Tiropitta
Cheese pie

Μεζές
Mezes
Large number of small appetisers served as they are ready

Καλαμάρι
Kalamari
Fried baby squid

Κεφτέδες
Keftedes
Meatballs in sauce

Σουβλάκι
Souvlaki
Grilled meat on a skewer

GETTING AROUND

Public Transport

Where is the bus stop/coach station/nearest metro station?
Πού είναι η στάση λεωφορείων/ο σταθμός των πούλμαν/το πλησιέστερο μετρό;
Pu ine i stasi leoforion/o stathmos ton pullman/to plisiestero metro?

When is the next/last bus to ...?
Πότε είναι το επόμενο/ τελευταίο λεωφορείο για την ...;
Pote ine to epomeno/telefteo leoforio ya tin ...?

How much is the fare to the city centre (downtown)/ railway (railroad) station/ airport?
Πόσο κάνει το εισιτήριο για το κέντρο της πόλης/το σιδηροδρομικό σταθμό/το αεροδρόμιο;
Poso kani to isitirio ya to kentro tis

polis/to sidirodromiko stathmo/to aerodromio?

Will you tell me when to get off?
Μου λέτε πού να κατέβω;
Mu lete pu na katevo?

Does this bus go to ...?
Αυτό το λεωφορείο πάει στο ...;
Afto to leoforio pai sto ...?

Which number bus goes to ...?
Ποιο λεωφορείο πηγαίνει στο ...;
Pio leoforio piyeni sto ...?

May I have a single (one-way)/return (round-trip)/day ticket/book of tickets?
Μπορώ να έχω μονό/μετ' επιστροφής/ημερήσιο εισιτήριο/δεσμιδα εισιτηρίων;
Boro na eho mono/met epistrofis/ imerisio isitirio/desmida isitirion?

Taxis (Ταξί)

I would like to go to ... How much will it cost?
Θα ήθελα να πάω στο ... πόσο θα μου στοιχίσει;
Tha ithela na pao sto ... poso tha mu stihisi?

Please may I stop here?
Παρακαλώ σταματήστε εδώ;
Parakalo stamatiste edo?

I would like to order a taxi today/tomorrow/at 2pm to go from ... to ...
Θα ήθελα να κλεισω ταξί σήμερα/αύριο/στις δυο μ.μ. να με πάρει από το ... στο ...
Tha ithela na kliso taxi simera/ avrio/stis dio to apoyevma na me pari apo to ... sto ...

Entertainment

Can you recommend a good bar/nightclub?
Μπορείτε να μου συστήσετε ένα καλό μπαρ/νυχτερινό κέντρο;
Borite na mu sistisete ena kalo bar/nihterino kentro?

Do you know what is on at the cinema (playing at the movies)/theatre at the moment?
Ξέρετε τι παίζεται τώρα στο σινεμά/στο θέατρο;
Xerete ti pezete tora sto cinema/sto theatro?

I would like to book (purchase) ... tickets for the matinee/evening performance on Monday
Θα ήθελα να κρατήσω ... εισιτήρια για απογευματινή/ βραδινή παράσταση τη Δευτέρα
Tha ithela na kratiso ... isitiria ya apoyevmatini/vradini parastasi ti Deftera

What time does the film/ performance start?
Τί ώρα αρχίζει η ταινία/η παράσταση;
Ti ora arhizi i tenia/i parastasi?

COMMUNICATIONS

Post

How much will it cost to send a letter/postcard/this package to Britain/America/ Canada/Australia/New Zealand?
Πόσο θα στοιχίσει να στείλω μια επιστολή/καρτ ποστάλ/ αυτό το πακέτο στη Βρετανία/ Αμερική/Καναδά/Νέα Ζηλανδία;
Poso tha stihisi na stilo mia epistoli/card postale/afto to paketo sti Vretania/Ameriki/Canada/ Nea Zilandia?

I would like one stamp/two stamps
Θα ήθελα ένα γραμματόσημο/ δύο γραμματόσημα
Tha ithela ena grammatosimo/dio grammatosima

I'd like ... stamps for postcards to send abroad, please
Θα ήθελα ... γραμματόσημα για καρτποστάλ να τις στείλω στο εξωτερικό, παρακαλώ
Tha ithela ... gramatosima ya card postale na tis stilo sto exoteriko, parakalo

Phones

I would like to make a telephone call/reverse the charges to (make a collect call to) ...
Θα ήθελα να τηλεφωνήσω/ να αντιστρέφω το κόστος στο ...
Tha ithela na tilefoniso/na antistrepso to kostos ...

Which coins do I need for the telephone?
Ποια κέρματα χρειάζομαι για το τηλέφωνο;
Pia kermata hriazome ya to tilefono?

The line is engaged (busy)
Η γραμμή είναι κατειλημμένη
I grami ine katilimeni

The number is ...
Ο αριθμός είναι ...
O arithmos ine ...

Hello, this is ...
Εμπρός είμαι ...
Empros, ime ...

Please may I speak to ...?
Μπορώ να μιλήσω στον/ στην ...;
Boro na miliso ston/stin ...?

He/she is not in at the moment. Please can you call back?
Δεν είναι εδώ αυτή τη στιγμή. Μπορείτε να ξανακαλέσετε;
Den ine edo avti ti stigmi. Borite na xanakalesete?

SHOPPING

Shops

Βιβλιοπωλείο/Χαρτοπωλείο
Vivliopolio/Hartopolio
Bookshop/Stationery

Κατάστημα Κοσμημάτων/Δώρων
Katastima Kosmimaton/Thoron
Jeweller/Gifts

Υποδήματα
Ipodimata
Shoes

Είδη Κιγκαλερίας
Idi Kingalerias
Hardware

Κομμωτήριο (ανδρών)/(γυναικών)
Komotirio (andron)/(ginekon)
Hairdresser (men's)/(women's)

Αρτοποιείο
Artopiio
Baker

Σουπερμάρκετ
Supermaket
Supermarket

Φωτογραφείο
Photographio
Photo Shop

Ταξιδιωτικός Πράκτορας
Taxidiotikos Praktoras
Travel Agent

Φαρμακείο
Farmakio
Pharmacy

In the Shops

What time do the shops open/close?
Τι ώρα ανοίγουν/κλείνουν τα καταστήματα;
Ti ora anigun/klinun ta katastimata?

Where is the nearest market?
Πού είναι η κοντινότερη αγορά;
Pu ine i kontinoteri agora?

Can you show me the one in the window/this one?
Μπορείτε να μου δείξετε κάτι που είδα στη βιτρίνα/αυτό εδώ;
Borite na mu dixete kati pu ida sti vitrina/afto edo?

Can I try this on?
Μπορώ να το δοκιμάσω;
Boro na to dokimaso?

What size is this?
Τι μέγεθος είναι;
Ti meyethos ine?

This is too large/too small/too expensive
Είναι πολύ μεγάλο/μικρό/ακριβό
Ine poli megalo/mikro/akrivo

Do you have any others?
Εχετε άλλα;
Ehete ala?

My size is ...
Το νούμερό μου είναι ...
To numero mu ine ...

Where is the changing room/children's/cosmetic/ladieswear/menswear/food department?
Πού είναι το δοκιμαστήριο/το παιδικό τμήμα/το τμήμα καλλυντικών/γυναικείων/ανδρικών/τροφίμων;
Pu ine to dokimastirio/to pediko tmima/to tmima kalintikon/ginekion/andrikon/trofimon?

I would like ... a quarter of a kilo/half a kilo/a kilo of bread/butter/cheese/ham/tomatoes
Θα ήθαλα ... ένα τέταρτο κιλό/ μισό κιλό/ένα κιλό ψωμί/βούτυρο/τυρί/ζαμπόν/τομάτες
Tha ithela ... ena tetarto kilo/miso kilo/ena kilo psomi/vutiro/tiri/zambon/tomates

How much is this?
Πόσο κάνει αυτό;
Poso kani afto?

I'll take this one, thank you
Θα πάρω αυτό εδώ, ευχαριστώ
Tha paro afto edo, efharisto

Do you have a carrier (shopping) bag?
Εχετε μία σακούλα;
Ehete mia sakula?

Do you have anything cheaper/larger/smaller/of better quality?
Εχετε τίποτα φτηνότερο/μεγαλύτερο/μικρότερο/καλύτερης ποιότητας;
Ehete tipota ftinotero/megalitero/mikrotero/kaliteris piotitas?

I would like a film for this camera
Θα ήθελα ένα φιλμ για αυτή την φωτογραφική μηχανή
Tha ithela ena film ya afti tin fotografiki mihani

I would like some batteries, the same size as this old one
Θα ήθελα μερικές μπαταρίες, του ίδιου μεγέθους, όπως αυτή η παλιά
Tha ithela merikes bataries, tu idiu meyethus, opos afti i palia

Would you mind wrapping this for me, please?
Θα μπορούσατε να μου το τυλίξετε, παρακαλώ;
Tha borusate na mu to tilixete, parakalo?

Sorry, but you seem to have given me the wrong change
Συγγνώμη αλλά φαίνεται ότι μου δώσατε λάθος ρέστα
Signomi, alla fenete oti mu dosate lathos resta

MOTORING

Car Hire (Rental)

I have ordered (rented) a car in the name of ...
Νοίκιασα αυτοκίνητο στο όνομα ...
Nikiasa aftokinito sto onoma ...

How much does it cost to hire (rent) a car for one day/ two days/a week?
Πόσο στοιχίζει να νοικιάσω αυτοκίνητο για μία μέρα/δύο μέρες/μία εβδομάδα;
Poso stihizi na nikiaso aftokinito ya mia mera/dio meres/mia evdomada?

Is the tank already full of petrol (gas)?
Μήπως το ντεπόζιτο είναι ήδη γεμάτο με βενζίνη;
Mipos to deposito ine idi yemato me venzini?

Is insurance and tax included? How much is the deposit?
Περιλαμβάνει ασφάλεια και φόρο; Πόσο είναι η προκαταβολή;
Perilamvani asfalia ke foro? Poso ine prokatavoli?

By what time must I return the car?
Μέχρι πότε πρέπει να επιστρέψω το αυτοκίνητο;
Mehri pote prepi na epistrepso to aftokinito?

I would like a small/large/ family/sports car with a radio/cassette player
Θα ήθελα ένα μικρό/μεγαλό/ οικογενειακό/σπορ αυτοκίνητο με ράδιο/κασετόφωνο
Tha ithela ena mikro/megalo ikoyeniako/spor aftokinito me radio/kassetofono

Do you have a road map?
Εχετε χάρτη οδικού δικτύου;
Ehete harti odiku diktiu?

Parking

How long can I park here?
Για πόσο διάστημα μπορώ να παρκάρω εδώ;
Ya poso diastima boro na parkaro edo?

Is there a car park near here?
Υπάρχει χώρος σταθμεύσεως κάπου εδώ;
Iparhi horos stathmefseos kapu edo?

At what time does this car park close?
Τι ώρα κλείνει ο χώρος σταθμεύσεως;
Ti ora klini o horos stathmefseos?

Signs and Notices

Μονόδρομος
Monodromos
One way

Απαγορεύεται η είσοδος
Apagorevete i isodos
No entry

MOTORING

GREEK

Απαγορεύεται η στάθμευση
Apagorevete i stathmefsi
No parking

Παρακαμπτήριος
Parakamptirios
Detour (diversion)

Σταμάτημα/Stop
Stamatima/Stop
Stop

Δώσε προτεραιότητα
Dose protereotita
Give way (yield)

Ολισθηρός δρόμος
Olisthiros dromos
Slippery road

Απαγορεύεται η προσπέραση
Apagorevete i prosperasi
No overtaking

Κίνδυνος!
Kindinos!
Danger!

At the Filling Station (Βενζινάδικο)

Unleaded (lead-free)/ standard/premium/diesel
Αμόλυβδη/απλή (Regular)/ σούπερ (Super)/ντήζελ
Amolivdi/apli/super/dizel

Fill the tank please
Γεμίστε το ντεπόζιτο παρακαλώ
Gemiste to depozito parakalo

Do you have a road map?
Εχετε χάρτη οδικού δικτύου;
Ehete harti odiku diktiu?

How much is the car wash?
Πόσο κοστίζει το πλύσιμο αυτοκινήτου;
Poso kostizi to plisimo aftokinitu?

Breakdowns

I've had a breakdown at ...
Το αυτοκίνητο χάλασε στη ...
To aftokinito halase sti ...

I am a member of the ... [motoring organisation]
Είμαι μέλος της ...
Ime melos tis ...

I am on the road from ... to ...
Είμαι στο δρόμο από ... στο/στη ...
Ime sto dromo apo ... sto/sti ...

I can't move the car. Can you send a tow-truck?
Δεν μπορώ να κινήσω το αυτοκίνητο. Μπορείτε να στείλετε ρυμουλκό;
Den boro na kiniso to aftokinito. Borite na stilete rimulko?

I have a flat tyre
Εχω ξεφουσκωμένο λάστιχο
Eho xefuskomeno lastiho

The windscreen (windshield) has smashed/cracked
Το παρμπρίζ έσπασε/ράγισε
To parbriz espase/ragise

There is something wrong with the engine/brakes/ lights/steering/gearbox/ clutch/exhaust
Κάτι δεν πάει καλά με τη/τα μηχανή/φρένα/φώτα/τιμόνι/τα χύτητες/συμπλέκτη/εξάτμιση
Kati den pai kala me ti/ta mihani/frena/fota/timoni/tahitites/sibl ekti/exatmisi

It's overheating
Υπερθερμαίνεται
Iperthermenete

It won't start
Δεν ξεκινά
Den xekina

Where can I get it repaired?
Πού μπορώ να το επισκευάσω;
Pu boro na to episkevaso?

Can you take me there?
Μπορείτε να με πάτε εκεί;
Borite na me pate eki?

Will it take long to fix?
Πόση ώρα θα κάνετε να το επισκευάσετε;
Posi ora tha kanete na to episkevasete?

How much will it cost?
Πόσο θα κοστίσει;
Poso tha kostisi?

Please can you pick me up/give me a lift?
Παρακαλώ μπορείτε να με πάρετε στο αυτοκίνητό σας;
Parakalo borite na me parete sto aftokinito sas?

Accidents and Traffic Offences (Violations)

Can you help me? There has been an accident
Μπορείτε να με βοηθήσετε; Εχει συμβεί κάποιο ατύχημα
Borite na me voithisete? Ehi simvi kapio atihima

Please call the police/an ambulance
Παρακαλώ καλέσετε την αστυνομία/ασθενοφόρο
Parakalo kalesete tin astinomia/asthenoforo

Is anyone hurt?
Εχει τραυματιστεί κανείς;
Ehi travmatisti kanis?

I'm sorry, I didn't see the sign
Συγγνώμη, δεν πρόσεξα την πινακίδα
Signomi, den prosexa tin pinakida

Must I pay a fine? How much?
Πρέπει να πληρώσω; Πόσα;
Prepi na pliroso prostimo? Posa?

Δείξτε μου τα χαρτιά σας
Dixte mu ta hartia sas
Show me your documents

GREEK

HEALTH

Pharmacy (Φαρμακείο)

Do you have anything for a stomach ache/headache/sore throat/toothache?
Εχετε κάτι για στομαχόπονο/πονοκέφαλο/ερεθισμένο λαιμό/πονόδοντο;
Ehete kati ya stomahopono/ponokefalo/erethismeno lemo/ponodonto?

I need something for diarrhoea/constipation/a cold/a cough/insect bites/sunburn/travel (motion) sickness
Χρειάζομαι κάτι για τη διάρροια/δυσκοιλιότητα/κρύο/βήχα/τσιμπήματα εντόμων/ηλιοκαύματα/ναυτία
Hriazome kati ya ti diarria/dispepsia/krio/vinha/tsimpimata entomon/iliokavmata/naftia.

How much/how many do I take?
Πόσο/Πόσα να παίρνω;
Poso/posa na perno?

How often do I take it/them?
Κάθε πόση ώρα να το/τα παίρνω;
Kathe posi ora na to/ta perno?

I am/he is/she is taking this medication
Παίρνω/παίρνει αυτό το φάρμακο
Perno/perni afto to pharmako

How much does it cost?
Πόσο κοστίζει;
Poso kostizi?

Can you recommend a good doctor/dentist?
Μπορείτε να μου συστήσετε ένα καλό γιατρό/οδοντογιατρό;
Borite na mu sistisete ena kalo yatro/odontoyatro?

Is it suitable for children?
Είναι κατάλληλο για παιδιά;
Ine katallilo ya pedia?

Doctor (Γιατρός)

I have a pain here/in my arm/leg/chest/stomach
Πονάω εδώ/στο βραχίονά μου/στη γάμπα/στο στήθος/στο στομάχι
Ponao edo/sto vrahiona mu/sti gamba/sto stithos/sto stomahi

Please call a doctor, this is an emergency
Παρακαλώ τηλεφωνήστε σε ένα γιατρό, είναι επείγουσα κατάσταση
Parakalo tilefoniste se ena yatro, ine epigusa katastasi

I would like to make an appointment to see the doctor
Θα ήθελα να κλείσω ραντεβού για να δω τον γιατρό
Tha ithela na kliso rantevu ya na tho ton yatro

I am diabetic/pregnant
Είμαι διαβητικός/έγκυος
Ime diavitikos/engios

I need a prescription for ...
Θέλω συνταγή για ...
Thelo sintayi ya ...

Can you give me something to ease the pain?
Μπορείτε να μου δώσετε κάτι για να καταπραΰνει τον πόνο;
Borite na mu dosete kati gia na kataptraini ton pono?

I am/he is/she is allergic to penicillin
Είμαι/είναι/αλλεργικός(ή) στην πενικιλίνη
Ime/ine/alergikos(i) stin penicilini

Πονάει;
Ponai?
Does this hurt?

Πρέπει να πάτε/πάει στο νοσοκομείο
Prepi na pate/pai sto nosokomio
You must/he must/she must go to hospital

Παίρνετε αυτά μία φορά/δύο/τρεις φορές την ημέρα
Pernete afta mia fora/dio/tris fores tin imera
Take these once/twice/three times a day

I am/he is/she is taking this medication
Παίρνω/παίρνει αυτό το φάρμακο
Perno/perni afto to pharmako

I have medical insurance
Εχω ασφάλεια νοσοκομειακής περίθαλψης
Echo asfalia nosokomiakis perithalpsis

Dentist (Οδοντίατρος)

I have toothache
Νοιώθω πονόδοντο
Niotho ponodonto

My filling has come out
Βγήκε το σφράγισμα
Vgike to sfrayisma

I do/do not want to have an injection first
Θέλω/δεν θέλω να έχω πρώτα ένεση
Thelo/den thelo na eho prota enesi

EMERGENCIES

Help!
Βοήθεια!
Voithia!

Fire!
Πυρκαγιά!
Pirkaya!

Stop!
Σταματήστε!
Stamatiste!

Call an ambulance/a doctor/the police/the fire brigade!
Τηλεφωνήστε για ασθενοφόρο/γιατρό/αστυνομία/την πυροσβεστική!
Tilefoniste yia asthenoforo/yatro/astinomia/tin pirosvestiki!

Please may I use a telephone?
Παρακαλώ μπορώ να χρησιμοποιήσω το τηλέφωνο;
Parakalo boro na hrisimopiiso to tilefono?

I have had my traveller's cheques/credit cards/handbag/ rucksack/luggage/wallet/ passport/mobile phone stolen
Μου κλέψανε τις ταχυδρομικές μου επιταγές/τις πιστωτικές μου κάρτες/τη τσάντα μου/ τον εκδρομικό σάκο/τις αποσκευές/το πορτοφόλι μου/το διαβατήριο/ το κινητό τηλέφωνο
Mu klepsane tis tahidromikes mu epitayes/tis pistotikes mu kartes/tin tsanta mu/ton ekdromiko sako/tis aposkeves/to portofoli mu/to diavatirio/to kinito tilefono

May I please have a copy of the report for my insurance claim?
Παρακαλώ μπορώ να έχω ένα αντίγραφο της έκθεσης για την ασφάλειά μου;
Parakalo boro na eho ena andiwrafo tis ekthesis ya tin asfalia mu?

Can you help me, I have lost my daughter/son/my companion(s)?
Μπορείτε να με βοηθήσετε, έχασα τη κόρη μου/τον γιο μου/το σύντροφό μου (τους συντρόφους μου);
Borite na me voithisete, ehasa ti kori mu/ton yo mu/to sindrofo mu (tus sindrofus mu)?

Please go away/leave me alone
Παρακαλώ φύγετε/αφήστε με
Parakalo fiyete/afiste me

I'm sorry
Λυπάμαι
Lipame

I want to contact the British/ American/Canadian/Irish/ Australian/New Zealand/ South African consulate
Θέλω να επικοινωνήσω με το Βρετανικό/Αμερικανικό/ Καναδικό/Ιρλανδικό/ Αυστραλιανό/Νέας Ζηλανδίας/Νοτίου Αφρικής Προξενείο
Thelo na epikinoniso me to Vretaniko/Amerikaniko/Kanadiko/Irla ndiko/Avstraliano/Neas Zilandias/Notiu Afrikis Proxenio

I'm/we're/he is/she is/they are ill
Είμαι/είμαστε/αυτός είναι/αυτή είναι/αυτοί είναι άρρωστος (άρρωστη) (άρρωστοι)
Ime/Imaste/aftos ine/afti ine/afti ine arostos (masc)/*arosti*(fem)/*arosti* (pl)

I'm/we're/he is/she is/they are lost
Είμαι/είμαστε/αυτός είναι/αυτή είναι/αυτοί είναι
Έχω/εχουμε/εχει/εχουν χαθεί
Ime/Imaste/aftos ine/afti ine/afti ine Eho/ehume/ehi/ehun hathi

I'm/we're/he is/she is/they are injured
Είμαι/είμαστε/αυτός είναι/ αυτή είναι/αυτοί είναι τραυματισμένος/ τραυματισμένη/ τραυματισμένοι
Ime/Imaste/aftos ine/afti ine/afti ine travmatismenos (masc)/ *travmatismeni* (fem)/ *travmatismeni* (pl)

HUNGARIAN

INTRODUCTION

Hungarian, or Magyar, is distantly related to Finnish and Estonian, but is utterly unlike the languages of the other main linguistic groups of Europe. German is widespread as a second language.

Hungarian is undoubtedly a difficult language to master, and Hungarians are well aware of this, but you should nevertheless try to learn a few greetings, as silence when entering a shop, for instance, is considered rude.

Prepositions are replaced by suffixes. Each suffix has two forms: choose one that sounds harmonious with the noun/place name. There is no specific gender in the Hungarian language, therefore there is no difference in the words for 'he/she/it'.

Addresses for Travel and Tourist Information

New Zealand: *Hungarian Consulate-General,* PO Box 29-039, Wellington 6030; tel: (04) 973 7507; fax: (04) 973 7509.

UK: *Hungarian National Tourist Office,* 46 Eaton Place, London SW1X 8AL; tel: (020) 7823 1032; fax: (020) 7823 1459.

USA: *IBUSZ Hungarian Travel Company,* 1 Parker Plaza, #1104, Fort Lee, NJ 07024; tel: (201) 592 8585.

Official tourism websites: www.hungarywelcomesbritain.com (UK); www.gotohungary.com (USA).

Hungary Facts

CAPITAL: Budapest
CURRENCY: Forints (Ft); 1 Forint = 100 filler.
OPENING HOURS: Food/Tourist Shops, markets open Sun. Banks: National Bank of Hungary: Mon–Fri 1030–1400; Commercial Banks: Mon–Thur 0800–1500, Fri 0800–1300. Food shops: Mon–Fri 0700–1900; others: 1000–1800 (Thur until 1900); shops close for lunch and half-day on Sat (1300). Museums: Tues–Sun 1000–1800.
TELEPHONES: To dial in, +36. Outgoing, 00 and the country code. Police, 107. Fire, 105. Ambulance, 104.
PUBLIC HOLIDAYS: 1 Jan; 15 Mar; Easter Monday; 1, 8 May; 20 Aug; 23 Oct; 24–26 Dec.

Technical Language Hints

- You will notice there are different suffixes added onto the ends of words – e.g. -ban/-ben (in). These two options are for 'vowel harmony'. Hungarian has two kinds of vowels: open, and closed:

- Open Vowels: e, é, i, í, ö, ő, ü, and ű

  e.g.: kérem *[kehrem]*, segítsen *[shegitshen]*, önöknél *[yuonyuoknehk]*, etc.

- Closed Vowels: a, á, o, ó, u, and ú

  e.g.: lámpámat *[lahmpahmat]*, hálózsákomat *[hahlohzhakomaht]*

- For example, take the word "ház" (house): here you would use the ending "-ban", so that both vowels are in the "closed" group and two similar sounds are made sequentially.

ESSENTIALS

Alphabet and Pronunciation

	Name	Pronounced
A, a	*o*	**o as in clock**
Á, á	*ah*	**ah as in father**
B, b	*bay*	**as in boy**
C, c	*tsay*	**ts as in cats**
Cs, cs	*chay*	**ch as in chug**
D, d	*day*	**d as in do**
Dz, dz		**ds as in feeds**
Dzs, dzs		**j as in jeans**
E, e	*eh*	**e as in set**
É, é		**eh as grey**
F, f	*eff*	**f as in find**
G, g	*gay*	**hard g as in go**
Gy, gy		**dy as in British pronunciation of duke**
I, i	*ee*	**i as in sit**
Í, í	*ee*	**ee as in machine**
J, j	*yay*	**y as in yes**
K, k	*kah*	**k as in keep**
L, l	*el*	**l as in low**
Ly, ly		**y as in yes (the l is silent)**
M, m	*em*	**as in mother**
N, n	*en*	**n as in no**
Ny, ny		**ny as in canyon**
O, o	*o*	**o as clock**
Ó ó	*aw*	**aw as in law**
Ö, ö	*oo*	**short oo as in zoo**
Ő, ő	*ur*	**as the vowel sound in fur**
P, p	*pay*	**as in pirate**
Q, q		**k sound as in cheque**
R, r	*air*	**slightly rolled rr sound**
S, s	*esh*	**sh as in sugar**
Sz, sz	*ess*	**s as in see**
T, t	*tay*	**t as in top**
Ty, ty		**ty as in met you**
U, u	*oo*	**short oo as in zoo**
Ú, ú	*ooh*	**long oo as in cool**

Ü, ü	*ew*	**ew as in feud**	X, x	*ex*	**x as in tax**
Ű, ű	*eew*	**eew as in feud but longer**	Y, y	*eepseelon*	**ee as in see**
V, v	*vay*	**v as in value**	Z, z	*zat*	**z as in zebra**
W, w	*dooplo vay*	**v as in value**	Zs, zs		**zh like the sound of the s in treasure**

Basic Words and Phrases

Yes
Igen
Ee-gehn

No
Nem
Nehm

Please
Kérem
Kay-rehm

Thank you
Köszönöm
Kuh-suh-nuhm

Hello
Szervusz
Sehr-voos

Goodbye
Viszontlátásra
Vee-sohnt-lah-tahsh-ro

Excuse me
Elnézést
Ehl-nay-zaysht

Sorry
Bocsánat
Bo-chah-not

How
Hogyan
Hoh-djon

When
Mikor
Mee-kohr

Why
Miért
Mee-ayrt

What
Mi
Mee

Who
Ki
Kee

That's O.K.
Rendben van.
Rhend-ben von

Perhaps
Esetleg
Eh-shet-leg

To
-be/ba,-hez/hoz/höz,-ig
-beh/bo,-hehz/hohz/huhz,-eeg

From
-ből/ból,-tól/től
-burl/bohl,-tohl/turl

To & From: Always choose the vowel sound which resembles the sound of the destination

Here
Itt
Eett

There
Ott
Ohtt

I don't understand
Nem értem
Nehm ayr-tehm

I don't speak Hungarian
Nem beszélek magyarul
Nehm beh-say-lehk mo-djo-rool

Do you speak English?
Beszél angolul?
Beh-sayl on-goh-lool?

Can you please write it down?
Írja le, kérem?
Eer-yo leh, kay-rehm?

Please can you speak more slowly?
Kérem, beszéljen lassabban?
Kay-rehm, beh-sayl-yehn losh-shob-bon?

Greetings

Good Morning/Good Afternoon/Good Evening/Good Night
Jó reggelt/Jó napot/Jó estét/ Jó éjszakát kívánok
Joh rehg-gehlt/Joh no-poht/ Joh ehsh-tayt/Joh ahy-so-kaht kee-vah-nohk

Pleased to meet you
Örülök, hogy megismerhettem
Uh-rew-luhk hohdj mehg-eesh-mehr-heht-tehm

How are you?
Hogy van?
Hohdj von?

I am well, thank you. And you?
Köszönöm, jól. És Ön?
Kuh-suh-nuhm johl. Aysh Uhn?

My name is ...
A nevem ...
O neh-vehm ...

This is my friend/boyfriend/ girlfriend/husband/wife/ brother/sister
Ez az én barátom/udvarlóm/ barátnőm/férjem/feleségem/ fiútestvérem/lánytestvérem
Ehz oz ayn bo-rah-tohm/ood-vor-lohm/bo-raht-nurm/feh-leh-shay-gehm/fee-oo-tehsht-vay-rehm/lahnj-tehsht-vay-rehm

Where are you travelling to?
Hova utazik?
Hoo-vo oo-to-zek?

I am/we are going to ...
...-ba/be/ra/re utazom/utazunk
...-bo/beh/ro/reh oo-to-zohm/oo-to-zoonk

How long are you travelling for?
Milyen hosszú lesz az utazása?
Mee-yehn hohs-soo lehs oz oo-to-zah-sho?

Where do you come from?
Hová valósi Ön?
Hoh-vah vo-loh-she Uhn?

I am/we are from... Australia/Britain/Canada/ America
Én/mi ...-ból/ből vagyok/ vagyunk ... Ausztráliából/ NagyBritanniából/Kanadából/ Amerikából
Eyn/mee ...-bohl/burl vo-djohk /vo-djoonk Aust-rah-lee-ah-bohl/ Nodj-Britanni-ah-bohl/Kanadah-bohl/ Amerikah-bohl

We are on holiday
Szabadságon vagyunk
So-bod-shah-gohn vo-djoonk

This is our first visit here
Először vagyunk itt
Eh-lur-suhr vo-djoonk eet

How old are you?
Hány éves Ön?
Hahnj ay-vehsh Uhn?

I am .... years old
... éves vagyok
... ay-vehsh vod-yohk

I am a business person/ doctor/journalist/manual worker/administrator/ scientist/student/teacher

HUNGARIAN

Üzletember/orvos/újságíró/munkás/adminisztrátor/tudós/diák/tanár/vagyok
Ewz-leht-ehm-behr/ohr-vohsh/oohy-shayg-ee-roh/moon-kahsh/od-mee-neest-rah-tohr/too-dohsh/dee-ahk/to-nahr/vod-yohk

I am waiting for my husband/wife/boyfriend/girlfriend
Várom a férjemet/feleségemet/barátomat/barátnőmet
Vah-rohm o fayr-yeh-meht/feh-leh-shay-geh-meht/bo-rah-toh-mot/bo-raht-nur-meht

Would you like/may I have a cigarette?
Kér egy cigarettát? Kérhetnék egy cigarettát?
Kayr ehdj tzee-go-reht-taht? Kayr-heht-nayk ehdj-tsee-go-reht-that?

Do you mind if I smoke?
Nem zavarja, ha rágyújtok?
Nehm zo-vor-yah, ho rah-djooy-tohk?

Do you have a light?
Adna egy kis tüzet?
Od-no ehdj keesh tew-zeht?

Days

Monday
Hétfő
Hayt-fur

Tuesday
Kedd
Kehdd

Wednesday
Szerda
Sehr-do

Thursday
Csütörtök
Chew-tuhr-tuhk

Friday
Péntek
Payn-tehk

Saturday
Szombat
Sohm-bot

Sunday
Vasárnap
Vo-shahr-nop

Morning
Reggel
Rehg-gehl

Afternoon/Evening/Night
Délután/Este/Éjszaka
Dayl-oo-tahn/Ehsh-teh/Ay-so-ko

Yesterday/ Today/Tomorrow
Tegnap/Má/Holnap
Tehg-nop/ Mah/Hohl-nop

Numbers

Zero
Nulla
Nool-lo

One
Egy
Ehdj

Two
Kettő
Kayt-tur

Three
Három
Hah-rohm

Four
Négy
Naydj

Five
Öt
Uht

Six
Hat
Hot

Seven
Hét
Hayt

Eight
Nyolc
Njohlts

Nine
Kilenc
Kee-lehnts

Ten
Tíz
Teez

Eleven
Tizenegy
Tee-zehn-ehdj

Twelve
Tizenkettő
Tee-zehn-keht-tur

Thirteen
Tizenhárom
Tee-zehn-hahrohm

Fourteen
Tizennégy
Tee-zehn-naydj

Fifteen
Tizenöt
Tee-zehn-uht

Sixteen
Tizenhat
Tee-zehn-hot

Seventeen
Tizenhét
Tee-zehn-hayt

Eighteen
Tizennyolc
Tee-zehn-njolhlts

Nineteen
Tizenkilenc
Tee-zehn-kee-lehnts

Twenty
Húsz
Hoos

Twenty-one
Huszonegy
Hoo-sohn-ehdj

Twenty-two
Huszonkettő
Hoo-sohn-keht-tur

Thirty
Harminc
Hor-meents

Forty
Negyven
Nehdj-vehn

Fifty
Ötven
Urt-vehn

Sixty
Hatvan
Hot-von

Seventy
Hetven
Heht-vehn

Eighty
Nyolcvan
Njolts-von

Ninety
Kilencven
Kee-lents-vehn

One hundred
Száz
Sahz

Five hundred
Ötszáz
Uht-sahz

One thousand
Ezer
Eh-zehr

One million
Millió
Mil-lee-oh

Time

What time is it?
Mennyi az idő?/Hány óra van?
Menj-njee os ee-dur?/Hahnj ooh-ro von?

It is ...
Most ... óra van
Mosht ... oh-ro von

9.00
Pontosan kilenc óra
Pohn-toh-shon kee-lehnts oh-ro

9.05
Öt perccel múlt kilenc
Uht pehrts-tsehl moolt kee-lehnts

9.15
Negyed tíz
Neh-djehd teez

9.20
Öt perccel múlt negyed tíz
Uht pehrts-tsehl moolt neh-djehd teez

9.30
Fél tíz
Fayl teez

9.35
Öt perccel múlt fél tíz
Uht pehrts-tsehl moolt fayl teez

9.40
Öt perc múlva háromnegyed tíz lesz
Uht pehrts mool-vo hah-rohm-neh-djehd teez lehs

9.45
Háromnegyed tíz
Hah-rohm-neh-djehd teez

9.50
Öt perccel múlt háromnegyed tíz
Uht pehrts-tsel moolt hah-rohm-neh-djehd teez

9.55
Öt perc múlva tíz lesz
Uht pehrts mool-vo teez lehs

Midday/Midnight
Dél/Éjfél
Dayl/Ay-fayl

Money

I would like to change these traveller's cheques/this currency
Be szeretném váltani az úticsekkeket/ezt a valutát
Beh seh-reht-naym vahl-to-nee oz oo-tee-chehk-keh-keht/ehzt o vo-loo-taht

How much commission do you charge? (What is the service charge?)
Mennyi a jutalékdíj?
Mehnj-njee o joo-to-layk-deey?

Can I obtain money with my Mastercard?
Vehetek fel pénzt a Mastercard-omról?
Veh-heh-tehk fehl paynzt o Mastercard-ohm-roohl?

Where is the nearest ATM?
Hol van a legközelebbi bankautomata?
Hol von o lehg-kew-zeh-lehbee bonk-auto-moto?

My name is ... Some money has been wired to here for me to collect
Nevem ... Ide átutaltak nekem pénzt. Fel szeretném venni
Neh-vehm ... Eedeh ayt-oo-tol-tok neh-kehm paynzt. Fehl seh-reht-nahm vehn-nee

ARRIVING AND DEPARTING

Airport

Excuse me, where is the check-in desk for ... airline?
Legyen szíves, mondja meg, hol van a regisztrálás a ... járatra?
Leh-djehn see-vehsh, mohnd-jo mehg, hohl von o reh-geest-rah-lash o ... jah-rotro?

What is the boarding gate for my flight?
Melyik kapunál kell beszállni a járatomra?
Meh-yeek ko-poo-nahl kehll beh-sahll-nee o jah-ro-tohm-ro?

What is the time for my flight?
Hánykor van a beszállás a járatomra?
Hahnj-kohr von o beh-sahl-lahsh o jah-ro-tohm-ro?

How long is the delay likely to be?
Mennyi a várható késés?
Mehnj-njee o vahr-ho-toh kay-shaysh?

Where is the duty-free shop?
Hol van a duty free üzlet?
Hohl von o duty free ewz-leht?

Which way is the luggage reclaim?
Merre kell mennem a poggyász kiadásához?
Mehr-reh kehll mehn-nehm o pohdj-djahs kee-o-dah-shah-hohz?

I have lost my luggage. Please can you help?
Elvesztettem a poggyászomat. Tudna nekem segíteni?
Ehl-vehs-teht-tehm o pohdj-djah-soh-mot. Tood-no neh-kehm sheh-gee-teh-nee?

I am flying to ...
...-ba/be repülök
...-bo/beh reh-puew-luhk

Where is the bus for the city centre?
Honnan indul a busz a városközpont felé?
Hohn-non een-dool o boos o vah-rohsh-kuhz-pohnt feh-lay?

Trains and Boats

Where is the ticket office/information desk?
Hol van a jegypénztár/ információ?
Hohl von o yehdj-paynz-tahr/ infor-mah-tsee-oh?

Which platform does the train/speedboat/ferry to ... depart from?
Melyik peronról indul a ... -ba/be menő vonat/hajó/ komp?
Meh-yeek peh-rohn-rohl een-dool o ... –bo/-beh meh-nur voh-not/ho-yoh/kohmp?

Where is platform ...?
Merre van a ... peron?
Mehr-reh von a ... peh-rohn?

When is the next train/boat to ...?
Mikor indul a következő vonat/hajó ...-ba/be?
Mee-kohr een-dool o kuh-veht-keh-zur voh-not/ho-yoh ... – bo/beh?

Is there a later train/boat to...?
Van későbbi vonat/hajó ... -ba/be?
Von kay-shurb-bee voh-not/ho-yoh ...-bo/beh?

Notices and Signs

Büfékocsi (Étkezőkocsi)
Bew-fay-koh-chee (Ayt-keh-zur-koh-chee)
Buffet (Dining) Car

Busz
Boos
Bus

Ivóvíz/nem ivóvíz
Ee-voh-veez/nehm ee-voh-veez
Drinking/Non-drinking water

Bejárat
Beh-rah-rot
Entrance

Kijárat
Kee-yah-rot
Exit

Kórház
Kohr-hahz
Hospital

Tudakozó
Too-do-koh-zoh
Information

Poggyászmegőrző
Pohdj-djahs-mehg-urr-zur
Left Luggage (Baggage Claim)

Önkiszolgáló poggyászmegőrző
Uhn-kee-sohl-gah-loh-pohdj-djahs-meg-urr-zur
Luggage Lockers

Posta
Pohsh-to
Post Office

Peron
Peh-rohn
Platform

Vasútállomás
Vah-shooht-ahl-loh-mahsh
Railway (Railroad) Station

Repülőtér
Reh-pew-lur-tayr
Airport

Rendőrkapitányság
Rehn-dur-ko-pee-tahnj-shahg
Police Station

Kikötő
Kee-kuh-tur
Port

Étterem
Ayt-teh-rehm
Restaurant

Dohányzóknak/Nem dohányzóknak
Doh-hahnj-zohk-nok/Nehm doh-hahnj-zohk-nok
Smoking/Non Smoking

Telefon
Teh-leh-fohn
Telephone

Jegypénztár
Yehdj-paynz-tahr
Ticket Office

Check-in ablak
Check-in ob-lok
Check-in desk

Menetrend
Meh-neht-rehnd
Timetable

WC
Vay-tsay
Toilets(Restrooms)

Női/Férfi
Nyr-ee/Fayr-fee
Ladies/Gentlemen

Metró
Meht-roh
Underground(Subway)

Váróterem
Vah-roh-teh-rehm
Waiting Room

Buying a Ticket

I would like a first-class/second-class/third class-single (one-way)/return (round trip) ticket to...
Jegyet kérek első osztályra/ másodosztályra/ harmadosztályra egy irányban/oda-vissza ... ig
Yeh-djeht kay-rehk ehl-shur ohs-tahy-ro/mah-shohd-ohs-tahy-ro/hor-mod-

ohs-tayy-ro ehdj ee-rahnj-bon/oh-do-vees-so ... eeg

Is it an express (fast) train/ bus?
Ez express vonat/busz?
Ehz ehx-prehs voh-not/boos?

Is my rail pass valid on this train/ferry/bus?
A vasúti bérletem érvényes erre a vonatra/kompra/buszra?
O vo-shoo-tee bayr-leh-tehm ayr-vay-njehsh ehr-reh o voh-not-ro/kohmp-ro/boos-ro?

I would like an aisle/window seat
Folyosó menti/ablak melletti helyet kérek
Foh-yoh-shoh mehn-tee/ob-lok mehl-leht-tee heh-yeht kay-rehk

No smoking/smoking please
Nemdohányzó/dohányzó kocsiba kérek jegyet
Nehm-doh-hahnj-zoh/doh-hanynj-zoh koh-csee-bo kay-rehk yeh-djeht

We would like to sit together
Egymás mellett szeretnénk ülni
Ehdj-mahsh mehl-leht seh-reht-naynk-eewl-nee

I would like to make a seat reservation
Helyjegyet szeretnék rendelni
Hehy-yeh-djeht seh-reht-nayk rehn-dehl-nee

I would like to reserve a couchette/sleeper for one person/two people/my family
Szeretnék helyet foglalni couchettebe/hálókocsiba egy személyre/két személyre/ családomnak
Seh-reht-nayk heh-yeht fohg-lol-nee couchette-beh/hah-loh-koh-chee-bo ehdj seh-may-reh/kayt she-may-reh/cho-lah-dohm-nok

I would like to reserve a cabin
Hajófülkét szeretnék foglalni
Ho-yoh-fewl-kayt seh-reht-nayk fohg-lol-nee

Timetables (Schedules)

Érkezés
Ayr-keh-zaysh
Arrive

Megállóhelyek (Megállók)
Mehg-ahl-loh-heh-yehk (Mehg-ahl-lohk)
Calls (Stops at)

Étkezés
Ayt-keh-zaysh
Catering Service

Átszállás ...-ra/-re
Aht-sahl-lash ... -ro/reh
Change At...

Csatlakozás/Útvonal
Chot-lo-koh-zahsh/Oht-vohh-nol
Connection/Via

Naponta
No-pohn-to
Daily

Negyven percenként
Nehdj-vehn pehr-tsehn-kaynt
Every 40 minutes

Első osztály
Ehl-shur ohs-tahy
First Class

Óránként
Oh-rahn-kaynt
Hourly

Helyjegyfoglalás ajánlott
Hehy-yehdj-fohg-lo-lahsh o-jahn-lohtt
Seat Reservations are recommended

Második osztály
Mah-shoh-deek ohs-tahy
Second Class

Kiegészitő díj fizetendő
Kee-eh-gay-see-tur deey fee-zeh-tehn-dur
Supplement Payable

Luggage

How much will it cost to send (ship) my luggage in advance?
Mennyibe kerül, ha előre küldöm a poggyászomat?
Mehnj-njee-beh keh-rewl, ho eh-lur-reh kewl-duhm o pohdj-djah-soh-mot?

Where is the left luggage (baggage claim) office?
Hol van a poggyászmegőrző?
Hohl von o pohdj-djahs-mehg-urr-zur?

What time do you open/close?
Hánykor nyitnak/zárnak?
Hahnj-kohr njeet-nok/zahr-nok?

Where are the luggage trolleys (carts)?
Hol vannak a poggyászkocsik?
Hohl von-nok o pohdj-djahs-koh-cheek?

Where are the lockers?
Hol van az önkiszolgáló poggyászmegőrző?
Hohl von oz uhn-kee-sohl-gah-loh pohdj-djahs-mehg-urr-zur?

I have lost my locker key
Elvesztettem a poggyászmegőrző kulcsomat
Ehl-vehs-teht-tehm o pohdj-djahs-meg-urr-zur kool-choh-mot

On Board

Is this seat free?
Szabad ez a hely?
So-bod ehz o hehy?

Excuse me, you are sitting in my reserved seat
Bocsánat, de Ön az én foglalt helyemen ül
Boh-chah-not, deh Uhn oz ayn fohg-lolt heh-yeh-mehn ewl

Which station is this?
Ez melyik állomás?
Ehz meh-yeek ahl-loh-mahsh?

What time is this train/bus/ferry/flight due to arrive/depart?
Hánykor érkezik/indul ez a vonat/busz/komp/repülő?

Hahnj-kohr ayr-keh-zeek/een-dool ehz o voh-not/boos/kohmp/reh-puh-lur?

Travelling with Children

Do you have a high chair/ babysitting service/cot?
Van itt etetőszék/ gyermekvigyázó/gyermekágy?
Von eett eh-teh-tur-sayk/djehr-mehk-vee-djah-zoh/djehr-mehk-ahdj?

Where is the nursery/ playroom?
Hol van a bölcsöde/játékszoba?
Hohl von o buhl-chuh-deh/yah-tayk-soh-bo?

Where can I warm the baby's bottle?
Hol lehet felmelegíteni a cumisüveget?
Hohl leh-heht fehl-meh-leh-gee-teh-nee o tsoo-meesh-ew-veh-geht?

Customs and Passports

Kérem az útleveleket
Kay-rehm oz ooht-leh-veh-leh-keht
Passports please

I have nothing to declare
Nincs vámolnivalóm
Neench-vah-mohl-nee-vo-lohm

I have wine/spirits (alcohol)/tobacco to declare
Bor/szeszes italok/dohányáru elvámolnivalóm van
Bohr/seh-sehsh ee-to-lohk/ doh-hahny-ah-roh ehl-vah-mohl-nee-vo-lohm von

I will be staying for ... days/weeks/months
... napot/hetet/hónapot szeretnék itt tartózkodni
... noh-poht/heh-teht/hoh-noh-poht seh-reht-nayk eett tor-tohz-kohd-nee

SIGHTSEEING

Asking the Way

Excuse me, do you speak English?
Elnézést, beszél angolul?
Ehl-nay-zaysht, beh-sayl on-goh-lool?

Excuse me, can you help me please?
Bocsánat, tudna nekem segíteni?
Boh-tsah-not, tood-no neh-kehm sheh-gee-teh-nee?

Where is the Tourist Information Office?
Hol van az Utazási Iroda?
Hohl von oz Oo-to-zah-shee Ee-roh-do?

Excuse me, is this the right way to ... the cathedral/the tourist office/the castle/the old town?
Elnézést, jó felé megyek a templomhoz/utazási irodához/várhoz/belváros felé?
Ehl-nay-zaysht, joh feh-leh med-yek o tehmp-lohm-hohz/oo-to-zah-shee ee-roh-dah-hohz/vahr-hohz/behl-vah-rosh feh-lay?

Can you tell me the way to the railway station/bus station/taxi rank/city centre/beach?

SIGHTSEEING

Hogy jutok el a pályaudvarhoz/autóbuszállomáshoz/taxiállomáshoz/belvárosba/strandra?
Hohdj joo-tohk ehl o pah-yo-ood-vahr-hohz/au-toh-boos-ahl-loh-mahsh-hohz/taxi-ahl-loh-mahsh-hohz/behl-vah-rohsh-bo/shtrond-ro?

Első/második forduló balra/jobbra/egyenesen előre
Ehl-shur/mah-shoh-deek fohr-doo-loh bol-ro/johb-ro/eh-djeh-neh-shehn eh-lur-reh
First/second/left/right/straight ahead

A sarkon/A lámpánál
O shor-kohn/O lahm-pah-nahl
At the corner/At the traffic lights

Where is the nearest police station/nearest post office?
Hol van a legközelebbi rendőrkapitányság/legközelebb bi posta?
Hohl von o lehg-kuh-zeh-lehb-bee rehn-dur-ko-pee-tahnj-sahg/lehg-kuh-zeh-lehb-bee pohsh-to?

Is it near/far?
Közel/messze van?
Kuh-zehl/mehs-seh von?

Do I need to take a taxi/catch a bus?
Taxival/busszal kell mennem?
Taxi-vol/boos-sol kehl mehn-nehm?

Do you have a map?
Van Önnél térkép?
Von Uhn-nayl tayr-kayp?

Can you point to it on my map?
Meg tudná ezt mutatni a térképemen?
Mehg tood-nah ehzt moo-tot-nee o tayr-kay-peh-mehn?

Thank you for your help
Köszönöm a segítségét
Kuh-suh-nuhm o sheh-geet-say-gayt

How do I reach the motorway/main road?
Hogyan jutok el az autópályára/a főútra?
Hohd-jon yoo-tohk ehl oz auto-pah-yah-ro/o fur oht-ro?

I think I have taken the wrong turning
Azt hiszem, rossz helyen kanyarodtam be
Ozt hee-sehm, rohss heh-yehn ko-njo-rohd-tom beh

I am looking for this address
Ezt a címet keresem
Ehzt o tsee-meht keh-reh-shehm

I am looking for the ... hotel
A ... szállodát keresem
O .... sahl-loh-daht keh-reh-shehm

How far is it to ... from here?
Milyen messze van ez innen ...?
Mee-yehn mehs-she von ehz een-nehn... ?

Menjen tovább ... kilométert egyenesen
Mehn-yehn toh-vahbb ... kee-loh-may-tehrt eh-djeh-neh-shehn
Carry straight on for ... kilometres

A következő sarkon forduljon jobbra/balra
O kuh-veht-keh-zur shor-kohn

fohr-dool-yohn yohbb-ro/bol-ro
Take the next turning on the right/left

A következő kereszteződésnél/ lámpánál kanyarodjon jobbra/ balra
O kuh-veht-keh-zur keh-rehs-teh-zur-daysh-nayl fohr-dool-yohn yohbbro/ bol-ro
Turn right/left at the next crossroads/traffic lights

Rossz irányba megy
Rohss ee-rahnj-bo mehdj
You are going in the wrong direction

Where is the cathedral/ church/museum/pharmacy?
Hol van a katedrális/templom/ múzeum/gyógyszertár?
Hol von o ko-tehd-rah-leesh/tehmp-lom/mooh-zeh-oom/djohdj-zehr-tahr?

How much is the admission/ entrance charge?
Mennyibe kerül a belépőjegy?
Mehnj-njee-beh keh-rewl o beh-lay-pur-yehdj?

Is there a discount for children/students/senior citizens?
Van engedmény gyerekeknek/diákoknak/nyugdí jasoknak?
Von ehn-gehd-maynj-djeh-reh-kehk-nehk/dee-ah-kohk-nok/njoog-dee-yo-shohk-nok?

What time does the next guided tour (in English) start?
Mikor indul a következő csoport (angol nyelven)?
Mee-kohr een-dool o kuh-veht-keh-zur choh-pohrt (on-gohl njehl-vehn)?

One/two adults/children please
Egy/két felnőtt/gyerek jegyet kérek
Ehdj/kayt fehl-nurtt/djeh-rehk yeh-djet kay-rehk

May I take photographs here?
Szabad itt fényképezni?
So-bod eett faynj-kay-pehz-nee?

At the Tourist Office

Do you have a map of the town/area?
Van Önöknek várostérképük/ körzeti térképük?
Von Uhn-nuhk-nehk vah-rosh-tayr-kay-pewklkuhr-zeh-tee tayr-kay-pewk?

Do you have a list of accommodation?
Van Önöknek szállodalistájuk?
Von Uh-nuhk-nehk sahl-loh-do-leesh-tah-yook?

Can I reserve accommodation?
Foglalhatok szállást?
Fohg-lol-ho-tohk sahl-lahsht?

ACCOMMODATION

Hotels

I have a reservation in the name of..
Szobát foglaltam ... névre
Soh-baht fohg-lol-tom ... nayv-reh

I wrote to/faxed/telephoned you last month/last week
Levelet/faxot küldtem/ telefonáltam Önöknek a múlt hónapban/múlt héten
Leh-veh-leht/fax-oht kewld-tehm/tele-foh-nahl-tom Uh-nuhk-nehk o moolt hoh-nop-bon/moolt hay-tehn

Do you have any rooms free?
Van szabad szobájuk?
Von so-bod soh-bah-yook?

I would like to reserve a single/double room with bath (shower)/without bath (shower)
Foglalni szeretnék egy egyágyas/kétágyas szobát fürdőszobával (zuhanyozóval)/ fürdőszoba (zuhanyozó) nélkül
Fohg-lol-nee seh-reht-nayk ehdj ehdj-ah-djosh/kayt-ah-djosh soh-baht fewr-dur-soh-bah-vol (zoo-ho-njoh-zoh-vol) fewr-dur-soh-bah (zoo-ho-njoh-zoh) nayl-kewl

I would like bed/breakfast/ (room and) full board
Szállást/reggelit/(szobát és) teljes panziót kérek
Sahl-lahsht/rehg-geh-leet/(soh-baht aysh) tehl-yesh pon-zee-oht kay-rehk

How much is it per night?
Mennyibe kerül ez egy éjszakára?
Mehnj-njee-beh keh-rewl ehz ehdj ayy-so-kah-ro?

Is breakfast included?
A reggeli is benne van az árban?
O rehg-geh-lee eesh behn-neh von oz ahr-bon?

Do you have any cheaper rooms?
Van olcsóbb szobájuk?
Von ohl-chohbb soh-bah-yook?

I would like to see/take the room
Megnézném/kivenném a szobát
Mehg-nayz-naym/kee-vehn-naym o soh-baht

I would like to stay for ..... nights
... napot szeretnék maradni
... no-pot seh-reht-nayk mo-rod-nee

The shower/light/tap/hot water doesn't work
A zuhanyozó/villany/ csap/melegvíz nem működik
O zoo-ho-njoh-zoh/veel-lonj/chop/meh-lehg-veez nehm meew-kuh-deek

At what time/where is breakfast served?
Hánykor/hol van a reggeli?
Hahnj-kohr/hohl von o rehg-geh-lee?

What time do I have to check out?
Mikor kell kijelentkeznem?
Mee-kohr kehll kee-yeh-lehnt-kehz-nehm?

Can I have the key to room number...?
Megkaphatnám a ...-as/-os/-es szoba kulcsát?
Mehg-kop-hot-nahm o ...-osh/-ohsh/-ehsh soh-bo kool-chaht?

My room number is...
A szobaszámom ...
O soh-bah-sah-mohm ...

My room is not satisfactory/ not clean enough/too noisy. Please can I change rooms?
A szobám nem megfelelő/ piszkos/túl zajos. Cserélhetnék szobát?
O soh-bahm nehm mehg-feh-lehl-lur/pees-kohsh/tool zo-yohsh. Cheh-rayl-heht-nayk soh-baht?

Where is the bathroom?
Hol van a fürdőszoba?
Hohl von o fewr-dur-soh-bo?

Do you have a safe for valuables?
Van Önöknél értékmegőrző?
Von Uh-nuhk-nayl ayr-tayk-mehg-urr-zur?

Is there a laundry/do you wash clothes?
Van maguknál mosoda/mosnak-e ruhát?
Von mo-gook-nahl moh-shoh-do/mohsh-nok-eh roo-haht?

I would like an air-conditioned room
Légkondicionált szobát szeretnék
Layg-kohn-dee-tsee-oh-nahlt soh-baht seh-reht-nayk

Do you accept traveller's cheques/credit cards?
Elfogadnak úticsekkeket/ hitelkártyát?
Ehl-foh-god-nok oo-tee-chehk-keht/hee-tehl-kahr-tjayt?

May I have the bill please?
Kérhetem a számlát?
Kayr-heh-tehm o sahm-laht?

Excuse me, I think there may be a mistake in this bill.
Elnézést kérek, de azt hiszem, téves a számla
Ehl-nay-zaysht kay-rehk, deh ozt hee-sehm, tay-vehsh o sahm-lo

Youth Hostels

How much is a dormitory bed per night?
Mennyibe kerül a hálóteremben egy ágy egy éjszakára?
Mehnj-njee-beh keh-rewl o hah-loh-teh-rehm-behn ehdj ahdj ehdj ayy-so-kah-ro?

I am/am not an HI member.
Tagja vagyok/nem vagyok tagja a HI-nek
Tog-yo vo-djohk/nehm vo-djohk tog-yo o HI-nehk

May I use my own sleeping bag?
Használhatom a saját hálózsákomat?
Hos-nahl-ho-tom o sho-yaht hah-loh-zhay-koh-mot?

What time do you lock the doors at night?
Este hánykor zárják be a kaput?
Ehsh-teh hahnj-kohr zahr-jahk beh o ko-poot?

Camping

May I camp for the night/two nights?
Maradhatok egy/két éjszakára?
Mo-rod-ho-tohk ehdj/kayt ayy-so-kah-ro?

Where can I pitch my tent?
Hol üthetem fel a sátramat?
Hohl ewt-heh-tehm fehl o shaht-roh-mot?

How much does it cost for one night/week?
Mennyibe kerül ez egy éjjelre/egy hétre?
Meehnj-njee-beh keh-rewl ehz ehdj ayy-yehl-reh/ehdj hayt-reh?

Where are the washing facilities?
Hol van a fürdőszoba-zuhanyozó?
Hohl von o fewr-dur-soh-bo - zoo-ho-njoh-zoh?

Is there a restaurant/ supermarket/swimming pool on site/nearby?
Van itt a közelben/a kempingben étterem/ supermarket/uszoda?
Von eett o kuh-zehl-behn/o kehm-peeng-behn ayt-teh-rehm/supermar-ket/oo-soh-do?

Do you have a safety deposit box?
Van Önöknél értékmegőrző?
Von Uh-nuhk-nayl ayr-tayk-mehg-urr-zur?

EATING AND DRINKING

Cafés and Bars

I would like a cup of/two cups of/another coffee/tea
Szeretnék egy csésze/két csésze kávét/még egy kávét/teát
Seh-reht-nayk ehdj chay-seh/kayt chay-she kah-veht/mayg ehdj kah-veht/teh-aht

With/without milk
Tejjel/tej nélkül
Tehy-yehl/tehy nayl-kewl

With/without sugar
Cukorral/cukor nélkül
Tsoo-kohr-rol/tsoo-kohr nayl-kewl

I would like a bottle/glass/two glasses of mineral water/red wine/white wine, please
Szeretnék egy üveg/pohár/ két pohár ásványvizet/vörös bort/fehér bort
Seh-reht-nayk ehdj ew-vehg/ poh-hahr/kayt poh-hahr ahsh-vahnj-vee-zeht/vuh-ruhsh bohrt/ feh-hayr bohrt

I would like a beer/two beers, please
Szeretnék egy sört/két sört
Seh-reht-nayk ehdj suhrt/kayt suhrt

Please may I have some ice?
Kaphatnék egy kis jeget?
Kop-hot-nayk ehdj kees yeh-geht?

Do you have any matches/cigarettes/cigars?
Van Önöknél gyufa/cigaretta/szivar?
Von uh-nuhk-nayl djoo-fo/tsee-go-reht-to/see-vor?

Restaurants

Can you recommend a good/cheap restaurant in this area?
Tudna ajánlani egy jó/nem drága éttermet a környéken?

Tood-no o-yahn-lo-nee ehdj joh/nehm drah-go ayt-tehr-meht o kuhr-njay-kehn?

I would like a table for ... people
Szeretnék egy asztalt ... személyre
Seh-reht-nayk ehdj os-tolt ... seh-mayy-reh

Do you have a non-smoking area?
Van maguknál nemdohányzó terem?
Von mo-gook-nahl nehm-doh-hahnj-zoo teh-rehm?

Waiter/Waitress!
Pincér/Pincérnő!
Pin-cayr/pin-cayr-nur!

Excuse me, please may we order?
Kérem, rendelhetünk?
Kay-rehm, rehn-dehl-heh-tewnk?

Do you have a set menu/ children's menu/wine list ... in English?
Van komplett menüjük/gyer-mek menüjük/itallapjuk?
Von komp-lett meh-new-yewk/djehr-mehk meh-new-yewk/ee-tol-lop-yook?

Do you have any vegetarian dishes?
Van vegetariánus ételük?
Von veh-geh-to-ri-ah-noosh ay-teh-lewk?

Do you have any local specialities?
Vannak helyi specialitásaik?
Von-nok heh-yee shpeh-tsee-o-lee-tah-sho-eek?

Are vegetables included?
A zöldségek benne vannak az árban?
O zuhld-shay-gehk behn-neh von-nok oz ahr-bon?

Could I have it well-cooked/medium rare please?
Kaphatnám ezt jól megsülten/félig sülten?
Kop-hot-nahm ehzt johl mehg-shewl-tehn/fay-leeg shewl-tehn?

What does this dish consist of?
Miből készült ez az étel?
Mee-burl kay-sewlt ehz oz ay-tehl?

I am a vegetarian. Does this contain meat?
Vegetáriánus vagyok. Van ebben hús?
Veh-geh-tah-ree-ah-nosh vodjok. Von ehb-behn hoosh?

I do not eat nuts/dairy products/meat/fish
Nem eszem dióféléket/ tejtermékeket/húst/halat
Nehm eh-sehm dee-oht-feh-leh-ket/tehy-tehr-may-keh-keht/hoosht/ ho-lot

Not (very) spicy please
Kérem, ne legyen (nagyon) erős
Kay-rehm, neh-leh-djehn (no-djohn) eh-rursh

I would like the set menu please
Kérem szépen a menüt
Keh-rehm say-pehn o meh-newt

HUNGARIAN

We have not been served yet
Még nem szolgáltak ki minket
Mayg nem sol-gahl-tok kee meen keht

Please bring a plate/knife/fork
Kérem, hozzon tányért/kést/villát
Kay-rehm, hoz-zon tah-njayrt/kaysht/vee-llaht

Excuse me, this is not what I ordered
Bocsánat, de nem ezt rendeltem
Boh-chah-not, deh nehm ehzt rehn-dehl-tehm

May I have some/more bread/water/coffee/tea?
Kérhetnék még egy kis kenyeret/vizet/kávét/teát?
Kayr-heht-nayk mayg ehdj keesh keh-njeh-reht/vee-zeht/kah-vayt/teh-aht?

May I have the bill please?
Kérhetem a számlát?
Kayr-heh-tehm o sahm-laht?

Does this bill include service?
A kiszolgálás benne van az árban?
O kee-sohl-gahl-lash behn-neh von oz ahr-bon?

Do you accept traveller's cheques/Mastercard/US dollars?
Elfogadnak úticsekkeket/Mastercard hitelkártyát/USA dollárt?
Ehl-foh-god-nok oo-tee-chehk-keht/Mastercard hee-tehl-kahr-tjayt/USHAH dohl-lahrt?

Can I have a receipt please?
Kaphatnék nyugtát a számláról?
Kop-hot-nayk njoog-taht o sahm-lah-rohl?

Where is the toilet (restroom) please?
Hol van a WC?
Hohl von o aya-tsay

On the Menu

Reggeli/Ebéd/Vacsora
Rehg-geh-lee/Eh-bayd/Votso-ro
Breakfast/Lunch/Dinner

Előételek
Eh-lur-ay-teh-lehk
First Courses

Levesek
Leh-veh-shehk
Soups

Fő ételek
Fur ay-teh-lehk
Main Courses

Halételek
Hahl-ay-teh-lehk
Fish Dishes

Húsételek
Hohsh-ay-teh-lehk
Meat Dishes

Marhahús
Morho-hoo-sh
Beef

Sült (hús, hal) szelet
Shewlt (hoosh, hol) seh-leht
Steak

Disznóhús
Dees-no-hoosh
Pork

Borjúhús
Bohr-yoo-hoosh
Veal

Csirkehús
Tseer-keh-hoosh
Chicken

Báránlyhús
Bah-rahnj-hoosh
Lamb

Sonka
Shon-ko
Ham

Vegetáriánus ételek
Veh-geh-tah-ree-ah-noosh ay-teh-lehk
Vegetarian Dishes

Zöldségek/Főzelékek
Zewld-shay-ghek/Fur-ze-ley-kehk
Vegetables

Rósejbni (hasábburgonya)
Rosh-ayb-nee (hoh-sayb-boor-goh-njo)
Chips (french fries)

Főtt/Hirtelen sült burgonya/burgonyapüré
Furt/Heer-teh-lehn shewlt boor-goh-njo/boor-goh-njo-pew-ray
Boiled/sauté/mashed potatoes

Rizs
Reezh
Rice

Desszertek
Dehs-sehr-tehk
Desserts

Fagylalt
Fodj-lolt
Ice cream

Torta
Tor-to
Cakes

Sütemény
Shew-teh-may-nj
Pastries

Gyümölcs
Djew-muh-lts
Fruit

Kenyér
Kehnj-ayr
Bread

Péksütemény (Kifli/Zsemle)
Payk-shew-teh-may-nj (Keef-lee/Zhehm-leh)
Rolls

Piritós
Pee-ree-tawsh
Toast

Vaj
Voy
Butter

Só/bors
Shaw/borrsh
Salt/pepper

Cukor
Tsoo-kohr
Sugar

Ételspecialitások
Ay-tehl-shpeh-tsee-o-lee-tah-shohk
Specialities

Helyi specialitások
Hehy-ee shpeh-tsee-o-lee-tay-shock
Local specialities

Napi menü
Nopeh meh-new
Set Menu

Borlista
Bohr-lee-shto
Wine list

Vörösbor
Vuh-ruhsh-bohr
Red wines

Fehérbor
Feh-hayr-bohr
White wines

Világos vörös bor
Vee-lah-gosh vuh-ruhsh bohr
Rosé wines

Habzóbor
Hobzo-bohr
Sparkling wines

Sör
Shuhr
Beer

Palackozott sör/Csapolt sör
Po-lots-ko-zott shuhr/Tso-polt shuhr
Bottled beer/Draught (draft) beer

Alkoholmentes italok
Ol-ko-hol-mehn-tehsh ee-to-lok
Non-alcoholic drinks

Ásványvíz
Aysh-vaynj-veez
Mineral water

HUNGARIAN

Gyümölcslevek
Djew-muhlts-leh-vehk
Fruit juices

Narancslé
No-ronts-lay
Orange juice

Limonádé	Jég
Lee-mo-nah-day	*Jaygh*
Lemonade	**Ice**

Tejeskávé/feketekávé/eszpresszó kávé
Teh-yesh-kah-vay/fehkehteh-kah-vay/espresso kay-vay
White coffee/black coffee/espresso coffee

Tea tejjel/citrommal
Teh-a tehj-jehl/tseet-rom-mol
Tea with milk/with lemon

Kakaó	Tej
Koko-aw	*Tehj*
Chocolate (drink)	**Milk**

Falatkák/Könnyű ételek
Fo-lot-kahk/Kuhnj-njew ay-teh-lehk
Snacks/Light meals

Saláták	Szendvicsek
Sho-lah-tahk	*Sehnd-vww-tschehk*
Salads	**Sandwiches**

Tojás	Kolbász/Virsli
Toy-ahsh	*Kohl-bahs/Veer-shlee*
Eggs	**Sausage**

Főtt tojás/tükörtojás/rántotta
Furt toy-ashsh/tew-kuhr tohy-ash/rahn-tot-to
Boiled/fried/scrambled eggs

Typical Local Dishes

Tyúkhúsleves
Tjohk-hohsh-leh-vesh
Chicken soup

Gyümölcsleves
Djew-muhlch-leh-vesh
Fruit Soup

Sült pisztráng
Sheewlt peest-rahng
Fried Trout

Töltött palacsinta
Tuhl-tuhltt po-lo-cheen-to
Pancakes with filling

Pálinka
Pah-leen-ko
Strong alcoholic drink

GETTING AROUND

Public Transport

Where is the bus stop/coach stop/nearest metro station?
Hol van az autóbuszmegálló/távolsági-buszmegálló/legközelebbi metróállomás?
Hohl von oz auto-boos-mehg-ahl-loh/tah-vohl-shah-gee-boos-mehg-ahl-loh/lehg-kuh-zeh-lehb-bee metro-ahl-loh-mahsh?

When is the next/last bus to...?
Mikor indul a következő/utolsó busz ...-ba/be?
Mee-kohr een-dool a kuh-veht-keh-zur boos … –bo/beh?

How much is the fare to the city centre (downtown)/ railway station/airport?
Mennyi a viteldíj a városközpontig/pályaudvarig/ repülőtérig?
Mehnj-njee o vee-tehl-deey o vah-rohsh-kuhz-pohnt-eeg/pah-yo-ood-vo-reeg/reh-pew-lur-tay-reeg?

Will you tell me when to get off?
Szólna, amikor le kell szállnom?
Sohl-no, o-mee-kohr leh kehll sahll-nohm?

Does this bus go to...?
Ez a busz megy...-ig?
Ehz o boos mehdj ...-eeg?

Which number bus goes to...?
Hányas busz megy ...-ig?
Hah-njos boos mehdj .... eeg?

May I have a single (one way)/return (round trip)/day ticket/book of tickets?
Szeretnék egy jegyet egy irány-ban/oda-vissza (menettérti jegyet)/egésznapos bérletet/jegytömböt?
Seh-reht-nayk ehdj-yeh-djeht ehdj ee-rahnj-bon/oh-do-vees-so (meh-neht-tay-ree yeh-djeht)/eh-gays-no-pohsh bayr-leh-teht/yehdh-tuhm-buht?

Taxi (Taxi)

I would like to go to ... How much will it cost?
...-ba/-be szeretnék eljutni. Mennyibe fog ez kerülni?
...-oa/-beh seh-reht-nayk ehl-joot-nee. Mehnj-njee-beh fohg ehz keh-rewl-nee?

Please may I stop here?
Kérem, álljon meg itt?
Kay-rehm ahll-yohn mehg eett?

I would like to order a taxi today/tomorrow at 2pm to go from...to...
Taxit szeretnék rendelni mára/holnapra két órára, hogy ...-ból/-ből ...-ig menjek
Taxit seh-reht-nayk rehn-dehl-nee mah-ro/hohl-nop-ro kayt oh-rah-ro, hodj ... bool/bur ... eeg mehn-yehk

Entertainment

Can you recommend a good bar/nightclub?
Tudna ajánlani egy jó bárt/éjszakai klubot?
Tood-no o-yahn-lo-nee ehdj joh bahrt/ay-so-ko-ee kloob-oht?

Do you know what is on at the cinema (playing at the movies)/theatre at the moment?
Meg tudná mondani, hogy mi megy most a mozikban/ szinházakban?
Mehg tood-nah mohn-do-nee, hohdj mee mehdj mohsht o moh-zeek-bon/seen-hahz-ok-bon?

I would like to book (purchase) ... tickets for the matinee/evening performance on Monday
Szeretnék ... jegyet rendelni/venni a hétfő délutáni/esti előadásra

HUNGARIAN

Seh-reht-nayk ... yeh-djeht rehn-dehl-nee/vehn-nee o hayt-fur dayl-oo-tah-nee eh-lur-o-dahsh-ro

What time does the film/ performance start?
Hánykor kezdődik a film/az előadás?
Hahnj-kohr kehz-dur-deek o film/oz eh-lur-o-dahsh?

COMMUNICATIONS

Post

How much will it cost to send a letter/postcard/this package to Britain/Ireland/ America/Canada/Australia/ New Zealand?
Mennyibe kerül egy levelet/képeslapot/ezt a küldeményt feladni Angliába/ Irországba/Amerikába/ Kanadába/Ausztráliába/ Új Zélandba?
Mehnj-njee-beh keh-rewl ehdj leh-vehl-leht/kay-pehsh-lo-poht/ehzt o kewl-deh-maynjt fehl-od-nee Ong-lee-ah-bo/Amerikah-bo/Ko-no-dah-bo/ Aoost-rah-lee-ah-bo/Ohy-zay-lond-bo?

I would like one stamp/two stamps
Kérek egy/két bélyeget
Kay-rehk ehdj/kayt bay-yeh-geht

I'd like ... stamps for postcards to send abroad, please
Kérek ... képeslapra való nemzetközi bélyeget
Kay-rehk ... kay-pehsh-lop-ro vah-loh nehm-zeht-kuh-zee bay-yeh-geht

Phones

I would like to make a telephone call/reverse the charges to (make a collect call to)...
Szeretnék telefonálni/telefonál-ni a hívott szám költségére ... -ba/-be
Seh-reht-nayk teh-leh-foh-nahl-nee/teh-leh-foh-nahl-nee o hee-vohtt sahm kuhlt-say-gay-reh ... -bo/-beh

Which coins do I need for the telephone?
Milyen érmékkel lehet telefonálni?
Mee-yehn ayr-mayk-kehl leh-heht telefonahl-nee?

The line is engaged (busy)
Foglalt a vonal
Fohg-lahlt o voh-nol

The number is...
A szám ...
O sahm ...

Hello, this is...
Halló, ... vagyok
Hallo, ... vah-djohk

Please may I speak to ..?
Kérem, beszélhetnék ... val/-vel?
Keh-rehm, beh-sayl-heht-nayk ... voll-vehl?

He/she is not in at the moment. Please can you call back?
Most nincs bent. Kérem, hívja később?
Mohsht neench behnt. Kay-rehm heev-jo kay-surbb?

SHOPPING

Shops

Könyvesbolt/Papírbolt
Kuhnj-vehsh-bohlt/Pap-eer-bohlt
Bookshop/Stationery

Ékszerbolt/Ajándékbolt
Ayk-sehr-bohlt/O-yahn-dayk-bohlt
Jeweller/Gifts

Cipőbolt
Tsee-pur-bohlt
Shoes

Ruhabolt
Roo-ho-bohlt
Clothes

Mosoda
Moh-shoh-do
Laundry

Háztartási cikkek
Hahz-tor-tah-shee tseek-kehk
Hardware

Fodrász
Fohd-rahs
Hairdresser

Pék
Payk
Baker

Szupermarket
Supermarket
Supermarket

Fotóüzlet
Foh-toh-ewz-leht
Photo Shop

Utazási iroda
Oh-to-zah-shee ee-roh-do
Travel Agent

Gyógyszertár
Djohdj-zehr-tahr
Pharmacy

In the Shops

What time do the shops open/close?
Mikor nyitnak/zárnak a boltok?
Mee-kohr nn-y-eet-nok/zahr-nok o bohl-tohk?

Where is the nearest market?
Hol van a legközelebbi piac?
Hohl von o lehg-kuh-zeh-lehb-bee pee-ots?

Can you show me the one in the window/this one?
Megmutatná nekem a kirakatban levőt/ezt?
Megh-moo-tot-nah neh-kehm o kee-ro-kot-bon leh-vurt/ehzt?

Can I try this on?
Felpróbálhatom?
Fehl-proh-bahl-ho-tom?

What size is this?
Ez hányas méret?
Ehz hah-njosh may-reht?

This is too large/too small/too expensive. Do you have any others?
Ez túl nagy/túl kicsi/túl drága. Más van?
Ehz toohl nogj/tool kee-chee/tool drah-go. Mahsh von?

My size is...
Az én méretem ...
Oz ehn may-reh-tehm ...

Where is the changing room/children's/cosmetic/ ladieswear/menswear/food department?
Hol van a próbafülke/ gyermekosztály/parfümosztály/ nőiruha osztály/férfiruha osztály/élelmiszerosztály?
Hohl von o proo-bah-fewl-keh/djehr-mehk-ohs-tahy/por-fewm-ohs-tahy/nur-ee-roo-hah ohs-tahy/ay-lehl-mee-sehr-ohs-tahy?

I would like ... a quarter of a kilo/half a kilo/a kilo of bread/butter/ham/this fruit
Kérek ... huszonöt deka/fél kiló/kiló kenyeret/vajat/ sonkát/ebből a gyümölcsből
Kay-rehk ... hoo-sohn-uht deh-ko/fayl kee-loh keh-njeh-reht/vo-jot/sohn-kaht/ehb-bur o djew-muhlch-burl

How much is this?
Mennyibe kerül ez?
Mehnj-njee-beh keh-rewl ehz?

I'll take this one, thank you
Ezt megveszem, köszönöm
Ehzt mehg-veh-sehm, kuh-suh-nuhm

Do you have a carrier (shopping) bag?
Kérhetek egy nylonzacskót?
Kayrheh-tehk edj nehylon-zochkawt?

Do you have anything cheaper/larger/smaller/ of better quality?
Van Önnek ennél olcsóbb/ nagyobb/kisebb/jobb minőségű?
Vahn Uhn-nehk ehn-nayl ohl-csohbb/no-gyobb/kee-sehbb/johbb mee-nur-shay-geew?

I would like a film/to develop this film for this camera
Szeretnék ehhez a fényképezőgéphez filmet venni/filmet előhívatni
Seh-reht-nayk eh-hez o faynj-kay-peh-zur-gayp-hehz feel-meht vehn-nee/feel-meht elur-hee-vot-nee

I would like some batteries, the same size as this old one
A régivel azonos méretű elemet szeretnék
O ray-gee-vehl o-zoh-nohsh may-reh-teew eh-leh-meht seh-reht-nayk

Would you mind wrapping this for me, please?
Kérem, becsomagolná ezt nekem?
Kay-rehm, beh-choh-mo-gohl-nah ehzt neh-kehm?

Sorry, but you seem to have given me the wrong change
Elnézést, de úgy látszik, rosszul adott nekem vissza a pénzből
Ehl-nay-zaysht, deh oogj laht-sik, rohs-sool o-dohtt neh-kehm vees-so o paynz-burl

MOTORING

Car Hire (Rental)

I have ordered (rented) a car in the name of...
Rendeltem (kibéreltem) egy autót ... névre
Rehn-dehl-tehm (kee-bay-rehl-tehm) ehdj autoht ... nayv-reh

How much does it cost to hire (rent) a car for one day/two days/a week?
Mennyibe kerül az autótbérlés (kölcsönzés) egy napra/két napra/egy hétre?
Mehnj-njee-beh keh-rewl oz auto-bayr-laysh (kuhl-chuhn-zaysh) ehdj nop-ro/kayt nop-ro/ehdj hayt-reh?

Is the tank already full of petrol (gas)?
A benzintartály már tele van üzemanyaggal?
A behn-zeen-tor-tayy mahr teh-leh von ew-zehm-o-njog-gol?

Is insurance and tax included? How much is the deposit?
A biztositás és az adó is benne van az árban? Mennyi a letét nagysága?
O beez-toh-shee-tahsh aysh oz o-doh eesh behn-neh von oz ahr-bon? Mehnj-njee o leh-tayt nogy-shah-go?

By what time must I return the car?
Hány órára kell visszahoznom az autót?
Hahnj oh-rah-ro kehll vees-so-hohz-nohm oz autoht?

I would like a small/large/family/sports car with a radio/cassette
Szeretnék egy kis/nagy/családi/sport autót kölcsönözni rádióval/magnóval
Seh-reht-nayk ehdj keesh/nodj/cho-lah-dee/shport autoht kuhl-chuh-nuhz-nee rah-dee-oh-vol/mog-noh-vol

Do you have a road map?
Van Önöknek autótérképe?
Von Uh-nuhk-nehk autoh-tayr-kay-peh?

Parking

How long can I park here?
Meddig lehet itt állni?
Mehd-deeg leh-heht eett ahl-nee?

Is there a car park near here?
Van itt a közelben parkolóhely?
Vahn eett o kuh-zehl-behn por-koh-loh-hehy?

At what time does this car park close?
Hánykor zár ez a parkolóhely?
Hahnj-kohr zahr ehz o por-koh-loh-hehly?

Signs and Notices

Egyirányú forgalom
Ehdj-ee-rah-njoo fohr-go-lom
One way

Behajtani tilos
Beh-hoj-toh-nee tee-lohsh
No entry

Parkolni tilos
Pahr-kohl-nee tee-lohsh
No parking

Terelőút
Teh-reh-lur-oot
Detour (Diversion)

Stop
Shtop
Stop

Elsőbbségadás kötelező
Ehl-shurbb-shayg-o-dahsh kuh-teh-leh-zur
Give way (Yield!)

Csúszós út
Choo-soosh oot
Slippery road

Előzni tilos
Eh-lurz-nee tee-lohsh
No overtaking

Veszély!
Veh-sayy!
Danger!

At the Filling Station
(A Benzinkútnál)

Unleaded (lead free)/ standard/premium/diesel
Ólommentes/normál/szuper benzin/dízelolaj
Oh-lohm-mehn-tehsh/nohr-mahl/soo-pehr behn-zeen/dee-eh-zehl-oh-loy

Fill the tank please
Kérem, töltse tele a tankot
Kah-rehm, tuhlt-sheh teh-leh o tonkoht

Do you have a road map?
Van Önöknek autótérképe?
Von Uh-nuhk-nehk autoh-tayr-kay-peh?

How much is the car wash?
Mennyibe kerül a kocsimosás?
Mehnj-njee-beh keh-rewl o ko-chee-moh-shahsh?

Breakdowns

I've had a breakdown at ...
Elromlott a kocsim ...-n/-en/-on
Ehl-rohm-lohtt o koh-cheem...-n/ -ehn/-ohn

I am a member of the ... [motoring organisation]
A ... tagja vagyok
Ah ... tog-yo vodjok

I am on the road from... to...
A ...-ból/-ből ...-ba/-be vezető úton vagyok
A ...-bohl/-burly ...-bo/-beh veh-zeh-tur oo-tohn vo-gyohk

I can't move the car. Can you send a tow-truck?
Nem tudom elindítani a kocsit. Tudna küldeni egy vontatót?
Nehm too-dohm ehl-een-dee-to-nee o koh-cheet. Tood-no kewl-deh-nee ehdj vohn-to-toht?

I have a flat tyre
Defektet kaptam
Deh-fehk-teht kop-tom

The windscreen (windshield) has smashed/cracked
A szélvédő eltörött/elrepedt
O sayl-vay-dur ehl-tuh-ruhtt/ehl-reh-pehdt

There is something wrong with the engine/brakes/ lights/steering/gearbox/clutch /exhaust.
Valami baj van a motorral/ fékkel/fényszórókkal/ kormánnyal/sebességváltóval/ kipufogócsővel
Vah-lo-mee boj von o moh-toh-rroll/ fayk-kehl/faynj-soh-rohk-kol/kohr-

mahnj-njol/seh-behsh-shayg-vahl-too-vol/kee-poof-foh-goh-chur-vehl

It's overheating
Túlmelegszik
Tool-meh-lehg-seek

It won't start
Nem indul
Nehm een-dool

Where can I get it repaired?
Hol lehet ezt megjavíttatni?
Hohl leh-het ehzt mehg-yo-veet-toht-nee?

Can you take me there?
Elvinne engem oda?
Ehl-veen-neh ehn-gehm ohdo?

Will it take long to fix?
Sokáig tart a javítás?
Shoh-kah-eeg tort o ja-vee-tahsh?

How much will it cost?
Mennyibe kerül a javítás?
Mehnj-njee-beh ekh-rewl o ja-vee-tahsh?

Please can you pick me up/give me a lift?
Kérem, elvinne engem?
Kay-rehm, ehl-veen-neh ehn-gehm?

Accidents and Traffic Offences (Violations)

Can you help me? There has been an accident
Tudna segíteni? Baleset történt
Tood-no sheh-gee-teh-ni? bol-eh-sheht tuhr-taynt

Please call the police/an ambulance
Kérem hívja a rendőrséget/mentőket
Kay-rehm heev-yo o rehn-dur-shay-geht/mehn-tur-keht

Is anyone hurt?
Megsebesült valaki?
Meg-she-beh-shewlt vo-loki?

I'm sorry, I didn't see the sign
Bocsánat, nem vettem észre a jelzőtáblát
Boh-chah-not, nehm veht-tehm ays-reh o yehl-zur-tahb-laht

Must I pay a fine? How much?
Büntetést kell fizetnem? Mennyit?
Bewn-teh-taysht kehl fee-zeht-nehm? Mehnj-njeet?

Kérem, mutassa az iratait
Kay-rehm, moo-to-sso oz ee-ro-to-eet
Show me your documents

HEALTH

Pharmacy (Gyógyszertár)

Do you have anything for a stomach ache/headache/sore throat/toothache?
Van Önnek valami hasfájás/fejfájás/torokgyulladás/fogfájás ellen?
Vahn Uhn-nehk vo-lo-mee hosh-fah-yahsh/fehy-fah-yahsh/toh-rohk-djool-lah-dahsh ehl-lehn?

I need something for diarrhoea/constipation/a cold/a cough/insect bites/sunburn/travel (motion) sickness
Nekem kell valami hasmenés/

székrekedés/megfázás/köhögés/szúnyogcsípés/leégés/tengeribetegség ellen
Neh-kehm kehll vo-loh-mee hosh-meh-naysh/sayk-reh-keh-daysh/mehg-fah-zahsh/soo-njohg-chee-paysh/tehn-geh-ree-beh-tehg-shayg ehl-lehn

How much/how many do I take?
Mennyit/hány darabot kell bevennem?
Mehnj-njeet/hahnj do-ro-boht kehll beh-vehn-nehm?

I am taking anti-malaria tablets/these pills
Malária elleni tablettákat/ezeket a kapszulákat szedem
Mah-lah-ree-o ehl-lehnee tob-leht-tah-kot/eh-zeh-keht o kop-soo-lah-kot seh-dehm

How often do I take it/them?
Milyen gyakran kell ezt/ezeket bevennem?
Mee-lyehn djok-ron kehll ehzt/eh-zeh-keht beh-vehn-nehm?

I am/he is/she is taking this medication
Ezt a gyógyszert szedem/szedi
Ehzt o djoodj-sehrt seh-dehm/seh-dee

How much does it cost?
Mennyibe kerül ez?
Mehnj-njee-beh keh-rewl ehz?

Can you recommend a good doctor/dentist?
Tudna ajánlani egy jó orvost/fogorvost?
Tood-no o-jahn-lo-nee ehdj jooh ohr-vohsht/fohg-ohr-vohsht?

Is it suitable for children?
Ez gyerekeknek is való?
Ehz djeh-reh-kehk-nehk eesh vo-loh?

Doctor (Orvos)

I have a pain here/in my arm/leg/chest/stomach
Nekem fáj itt/a kezem/a lábam/a mellkasom/a hasam
Neh-kehm fahy eett/o keh-zehm/o lah-bohm/o mehll-ko-shohm/o ho-shohm

Please call a doctor, this is an emergency
Kérem, hívja sürgősen az orvost
Kay-rehm, heev-yoh shewr-gur-shehn oz ohr-vohsht

I would like to make an appointment to see the doctor
Szeretnék bejelentkezni az orvoshoz
She-reht-nayk beh-yeh-lehnt-kehz-nee oz ohr-vohsh-hohz

I am diabetic/pregnant
Diabetikus/terhes vagyok
Diabeti-koosh/tehr-hehsh vo-djohk

I need a prescription for…
Nekem recept kell ...-ra/re
Neh-kehm reh-tsept kehll ... ro/reh

Can you give me something to ease the pain?
Tudna nekem adni valami fájdalomcsillapítót?
Tood-no neh-kehm od-nee vo-lo-mee fahy-do-lohm-cheel-lo-pee-toht?

I am/he is/she is/allergic to penicillin
Nekem allergiám/neki allergiája van penicillinre
Neh-kehm allehr-gee-ahm/neh-kee allehr-gee-ahyo von penni-tsee-leen

Fáj itt?
Fahy eett?
Does this hurt?

Korházba kell mennie
Kohr-hahz-bo kehl mehn-nee-eh
You must/he must/she must go to hospital

Naponta egyszer/kétszer/háromszor vegye ezt be
No-pohn-to ehdj-sehr/kayt-sehr/hah-rohm-sohr veh-djeh ehzt beh
Take these once/twice/three times a day

I am/he is/she is taking this medication
Ezt a gyógyszert szedem/szedi
Ehzt o djoodj-sehrt seh-dehm/seh-dee

I have medical insurance
Van egészségbiztosításom
Von eh-gays-shayg-beez-toh-shee-tah-shohm

Dentist (Fogorvos)

I have toothache/my filling has come out
Fáj a fogam/kiesett a tömés
Fahy o foh-gom/kee-eh-shehtt o tuh-maysh

I do/do not want to have an injection first
Akarok/nem akarok injekciót előtte
O-ko-rohk/nehm o-ko-rohk een-yehk-tsee-oht eh-lurt-teh

EMERGENCIES

Help!
Segítség!
Sheh-geet-shayg!

Fire!
Tűz!
Teewz!

Stop!
Állj!
Ahlly!

Call an ambulance/a doctor/the police/the fire brigade!
Hivja a mentőket/orvost/rendőrséget/tűzoltókat!
Heev-yo o mehn-tur-keht/ohr-vohsht/rehn-dur-shay-geht/teewz-ohl-tooh-kot!

Please may I use a telephone?
Telefonálhatok innen?
Teh-leh-foh-nahl-ho-tok een-nehn?

I have had my traveller's cheques/credit cards/ handbag/rucksack/luggage/ wallet/passport/mobile phone stolen
Ellopták az úticsekkjeimet/ hitelkártyámat/táskámat/ hátizsákomat/poggyászomat/ pénztárcámat/útlevélemet/ mobiltelefonomat
Ehl-lohp-tahk oz oo-tee-chehk-yeh-ee-meht/hee-tehl-kahr-tjah-mot/ tahsh-kah-mot/hah-tee-zhay-koh-mot/pohdj-djah-soh-mot/paynz-tahr-tsah-mot/oot-leh-vayl-emet/mo-beel-teh-leh-fonoh-mot

May I please have a copy of the report for my insurance claim?
Megkaphatom a biztosítási igény-bejelentésem másolatát?
Mehg-kop-ho-tom o beez-to-shee-taay-shee ee-ganj-beh-jeh-lehn-tay-shehm mah-sho-lo-taht?

Can you help me, I have lost my daughter/son/my companion(s)
Kérem segítsen, nem találom a lányomat/fiamat/a társa(i)mat
Kay-rehm sheh-geet-shehn, nehm to-lah-lohm o lah-njoh-mot/ fee-o-mot/o tahr-so-(ee)-mot

Please go away/leave me alone!
Menjen innen! Hagyjon engem békén!
Mehn-yehn een-nehn! Hodj-yohn ehn-gehm bay-kayn!

I'm sorry
Bocsánat
Bo-chah-not

I want to contact the British/American/Canadian/ Irish/Australian/ New Zealand/South African consulate
Fel akarom hívni a Brit/ Amerikai/Kanadai/Ausztrál/ Új-Zélandi/Dél-Afrikai Konzulátust
Fehl o-ko-rohm heev-nee o Breet/Amerika-ee/Kah-nah-dah-Eeaust-rahl/Ooy-Zay-lon-dee/Dayl-Of-ree-koee Kohn-zoo-lah-toohsht

I'm/we're/he is/she is/ill/lost/ injured
Beteg vagyok/betegek vagyunk/ő beteg/eltévedtem/ eltévedtünk/ő eltévedt/ megsebesültem/megsebesültünk/megsebesült
Beh-tehg vo-djohk/beh-the-gehk vo-djoonk/ur beh-tehg/ehl-tay-vehd-tehm/ehl-tay-vehd-tewnk/ur ehl-tay-vehdt/mehg-sheh-beh-shewl-tehm/mehg-sheh-beh-shewl-tewnk/ur mehg-sheh-beh-shewlt

They are/ill/lost/injured
Betegek/eltévedtek/ megsebesültek
Beh-the-gehk/ehl-tay-vehd-tehk/mehg-sheh-beh-shewl-tehk

ITALIAN

INTRODUCTION

Italian, the closest to the original Latin of all the 'Romance' languages, is spoken in the southern cantons of Switzerland as well as the Italian peninsula and surrounding islands. Local dialects vary greatly from standard Italian, since Italy consisted of a large number of independent states for most of its history. The pure form of the language, derived from the dialect of Tuscany, is understood and spoken everywhere.

Addresses for Travel and Tourist Information

Australia: *Italian Government Tourist Office,* 46 Market Street, Level 4, Sydney NSW 2000; tel: (02) 9262 1666; fax: (02) 9262 1677.

Canada: *Italian Government Tourist Board,* 175 Bloor St E., Suite 907, South Tower, Toronto, Ontario M4W 3R8; tel: (416) 925 4882; fax: (416) 925 4799.

UK: *Italian State Tourist Board (ENIT),* 1 Princes St, London W1B 2AY; tel: (020) 7408 1254; fax: (020) 7399 3567.

USA: *Italian Government Travel Office,* Rockefeller Center, 630 Fifth Ave, New York, NY 10111; tel: (212) 245 4822. *Italian Government Travel Office,* 500 N. Michigan Ave, Chicago, IL 60611; tel: (312) 644 0990. *Italian Government Travel Office,* 12400 Wilshire Blvd, #550, Los Angeles, CA 90025; tel: (310) 820 0098.

Official tourism website: www.enit.it.

Italy Facts

CAPITAL: Rome (Roma)
CURRENCY: Euro (€). €1 = 100 cents.
OPENING HOURS: Banks: Mon–Fri 0830–1330 and 1445–1615.
Shops: Mon–Fri 0800–1330 and 1600–1900; Sat 0800–1330.
Museums: generally Tues–Sat 0900–1900, Sun 0900–1300.
TELEPHONES: To dial in, +39. Outgoing, 00 plus the country code.
Police, 112. Fire, 115. Ambulance, 113.
PUBLIC HOLIDAYS: 1, 6 Jan; Easter Monday; 1 May; 15 Aug; 1 Nov; 8, 25, 26 Dec. There are also many local saint's days and other festivals.

Technical Language Hints

It is not a difficult language to pick up because its spelling is entirely regular, there are no unexpected quirks of pronunciation, and accented characters are few.

ESSENTIALS

Alphabet and Pronunciation

The letters J (ee lungo), K (cappa), W (voo doppia), X (iks) and Y (ipsilon) are used only to spell foreign words and names.
Note: Double letters, such as ll, are pronounced distinctly as two letters.

	Name	Pronounced
A a	*a*	**short as in hat; long a is a longer version of the same sound, not like the a in father**
B b	*bee*	**like English b**
C c	*chi*	**c or cc are like English k before a, o or u, but like English ch of church before e or i; ch is always like a k**
D d	*dee*	**like English d**
E e	*eh*	**short as in get; long as in hey**
F f	*effeh*	**like English f**
G g	*gee*	**g or gg are like English hard g as in garden before a, o or u, but like English g of gender before e or i; gh is always a hard g; gl is pronounced ly as in schoolyard; gn is pronounced ny as in canyon**
H h	*akka*	**not pronounced**
I i	*ee*	**short i as in sit; long i an ee sound as in machine**
L l	*elley*	**like English l**
M m	*emmeh*	**like English m**
N n	*enneh*	**like English n**
O o	*o*	**short o as in got; long o an aw sound as in shore**
P p	*pee*	**like English p**
Q q	*koo*	**qu always a kw sound, as in queen**
R r	*erreh*	**a trilled r like the Scottish r**
S s	*esseh*	**like English z in lazy; ss is hard s sound, like the s of sea, but pronounced as two distinct ss's**
T t	*tee*	**like English t**
U u	*oo*	**long oo sound as in cool**
V v	*voo*	**like English v**
Z z	*zehta*	**soft z as in zoo, or some times like zz, which is pronounced either as ts, as in cats, or ds, as in lads**

ESSENTIALS

ITALIAN

Basic Words and Phrases

Yes
Si
See

No
No
Noh

Please
Per favore
Perr fahvawreh

Thank you
Grazie
Grahtsyeh

Hello
Salve
Sahlveh

Goodbye.
Arrivederci
Arreevehderrchee

Excuse me
Chiedo scusa
Kyehdaw skooza

Sorry
Scusi
Skoozee

How
Come
Cawme

When
Quando
Kwahndaw

Why
Perché
Perrkeh

What
Che
Keh

Who
Chi
Kee

That's O.K.
Va bene
Vah behneh

Perhaps
Forse
Forrseh

To
A
Ah

From
Da
Dah

Here
Qui
Kwee

There
Là
Lah

I don't understand
Non capisco
Nawn kahpeescaw

I don't speak Italian
Non parlo italiano
Nawn parrlaw itahlyahnaw

Do you speak English?
Parla inglese?
Parrla eenglehzeh?

Can you please write it down?
Potrebbe scriverlo, per favore?
Pawtrebbeh screevehrrlaw, perr fahvawreh?

Please can you speak more slowly?
Potrebbe parlare più lentamente, per favore?
Pawtrebbeh pahrrlahrreh pyoo lehntahmehnteh, perr fahvawreh?

Greetings

Good morning/good afternoon/good evening/goodnight
Buon giorno/buon pomeriggio/buona sera/buona notte
Booawn geeyawrnaw/booawn pawmehreehdjaw/booawnah sehrah/booawnah nawtteh

Pleased to meet you
Piacere
Pyahchehreh

How are you?
Come sta?
Cawmeh stah?

I am well thank you. And you?
Bene, grazie. E lei?
Behneh grahtsyeh. Eh ley?

My name is . . .
Mi chiamo . . .
Mee kyahmaw . . .

This is my friend/ boyfriend/girlfriend/ husband/wife/brother/ sister
Le presento il mio amico/il mio ragazzo/la mia ragazza/ mio marito/mia moglie/ mio fratello/mia sorella
Leh prehsentaw eel myaw ahmeecaw/eel myaw rahgatsaw/lah myah rahgatsa/myaw mahreetaw/myah mawlyeh/myaw fraht ellaw/myah sawrella

Where are you travelling to?
Dov' è diretto?
Dawveh deerettaw?

I am/we are going to . . .
Vado/andiamo a . . .
Vahdaw/ahndyahmaw ah . . .

How long are you travelling for?
Per quanto tempo sarà in viaggio?
Perr kwahntaw tempaw sahrah een veehadjaw?

Where do you come from?
Da dove viene?
Dah dawveh vyehneh?

I am/we are from Australia/ Britain/Canada/America/ New Zealand
Vengo/veniamo da Australia/Gran Bretagna/ Canada/America/Nuova Zelanda
Vehngaw/vehnyahmaw dah Grahn Ahoostrahlia/Brehtanya/Cahnada/ Ahmehreeca/Noohawva Tsehlahnda

We are on holiday
Siamo in vacanza
Seeyahmaw een vahkahntsah

This is our first visit here
Questa è la nostra prima visita qui
Kwehstah eh lah nawstrah preemah veeseetah kwee

How old are you?
Quanti anni ha (formal)/hai (informal)?
Kwantee an-nee a/ayee?

I am ... years old
Ho ... anni
Aw ... an-nee

I am a business person/ doctor/journalist/manual worker/administrator/ scientist/student/teacher
Sono imprenditore/medico/ giornalista/ lavoratore/scienziato (scienziata fem.)/studente (studentessa fem.)/insegnante
Sawnaw eemprendeetawreh/mehdeekoh/ jornaleesta/lahvohrahtawreh/ shee-entseeahtaw (shee-ntseeahta)/ stoodenteh (stoodentes-sa) /insenyanteh

I am waiting for my husband/wife/boyfriend/ girlfriend
Sto aspettando mio marito/mia moglie/il mio fidanzato/la mia fidanzata
Staw ahspehtahndaw meeaw mahreetaw/meeah mawlyeh/eel meeaw feedahntsahtaw/lah meeah feedahntsahtah

Would you like/May I have a cigarette?
Vuole una sigaretta?/Potrebbe darmi una sigaretta?
Vooh leh oona seegahretta?/Pawtrebbeh darrmee oona seegahretta?

Do you mind if I smoke?
Le spiace se fumo?
Leh speehacheh seh foomaw?

Do you have a light?
Mi fa accendere?
Me fah acchendereh?

Days

Monday
Lunedì
Loonehdee

Tuesday
Martedì
Marrtehdee

Wednesday
Mercoledì
Merrcawlehdee

Thursday
Giovedì
Jawvehdee

Friday
Venerdì
Venerrdee

Saturday
Sabato
Sahbahtaw

Sunday
Domenica
Dawmehneeca

Morning
Mattino
Mahtteenaw

Afternoon
Pomeriggio
Pawmehreedjaw

Evening
Sera
Sehra

Night
Notte
Notteh

Yesterday/Today/Tomorrow
Ieri/Oggi/Domani
Yeree/Odjee/Dawmahnee

Numbers

Zero
Zero
Tsehraw

One
Uno
Oonaw

Two
Due
Dweh

Three
Tre
Treh

Four
Quattro
Kwahttraw

Five
Cinque
Cheenkweh

Six
Sei
Say

Seven
Sette
Setteh

Eight
Otto
Ottaw

Nine
Nove
Noveh

Ten
Dieci
Dyehchee

Eleven
Undici
Oondeechee

Twelve
Dodici
Dawdeechee

Thirteen
Tredici
Trehdeechee

Fourteen
Quattordici
Kwahttrrdeechee

Fifteen
Quindici
Kweendeechee

Sixteen
Sedici
Sedeechee

Seventeen
Diciassette
Deechassetteh

Eighteen
Diciotto
Deechottaw

Nineteen
Diciannove
Deechannoveh

Twenty
Venti
Ventee

Twenty-one
Ventuno
Ventoonaw

Twenty-two
Ventidue
Venteedweh

Thirty
Trenta
Trenta

Forty
Quaranta
Kwahrahnta

Fifty
Cinquanta
Cheenkwahnta

Sixty
Sessanta
Sessahnta

Seventy
Settanta
Settahnta

Eighty
Ottanta
Ottahnta

Ninety
Novanta
Novahnta

One hundred
Cento
Chentaw

Five hundred
Cinquecento
Cheenkwech-entaw

One thousand
Mille
Meelleh

One million
Un milione
Oon meellyawneh

Time

What time is it?
Che ore sono?
Keh awreh sawnaw?

It is . . .
Sono le . . .
Sawnaw leh . . .

9.00
Nove
Noveh

9.05
Nove e cinque
Noveh eh cheenkweh

9.15
Nove e quindici
Noveh eh kweendechee

9.20
Nove e venti
Noveh eh ventee

9.30
Nove e trenta
Noveh eh trenta

9.35
Nove e trentacinque
Noveh eh trentacheenkweh

9.40
Nove e quaranta
Noveh eh kwahranta

9.45
Nove e quarantacinque
Noveh eh kwahran tacheenkweh

9.50
Nove e cinquanta
Noveh eh cheenkwahnta

9.55
Nove e cinquantacinque
Noveh eh cheenkwahntacheenkweh

12.00/midday/midnight
Dodici/mezzogiorno/mezzanotte
Dohdychee/metsawjorrnaw/metsanotteh

Money

I would like to change these traveller's cheques/this currency
Vorrei cambiare questi assegni turistici/questa valuta
Vawrray cahmbyahreh kwestee assenee tooreesteechee/kwesta vahloota

How much commission do you charge? (What is the service charge?)
Qual' è la vostra commissione?
Kwal eh lah vostra commeesiawneh?

Can I obtain money with my Mastercard?
Posso incassare contanti con la Mastercard?
Pawssaw eencassahreh cawntahntee con lah Mastercard?

Where is the nearest ATM?
Dov'è il bancomat più vicino?
Dawveh eel bankomaht pyoo veecheenaw?

My name is ... Some money has been wired to here for me to collect
Mi chiamo ... Mi hanno fatto un vaglia telegrafico e vorrei ritirarlo
Mee keeahmaw ... Mee annaw fattaw oon valyah tehlehgrafeekaw e vorreyee reeteerahrlaw

ARRIVING AND DEPARTING

Airport

Excuse me, where is the check-in desk for ... airline?
Mi scusi, dov' è il banco accettazioni per la linea aerea ...?
Mee scoozee, dawveh eel bahnkaw ahchettatsyawnee perr lah leenayah ah-aerrhayah ...?

What is the boarding gate/ time for my flight?
Qual' è il cancello di imbarco/ l'orario del mio volo?
Kwaaleh eel kahnchehlaw dee ihmbahrcaw/lawrahreeaw del meeoh vawloh?

How long is the delay likely to be?
Qual' è il ritardo previsto?
Kwaaleh eel rreehtahrdaw prehveestaw?

Where is the duty-free shop?
Dov' è il duty-free?
Dawveh eel duty-free?

Which way is the luggage reclaim?
Dove si trova il recupero bagagli?
Dawveh see trawvah eel rehkupehrraw bahgahlyee?

I have lost my luggage. Please can you help?
Ho perso i bagagli. Può aiutarmi?
Aw pairsaw ee baggalyee. Poo-oh ayootarmee?

I am flying to ...
Ho un volo per ...
Aw oon vawlaw pair ...

Where is the bus for the city centre?
Dove posso prendere l'autobus per il centro?
Dawveh pawssaw prendereh lahutobhuss perr eel chentraw?

Trains and Boats

Where is the ticket office/ information desk?
Dov'è la biglietteria/l'ufficio informazioni?
Dawv e h lah eelyetteryha/ looffeechaw eenformahtseeawnee?

Which platform does the train to ... depart from?
Da quale binario parte il treno per ...?
Dah kwahley binahriaw pahrteh eel trehnaw pair ...?

Which platform does the speedboat/ferry to ... depart from?
Da quale molo parte l'aliscafo/il ferryboat per ...?
Dah kwahley mawlaw pahrteh laliscafaw/eel ferryboat pair ...?

Where is platform ...?
Dov' è il binario ...?
Dawvèh eel binahriaw ...?

When is the next train/boat to ...?
A che ora parte il prossimo treno/la prossima nave per...?
A keh awrah pahrteh eel prossimo trehnaw/la prossimah nahveh pair...?

Is there a later train/boat to ...?
C'è un treno/una nave per ... che parte più tardi?
Cheh oon trehnaw/oona nahveh pair ... keh pahrteh pyoo tardee?

Notices and Signs

Carrozza rinfreschi
Carrotsa reenfreskee
Buffet (Dining) Car

Autobus
Ahootawboos
Bus

Acqua potabile/non potabile
Aqua pawtahbeeleh/non pawtahbeeleh
Drinking/Non-drinking water

Entrata
Entrahta
Entrance

Uscita
Oosheeta
Exit

Ospedale
Ospedahleh
Hospital

Informazioni
Eenformahtsyawnee
Information

Bagaglio depositato
Bahgalyaw depawseetahtaw
Left Luggage (Baggage Claim)

Armadietti per bagagli
Armahdyettee perr baghgalee
Luggage Lockers

Ufficio postale
Ooffeechaw pawstahleh
Post Office

Binario
Binahriaw
Platform

Stazione ferroviaria
Stahtsyawneh ferrawvyarya
Railway (Railroad) Station

Aeroporto
Ahaerrhawpawrrtaw
Airport

Stazione di polizia
Stahtsiawneh dee politseeah
Police station

Porto
Pawrrtaw
Port

Ristorante
Reestawrahnteh
Restaurant

Per fumatori/non fumatori
Perr foomahtawree/non foom-ahtawree
Smoking/Non-Smoking

Telefono
Telehfawnaw
Telephone

Biglietteria
Beelyetterya
Ticket Office

Banco accettazioni
Bahnkaw ahchettahtsyawnee
Check-in Desk

Orario
Awraryaw
Timetable (Schedule)

Bagni
Banyee
Toilets (Restrooms)

Signore/Signori
Seenyawreh/Seenyawree
Ladies/Gentlemen

Metropolitana
Metrawpawleetahna
Underground (Subway)

Sala d'attesa
Sahla dahttehsa
Waiting Room

Buying a Ticket

I would like a first-class/second-class single (one-way)/return (round-trip) ticket to . . .
Vorrei un biglietto di sola andata/andata e ritorno di prima classe/di seconda classe per ...
Vawrray oon beelyettaw dee sawlah ahndahta/ahndahta eh reetawrnaw dee preema classeh/dee seconda classeh perr . . .

Is it an express (fast) train/bus?
È un treno/autobus espresso?
E oon trehnaw/a-ootoboos ehspressaw

Is my rail pass valid on this train/ferry/bus?
Il mio abbonamento è valido su questo treno/traghetto/autobus?
Eel meeoh abhawnahmentaw eh vahleedhaw soo kwestaw trehnaw/trahgehtaw/ahootawboos?

I would like an aisle/window seat
Vorrei un posto vicino al corridoio/al finestrino
Vawrray oon pawstaw veecheenaw ahl correedoyaw/ahl feenestreenaw

No smoking/smoking, please
Per favore nello scompartimento per fumatori/non fumatori
Perr fahvawreh nehllo scomparteementaw peer foomahtawree /non foomahtawree

We would like to sit together
Vorremmo sedere vicini
Vawrremmaw sehdehreh veecheenee

I would like to make a seat reservation
Vorrei prenotare un posto.
Vawrray prehnawtahreh oon pawstaw

I would like to reserve a couchette/sleeper for one person/two people/my family
Vorrei prenotare una cuccetta/ una cabina per una persona/ due persone/la mia famiglia
Vawrray prehnawtareh oona coocchetta/oona cahbeena perr oona perrsawna/dweh perrsawneh/lah myah fahmeelya

I would like to reserve a cabin
Vorrei prenotare una cabina
Vawrray prehnawtahrreh oonah kahbeenah

Timetables (Schedules)

Arrivare
Arreevahreh
Arrive

Ferma a
Ferrma ah
Calls (Stops) at

Servizio ristorazione
Serveetsyaw reestohrahtsiawneh
Catering Service

Cambiare a
Cahmbyareh ah
Change at

Coincidenza/Via
Coincheedentsa/Veeha
Connection/Via

Giornaliero
Jawrnahlyeraw
Daily

Ogni 40 minuti
Awnee 40 meenootee
Every 40 minutes

Prima classe
Preema classeh
First Class

Ogni ora
Awnyee awra
Hourly

Si raccomanda la prenotazione dei posti
See rahckawmahnda la prehnawtatsyawneh day pawstee
Seat reservations are recommended

Seconda classe
Secawnda classeh
Second Class

Supplemento esigibile
Soopplehmentaw eseejeebeeleh
Supplement Payable

I T A L I A N

Luggage

How much will it cost to send (ship) my luggage in advance?
Quanto costa la spedizione anticipata del mio bagaglio?
Kwahntaw cawstah la spehdeet-syawneh ahnteecheepahta del myaw bahgalyaw?

Where is the left luggage (baggage claim) office?
Dov' è il deposito bagagli?
Dawv eh eel dehpawseetaw bahgahlyee?

What time do you open/ close?
A che ora aprite/chiudete?
Ah keh awra ahpreeteh/kewdehteh?

Where are the luggage trolleys (carts)?
Dove sono i carrelli portabagagli?
Dawveh sawnaw ee carrellee porrtahbahgalee?

Where are the lockers?
Dove sono gli armadietti?
Dawveh sawnaw lyee ahrmahdyetee?

I have lost my locker key
Ho perso la chiave del mio armadietto
Aw perrsaw lah kyahveh del myaw armahdyettaw

On Board

Is this seat free?
È libero questo posto?
Eh leebehraw kwestaw pawstaw?

Excuse me, you are sitting in my reserved seat
Scusi, Lei siede nel mio posto riservato
Scoozee, Lay syedeh nel myaw pawstaw reeservahtaw

Which station is this?
Che stazione è?
Keh stahtsyawneh eh?

What time is this train/bus/ ferry/flight due to arrive/ depart?
A che ora è previsto l'arrivo/ la partenza di questo treno/ autobus/volo?
Ah keh awrah eh prehveestaw lahrreevaw/lah pahrrtehntsah dee kwestaw trehnaw/ ahootawboos/vawlaw?

Travelling with Children

Do you have a high chair/ babysitting service/cot?
Ha un seggiolone/dei baby sitter/un lettino?
Ah oon sedjawlawneh/day baby sitter/oon letteenaw?

Where is the nursery/ playroom?
Dov' è la camera dei bambini/la stanza dei giochi?
Dawveh lah cahmera day bahmbee-nee/las stantsa day jawkee?

Where can I warm the baby's bottle?
Dove posso riscaldare il biberon?
Dawveh pawssaw reescahldareh eel beebehron?

Customs and Passports

Passaporti per favore!
Passaporrtee perr fahvawreh!
Passports, please!

I have nothing to declare/wine/spirits (alcohol)/ tobacco to declare
Non ho nulla da dichiarare/ho vino/alcolici/tabacco da dichiarare
Non aw noollah dah deekyarareh/ aw veenaw/ahlcoleechee/tahbah ckaw dah deekyarareh

I will be staying for ... days/ weeks/months
Mi tratterrò per ... giorni/ settimane/mesi
Mee trahtterraw perr ...jawrnee/set-teemahneh/mehzee

SIGHTSEEING

Asking the Way

Excuse me, do you speak English?
Mi scusi, parla inglese?
Mee scoozee, parrla eenglehzeh?

Excuse me, can you help me please?
Mi scusi, potrebbe gentilmente aiutarmi?
Mee skoozee, potrebbeh jenteelmenteh ayootarmee?

Where is the Tourist Information Office?
Dov' è l'Ufficio informazioni turistiche?
Dawv e h l'ooffeechaw eenforrmaht-syawnee tooreesteekeh?

Excuse me, is this the right way to ...?
Mi scusi, è questa la strada per ...?
Mee scoozee, eh kwehstah lah strahda perr ...?

...the cathedral/the Tourist Information Office/the castle/ the old town
... la cattedrale/l'ufficio informazioni turistiche/il castel-lo/la città vecchia
... lah kahttehdrahleh/looffeechaw eenforrmahtsyawnee tooreesteekeh/ eel kahstehllaw/lah cheetta vehkyah

Can you tell me the way to the railway (railroad) station/bus station/taxi rank (stand)/city centre (downtown)/beach?
Sa indicarmi la strada per andare alla stazione ferroviaria/ alla stazione degli autobus/al posteggio dei tassì/al centro città/alla spiaggia?
Sah eendeecarrmee lah strahda perr ahndarch ahlla stahtsyawneh ferrawvyarya/ahlla stahtsyawneh delee ahootawboos/ahl pawstedjaw day tassee/ahl chentraw cheetteh/ahlla spyadjya?

Prenda la prossima/la seconda/ a sinistra/a destra/Vada sempre diritto
Prehnda lah prawsseema/lah secawnda ah seeneestra/ah destra/Vahda sempreh deereettaw
First/second/left/right/go straight ahead

All'angolo/al semaforo
Al langawlaw/al sehmahforaw
At the corner/at the traffic lights

SIGHTSEEING

I T A L I A N

Where is the nearest police station/post office?
Dov' è il più vicino posto di polizia/ufficcio postale?
Dawv e h eel pyoo veecheenaw pawstaw dee pawleetsya/ ooffechaw pawstahle?

Is it near/far?
È vicino/lontano?
E veecheenaw/lontahnaw?

Do I need to take a taxi/catch a bus?
Devo prendere un tassì/l'autobus?
Dehvaw prendehreh oon tassee/lahootawboos?

Do you have a map?
Ha una cartina?
Ah oonah carteenah?

Can you point to it on my map?
Può indicarmelo sulla mappa?
Pooh o h eendeecarrmehlaw soolla mappa?

Thank you for your help
Grazie dell'aiuto
Grahtsyeh dell ahyootaw

How do I reach the motorway/main road?
Come si arriva all'autostrada/ strada principale?
Cawmeh see ahrreevah alahootaw-strahdah/strahdah preencheep-ahleh?

I think I have taken the wrong turning
Penso di aver preso la svolta sbagliata
Pehnsaw dee avehr prehsaw lah svawltah sbahlyahtah

I am looking for this address
Sto cercando questo indirizzo
Staw cherkahndaw kwestaw eendeereetsaw

I am looking for the ... hotel.
Sto cercando l'hotel ...
Staw cherkahndaw lotehl ...

How far is it to .. . from here?
Quanto dista ... da qui?
Kwantaw deestah ... dah kwee?

Vada dritto per ... chilometri
Vahdah dreetaw perr ... keehlawme-htree
Carry straight on for ... kilometres

Prenda la prossima svolta a destra/sinistra
Prehndah lah prawseehmah svawl-tah ah dehstrah/seeneestrah
Take the next turning on the right/left

Giri a destra/sinistra al prossimo incrocio/semaforo
Djyree ah dehstrah/seeneestrah ahl prawseemaw eencrawchyaw/ sehmahfawraw
Turn right/left at the next crossroads/traffic lights

Sta andando nella direzione sbagliata
Stah ahndahndaw nehllah deereht-syawneh sbahlyahtah
You are going in the wrong direction

Where is the cathedral/ church/museum/pharmacy?
Dov' è la cattedrale/la chiesa/il museo/la farmacia?
Dawv lah cattehdrahleh/lah

kyehza/eel moozehaw/lah farmahchheeah?

How much is the admission/entrance charge?
Qual' è la tariffa d'ingresso?
Kwahleh lah tahreeffa deengressaw?

Is there a discount for children/students/senior citizens?
I bambini/gli studenti/i pensionati hanno diritto a una riduzione?
Ee bahmbeenee/lee stoodentee/ee pensyawnahtee annaw deereettaw ah oona reedootsyawneh?

What time does the next guided tour (in English) start?
A che ora ha inizio la prossima visita guidata (in Inglese)?
Ah keh awra ah eeneetsyaw lah prosseemah veeseeta goohedahta (in eenglehzeh)?

One/two adults/children, please
Un adulto/due adulti/due bambini per favore
Oon ahdooltaw/dweh ahdooltee/dweh bahmbeenee perr fahvawreh

May I take photographs here?
Posso fare fotografie qui?
Payssaw fahreh fotografyeh kwee?

At the Tourist Office

Do you have a map of the town/area?
Ha una mappa della città/della zona?
Ah oona mahppa della cheettah/della zawna?

Do you have a list of accommodation?
Ha un elenco di alloggi?
Ah oon ehlehnkaw dee ahlawdjee?

Can I reserve accommodation?
Posso prenotare qui l'alloggio?
Pawssaw prenotahre kwee lallodjaw?

ACCOMMODATION

Hotels

I have a reservation in the name of . . .
Ho una prenotazione per . . .
Aw oona prehnawtahtsyawneh perr

I wrote to/faxed/telephoned you last month/last week
Vi ho scritto/inviato un fax/telefonato il mese scorso/la settimana scorsa
Vee haw skreehtaw/eenveeahtaw oon fax/tehlehfonahtaw eel mehseh skawhrsaw/lah sehteemahnah skawrsah

Do you have any rooms free?
Avete camere libere?
Ahvehteh kahmehreh leebehreh?

I would like to reserve a single/double room with/without a bath/shower
Vorrei prenotare una camera singola/matrimoniale con/senza bagno/doccia
Vawrray prehnawtahreh oona cahmehra seengawlah/mahtreemawnyahleh con/sentsa bahnyaw/doccha

I T A L I A N

I would like bed/breakfast/ (room and) full board
Vorrei una camera con colazione/pensione completa
Vawrray oona cahmehra con cawlahtsyawneh/pensyawneh com-plehta

How much is it per night?
Quant' è per notte?
Kwahnt e h perr notteh?

Is breakfast included?
È compresa la colazione?
Eh comprehsa lah cawlatsyawneh?

Do you have any cheaper rooms?
Ha delle camere più economiche?
Ah delleh cahmehreh pyoo ehcawnohmikeh?

I would like to see/take the room
Vorrei vedere/prendere la camera
Vorreyi vehdereh/prendereh

I would like to stay for ... nights
Vorrei alloggiare per ... notti
Vawrray allawdjahreh perr ... nottee

The shower/light/tap/hot water doesn't work
La doccia/luce/rubinetto/acqua calda non funziona
Lah dawcheeah/loocheh/roobeeneht-taw/ahkwah caldah nawn foontsyawnah

At what time/where is breakfast served?
A che ora/dove viene servita la colazione?
Ah keh awra/dawveh vyeneh ser-rveeta lah cawlahtsyawneh?

What time do I have to check out?
A che ora devo lasciare libera la camera?
Ah keh awra dehvaw lahshareh lee-behra lah cahmehra?

Can I have the key to room number ...?
Posso avere la chiave della camera numero ...?
Payssaw ahvehreh lah keeyahveh dehlah noohmehraw ...?

My room number is . . .
La mia camera ha il numero . . .
Lah myah cahmehra ah eel noomehraw . . .

My room is not satisfactory/ not clean enough/too noisy. Please can I change rooms?
La camera non è di mio gradimento/non è molto pulita/è troppo rumorosa. Potrei averne un'altra per cortesia?
Lah kahmerah nawn e dee meeaw gradeementaw/nawn e moltaw poolitah/e troppaw roomorawsah. Potreyi avairneh oon altrah pair kortezeeah?

Where is the bathroom?
Dov'è il bagno?
Dawveh eel banyaw?

Do you have a safe for valuables?
C'è una cassetta di sicurezza per gli oggetti di valore?
Cheh oonah kassettah dee seekooretsah pairl-yi odjetti dee valawreh?

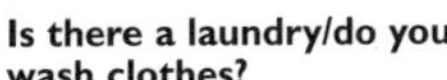

Is there a laundry/do you wash clothes?
C'è una lavanderia/è possibile lavare gli abiti?
Cheh oona lavandereeah/e posseebeeleh lavahrehl-yi ahbeetee?

I would like an air-conditioned room
Desidero una camera con aria condizionata
Dehseedehraw oona kahmerah con ahreeah condeetsionahtah

Do you accept traveller's cheques/credit cards?
Accettate assegni turistici/carte di credito?
Achetahteh asehnyee tooreesteechee/kahrrteh dee krehdeehtaw?

May I have the bill please?
Mi dà il conto per favore
Mee dah eel cawntaw perr fahvawreh

Excuse me, I think there is a mistake in this bill
Mi scusi, credo ci sia un errore nel conto
Mee scozee, kredaw chee syah oon errawreh nel cawntaw

Youth Hostels

How much is a dormitory bed per night?
Quant' è un letto in dormitorio per notte?
Kwahnteh oon lettaw een dormeetawryaw perr notteh?

I am/am not an HI member
Sono/non sono membro dell'Associazione Internazionale Ostelli della Gioventù
Sawnaw/non sawnaw membraw dell Assawchahtsyawne Eenterrnahtsyawnahleh Ostelee della Jovehntoo

May I use my own sleeping bag?
Posso usare il mio sacco a pelo?
Pawssaw oozahreh eel myaw saccaw ah pehlaw?

What time do you lock the doors at night?
A che ora chiudete le porte la notte?
Ah keh awra kewdehte leh porrteh lah notteh?

Camping

May I camp for the night/two nights?
Posso accamparmi qui per la notte/due notti?
Pawssaw accahmparmee kwee perr lah notteh/dweh nottee?

Where can I pitch my tent?
Dove posso piantare la tenda?
Dawveh pawssaw pyahntareh lah tenda?

How much does it cost for one night/week?
Qual' è la tariffa per una notte/una settimana?
Kwaleh lah tahreeffa perr oona notteh/oona setteemahna?

Where are the washing facilities?
Dove sono le lavanderie?
Dawveh sawnaw leh lavahndehryeh?

Is there a restaurant/ supermarket/swimming pool on site/nearby?
C'è un ristorante/un supermercato/una piscina al campeggio/nelle vicinanze?
Cheh oon reestawrahnteh/oon soop-errmerrcahtaw/oona peesheena ahl cahmpedjaw/nelleh veecheenah-ntseh?

Do you have a safety deposit box?
C'è una cassaforte?
Cheh oona cassahforrteh?

EATING AND DRINKING

Cafés and Bars

I would like a cup of/two cups of/another coffee/tea
Vorrei una tazza di/due tazze di/un altro caffè/tè
Vawrray oona tatsa dee/dweh tatseh dee/oon ahltraw calfe/teh

With/without milk/sugar
Con/senza latte/zucchero
Con/sentsa latteh/tsoockehraw

I would like a bottle/glass/ two glasses of mineral water/ red wine/white wine, please
Per cortesia, vorrei una bottiglia/un bicchiere/due bicchieri d'acqua minerale/ vino rosso/vino bianco
Peer corrtehzya, vawrray oona bot-teelya/oon beeckyereh/dweh beecky-eree daqua meenehrahleh/veenaw rawssaw/veenaw byahncaw

I would like a beer/two beers, please
Per cortesia, vorrei una birra/due birre
Perr corrteshzya, vawrray oona beerra/dweh beerreh

Please may I have some ice?
Può darmi del ghiaccio?
Poohoh darrmee del ghyacchaw?

Do you have any matches/ cigarettes/cigars?
Vendete fiammiferi/sigarette/ sigari?
Vendehteh fyammeefehree, see-gahretteh, seegaree?

Restaurants

Can you recommend a good/ cheap restaurant in this area?
Può raccomandarmi un buon ristorante/un ristorante economico in questa zona?
Poohoh raccomahndarmee oon boohon reestawrahnteh/oon reestawrahnteh ehcawnawmeecaw een kwesta zawna?

I would like a table for ... people
Vorrei un tavolo per ... persone
Vawrray oon tahvawlaw perr ... perr-sawneh

Do you have a non-smoking area?
Avete un'area non fumatori?
Ahvehteh oonahrreyah nawn foom-ahttawree?

Waiter/Waitress!
Cameriere/cameriera!
Cahmehryereh/cahmehryera!

Excuse me, please may we order?
Mi scusi, possiamo ordinare per favore?
Mee skoozee, posseeahmaw ordeenahreh perr fahvawreh?

Do you have a set menu/ children's menu/wine list in English?
Ha un menù fisso/un menù per bambini/una lista dei vini in Inglese?
Ah oon mehnoo feessaw/oon mehnoo perr bambeenee/oona leesta day veenee in eenglehzeh?

Do you have any vegetarian dishes?
Per favore, ha dei piatti vegetariani?
Perr fahvawreh, ah day pyattee vehgehtahryanee?

Do you have any local specialities?
Avete qualche specialità locale?
Ahvehteh kwalkeh spehchiahleehtah lawkahleh?

Are vegetables included?
Sono incluse anche le verdure?
Sawnaw eenclooseh ahnkeh leh vehrdooreh?

Could I have it well-cooked/medium/rare please?
Potrei averlo ben cotto/ mediamente cotto/poco cotto, per favore?
Pawtray ahvehrlaw behn cawtaw/mehdeeyahmehnteh cawtaw/pawcaw cawtaw perr fah-vawreh?

What does this dish consist of?
Quali sono gli ingredienti di questo piatto?
Kwahlee sawnaw lee eengrehdyehn-tee dee kwestaw pyattaw?

I am a vegetarian. Does this contain meat?
Sono vegetariano/vegetariana (fem.). Contiene carne?
Sawnaw vejetahreeahnaw/veje-tahreeahnah). Contyehneh kahrneh?

I do not eat nuts/dairy products/meat/fish
Non mangio noci/latticini/carne/ pesce
Nawn manjaw nawchee/latteechee-nee/kahrneh/pehsheh

Not (very) spicy, please
Non (molto) piccante, per favore
Nawn (moltaw) peek-kanteh, pair favawreh

I would like the set menu, please
Vorrei il menù fisso
Vawrray eel mehnoo feessaw

We have not been served yet
Non ci hanno ancora serviti
Non chee annaw ahncawra serrveetee

Please bring a plate/knife/fork.
Gentilmente, può portarmi un piatto/un coltello/una forchetta?
Jenteelmenteh, poo-oh portahmee oon piahttaw/oon coltellaw/oona forkehttah?

ITALIAN

EATING AND DRINKING

Excuse me, this is not what I ordered
Mi scusi, questo non è quello che ho ordinato
Mee scoozee, kwehstaw nawn eh kwellaw keh haw awrdeehnahtaw

May I have some/some more bread/water/coffee/tea?
Può darmi del/dell'altro pane/caffè/tè?
Poo-oh darrmee del/dellahltraw pahneh/caffeh/teh?

May I have the bill, please?
Mi dà il conto, per favore
Mee dah eel cawntaw, perr fahvawreh

Does this bill include service?
Il conto include il servizio?
Eel cawntaw eencloodeh eel serrveetsyaw?

Do you accept traveller's cheques/Mastercard/US dollars?
Accettate assegni turistici/Mastercard/dollari USA?
Acchettahteh assenee tooreesteechee/Mastercard/ dollahree oo ez ah?

Can I have a receipt, please?
Potrei avere la ricevuta, per favore?
Pawtray ahvehreh lah reechevootah, perr fahvawreh?

Where is the toilet (restroom), please?
Dov' è il bagno, per cortesia?
Dawveh eell banyaw, perr corrtezya?

On the Menu

Colazione/Pranzo/Cena
Colahtseeawneh/Prandzaw/ Chehnah
Breakfast/Lunch/Dinner

Primi piatti
Preemee pyattee
First courses

Zuppe
Zooppeh
Soups

Piatti principali
Pyattee preencheepahlee
Main courses

Piatti di pesce
Pyattee dee pesheh
Fish dishes

Piatti di carne
Pyattee dee kahrneh
Meat dishes

Manzo
Mantsaw
Beef

Bistecca
Beestekkah
Steak

Maiale
Myahleh
Pork

Vitello
Veetellaw
Veal

Pollo
Pawllaw
Chicken

Agnello
Anyellaw
Lamb

Prosciutto
Proshoot-taw
Ham

Piatti vegetariani
Pyattee vehjehtaryanee
Vegetarian dishes

Verdure
Vairdooreh
Vegetables

Patatine fritte
Pahtahteeneh freet-teh
Chips (french fries)

Patate lesse/rosolate/passate
Pahtahteh lesseh/rawsawlahteh/ passahteh
Boiled/sauté/mashed potatoes

Riso
Reezaw
Rice

Formaggio
Fawrmahdyiaw
Cheese

Dessert
Dehssehrt
Desserts

Gelato
Jelahtaw
Ice cream

Dolci/torte
Dochee/tawrteh
Cakes

Paste
Pasteh
Pastries

Frutta
Froot-tah
Fruit

Pane
Pahneh
Bread

Panini
Pahneenee
Rolls

Toast
Toast
Toast

Burro
Boorraw
Butter

Sale/pepe
Sahleh/pepeh
Salt/pepper

Zucchero
Tsookeraw
Sugar

Menu fisso
Menoo feessaw
Set Menu

Specialità
Spehcheeyahleeht»h
Specialities

Specialità locali
Specheeahlitah lawkahlee
Local specialities

Lista dei vini
Leestah dehyi veenee
Wine list

Vini rossi
Veenee raws-see
Red wines

Vini bianchi
Veenee beeankee
White wines

Vini rosati
Veenee rawzahtee
Rosé wines

Vini frizzanti
Veenee freetsantee
Sparkling wines

Birra
Beerah
Beer

Birra in bottiglia/alla spina
Beerah in botteelyah/alla speenah
Bottled beer/draught (draft) beer

Bevande non alcoliche
Bevandeh nawn alkoleekeh
Non-alcoholic drinks

Acqua minerale
Akkwah meenerahleh
Mineral water

Succhi di frutta
Sookkee dee froot-tah
Fruit juices

Succo d'arancia
Sookaw darancheeah
Orange juice

Limonata
Leemonahtah
Lemonade

Ghiaccio
Gyeeahchaw
Ice

Caffé macchiato/caffé lungo/caffé espresso
Kaffeh makkeeahtaw/kaffeh loongaw/kaffeh espressaw
White coffee/black coffee/espresso coffee

Tè con latte/con limone
Teh con lahtteh/con leemawneh
Tea with milk/with lemon

Cioccolata
Chokkolahtah
Chocolate (drink)

Latte
Lahtteh
Milk

Spuntino/pasto leggero
Spoonteenaw/pastaw ledjairaw
Snacks/Light meals

Insalate
Insalahteh
Salads

Panini imbottiti/sandwich
Pahneenee imbotteetee/sandwich
Sandwiches

Uova
Wawvah
Eggs

Salsiccia
Salseecheeah
Sausage

Uova sode/fritte/sbattute
Wawvah sawdeh/freetteh/sbattooteh
Boiled/fried/scrambled eggs

Typical Local Dishes

Bucatini all'amatriciana
Bookateenee ahl lahmah-treech-ahnah
Pasta tubes in a pepper and tomato sauce

Saltimbocca alla romana
Saltimbokka ahl-lah rawmahnah
Veal with a slice of ham, cheese and sage

Bistecca alla fiorentina
Beestekka al-lah feeohrehnteenah
Grilled steak with pepper, lemon juice and parsley

Fegato alla veneziana
Fehgahtoh ahl-lah vehnehtseeahnah
Thin calf's liver fried with onions

Zabaglione
Dzahbahlyohneh
Warm dessert of egg yolks, Marsala wine and sugar

GETTING AROUND

Public Transport

Where is the bus stop/coach station/nearest metro (subway) station?
Dov' è la fermata degli autobus/la stazione delle corriere/la più vicina stazione della metropolitana?
Dawveh lah ferrmahta delee ahootawboos/lah stahtsyawneh delleh corryereh/lah pyoo veecheena stahtsyawneh della metropawlee-tahna?

When is the next/last bus to ..?
A che ora è il prossimo/l'ultimo autobus per ...?
Ah keh awra e h eel prawssemaw/loolteemaw ahootawboos perr ...?

How much is the fare to the city centre (downtown)/ railway (railroad) station/ airport?
Qual' è la tariffa per il centro/ la città stazione ferroviaria/ l'aeroporto?
Kwahleh lah tahreeffa perr eel chentraw cheett»h/lah stahtsyawne ferrawvyarya/l'aheraoporrtaw?

Will you tell me when to get off?
Può dirmi quando devo scendere?
Pooh-oh deerrmee kwahndaw dehvaw shendehreh?

Does this bus go to ...?
Quest'autobus va a ...?
Kwest ahootawboos vah ah ...?

Which number bus goes to ?
Quale autobus va a ...?
Kwahleh ah-ootawboos vah ah ...?

May I have a single (one-way)/return (round-trip)/ day ticket/book of tickets?
Vorrei un biglietto di sola andata/di andata e ritorno valido per un giorno/un blocchetto di biglietti
Vawrray oon beelyettaw dee sawla ahndahta/dee ahndahta eh reetorrnaw vahleedaw perr oon jawrnaw/ oon blawckettaw dee beelyettee

Taxis (Tassi)

I would like to go to ... How much will it cost?
Vorrei andare a ... , quant' è?
Vawrray ahnahre ah ... kwahnteh?

Please may I stop here
Fermi qui, per cortesia
Ferrmee koohee perr corrtehzya

I would like to order a taxi today/tomorrow/at 2pm to go from ... to ...
Vorrei prenotare un tassì per oggi/per domani/per le quattordici che mi porti da ... a ...
Vawrray prehnawtahreh oon tassee perr odjee/perrdawmahnee/perr leh kwahttorrdeechee keh mee porrtee dah ... ah . . .

Entertainment

Can you recommend a good bar/nightclub?
Può raccomandarmi un buon bar/locale notturno?
Pooh-oh rahccawmahdarrmee oon bwon barr/lawcahleh nawttoorrnaw?

Do you know what is on at the cinema (playing at the movies)/theatre at the moment?
Conosce il programma del cinema/teatro?
Cawnawsheh eel prawgramma del ceenema/tehatraw?

I would like to book (purchase) ... tickets for the matinee/evening performance on Monday
Vorrei prenotare ... posti per la matinée/lo spettacolo serale di lunedì
Vawrray prehnawtahre ... pawstee perr lah mateeneh/law spettah-cawlaw sehrahleh dee loonehdee

What time does the film/ performance start?
A che ora incomincia il film/lo spettacolo?
Ah keh awra eencawmeencha eel film/law spettahcawlaw?

COMMUNICATIONS

Post

How much will it cost to send a letter/postcard/this package to Britain/Ireland/ America/Canada/Australia/ New Zealand?
Qual' è la tariffa per l'invio di una lettera/cartolina postale/di questo pacco in Gran Bretagna/ Irlanda/ America/Canada/ Australia/Nuova Zelanda?
Kwahleh lah tahreeffa perr l'een-vyaw dee oona lettehra/car-rtawleena pawstahle/dee kwehstaw pahccaw een Grahn Brehtanya/ Eerrlahnda/Ahmehreeca/Cahnada/A hoostrahlia/Noohawva Tsehlahnda?

I would like one stamp/two stamps
Vorrei un francobollo/due francobolli
Vawrray oon frahncawbawllaw/dweh francawbawllee

I'd like ... stamps for postcards to send abroad, please
Vorrei ... dei francobolli per delle cartoline da inviare all'estero, per favore
Vawrray ... dey frahnkawbawlee perr dehleh kahrtawleeneh dah een-veeyahreh ahlehstehraw, perr fah-vawreh

Phones

I would like to make a telephone call/reverse the charges to (make a collect call) to ...
Vorrei fare una telefonata/a carico del destinatario a ...
Vawrray fahreh oona telefawnahta/ ah cahreecaw del desteenahtahryaw ah ...

Which coins do I need for the telephone?
Che monete devo usare con quest'apparecchio?
Keh mawnehteh dehvaw oozahreh con kwestaw appareckyaw?

The line is engaged (busy)
La linea è occupata
Lah leeneha eh occoopahta

The number is . . .
Il numero è . . .
Eel noomehraw eh . . .

Hello, this is . . .
Pronto, sono ...
Prawntaw, sawnaw ...

Please may I speak to ...?
Potrei parlare con ...?
Pawtray pahrlahreh kon ...?

He/she is not in at the moment. Can you call back?
Ora non c' è. Può richiamare?
Awrrah nawn cheh. Pooh-oh reekyahmahreh?

SHOPPING

Shops

Libreria/Cartoleria
Leebrehreeyah/Kahrtawlehreeyah
Bookshop/Stationery

Gioielleria/Articoli da regalo
Djaweeyehlehreeyah/Ahrteekawlee dah rehgahlaw
Jeweller/Gifts

Scarpe
Skahrpeh
Shoes

Ferramenta
Fehrrahmehntah
Hardware

Parrucchiere (per uomini)/(per donne)
Pahrrookyehreh (perr ooawmee-nee) (perr dawneh)
Hairdresser (men's)/(women's)

Panificio
Pahneefeechyaw
Baker

Supermercato
Soopehrmehrkahtaw
Supermarket

Fotografo
Fotografaw
Photo shop

Agenzia di viaggi
Ahjehntsyah dee veeyahdjee
Travel Agent

Farmacia
Fahrmahcheeah
Pharmacy

In the Shops

What time do the shops open/close?
A che ora aprono/chiudono i negozi?
Ah keh awra ahprawnaw/kewdaw-naw ee nehgotsee?

Where is the nearest market?
Dov' è il mercato più vicino?
Dawv eh eel mehrkahtaw pyoo veecheehnaw?

Can you show me the one in the window/this one?
Può mostrarmi quello in vetrina/questo?
Pooh oh mawstrahrmee kwehllaw een vehtreenah/kwehstaw?

Can I try this on?
Posso provarlo?
Pawssaw prawvarrlaw?

What size is this?
Di che misura è?
Dee keh meezoora eh?

This is too large/too small/too expensive
Questo è troppo grande/troppo piccolo/troppo caro
Kwestaw eh tropaw grahndeh/tropaw peekawlaw/trawpaw kahraw

Do you have any others?
Ne avete degli altri?
Neh ahvehteh delyee ahltree?

My size is . . .
La mia taglia è ...
Lah meeyah tahlyah eh ...

Where is the changing room/ children's/cosmetic/ ladieswear/menswear/food department?
Dov' è lo spogliatoio/il reparto bambini/cosmetici/ abbigliamento femminile/abbigliamento maschile/alimentari?
Dawv eh law spawlyahtoyaw/eel rehparrtaw bahmbeenee/cosmeteechee abbeelyahmentaw femmeeneeleh/ abbeelyahmentaw maskeeleh/ahleemehntahree?

I would like... a quarter of a kilo/half a kilo/a kilo of bread/butter/ham/tomatoes
Vorrei ... due etti e mezzo/mezzo chilo/un chilo di pane/burro/ formaggio/prosciutto/pomodori
Vawrray ... dweh ehttee eh metsaw/metsaw keelaw/oon keelaw dee pahneh/boorraw/forrmahdjaw/prawshoottaw/pawmawdoree

How much is this?
Quant' è?
Kwahnteh?

I'll take this one, thank you
Prenderò questo, grazie
Prehndehroh kwestaw, grahtsyeh

Do you have a carrier (shopping) bag?
Ha un sacchetto di plastica?
Ah oon sahckettaw dee plahsteeca?

Do you have anything cheaper/larger/smaller/of better quality?
Ha un articolo meno caro/più grande/più piccolo/di migliore qualità?
Ah oon arrteecawlaw mehnaw cahraw/pyoo grahndeh/pyoo peeckawlaw/dee meelyawreh kwahleetah?

I would like a film for this camera
Vorrei una pellicola per questa macchina fotografica
Vawrray oona pelleecawla perr kwesta mackeena fawtawgrahfeeca

I would like some batteries, the same size as this old one
Vorrei delle pile della stessa grandezza di quella vecchia
Vawrray delleh peeleh della stehssah grahndetsa dee kwella veckya

Would you mind wrapping this for me, please?
Le dispiacerebbe impacchettarmele?
Leh deespyahcherebbeh eempahckett-arrmehleh?

Sorry, but you seem to have given me the wrong change
Scusi, si è sbagliato nel darmi il resto se non erro
Scoozee, se eh sbahlyahtaw nel darrmee eel restaw seh non erraw

MOTORING

Car Hire (Rental)

I have ordered (rented) a car in the name of ...
Ho ordinato una vettura per ...
Aw ordeenahtaw oona vettoora per ...

How much does it cost to hire (rent) a car for one day/ two days/a week?
Quant' è il nolo di una vettura per un giorno/due giorni/una settimana?
Kwahnt eh eel nawlaw dee oona vettoora pehr oon jorrnaw/dweh joornee/oona setteemahna?

Is the tank already full of petrol (gas)?
Il serbatoio è pieno di benzina?
Eel serbahtoyaw eh pyehnaw dee bentseena?

Is insurance and tax included? How much is the deposit?
L'assicurazione e l'imposta sono comprese? Quant' è la caparra?
Lasseecoorahtsyawne eh leempaw-sta sawnaw cawmprehseh? Kwahnteh lah cahparra?

By what time must I return the car?
A che ora devo restituire la vettura?
Ah keh awra devaw restitoo-eereh lah vettoora?

I would like a small/large family/sports car with a radio/cassette
Vorrei una piccola/grande vettura/una familiare/una vettura sport con radio/mangianastri
Vawrray oona peeccawla grahndeh vettoora/oona fahmeelyareh oona vettoora sport con rahdyaw/ mahnjanastree

Do you have a road map?
Avete una carta stradale?
Ahvehteh oonah kahrtah strahdahleh?

Parking

How long can I park here?
Per quanto tempo posso parcheggiare qui?
Pehr kwantaw tehmpaw payssaw pahrkehdjahreh kwee?

Is there a car park near here?
C' è un parcheggio da queste parti?
Cheh oon pahrkehdjaw dah kwesteh pahrtee?

At what time does this car park close?
A che ora chiude il parcheggio?
Ah keh awrah keeyoodeh eel pahrkehdjaw?

Signs and Notices

Senso unico
Sehnsaw ooneekaw
One way

Divieto di accesso
Deeveeyehtaw dee ahchehssaw
No entry

ITALIAN

Divieto di sosta
Deeveeyehtaw dee sawstah
No parking

Deviazione
Dehveeyahtsyawneh
Detour (diversion)

Stop
Stop
Stop

Dare precedenza
Dahreh prehchehdehntsah
Give way (yield)

Strada sdrucciolevole
Strahdah sdroocheeyawlehvawle.
Slippery road

Divieto di sorpasso
Deeveeyehtaw dee sawrpahssaw
No overtaking

Pericolo!
Pereekawlaw!
Danger!

At the Filling Station
Distributore (di benzina)

Unleaded (lead-free)/ standard/premium/diesel
Carburante senza piombo/ normale/super/diesel
Kahrboorahnteh sehntsah peeyawm-baw/nawrmahleh/soopehrr/deezel

Fill the tank please
Il pieno, per favore
Eel peeyehnaw perr fahvawreh

Do you have a road map?
Avete una carta stradale?
Ahvehteh oonah kahrtah strahdahleh?

How much is the car wash?
Quanto costa l'autolavaggio?
Kwahntaw kawstah lahootawlahvahdjyoh?

Breakdowns

I've had a breakdown at . . .
Ho avuto un guasto a ...
Haw ahvootaw oon gwastaw ah ...

I am a member of the ... [motoring organisation]
Sono membro di ...
Sawnaw mehmbraw dee ...

I am on the road from ... to . . .
Sono sulla strada da ... a ...
Sawnaw soollah strahdah dah ... ah . . .

I can't move the car. Can you send a tow-truck?
Non posso spostare l'auto. Potrebbe mandare un carro attrezzi?
Nawn pawssaw spawstahreh lahootaw. Pawtrebbeh mahndahreh oon kahrraw ahtretzee?

I have a flat tyre
Ho una ruota a terra
Haw oonah rooawtah ah tehrrah

The windscreen (windshield) has smashed/cracked
Il parabrezza si è sfondato/ incrinato
Eel pahrahbretzah see eh sfawn-

dahtaw/eenkreenahtaw

There is something wrong with the engine/brakes/ lights/steering/gearbox/ clutch/exhaust
C' è qualcosa che non va con il motore/i freni/le luci/lo sterzo/il cambio/la frizione/lo scarico
Cheh kwahlkawsah keh nawn vah kawn eel mawtawreh/ee frehnee/leh loochee/law stehrtsaw/eel kahm-beeyaw/lah freetsyawneh/law skahreehkaw

It's overheating
È surriscaldato
Eh soorreeskahldhataw

It won't start
Non parte
Nawn pahrteh

Where can I get it repaired?
Dove posso ripararla?
Dawveh pawssaw reepahrarlah?

Can you take me there?
Mi ci potrebbe accompagnare?
Mee chee pawtrebbeh ahkawmpah-nyareh?

Will it take long to fix?
Ci vorrà molto tempo per ripararla?
Chee vawrrah mawltaw tehmpaw perr reepahrahrlah?

How much will it cost?
Quanto mi costerà?
Kwantaw mee kawstehreh?

Please can you pick me up/give me a lift?
Potrebbe venirmi a prendere/ darmi un passaggio?
Potrebbeh veneermee a prendereh/dahrmee oon passadjaw?

Accidents and Traffic Offences (Violations)

Can you help me? There has been an accident
Potrebbe aiutarmi? C' è stato un incidente
Pawtrebbeh ahyiootahrmee? Cheh stahtaw oon eencheedehnteh

Please call the police/an ambulance
Per favore, chiami la polizia/ un'ambulanza
Perr fahvawreh keeyahmee lah pawleetseeyah/oonamboolahntsah

Is anyone hurt?
Ci sono feriti?
Chee sawnaw fehreetee?

I'm sorry, I didn't see the sign
Mi scusi, non ho visto il cartello
Mee scoozee, nawn haw veestaw eel kahrtehllaw

Must I pay a fine? How much?
Devo pagare una multa? Quant'è?
Dehvaw pahgareh oonah mooltah? Kwant eh?

Mi mostri i documenti.
Mee mawstree ee dawcoomehntee
Show me your documents.

ITALIAN

HEALTH

Pharmacy (Farmacia)

Do you have anything for a stomach ache/headache/sore throat/toothache?
Ha un preparato per il mal di stomaco/mal di testa/mal di gola/mal di denti?
Ah oon prehpahrahtaw perr eel mahl dee stohmahcaw/mahl dee testa/ mahl dee gawla/mahl dee dehntee?

I need something for diarrhoea/constipation/a cold/a cough/insect bites/ sunburn/ travel (motion) sickness
Ho bisogno di un rimedio per la diarrea/la stitichezza/il raffreddore/la tosse/le punture di insetti/l'eritema solare/il mal di viaggio
Aw beesawnyaw dee oon reemehdyaw perr lah dyahrreha/lah steeteeketsa/eel rahffredawreh/lah tawsseh/leh poontooreh dee eensehttee/lehreetehma sawlahreh/eel mahl dee vyahdjaw

How much/how many do I take?
Quanto/quanti ne devo prendere?
Kwahntaw/kwahntee neh dehvaw prendehreh?

How often do I take it/them?
Ogni quanto devo prenderlo/prenderli?
Awnee kwahntaw dehvaw prenderrlaw/prendehrlee?

How much does it cost?
Quanto costa?
Kwahntaw cawsta?

I am/he is/she is taking this medication
Sto/egli sta/ella sta prendendo questa medicina
Staw/ehlyee stah/ehlah stah prehndehndaw kwestah mehdeecheenah

Can you recommend a good doctor/dentist?
Può raccomandarmi un buon medico/dentista?
Pooh-oh rhaccawmahndarrmee oon boohon mehdeecaw/denteesta?

Is it suitable for children?
È adatto per i bambini?
Eh ahdahttaw perr ee bahmbeenee?

Doctor (Medico)

I have a pain here/in my arm/leg/chest/stomach
Ho un dolore qui/nel braccio/nella gamba/nel petto/nello stomaco
Aw oon dawlawreh kwee/nel bracchaw/nella gahmba/nel pettaw/nellaw stohmahcaw

Please call a doctor, this is an emergency
La prego di chiamare un medico, è un'emergenza
Lah prehgaw dee kyahmahreh oon meh deecaw, eh oonemerrgentsa

I would like to make an appointment to see the doctor
Vorrei prendere un appuntamento con un medico
Vawrray prendehre oon ahppoontahmentaw con oon meh deecaw

I am diabetic/pregnant

Sono diabetica/incinta
Sawnaw dyahbe hteeca/eencheenta

I need a prescription for ...
Ho bisogno di una ricetta per ...
Aw beesohnyaw dee oona reechetta perr ...

Can you give me something to ease the pain?
Può prescrivermi qualcosa che allevii il dolore?
Pooh oh prehscreeverrmee kwahl cawsa keh allevee eel dawlawreh?

I am/he is/she is allergic to penicillin
Sono/egli è/ella è allergico/allergica (fem.) alla penicillina.
Sawnaw/ehlyee eh/ehlah eh allehrjeekaw/allehrjeekah ahlah pehneecheeleenah

Questo fa male?
Kwestaw fah mahleh?
Does this hurt?

Lei deve/egli deve/ella deve andare in ospedale
Ley dehveh/ehlyee dehveh/ehlah dehveh ahndahreh een awspehdahleh
You must/he must/she must go to hospital

Prenda queste una volta/due volte/tre volte al giorno
Prehndah kwesteh oonah vawltah/dooweh vawlteh/treh vawlteh ahl djeeyawrnaw
Take these once/twice/three times a day

I have medical insurance
Ho un'assicurazione medica
Haw oonahseekoorahtsyawneh mehdeekah

Dentist (Dentista)

I have toothache
Ho mal di denti
Aw mahl dee dentee

My filling has come out
È uscita l'otturazione
Eh oosheeta lawttoorahtsyawneh

I do/do not want to have an injection first
Voglio/non voglio l'anestetico
Vawlyaw/non vawlyaw lahnestehteecaw

EMERGENCIES

Help!
Aiuto!
Ahyootaw!

Fire!
Al fuoco!
Ahl fooawcaw!

Stop!
Ferma!
Fairmah!

Call an ambulance/a doctor/the police/the fire brigade!
Chiamate un'ambulanza/un medico/la polizia/i pompieri!
Kyahmahteh oon ahmboolahntsa/oon mehdeecaw/la pawleetsya/ee pompee-ehree!

Please may I use a telephone?
Posso usare il telefono per favore?
Possaw oozahreh eel tehlefawnaw pair favawreh?

EMERGENCIES

I
T
A
L
I
A
N

I have had my traveller's cheques/credit cards/purse/ handbag/rucksack/luggage/ wallet/passport/ mobile phone stolen
Mi hanno rubato gli assegni turistici/le carte di credito/il borsellino/la borsetta/lo zaino/il bagaglio/il portafoglio/ il passaporto/il cellulare
Mee annaw roobahtaw lee assenyee tooreesteechee/leh carrteh dee cre-deetaw/eel borrselleenaw/lah borrsetta/law tsaheenaw/eel bahgalyaw/eel porrtafawlyaw/eel passaportaw/eel chelloolahreh

May I please have a copy of the report for my insurance claim?
Potrei avere una copia del rapporto per la richiesta alla mia assicurazione?
Potrehyee avaireh oona copeeya del rapportaw pair lah reekee-ehstah alla meeah assikoorahtsiawneh?

Can you help me? I have lost my daughter/son/my companion(s)
Può aiutarmi? Ho perduto mia figlia/mio figlio/il mio compagno (i miei compagni)
Pooh-oh ahyootarrmee? Aw perrdootaw myah feelya/myaw feelyaw/eel meeaw companyaw (ee mee-ehyee compan-yee)

Please go away/leave me alone
Se ne vada/mi lasci in pace!
Seh neh vahda/me lahshee een pahcheh!

I'm sorry
Mi dispiace
Mee dispeeahcheh

I want to contact the British/American/ Canadian/Irish/Australian/ New Zealand/South African Consulate
Voglio contattare il Consolato Britannico/Americano/Canadese/ Irlandese/Australiano/ Neozelandese/Sudafricano
Vawlyaw kawntattahreh eel Kawnsawlahtaw Breetahnneekaw/ Ahmehreekahnaw/Kahnahdehseh/ Eerlahndehseh/Ahoostrahleeyahnaw/ Nehawzehlahndehseh/ Soodahfrikahnaw

I'm ill/lost/injured
Mi sento male/mi sono perso/sono ferito
Mee sentaw mahleh/mee sawnaw pairsaw/sawnaw fereetaw

We're ill/lost/injured
Ci sentiamo male/ci siamo persi/siamo feriti
Chee senteeahmaw mahleh/chee seeahmaw pairsi/seeahmaw fereetee

He is ill/lost/injured
Lui si sente male/lui si è perso/lui è ferito
Looee see senteh mahleh/looee see e pairsaw/looee e fereetaw

She is ill/lost/injured
Lei si sente male/lei si è persa/lei è ferita
Lehyee see senteh mahleh/lehyee see e pairsah/lehyee e fereetah

They are/ill/lost/injured
Si sentono male/si sono persi/sono feriti
See sentawnaw mahleh/see sawnaw pairsee/sawnaw fereetee

POLISH

INTRODUCTION

Polish is a Slavic tongue and therefore related to Russian, Czech and many other Eastern European languages. English is spoken to some extent in larger cities, particularly by younger people, though older inhabitants are more likely to speak German or French as a second language. Russian is understood but unpopular.

Addresses for Travel and Tourist Information

Australia: *Embassy,* 7 Turrana St, Yarralumla, ACT 2600; tel: (02) 6273 1208.

Canada: *Embassy,* 443 Daly Ave, Ottawa, Ontario K1N 6H3; tel: (613) 789 0468; fax: (613) 789 1218.

New Zealand: *Embassy,* 17 Upland Road, Kelburn, Wellington; tel: (04) 475 9453; fax: (04) 475 9458.

South Africa: *Embassy,* 14 Amos Street, Colbyn, Pretoria; tel: (12) 430 2631.

UK: *Polish National Tourist Office,* Level 3, Wester House, West Gate, London W5 1YY; tel: 08700 675010 (brochure line); fax: 08700 675011.

USA: *Polish National Tourist Office,* 275 Madison Ave, #1711, New York, NY 10016; tel: (212) 338 9412.

Official tourism website: www.visitpoland.org.

Poland Facts

CAPITAL: Warsaw, Warsawa (pronounced Varrshaava)

CURRENCY: Złoty (Zł), pronounced zwahti. Zł 1 = 100 groszy (pronounced groshi).

OPENING HOURS: Banks: Mon–Fri 0800–1600, with some open Sat 0900–1300. Shops: Mon–Sat 1000–1900, but some shops are open 24 hours. Museums: generally 1000–1600, closed Monday.

TELEPHONES: To dial in, +48. Outgoing, 0 for dial tone, 0 again and then the country code. Police, 997. Fire, 998. Ambulance, 999.

PUBLIC HOLIDAYS: 1, 6 Jan; Easter Monday; 1, 3 May; 15 Aug; 1, 11 Nov; 25, 26 Dec.

Technical Language Hints

Polish uses the Roman alphabet, but there are a few accented characters which are considered as separate letters, and there are some complexes of consonants which at first sight look unpronounceable to English speakers – szcz, for instance. 'Unvoiced' consonants at the end of a word are pronounced in a 'harder' way than their equivalents in the middle of a word – w, for example, which is normally pronounced like an English v, is like an English f when it occurs at the end of a word.

The word 'You' is translated in these phrases as 'Pan' (for men) and 'Pani' (for women). In other phrases the feminine form is denoted by (fem.).

ESSENTIALS

Alphabet and Pronunciation

	Name	Pronounced
A a	*ah*	**like the u in cut**
Ą ą	*awng*	**a nasalised long a**
B b	bey	**like b in butter**
C c	tsey	**like ts in cats**
Ć ć		**like ty in get you or like ch with the top of the tongue slightly forward**
ch		**like h in head**
cz		**like ch in church**
D d	dey	**like d in day**
dz		**like ds in adds up**
dż		**like j in jam**
dź		**like dy in would you or j in jam with the top of the tongue slightly forward**
E e	*ey*	**like e in bed**
F f	*ef*	**like f in fast**
G g	*gye*	**like g in go**
H h	*hah*	**like h in head**
I i	*ee*	**like e in he**
J j	*yot*	**like y in yes**
K k	*kah*	**like k in key**
L l	*el*	**like l in love**
Ł ł	*w*	**like w in wine**
M m	*em*	**like m in milk**
N n	*en*	**like n in no**
Ń ń	*ny*	**like ni in onion**

ESSENTIALS

O o	*oh*	**like o in not**
Ó ó		**like oo in boot or u in put**
P p	*pey*	**like p in pot**
Q	*koo*	**not found in Polish words**
R r	*air*	**rolled r as in Scottish pronunciation**
rz		**zh like s in pleasure**
S s	*ess*	**like s in stop**
Ś ś	*sh*	**like si in passion but with the top of the tongue slightly forward**
sz		**like sh in show**
szcz	*shch*	**as in fresh cheese**
T t	*tey*	**like t in top**
U u	*oo*	**like oo in boot or u in put**
V	*fow*	**not found in Polish words**
W w	*voo*	**like v in vest**
X	*iks*	**not found in Polish words**
Y y	*eegrek*	**like e in he**
Z z	*zet*	**like z in zest**
Ż ż	*zh*	**like s in pleasure**
Ź ź		**similar to ż but with the top of the tongue slightly forward**

Basic Words and Phrases

Yes Tak *Tak*	**No** Nie *Nyeah*
Please Proszę *Pro-sheh*	**Thank you** Dziękuję *Jen-koo-yair*
Hello (informal) Cześć *Cheshch*	**Goodbye** Do widzenia *Do vee-je-nyah*
Excuse Me/ Sorry Przepraszam *Pshe-pra-sham*	
How Jak *Yak*	**When** Kiedy *Kye-de*
Why Dlaczego *Dla-che-goe*	**What** Co *Tso*
Who Kto *Ktoh*	
That's O.K. To jest O.K. *Toe yest O.K.*	**Perhaps** Może *Mozhe*
To Do *Doe*	**From** Z/Skąd *Z/Skond*
Here Tutaj *Too-tigh*	**There** Tam *Tam*

I don't understand
Nie rozumiem
Nyeah ro-zoo-myem

I don't speak Polish
Nie mówię po polsku
Nyeah moo-vyair po pols-koo

Do you speak English?
Czy mówi Pan/Pani po angielsku?
Chy moo-vee pa-nee po an-gyels-koo?

Can you please write it down?
Czy mógłby Pan/mogłaby Pani to napisać?
Chy moogw-bi pan/ mogwah-bi pa-nee toh napisach?

Please can you speak more slowly?
Proszę mówić wolniej?
Pro-shair moo-vech vol-nyey?

Greetings

Good Morning/ Good Afternoon/Good Evening/ Good Night
Dzień dobry/Dobry wieczór/ Dobranoc
Jeny dobri /do-bri vie-choor/ do-bra-nots

Pleased to meet you
Miło mi Pana/Panią poznać
Mee-wo me pana/pa-nyom po-znach

How are you?
Jak się Pan/Pani miewa?
Yak sie pan/pa-nee mye-va?

I am well, thank you. And you?
Bardzo dobrze, dziękuję. A Pan/Pani?
Bar-zo do-bje, jen-koo-yair. ar pan/pa-nee?

My name is ...
Nazywam się ...
Nazyvam shiem ...

This is my friend/ boyfriend/ girlfriend/husband/wife/ brother/sister
To mój kolega/mój chłopak/ moja dziewczyna/mój mąż/ moja żona/mój brat/moja siostra
Toe mooy kollehga/mooy hwopak/ moya dzee-evcheena/mooy monj/moya zhona/moy brat/moya syostra

Where are you travelling to?
Dokąd Pan/Pani jedzie?
Doh-kond pan/pa-nee ye-jair?

I am/ we are going to ...
Jadę/Jedziemy do ...
Ya-dair/Yedziemmy doh ...

How long are you travelling for?
Na jak długo Pan/Pani jedzie?
Na yak dwoo-go pan/pa-nee yejair?

Where do you come from?
Skąd Pan/Pani pochodzi?
Skond pan/pa-nee po-ho-jee?

I am/we are from ... Australia/Britain/Canada/ America
Pochodzę/Pochodzimy z ... Australii/ Wielkiej Brytanii/Kanady/ Ameryki

Po-ho-dzair/Po-ho-dzimee z …
Aus-tra-lee/Yyel-kyey Bre-ta-nee/
Ka-na-de/Ame-ri-key

We are on holiday
Jesteśmy na wakacjach
Ye-ste-shme na va-ka-tsyah

This is our first visit here
To jest nasza pierwsza wizyta
Toh yest na-sha pier-vsha vee-ze-ta

How old are you?
Ile ma Pan/Pani lat?
Ee-lair ma pan/pa-nee lat?

I am ... years old
Mam ... lat
Mam ... lat

I am a business person/ doctor/journalist/manual worker/administrator/ scientist/student/teacher
Jestem biznesmenem lekarzem/dziennikarzem/ robotnikiem/urzędnikiem/ naukowcem/studentem/ nauczycielem
Ye-stem bi-znes-me-nem le-ka-jem/ je-nnee-ka-jem/ ro-bo-tnee-kyem/ oo-jen-dnee-kyem/now-kov-tsem/ stoo-den-tem/now-oo-chi-chairlem

I am waiting for my husband/ wife/boyfriend/girlfriend
Czekam na męża/żonę/ mojego chłopaka/moją dziewczynę
Che-kam na menja/zho-nair/ moyego hwopaka/moyanhg dzee-ehvcheenen

Would you like a cigarette?/May I have a cigarette?
Czy chciałby Pan/Pani zapalić?
Czy mogę zapalić?
Che hchawbi pan/pa-nee zapalitsh? /che mogair zapalitsh?

Do you mind if I smoke?
Czy pozwoli Pan/Pani, że zapalę?
Chy pozvoli pan/pa-nee je za-palair?

Do you have a light?
Czy mogę prosić o ogień?
Chy mo-gair proshitsh o ogieny?

Days

Monday
Poniedziałek
Po-niair-ja-wek

Tuesday
Wtorek
Vto-rek

Wednesday
Środa
Shro-da

Thursday
Czwartek
Chvar-tek

Friday
Piątek
Pyon-tek

Saturday
Sobota
So-bo-ta

Sunday
Niedziela
Nyair-je-la

Morning
Rano
Rano

Afternoon/Evening/Night
Popołudnie/Wieczór/Noc
Po-po-woo-dnye/vyair-choor/nots

Yesterday
Wczoraj
Vcho-ray

Tomorrow
Jutro
Yoo-troe

Today
Dzisiaj
Jishyay

Numbers

Zero
Zero
Zeroe

One
Jeden
Ye-den

Two
Dwa
Dva

Three
Trzy
Tshe

Four
Cztery
Chte-ri

Five
Pięć
Pyench

Six
Sześć
Shesch

Seven
Siedem
She-dem

Eight
Osiem
O-shem

Nine
Dziewięć
Je-vyench

Ten
Dziesięć
Je-shensh

Eleven
Jedenaście
Yede-nash-chair

Twelve
Dwanaście
Dva-nash-chair

Thirteen
Trzynaście
Tshe-nahsh-chair

Fourteen
Czternaście
Chtair-nash-chair

Fifteen
Piętnaście
Peeyent-nash-chair

Sixteen
Szesnaście
Shes-nash-chair

Seventeen
Siedemnaście
Shedem-nash-chair

Eighteen
Osiemnaście
Oshem-nash-chair

Nineteen
Dziewiętnaście
Jevyet-nash-chair

Twenty
Dwadzieścia
Dva-je-shchar

Twenty-one
Dwadzieścia jeden
Dva-je-shchar yeden

Twenty-two
Dwadzieścia dwa
Dva-je-shchar dva

Thirty
Trzydzieści
Tshee-je-shchee

Forty
Czterdzieści
Chtair-je-shchee

Fifty
Pięćdziesiąt
Peeyent-je-shont

Sixty
Sześćdziesiąt
Shesch-je-shont

Seventy
Siedemdziesiąt
She-dem-je-shont

Eighty
Osiemdziesiąt
Oshem-je-shont

Ninety
Dziewięćdziesiąt
Je-vyench-jeshont

One hundred
Sto
Sto

Five hundred
Pięćset
Peeyench-set

One thousand
Tysiąc
Ti-shonts

One million
Milion
Millyon

Time

What time is it?
Która jest godzina?
Ktoo-rah yest go-jee-nah?

It is ...
Jest ...
Yest ...

9.00
Dziewiąta
Je-vyon-ta

P O L I S H

9.05
Pięć po dziewiątej/dziewiąta pięć
Pyench poe je-vyon-tey/je-vyon-ta pyench

9.15
Piętnaście po dziewiątej/ kwadrans po dziewiątej/ dziewiąta piętnaście
Peeyent-nash-chair poe je-vyon-tey/ kva-drans poe je-vyon-tey/ je-vyon-ta peeyent-nash-chair

9.20
Dwadzieścia po dziewiątej/ dziewiąta dwadzieścia
Dva-je-shchar poe je-vyon-tey/ je-vyon-ta dva-je-shchar

9.30
W pół do dziesiątej/dziewiąta trzydzieści
V poow doe je-vyon-tey/je-vyon-ta tshe-je-shchee

9.35
Pięć po wpół do dziesiątej/ dziewiąta trzydzieści pięć
Pyench poe v poow doe je-vyon-tey/ je-vyon-ta tshe-je-shchee pyench

9.40
Za dwadzieścia dziesiąta/ dziewiąta czterdzieści
Za dva-je-shchar je-shont-ta/ je-vyon-ta chtair-je-shchee

9.45
Za piętnaście dziesiąta/ za kwadrans dziesiąta/ dziewiąta czterdzieści pięć
Za peeyent-nash-chair je-shont-ta/ za kva-drans je-shont-ta/ je-vyon-ta chtair-je-shchee pyench

9.50
Za dziesięć dziesiąta/ dziewiąta pięćdziesiąt
Za je-shensh je-shont-ta/ je-vyon-ta peeyent-je-shont

9.55
Za pięć dziesiąta/dziewiąta pięćdziesiąt pięć
Za pyench je-shont-ta/je-vyon-ta peeyent-je-shont pyench

12.00/Midday/Midnight
Dwunasta w południe/północ
Dvoo-nas-ta v po-woo-dniair/ poow-nots

Money

I would like to change these traveller's cheques/ this currency
Chciałbym/chciałabym wymienić te czeki podróżne/tą walutę
Hcha-wbem/hcha-wa-bem vem-ye-nech teh cheke po-droo-jneh/tom va-loo-tair

How much commission do you charge? (What is the service charge?)
Jaka jest opłata manipulacyjna?
Ya-ka yest opwata mani-poo-latsiyna?

Can I obtain money with my Mastercard?
Czy mogę uzyskać pieniądze za pomocą Mastercard?
Che mo-gair oo-ze-skach pier-nyon-ze za po-moe-tsom master-kard?

Where is the nearest ATM?
Gdzie jest najblişszy bankomat?
Gur-dj-yeah yest nay-bleesh-shee bank-oh-mat?

My name is ... Some money has been wired to here for me to collect
Nazywam się ... Czy mogę odebraç przekaz pieniężny
Nazeevam see-en ... Tchee mogeh oh-debr-ach pshe-kas pee-enee-enjnee

ARRIVING AND DEPARTING

Airport

Excuse me, where is the check-in desk for ... airline?
Przepraszam, gdzie jest odprava dla linii lotniczych ...?
Pshe-pra-sham gdjair yest odprava dla lee-nee lo-tnee-cheeh ...?

What is the boarding gate for my flight?
What is the time of my flight?
Z której sali odlotu?
O której godzinie jest odlot?
Z ktoo-rey sa-lee odlo-too?
O ktoo-rey go-jee-nyair yest od-lot?

How long is the delay likely to be?
Jakie będzie opóźnienie?
Ya-kyair ben-jair o-poo-jnyair-nair?

Where is the duty-free shop?
Gdzie jest sklep wolnocłowy?
Gdjair yest sklep volnoe-tswo-ve?

Which way is the luggage reclaim?
Gdzie jest odbiór bagażu?
Gdjair yest od-buer ba-ga-joo?

I have lost my luggage. Please can you help?
Zgubiłem bagaż. Czy mógłby mi Pan/mogłaby mi Pani pomóc?
Zgoo-bee-wem ba-gaj. Che moog-wbe me pan/mog-wa-be me pa-nee poe-moots?

I am flying to ...
Lecę do ...
Lair-tsair doe ...

Where is the bus for the city centre?
Skąd odjeżdża autobus do centrum?
Skond od-yeh-jdjah awto-boos doe tse-ntroom?

Trains and Boats

Where is the ticket office/ information desk?
Gdzie jest kasa biletowa/ informacja?
Gdjair yest ka-sah bee-le-toh-va/ in-for-ma-tsya?

Which platform does the train/speedboat/ferry to ... depart from?
Z którego peronu odjeżdża pociąg do ...?
Skąd odpływa motorówka/ prom do ...?
Z ktoo-rair-go pairo-noo od-yehj-ja poe-tsyong doe ...?
Skond od-pwe-vah mo-to-roov-ka/ prom doe ...?

Where is platform ...?
Gdzie jest peron ...?
Gjair yest pair-ron ...?

When is the next train/boat to ...?
O której godzinie jest następny pociąg/statek do ...?
O ktoo-rey go-jee-nyair na-stem-pne poe-tsyong/sta-tairk doe ...?

Is there a later train/boat to ...?
Czy jest późniejszy pociąg/statek do ...?
Che yest poo-jnyey-she poe-tsyong/sta-tairk doe ...?

Notices and Signs

Wagon restauracyjny
Va-gon re-sta-wra-tse-yne
Buffet (Dining) Car

Autobus
Awtoh-boos
Bus

Woda pitna/Woda niezdatna do picia
Vo-dah pee-tnah /vo-dah nyair zda-tna doe pee-chyah
Drinking/Non-drinking water

Wejście
Vey-shchair
Entrance

Wyjście
Veey-shchair
Exit

Szpital
Sh-pee-tal
Hospital

Informacja
In-for-ma-tsya
Information

Przechowalnia bagażu
Przehovalneeah bagaju
Left Luggage (Baggage Claim)

Schowki na bagaż
Se-hoe-vkee na ba-gaj
Luggage Lockers

Poczta
Po-chtah
Post Office

Peron
Pair-ron
Platform

Stacja kolejowa/Dworzec kolejowy
Stah-tsya ko-le-yo-va/Dvo-jets ko-le-yo-ve
Railway (Railroad) Station

Port lotniczy/Lotnisko
Port lo-tnee-che/Lot-nee-skoe
Airport

Policja
Po-lee-tsyah
Police Station

Port
Port
Port

Restauracja
Re-sta-wra-tsya
Restaurant

Dla palących
Dla niepalących/Zakaz palenia
Dla pa-lon-tse-h
Dla nyair pa-lon-tse-h/Za-kaz pa-lair-nyah
Smoking
Non Smoking

Telefon
Te-lair-fon
Telephone

Kasa biletowa
Ka-sa bee-lair-to-va
Ticket Office

Odprawa
Od-pra-vah
Check-in desk

Rozkład jazdy
Roz-kwad ya-zdi
Timetable

Toalety
Toe-a-lair-te
Toilets (Restrooms)

Damska/Męska
Dam-skah/Men-skah
Ladies/ Gentlemen

Metro
Metro
Underground (Subway)

Poczekalnia
Poe-chair-kal-nyah
Waiting Room (Subway)

Buying a Ticket

I would like a first-class/ second-class/third-class/single (one-way)/ return (round trip) ticket to ...
Poproszę o bilet pierwszej klasy/drugiej klasy/trzeciej klasy w jedną stronę/ powrotny do ...
Po-pro-she o bee-lairt pyer-vshey kla-si/droo-gyey kla-si/tsheh-chaey kla-si/v yednom stro-nair/po-vro-tni doe ...

Is it an express (fast) train/bus?
Czy to jest pociąg/autobus ekspresowy?
Che toh yest poe-tsyong/awtoh-boos expre-so-vi?

Is my rail pass valid on this train/ferry/bus?
Czy mój bilet jest ważny na ten pociąg/prom/autobus?
Che mooy bee-let yest va-jni na ten poe-tsyong/prom/awtoh-boos?

I would like an aisle/window seat
Chciałbym/Chciałabym (fem.) miejsce przy przejściu/przy oknie
Hcha-wbem/Hcha-wa-bim myey-stsair pshe pshey-shchool/ pshe o-knyair

No smoking/smoking please
Zakaz palenia/Wolno palić.
Za-kaz pa-lair-nyah/Vo-lnoe pa-leech

We would like to sit together
Chcielibyśmy siedzieć razem
Hche-lee-be-shme shair-jech ra-zem

I would like to make a seat reservation
Chciałbym/Chciałabym (fem.) zarezerwować miejsce
Hcha-wbem/Hcha-wa-bim za-rair-zer-vo-vach myey-stsair

I would like to reserve a couchette/sleeper for one person/two people/my family
Chciałbym/Chciałabym (fem.) zarezerwować kuszetkę/ miejsca w wagonie sypialnym dla jednej osoby/dla dwóch osób/dla rodziny
Hcha-wbem/Hcha-wa-bim za-rair-zer-vo-vach koo-shet-kair/myey-stsah v va-goe-nyair si-pyal-nim dla ye-dney o-so-bi/dvooh o-soob/ dla ro-jeene

I would like to reserve a cabin
Chciałbym/Chciałabym (fem.) zarezerwować kajutę
Hcha-wbem/Hcha-wa-bim za-rair-zer-vo-vach ka-yoo-tair

Timetables (Schedules)

Przyjazd
Pshe-yazd
Arrive

Przez/Przystanki
Pshehs /Pshi-stan-kee
Calls (Stops at)

Możliwość zakupu posiłku.
Moj-lee-voshch za-koo-poo po-siw-koo
Catering Service

Przesiadka
Pshair-sha-dkah
Change At

Połączenie/Przez
Po-won-che-nyair/Pshehs
Connection/ Via

Codziennie
Tsoe-jen-niair
Daily

Co 40 minut
Tsoe chtair-je-shchee mee-noot
Every 40 minutes

Pierwsza klasa
Pier-vsha kl-sa
First Class

Co godzinę
Coe goe-jee-nair
Hourly

Objęty rezerwacją miejsc
O-byen-ti re-zer-va-tsyanhg myeysts
Seat reservations are recommended

Druga klasa
Droo-gah kla-sah
Second Class

Dopłata
Doe-pwa-tah
Supplement Payable

Luggage

How much will it cost to send (ship) my luggage in advance?
Ile będzie kosztowało nadanie (wysłanie) bagażu wcześniej?
Ee-lair ben-jair koe-shtoh-vawoe na-da-nyair (vi-swa-nyair) ba-ga-joo vchair-shnyair?

Where is the left luggage (baggage claim) office?
Gdzie jest przechowalnia bagażu?
Gjair yest przehovalneeah bagaju?

What time do you open/ close?
O której jest otwarte/ zamknięte?
O ktoo-rey yest o-tvar-tair/ zam-knen-tair?

Where are the luggage trolleys (carts)?
Gdzie są wózki bagażowe?
Gjair som voo-zkee ba-ga-joe-vair?

Where are the lockers?
Gdzie są schowki na bagaż?
Gjair som s-hoe-vkee na ba-gaj?

I have lost my locker key
Zgubiłem/Zgubiłam (fem.) klucz od schowka
Zgoo-bee-wem/Zgoo-bee-wahm klooch od s-hoe-vkah

On Board

Is this seat free?
Czy to miejsce jest wolne?
Che toh myey-stsair yest volnair?

Excuse me, you are sitting in my reserved seat
Przepraszam, Pan/Pani siedzi na moim zarezerwowanym miejscu
Pshe-pra-sham Pan/Pa-nee syair-jee na mo-eem zarezervovaneem myey-stsoo

Which station is this?
Która to stacja?
Ktoo-rah toh sta-tsyah?

What time is this train/bus/ ferry/flight/ due to arrive/ depart?
O której godzinie jest planowy przyjazd/odjazd pociągu/auto-busu/promu przylot/odlot?
O ktoo-rey go-jee-nyair yest plan-ovi pshi-yazd/od-yazd poe-tsyon/goo/aw-to-boo-soo/pro-moo prshe-lot/od-lot?

Travelling with Children

Do you have a high chair/babysitting service/cot?
Czy macie fotelik dla dziecka/ opiekę nad dzieckiem/kojec?
Che ma-chair fo-te-leek dla je-tskah/ opye-kair nad jair-tskyem/ko-yets?

Where is the nursery/ playroom?
Gdzie jest kącik zabaw dla dzieci?
Gjair yest kon-cheek za-bav dla je-chee?

Where can I warm the baby's bottle?
Gdzie mogę zagrzać butelkę dla dziecka?
Gjair mo-gair zagr-jach boo-tel-kair dla je-tskah?

SIGHTSEEING

Customs and Passports

Poproszę o paszporty!
Po-pro-shair o pash-por-ti!
Passports please!

I have nothing to declare/ I have wine/spirits (alcohol)/ tobacco to declare
Nie mam nic od oclenia/ Mam wino/alkohol/wyroby tytoniowe do oclenia
Nyair mam nits doe o-tsle-nyah/ Mam veenoo/alcohol/ vi-ro-bee ti-to-nyo-veh doe o-tsle-nyah

I will be staying for ... days/ weeks/months
Mam zamiar zostać na ... dni/tygodni/miesięcy.
Mam za-myar zo-stach na ... dnee/ti-go-dnee/mye-syen-tsi

SIGHTSEEING

Asking the Way

Excuse me, do you speak English?
Przepraszam, czy mówi Pan/Pani po angielsku?
Pshe-pra-sham che moo-vee Pan/Pa-nee poe an-gyel-skoo?

Excuse me, can you help me please?
Przepraszam, czy mógłby mi Pan/mogłaby mi Pani pomóc?
Pshe-pra-sham che moog-wbe me Pan/mog-wa-be me Pa-nee po-moots?

Where is the Tourist Information Office?
Gdzie jest Biuro Informacji Turystycznej?
Gjair yest beu-ro In-for-ma-tsyee Too-ri-ste-chney?

Excuse me, is this the right way to ...?
Przepraszam, czy dojdę tędy do ...?
Pshe-pra-sham che doy-dair ten-di doe ...?

... the cathedral/the tourist Office/the castle/the old town
... katedry/biura turystycznego/ zamku/starego miasta?
... ka-tair-dri/byoo-rah too-ri-sti-chne-go/zam-koo/sta-re-go mya-stah

Can you tell me the way to the railway (railroad) station/bus station/taxi rank/city centre (downtown)/ beach?
Jak dojść do stacji kolejowej/ dworca autobusowego/ postoju taksówek/centrum miasta/plaży?
Yak doyshch doe sta-tsyee ko-le-yo-vay/dvortsah awto-boo-so-vego/ post-o-yoo tax-oovek/pla-ji?

Pierwsza/druga w lewo/w prawo/prosto
Prosto pier-vshah/droo-gah v lair-vo/v pra-vo/pro-sto
First/second/left/right/ straight ahead

Na rogu/Na światłach
Na ro-goo/Na shvya-twah
At the corner/At the traffic lights

Where is the nearest police station/post office?
Gdzie jest najbliższy posterunek policji/najbliższa poczta?

Gjair yest nay-blee-jshi po-ste-roo-nek po-lee-tsyee nay-blee-jshah po-chtah?

Is it near/ far?
Czy to jest blisko/daleko?
Che toh yest blee-sko/da-le-ko?

Do I need to take a taxi/catch a bus?
Czy muszę jechać taksówką/ autobusem?
Che moo-shair yehach tax-oo-vkom/ awto-boo-sem?

Do you have a map?
Czy ma Pan/Pani mapę?
Che ma Pan/Pa-nee ma-pair?

Can you point to it on my map?
Czy mógłby Pan/mogłaby Pani pokazać to na mapie?
Che moog-wbe Pan/mog-wa-be Pa-nee po-ka-zach na ma-pyair?

Thank you for your help
Dziękuję za pomoc
Jen-koo-yair za po-mots

How do I reach the motorway/main road?
Jak dojechać do autostrady/ głównej drogi?
Yak doe-ye-hach doe autostradee/ gwoo-vney dro-gee?

I think I have taken the wrong turning
Wydaje mi się, ze skręciłem w złym miejscu
Ve-da-yair me sie je skrair-chee-wem v zwem myey-stsoo

I am looking for this address
Szukam tego adresu
Shoo-kam te-go ad-re-soo

I am looking for the ... hotel
Szukam hotelu ...
Shoo-kam ho-te-loo ...

How far is it to ... from here?
Jak daleko jest do ...?
Yak da-le-ko yest doe ...?

Trzeba jechać prosto przez ... kilometrów
Tche-bah ye-hach pshez ... kee-lo-me-troov
Carry straight on for ... kilometres

Trzeba skręcić na najbliższym zakręcie w prawo/w lewo
Tche-bah skrair-cheech na nay-blee-jsheem za-krair-chair v pra-vo/v le-vo
Take the next turning on the right/left

Trzeba skręcić w prawo/w lewo na najbliższym skzyżowaniu/na najbliższych światłach
Tche-bah skrair-cheech v pra-vo/v le-vo na nay-blee-jsheem skshe-jova-nyoo/na nay-blee-jsheeh shvia-twah
Turn right/left at the next crossroads/traffic lights

Jedzie Pan/Pani w złym kierunku
Ye-jeh pan/pa-nee v zwem kye-roon-koo
You are going in the wrong direction

Where is the cathedral/ church/museum/pharmacy?
Gdzie jest katedra/kościół/ muzeum/apteka?
Gje yest katedra/koshchoow/ mooseum/a-pte-kah?

POLISH

How much is the admission/ entrance charge?
Ile kosztuje bilet wstępu?
Ee-lair ko-sh-too-yair bee-let vstem-poo?

Is there a discount for children/students/senior citizens?
Czy jest zniżka dla dzieci/ studentów/osób starszych?
Che yest znee-jkah dla jair-tsee/ stoo-den-toov/o-soob star-sheh?

What time does the next guided tour (in English) start?
O której godzinie jest następna wycieczka z przewodnikiem (w języku angielskim)?
O ktoo-rey go-jee-nyair yest na-stem-nah vi-che-chkah z pshair-vo-dnee-kyem (v yen-zi-koo an-gyel-skim)?

One/two adults/children please
Poproszę jeden bilet/dwa bilety dla dorosłych/dla dzieci
Po-pro-shair yeden bee-let/dva beeletty dla dorosweh/dla jair-tsee

May I take photographs here?
Czy wolno tutaj fotografować?
Che vol-no too-tigh fo-to-ghra-fo-vach?

At the Tourist Office

Do you have a map of the town/area?
Czy ma Pan/Pani mapę miasta/regionu?
Che ma Pan/Pa-nee ma-pair mya-stah/re-g-yo-noo?

Do you have a list of accommodation?
Czy ma Pan/Pani listę miejsc noclegowych?
Che ma Pan/Pa-nee lee-stair myeysts nots-le-go-veh?

Can I reserve accommodation?
Czy mogę zarezerwować nocleg?
Che mo-gair za-re-zer-vo-vach nots-leg?

ACCOMMODATION

Hotels

I have a reservation in the name of ...
Mam rezerwację na nazwisko ...
Mam re-ze-rva-tsyair na naz-vis-ko ...

I wrote to/faxed/telephoned you last month/last week
Napisałem list/dzwoniłem/ wysłałem faks w zeszłym miesiącu/tygodniu
Na-pee-sa-wem leest/zvo-nee-wem/ve-swa-wem fax v ze-shwem mye-syon-tsoo/ti-go-dnyoo

Do you have any rooms free?
Czy są wolne pokoje?
Che so vo-lne po-ko-yair?

I would like to reserve a single/double room with a bath/shower without a bath/ shower
Chciałbym/Chciałabym (fem.) zarezerwować jednoosobowy/ dwuosobowy pokój z wanną/ prysznicem bez wanny/ prysznica

Hcha-wbem/Hcha-wa-bim za-rair-zer-vo-vach ye-dno-o-so-bo-vi/dvoo-o-so-bo-vi po- kooy z va-nnom pri-shnee-tsem bes va nni/pri-shnee-tsah

I would like bed/breakfast/ (room and) full board
Chciałbym/Chciałabym (fem.) nocleg ze śniadaniem/ nocleg z pełnym wyżywieniem
Hcha-wbem/Hcha-wa-bem nots-leg ze shnya-da-nyem/nots-leg z pe-wnem ve-je-vye-nyem

How much is it per night?
Jaka jest cena noclegu?
Ya-ka yest tse-nah nots-le-goo?

Is breakfast included?
Czy śniadanie jest wliczone?
Che shnya-da-nyair yest vli-cho-nair?

Do you have any cheaper rooms?
Czy są tańsze pokoje?
Che so tan-shair po-ko-yair?

I would like to see/take the room
Chciałbym/Chciałabym (fem.) zobaczyć/wynająć ten pokój
Hcha-wbem/Hcha-wa-bim zo-ba-chech/vi-na-yonch ten po-kooy

I would like to stay for ... nights
Chciałbym/Chciałabym (fem.) zostać przez ... nocy
Hcha-wbem/Hcha-wa-bem zo-stach pshez ... no-tse

The shower/light/tap/hot water doesn't work
Prysznic/światło/kran/gorąca woda nie działa
Pri-shneets/shvia-twoh/kran/go-ron-tsa vo-da nyair ja-wa

At what time/where is breakfast served?
O której godzinie jest śniadanie?
O ktoo-rey go-jee-nyair yest shnya-da-nyair?

What time do I have to check out?
O której godzinie muszę się wyprowadzić?
O ktoo-rey go-jee-nyair moo-shair sie vi-pro-va-jeech?

Can I have the key to room number ...?
Poproszę o klucz do pokoju numer ...?
Po-pro-shair o klooch doe po-ko-yoo noo-mair ...?

My room number is ...
Mój pokój ma numer ...
Mooy po-kooy ma noo-mair ...

My room is not satisfactory./ It is not clean enough/too noisy. Please can I change rooms?
Nie jestem zadowolony/ zadowolona (fem.) z mojego pokoju./Jest brudno/zbyt głośno. Czy mogę prosić o inny pokój?
Nyair ye-stem za-do-vo-lo-ne/za-do-vo-lo-na z mo-ye-go po-ko-yoo/woo-jkah yest broo-dno/zbit gwo-shno pro-shair o in-ne po-kooy?

Where is the bathroom?
Gdzie jest łazienka?
Gjair yest wa-zyen-kah?

Do you have a safe for valuables?
Czy tutaj jest sejf?
Che too-tigh yest safe?

Is there a laundry/do you wash clothes?
Czy jest tutaj pralnia?
Che too-tigh yest pra-nyah?

I would like an air-conditioned room
Chciałbym/Chciałabym (fem.) pokój z klimatyzacją
Hcha-wbem/Hcha-wabim po-kooy z klee-ma-ti-za-tsyoh

Do you accept traveller's cheques/credit cards?
Czy mogę płacić czekami podróżnymi/kartą kredytową?
Che mo-gair pwa-cheech che-ka-mee po-droo-jne-me/kar-toh kre-de-toh-woh?

May I have the bill please?
Poproszę o rachunek?
Po-pro-shair o ra-hoo-neck?

Excuse me, I think there may be a mistake in this bill
Przepraszam, wydaje mi się, że w rachunku jest błąd
Pshe-pra-sham we-da-yair me sie je v ra-hoon-koo yest bwond

Youth Hostels

How much is a dormitory bed per night?
Ile kosztuje nocleg?
Ee-lair ko-shtoo-yair nots-leg?

I am/am not an HI member
Jestem/nie jestem członkiem organizacji turystycznej
Ye-stem/nyair ye-stem chwon-kyem orga-nee-za-tsyee too-re-ste-chney

May I use my own sleeping bag?
Czy mogę używać własnego śpiwora?
Che mo-gair oo-je-vach v-wa-sne-go shpee-vorah?

What time do you lock the doors at night?
O której godzinie zamyka się drzwi wieczorem?
O ktoo-rey go-jee-nyair za-me-kah sie jvee vye-cho-rem?

Camping

May I camp for the night/two nights?
Czy mogę rozbić tutaj namiot na jedną noc/dwie noce?
Che mo-ghair roz-beech too-tigh na-myot na ye-dnoh nots/dvyeh no-tsair?

Where can I pitch my tent?
Gdzie mogę rozbić namiot?
Gjair mo-ghair roz-beech na-myot?

How much does it cost for one night/week?
Ile kosztuje jedna noc/jeden tydzień?
Ee-lair ko-shtoo-yair ye-dnah nots/ye-den te-jen?

Where are the washing facilities?
Gdzie są łazienki?
Gjair so wa-jen-kee?

Is there a restaurant/ supermarket/swimming pool on site/nearby?
Czy jest restauracja/sklep/ basen/na kempingu/w pobliżu?
Gjair yest re-staw-ra-tsyah/sklep/basen na kem-peen-goo/v po-blee-joo?

Do you have a safety deposit box?
Czy jest tutaj schowek lub sejf?
Che yest too-tigh s-hoe-vek loob safe?

EATING AND DRINKING

Cafés and Bars

I would like a cup of/ two cups of/ another coffee/tea
Poproszę o jedną/dwie/jeszcze jedną kawę/herbatę
Po-pro-shair o ye-dnoh/dvyair/ye-shchair ye-dnoh ka-vair/herba-tair

With milk/sugar
Without milk/sugar
Z mlekiem/cukrem
Bez mleka/cukru
Z mle-kyem/tsoo-krem
Bez mle-kah/tsoo-kroo

I would like a bottle/glass/two glasses of mineral water/red wine/white wine, please
Poproszę o butelkę/szklankę/ dwie szklanki wody mineralnej/ butelkę/kieliszek/dwa kieliszki czerwonego wina/białego wina
Po-pro-shair o boo-tel-kair/shklan-kair/dvyair shklan-kee vo-de mee-ne-ral-nay/boo-tel-kair/kee-elishek/dva kee-elishkee cher-vo-ne-go vee-nah/bya-we-go vee-nah

I would like a beer/two beers, please
Poproszę o piwo/dwa piwa
Po-pro-shair o pee-vo/dvah pee-wah

Please may I have some ice?
Poproszę o lód?
Po-pro-shair o lood?

Do you have any matches/ cigarettes/cigars?
Czy można kupić zapałki/papierosy/cygara?
Che mo-jnah koo-peech za-paw-kee/pa-pye-ro-se/ci-ga-rah?

Restaurants

Can you recommend a good/ cheap restaurant in this area?
Czy mógłby Pan/mogłaby Pani polecić dobrą/tanią restaurację w tej okolicy?
Che moog-wbe pan/mog-wa-be pa-nee po-le-cheech do-broh/ta-nyoh re-staw-ra-tsyair v tey o-ko-lee-tse?

I would like a table for ... people
Poproszę o stolik dla ... osób.
Po-pro-shair o sto-leek dla ... o-soob

Do you have a non-smoking area?
Czy jest sala dla niepalących?
Che yest sa-la dla nyair-pa-lon-tseh?

Waiter/Waitress!
Kelner/Kelnerka!
Kelner/Kelnerka!

Excuse me, please may we order?
Przepraszam, chcielibyśmy/ chciałybyśmy (fem.) złożyć

zamówienie?
Pshe-pra-sham hche-lee-be-shme/hcha-le-be-shme zwo-jech za-moo-vye-nyair?

Do you have a set menu/children's menu/wine list/in English?
Czy macie menu/menu dla dzieci/kartę win w języku angielskim?
Che ma-chair me-nee/menu dla jechee/ka-rtair veen v yen-zi-koo an-gyel-skim?

Do you have any vegetarian dishes?
Czy macie dania jarskie?
Che ma-chair da-nya yarskye?

Do you have any local specialities?
Czy macie dania kuchni polskiej?
Che ma-chair da-nya koo-hnee pol-skyey?

Are vegetables included?
Czy warzywa są wliczone?
Che va-je-vah soh vlee-cho-neh?

Could I have it well-cooked/medium/rare please?
Poproszę o dobrze/średnio/lekko wysmażone?
Po-pro-shair o do-bjeh/shre-dnyo/lek-ko ve-sma-jo-ne?

What does this dish consist of?
Jakie są składniki tej potrawy?
Ya-kye soh skwa-dnee-kee tey po-tra-ve?

I am a vegetarian. Does this contain meat?
Jestem wegetarianinem/wegetarianką (fem.). Czy w tym daniu jest mięso?
Yestem vegetarianinem/vegetariankahng. Tchee fteem dah-nyoo yest myensoh?

I do not eat nuts/dairy products/meat/fish
Nie mogę jeść orzechów/produktów mlecznych/mięsa/ryb
Nyair mo-ghair ye-shch o-je-hoof/pro-doo-ktoof mle-chneh/myair-sah/rib

Not (very) spicy please
Proszę, żeby nie było (zbyt) pikantne
Pro-shair, je-be nyair be-woh (zbit) pee-kan-tne

I would like the set menu please
Poproszę o zestaw obiadowy
Po-pro-shair o ze-stav obiadove

We have not been served yet
Nie obsłużono nas jeszcze
Nye obswoozhono nas yeshche

Please bring a plate/knife/fork
Poproszę o talerz/nóś/widelec
Poh-proshair oh tah-lesh/noosh/vee-deh-lets

Excuse me, this is not what I ordered
Przepraszam, to nie jest to co zamówiłem/zamówiłam (fem.)
Pshe-pra-sham toh nyair yest toh coh za-moo-vee-wem/za-moo-vee-wam

May I have some/more bread/water/coffee/tea?
Poproszę o więcej chleba/wody/kawy/herbaty?
Po-pro-shair o vyen-tsey hle-bah/vo-de/ka-ve/herba-te?

May I have the bill please?
Poproszę o rachunek?
Po-pro-shair o ra-hoo-neck?

Does this bill include service?
Czy opłata za obsługę jest wliczona?
Che o-pwa-tah za ob-swoo-ghair yest vlee-chonah?

Do you accept traveller's cheques/Mastercard/ US dollars?
Czy mogę zapłacić czekami podróżnymi/Mastercard/ dolarami amerykańskimi?
Che mo-gair pwa-cheech che-ka-mee po-droo-jne-me/master-kard/ dola-ramee ameri-kan-skeemee?

Can I have a receipt please?
Poproszę o pokwitowanie/ paragon?
Po-pro-shair o po-kvee-toh-va-nyair/pa-ra-ghon?

Where is the toilet (restroom) please?
Przepraszam, gdzie jest toaleta?
Pshe-pra-sham ghjair yest toe-a-lair-tah?

On the Menu

Śniadanie/obiad/kolacja
Shnyah-dah-nyeah/oh-b-yahd/ koh-latsyah
Breakfast/Lunch/Dinner

Pierwsze danie
Pier-vsheh da-nyair
First Courses

Zupy
Zoo-pe
Soups

Główne danie
Gwoo-vneh da-nyair
Main Courses

Dania rybne
Da-nyair rib-ne
Fish Dishes

Dania mięsne
Da-nyair myair-snair
Meat Dishes

Wołowina
Vo-woe-veenah
Beef

Stek
Stehk
Steak

Wieprzowina
Wyep-shoh-veenah
Pork

Cielęcina
Chch-lcn-chee-nah
Veal

Kurczak
Koor-chuck
Chicken

Jagnięcina
Yag-nyen-chee-nah
Lamb

Szynka
Sheen-kah
Ham

Dania wegetariańskie
Da-nyair ve-ge-ta-ryan-skyair
Vegetarian Dishes

Warzywa
Vah-zhee-vah
Vegetables

Frytki
Freet-key
Chips (french fries)

Ziemniaki gotowane/sauté/ puree
Zyem-nyah-key goh-toh-vah-neh/sauté/pew-reh
Boiled/sauté/mashed potatoes

Ryż
Reezh
Rice

Desery
De-se-re
Desserts

Lody
Loh-dee
Ice cream

Ciasta
Chas-tah
Cakes

Ciastka
Chast-kah
Pastries

Owoce
O-voh-tseh
Fruit

Chleb
H-lep
Bread

Bułki
Boow-key
Rolls

Tosty
Tohsteh
Toast

Masło
Mah-swoh
Butter

Sól/pieprz
Sool/pyepsh
Salt/pepper

Cukier
Tsoo-kier
Sugar

Specjalność
Spe-tsyal-noshch
Specialities

Miejscowe dania
Mye-ys-tso-veh da-nyah
Local specialities

Zestaw obiadowy
Zestaf ob-ya-do-vee
Set Menu

Karta win
Kartah veen
Wine list

Wina czerwone
Vee-nah cher-vo-neh
Red wines

Wina białe
Veenah byaweh
White wines

Wina różowe
Veenah roozhoveh
Rosé wines

Wina musujące
Veenah moo-soo-yon-tseh
Sparkling wines

Piwo
Peevoh
Beer

Piwo w butelkach/Piwo z beczki
Peevo vboo-tell-kah/peevoh zbech-key
Bottled beer/Draught (draft) beer

Napoje bezalkoholowe
Nah-poyeh bez-alko-holo-veh
Non-alcoholic drinks

Woda mineralna
Vodah mee-neh-ralnah
Mineral water

Soki owocowe
Soh-key ovotsove
Fruit juices

Sok pomarańczowy
Sok poh-maran-choh-vee
Orange juice

Lemoniada
Leh-moh-nyah-dah
Lemonade

Lód
Lood
Ice

Kawa z mlekiem/czarna kawa/espresso
Kavah z mleh-kyem/char-nah kavah/espresso
White coffee/black coffee/espresso coffee

Herbata z mlekiem/z cytryną
Her-bah-tah z mleh-kyem/s tsit-rinom
Tea with milk/with lemon

Czekolada na gorąco
Cheh-koh-lah-dah nah go-rontsoh
Chocolate (drink)

Mleko
Mlekoh
Milk

Przekąski/Lekkie posiłki
Pshe-konskey/lek-kye poh-sheew-key
Snacks/Light meals

Sałatki
Sah-wat-key
Salads

Kanapki
Kah-nap-key
Sandwiches

Jajka
Yay-kah
Eggs

Kiełbasa
Kye-w-bah-sah
Sausage

Jajka gotowane/sadzone/jajecznica
Yay-kah goh-toh-vah-neh/sah-dzoh-neh/ya-yech-nee-tsah
Boiled/fried/scrambled eggs

Typical Local Dishes

Rosół
Ro-soow
Broth, usually served with noodles

Śledź w śmietanie
Shlej v shmye-ta-nyair
Herring in sour cream

Karp gotowany w jarzynach
Karp go-toh-va-ne v ya-jee-nah
Steamed carp with vegetables

Bigos
Bee-gos
Sauerkraut with mixed meats stew

Kotlet schabowy z kapustą
Kot-let sha-bo-ve s ka-poo-stoh
Breaded pork cutlet, traditionally served with cabbage

Pierogi
Pier-oghee
Dumplings stuffed with cabbage, mushrooms, meat or various fruits

Kasza gryczana z kwaśnym mlekiem
Kasha ghre-cha-nah s kva-shnim mle-kyem
Buckwheat with sour milk or buttermilk

Makowiec
Ma-ko-vyets
Traditional poppy seed roll

GETTING AROUND

Public Transport

Where is the bus stop/coach stop/nearest metro station?
Gdzie jest najbliższy przystanek autobusowy/metra?
Ghjair yest nay-blee-jshe pshe-sta-nek awto-boo-so-ve/metrah?

When is the next/last bus to ...?
O której godzinie jest następny/ostatni autobus do ...?
O ktoo-rey go-jee-nyair yest na-stem-pne/o-sta-tnee awto-boos doe ...?

POLISH

How much is the fare to the city centre (downtown)/ railway station/airport?
Ile kosztuje bilet do centrum miasta/dworca kolejowego/na lotnisko?
Ee-lair kosh-too-yeh bee-let doe tse-ntroom mya-stah/dvor-tsah ko-le-yo-ve-go/na lot-nis-koh?

Will you tell me when to get off?
Czy powie mi Pan/Pani kiedy wysiąść?
Che po-vye me pan/pa-nee kye-de ve-syonshch?

Does this bus go to ...?
Czy ten autobus jedzie do ...?
Che ten awto-boos ye-je doe ...?

Which number bus goes to ...?
Którym autobusem dojadę do ...?
Ktoo-rem awto-boo-sem do-ya-dair doe ...?

May I have a single (one way)/return (round trip)/day ticket/book of tickets?
Poproszę o bilet w jedną stronę/powrotny/bilet dzienny/ karnet?
Po-pro-shair o bee-let v ye-dnoh stro-nair/po-vrot-ne/bee-let jen-ne/ kar-net?

Taxis (Taxi)

I would like to go to ... How much will it cost?
Chciałbym/Chciałabym (fem.) dojechać do ... Ile będzie wynosić opłata?
Hcha-wbem/Hcha-wa-bem doe-ye-hach doe ... ee-lair beir-jair ve-no-sheech o-pwa-tah?

Please may I stop here?
Proszę się tu zatrzymać?
Pro-shair sheh too za-tshe-mach?

I would like to order a taxi today/tomorrow at 2pm to go from ... to ...
Chciałbym/Chciałabym (fem.) zamówić taksówkę na dzisiaj/jutro o godzinie drugiej z ... do ...
Hcha-wbem/Hcha-wa-bem za-moo-veech tax-oo-vkair na jee-shaigh/yoo-tro o goe-jee-nyair droo-ghey z ... doe

Entertainment

Can you recommend a good bar/nightclub?
Czy mógłby Pan/mogłaby Pani polecić dobry bar/klub nocny?
Che moog-wbe pan/mog-wa-be pa-nee po-le-cheech do-bre bar/kloob notsne?

Do you know what is on at the cinema (playing at the movies)/theatre at the moment?
Co jest teraz w kinach? Co grają w teatrze?
Tso yest te-ras v kee-nah? tso ghra-yom v teh-ah-tsheh?

I would like to book (purchase) ... tickets for the matinee/evening performance on Monday
Chciałbym/Chciałabym (fem.) zarezerwować/kupić ...

bilety na poranne/wieczorne przedstawienie w poniedziałek
Hcha-wbem/Hcha-wa-bimza-rair-zer-vo-vach/koo-peech ... bee-le-te na po-ran-ne/vye-chor-ne pshed-sta-vye-nyeh v po-nyair-ja-wek

What time does the film/ performance start?
O której zaczyna się film/przedstawienie?
O ktoo-rey za-che-nah sheh film/ pshed-sta-vye-nyeh?

COMMUNICATIONS

Post

How much will it cost to send a letter/postcard/this package to Britain/Ireland/ America/Canada/Australia/ New Zealand?
Ile kosztuje wysłanie listu/ pocztówki/tej paczki do Wielkiej Brytanii/Irlandii/Stanów Zjednoczonych/Kanady/ Australii/Nowej Zelandii?
Ee-lair ko-shtoo-yeh ve-swa-nyair lee-stoo/po-chtoo-vkee/tey pa-chkee doe vye-lkyey bre-ta-nee/ee-rlan-dee/sta-noov zye-dno-cho-neh/ka-na-de/aus-tra-lee/novey ze-lan-dee?

I would like one stamp/two stamps
Poproszę o jeden znaczek/dwa znaczki
Po-pro-shair o ye-den zna-chek/dva zna-chkee

I'd like ... stamps for postcards to send abroad, please
Poproszę o ... znaczki na pocztówki za granicę
Po-pro-shair o ... zna-chkee zah gra-nee-tsair

Phones

I would like to make a telephone call/reverse the charges to (make a collect call to) ...
Chciałbym/Chciałabym (fem.) zadzwonić ... na koszt odbiorcy
Hcha-wbem/Hcha-wabem za-jvo-neech ... nah kosht od-byor-tse

Which coins do I need for the telephone?
Których monet używa się do telefonu?
Ktoo-reh mo-net oo-je-vah sheh doe te-le-fo-noo?

The line is engaged (busy)
Linia jest zajęta
Lee-nyah yest za-yen-tah

The number is ...
To numer ...
Toh noo-merh ...

Hello, this is ...
Halo, mówi ...
Hah-loh, moo-vee ...

Please may I speak to ...?
Czy mogę rozmawiać z ...?
Che mo-ghair ro-zma-vyach z ...?

He/she is not in at the moment. Please can you call back?
Nie ma go/jej teraz w domu. Proszę zadzwonić później?
Nyair mah go/yey te-raz v do-moo Pro-shair za-jvo-neech poo-jney?

Where can I buy phone tokens or a phone card?
Gdzie mogę kupić żetony telefoniczne lub kartę telefoniczną?
Gjair mo-ghair koo-peech je-toh-ne te-le-fo-nee-chneh loob ka-rtair te-le-fo-nee-chnair?

SHOPPING

Shops

Księgarnia/Sklep papierniczy
Kshair-ghar-nyah/Sklehp pa-pier-neeche
Bookshop/Stationery

Jubiler/Pamiątki
Yoo-bee-lair/Pa-myont-kee
Jeweller/Gifts

Obuwie
O-boo-vyeh
Shoes

Odzież/Galanteria
O-djej/ga-lan-te-ryah
Clothes

Pralnia
Pral-nyah
Laundry

Artykuły metalowe
Arte-koo-we me-ta-lo-veh
Hardware

Fryzjer
Frez-yerr
Hairdresser

Piekarnia
P-ye-kar-nyah
Baker

Supermarket
Super-market
Supermarket

Fotograf
Fo-to-graf
Photo shop

Agencja turystyczna
A-ghen-tsyah too-re-ste-chnah
Travel Agent

Apteka
A-pte-kah
Pharmacy

In the Shops

What time do the shops open/close?
O której godzinie otwierają/zamykają sklepy?
O ktoo-rey go-jee-nyair otvyerayom/za-me-ka-yom skhle-pe?

Where is the nearest market?
Gdzie jest najbliższy targ?
Ghair yest nay-blee-jshe targ?

Can you show me the one in the window/ this one?
Proszę mi to pokazać/ Proszę mi pokazać to z wystawy?
Pro-shair me toh po-ka-zach/ pro-shair me po-ka-zach toh s ve-stah-ve?

Can I try this on?
Czy mogę to przymierzyć?
Che mo-ghair toh pshe-mye-jech?

What size is this?
Jaki to jest rozmiar?
Ya-kee toh yest roz-myarh?

This is too large/too small/too expensive. Do you have any others?
To jest zbyt duże/zbyt małe/zbyt drogie. Czy macie coś innego?
Toh yest zbit doo-jeh/zbit ma-weh/zbit dro-ghyeh. Che ma-che cosh in-ne-go?

My size is ...
Mój rozmiar to ...
Mooy roz-myarh toh ...

Where is the changing room/ children's/cosmetic/ ladieswear/menswear/food department?
Gdzie jest przymierzalnia? Gdzie jest dział dziecięcy/ kosmetyczny/damski/męski/ spożywczy?
Gjair yest pshe-mye-jal-nyah/ Gjair yest jyaw jair-chyen-tse/ ko-sme-te-chne/dam-skee/ men-skee/spo-je-vche?

I would like ... a quarter of a kilo/ half a kilo/ a kilo of bread/butter/ham/this fruit
Poproszę ... o ćwierć kilo/pół kilo/chleba/masła/szynki/tych owoców
Po-proshair ... o chvyerch kee-loh/ poow kee-loh/hle-bah/ma-swah/ she-nkee/teh o-vo-tsoov

How much is this?
Ile to kosztuje?
Ee-lair toh ko-shtoo-yeh?

I'll take this one, thank you
Poproszę o to
Po-pro-shair o toh

Do you have a carrier (shopping) bag?
Czy mogę prosić o torbę?
Chi mogem proshich o torbem?

Do you have anything cheaper/larger/smaller/ of better quality?
Czy macie coś tańszego/ większego/mniejszego/lepszej jakości?
Che ma-che cosh ta-nsheh-go/vyair-kshair-go/le-pshey ya-ko-shchee?

I would like a film for this camera. I would like this film developed
Poproszę o film do tego aparatu. Chciałbym/chciałabym (fem.) wywołać film
Po-pro-shair o film doh te-go a-pa-ra-too hcha-wbem/hcha-wa-bem ve-vo-wach film

I would like some batteries, the same size as this old one
Poproszę o kilka baterii tego samego rodzaju, jak te zużyte
Po-pro-shair o keel-kah ba-te-ree te-go sa-me-go ro-za-joo, yak teh zoo-je-teh

Would you mind wrapping this for me, please?
Czy byłby Pan uprzejmy/byłaby Pani uprzejma zapakować?
Che be-wbe pan uprzeymee/ beewabee/pa-nee oo-pshey-mah za-pa-ko-vach?

P O L I S H

Sorry, but you seem to have given me the wrong change
Przepraszam, wydaje mi się, że pomylił się Pan/pomyliła się pani przy wydawaniu
Pshe-pra-sham ve-da-ye me sheh je po-me-leew sheh Pan/po-me-leewah sheh pa-nee pshe ve-da-va-nyoo

MOTORING

Car Hire (Rental)

I have ordered (rented) a car in the name of ...
Zamówiłem (wynająłem) samochód na nazwisko ...
Za-moo-vee-wem (ve-na-yair-wem) sa-mo-ho-d nah na-zvee-sko ...

How much does it cost to hire (rent) a car for one day/ two days/ a week?
Ile kosztuje wynającie samochódu na jeden dzień/dwa dni/tydzień?
Ee-lair ko-shtoo-yeh ve-na-yair-chair sa-mo-ho-doo na ye-den jen/dva dnee/te-jen?

Is the tank already full of petrol (gas)?
Czy bak jest pełny?
Che bak yest pe-wne?

Is insurance and tax included? How much is the deposit?
Czy wliczono ubezpieczenie i podatek? Ile wynosi kaucja?
Che vlee-cho-no oo-bez-pye-che-nyeh ee po-da-tek? Ee-lair ve-no-shee kaw-tsyah?

By what time must I return the car?
O której godzinie muszę zwrócić samochód?
O ktoo-rey go-jee-nyair moo-shair zvroo-cheech sa-mo-hood?

I would like a small/large/ family/sports car with a radio/ cassette
Chciałbym/chciałabym (fem.) mały/duży/rodzinny samochód z radiem/magnetofonem
Hcha-wbem/hcha-wa-bem ma-we/doo-je/ro-jeen-ne sa-mo-hood s ra-dyem/ma-gne-toh-fo-nem

Do you have a road map?
Czy ma Pan/Pani mapę drogową?
Che ma pan/pa-nee ma-pair dro-go-vom?

Parking

How long can I park here?
Jak długo można tu parkować?
Yak dwoo-go mo-jnah too par-ko-vach?

Is there a car park near here?
Czy jest tu parking w pobliżu?
Che yest too par-keeng v po-blee-joo?

At what time does this car park close?
O której godzinie zamyka się parking?
O ktoo-rey go-jee-nyair za-me-kah sheh par-keeng?

Signs and Notices

Droga jednokierunkowa
Dro-gah ye-dno kye-roon-ko-vah
One way

Zakaz wjazdu
Za-kaz vya-zdoo
No entry

Zakaz parkowania
Za-kaz par-ko-va-nyah
No parking

Objazd
Ob-yazd
Detour (Diversion)

Stop
Stop
Stop

Dać pierwszeństwo przejazdu.
Dach pier-vshen-stvo pshe-yaz-doo
Give way (Yield)

Śliska droga
Shlee-skah dro-gah
Slippery road

Zakaz wyprzedzania
Za-kaz ve-pshe-za-nyah
No overtaking

Niebezpieczeństwo!/Uwaga!
Nyair-bez-pye-chen-stvo!/ Oo-va-gah!
Danger!

At the Filling Station (Stacja Benzynowa)

Unleaded (lead free)/ standard/premium/diesel
Bezołowiowa/zwyczajna/ super/diesel
Bez-owo-vyo-vah/zve-chay-nah/ soo-per/dee-zel

Fill the tank please
Pełny bak proszę
Pew-ne bak pro-shair

Do you have a road map?
Czy ma Pan/Pani mapę drogową?
Che ma pan/pa-nee ma-pair dro-go-vom?

How much is the car wash?
Ile kosztuje mycie samochodu?
Ee-lair ko-shtoo-yair me-chair sa-mo-ho-doo?

Breakdowns

I've had a breakdown at ...
Zepsuł mi się samochód w ...
Ze-psoow me sheh sa-mo-hood v ...

I am a member of the ... [motoring organisation]
Jestem członkiem ...
Yestem chwon-kyem ...

I am on the road from ... to ...
Jestem na drodze z ... do ...
Ye-stem nah dro-zair z ... doh ...

MOTORING

POLISH

I can't move the car. Can you send a tow-truck?
Nie mogę ruszyć. Czy może Pan/Pani przysłać samochód do holowania?
Nyair mo-ghair roo-shech. Che mo-jeh Pan/Pa-nee psh-swach sa-mo-hood doh ho-lo-va-nayah?

I have a flat tyre
Mam przebitą oponę
Mam pshe-bee-tom o-po-nair

The windscreen (windshield) has smashed/ cracked
Rozbiła się/pękła przednia szyba
Roz-bee-wah sheh/pen-kwah pshe-dnyah she-bah

There is something wrong with the engine/brakes/lights/ steering/gearbox/clutch/ exhaust
Coś się zepsuło w silniku/ hamulcach/swiatłach/kierownicy/skrzyni biegów/sprzęgle/ rurze wydechowej
Tsosh sheh ze-psoo-woh v sheel-nee-koo/ha-mool-tsah/shvya-twah/ kye-ro-vnee-tse skshe-ne bye-goof/ spshen-gleh/roo-jeh ve-de-ho-vey

It's overheating
Przegrzało się
Pshe-gja-wo sheh

It won't start
Nie chce zapalić
Nyair htseh za-pa-leech

Where can I get it repaired?
Gdzie to można naprawić?
Ghje toh mo-jnah na-pra-veech?

Can you take me there?
Czy może mnie Pan/Pani tam zawieźć?
Che mo-jeh mnyeh Pan/Pa-nee tam za-vyeshch?

Will it take long to fix?
Czy naprawa będzie długo trwała?
Che na-pra-vah ben-jeh dwoo-go trva-wah?

How much will it cost?
Ile to będzie kosztowało?
Ee-lair toh ben-jeh ko-sh-toh-va-woh?

Please can you pick me up/ give me a lift?
Czy mógłby Pan/czy mogłaby Pani mnie podwieźć?
Che moog-wbe Pan/mog-wa-be Pa-nee mnyeh pod-vye-shch?

Accidents and Traffic Offences (Violations)

Can you help me? There has been an accident
Proszę mi pomóc. Chodzi o wypadek
Proshem mi pomootz? Hodzhi o vipadek

Please call the police/an ambulance
Proszę wezwać policję/ pogotowie
Proshem vezvach policyem/ pogotohvye

Is anyone hurt?
Czy ktoś jest ranny?
Chi ktosh yest rannee?

I'm sorry, I didn't see the sign
Przepraszam, nie zauważyłem /zauważyłam (fem.) znaku
Pshe-pra-sham nyair za-oo-va-je-wem/za-oo-va-je-wam zna-koo

Must I pay a fine? How much?
Czy muszę zapłacić mandat? Ile to wynosi?
Che moo-shair za-pwa-cheech man-dat? Ee-lair to ve-no-shee?

Proszę pokazać dokumenty
Pro-shair po-ka-zach do-koo-men-te
Show me your documents

HEALTH

Pharmacy (Apteka)

Do you have anything for a stomach ache/ headache/ sore throat/ toothache?
Czy ma Pan/Pani coś na ból brzucha/ból głowy/ból gardła/ból zęba?
Che ma Pan/Pa-nee tsosh nah bool bjoo-hah/bool gwo-ve/bool gar-dwah/bool zem-bah?

I need something for diarrhoea/constipation/a cold/a cough/insect bites/ sunburn/travel (motion) sickness
Chciałbym/chciałabym (fem.) coś na biegunkę/zatwardzenie/ przeziębienie/kaszel/ukąszenie owada/oparzenie słoneczne/ chorobę lokomocyjną
Hcha-wbem/hcha-wa-bem tsosh nah bye-goon-kair/za-tvar-ze-nyeh/ pshe-jem-bye-nyeh/ka-shel/ oo-kon-sheh-nyeh o-va-dah/ o-pa-je-nyeh swo-ne-chneh/ ho-ro-bair lo-ko-mo-tsey-nom

How much/how many do I take?
W jakiej ilości mam to zażywać?
Y ya-kyey ee-lo-shchee toh za-je-vach?

I am taking anti-malaria tablets/these pills
Zażywam tabletki przeciw malarii/te tabletki
Za-je-vam ta-blet-kee pshe-cheef ma-la-ree/teh ta-ble-tkee

How often do I take it/them?
Jak często mam to zażywać?
Yak chen-sto mam toh za-je-vach?

I am/he is/she is taking this medication
Zażywam/on zażywa/ona zażywa to lekarstwo
Za-je-vam/on za-je-vah/onah za-je-vah toh le-kar-stvoh

How much does it cost?
Ile to kosztuje?
Ee-lair toh ko-shtoo-yeh?

Can you recommend a good doctor/dentist?
Czy mógłby Pan/mogłaby Pani polecić mi dobrego lekarza/dentystę?
Che moog-wbe pan/mog-wa-be pa-nee po-le-cheech me do-bre-go le-kajah/den-tes-tair?

Is it suitable for children?
Czy to można podawać dzieciom?
Che toh mo-jnah po-da-vach jaircham?

Doctor (Lekarz)

I have a pain here/in my arm/leg/chest/stomach
Boli mnie tutaj/ramię/noga/w klatce piersiowej/żołądek
Po-lee mnyeh too-tigh/ra-myeh/no-ghah/v klat-tse pier-syo-vey/jo-won-dek

Please call a doctor, this is an emergency
Proszę wezwać lekarza, to jest nagły przypadek
Pro-shair ve-zvach le-ka-jah, toh yest na-gwe pshe-pa-dek

I would like to make an appointment to see the doctor
Chciałbym/chciałabym (fem.) uzgodnić wizytę lekarską
Hcha-wbem/hcha-wa-bem oo-zgo-dneech vee-ze-tair le-kar-skom

I am diabetic
Mam cukrzycę
Mam tsoo-kshe-cair

I am pregnant
Jestem w ciąży
Ye-stem v tson-je

I need a prescription for ...
Potrzebuję receptę na ...
Po-tshe-boo-yair re-tse-ptair nah ...

Can you give me something to ease the pain?
Czy mógłbym/mogłabym (fem.) dostać coś przeciwbólowego?
Che moog-wbem/mog-wa-bem doh-stach tsosh pshe-tseev-boo-lo-ve-go?

I am/he is/she is allergic to penicillin
Jestem/on jest/ona jest uczulony/uczulona (fem.) na penicylinę
Ye-stem/on yest/onah yest oo-choo-lo-nah na pe-nee-tse-lee-neir

Czy to boli?
Che toh bo-lee?
Does this hurt?

Musi Pan/Pani iść do szpitala
Moo-shee pan/pa-nee ee-shch doh sh-pee-ta-lah
You must/ he must/ she must go to hospital

Zażywać raz/dwa razy/trzy razy dziennie
Za-je-vach ras/dva ra-ze/tshe ra-ze jen-nyeh
Take these once/twice/three times a day

I am/he is/she is taking this medication
Zażywam/on zażywa/ona zażywa to lekarstwo
Za-je-vam/on za-je-vah/onah za-je-vah toh le-kar-stvoh

I have medical insurance
Jestem ubezpieczony/ubezpieczona (fem.)
Ye-stem oo-bez-pye-cho-ne/oo-bez-pye-cho-nah

Dentist (Dentysta/Stomatolog)

I have toothache/my filling has come out
Boli mnie ząb/Wypadła mi plomba
Bo-lee mnyeh zomb/ve-pa-dwa me plombah

I want to have an injection first
I do not want to have an injection first
Chciałbym/Chciałabym (fem.) dostać najpierw zastrzyk.
Nie chciałbym/chciałabym (fem.) dostawać zastrzyku
Hcha-wbem/Hcha-wa-bem do-stach nay-pierf za-stshek.
Nyair hcha-wbem/hcha-wa-bem do-sta-vach za-stshe-koo

EMERGENCIES

Help!
Pomocy!
Po-mo-tse!

Fire!
Pożar!
Po-jar!

Stop!
Stop! Stój!
Stop/Stooy!

Call an ambulance/a doctor/ the police/the fire brigade!
Wezwać pogotowie/lekarza/ policję/straż pożarną!
Ve-zvach po-go-toh-vyeh/ le-ka-jah/po-lee-tsyehstraj po-jar-nom!

Please may I use a telephone?
Czy mogę skorzystać z telefonu?
Che mo-ghair sko-je-stach s te-le-fo-noo?

I have had my travellers' cheques/credit cards/ handbag/rucksack/luggage/ wallet/passport/mobile phone stolen
Skradziono moje czeki podróżne/moje karty kredytowe/moją torebkę/mój plecak/mój bagaż/mój portfel/ paszport/telefon komórkowy
Skra-jo-noh mo-yeh che-kee po-droo-jneh/mo-yeh kar-te kre-de-toh-veh/mo-yoh to-reb-kair/mooy ple-tsak/mooy ba-gaj/mooy port-fel/ pash-port/teh-lefon koh-moor-koh-vee

May I please have a copy of the report for my insurance claim?
Poproszę kopię raportu dla mojego towarzystwa ubez-pieczeniowego?
Poh-proshair oh kopyeh rah-portoo dlah moyego toh-vah-zhees-tvah oo-bes-pye-che-nyo-vegoh?

Can you help me?
I have lost my daughter
I have lost my son
I have lost my companion
I have lost my companions
Proszę mi pomóc?
Moja córka zgubiła się
Mój syn zgubił się
Mój znajomy zgubił się.
Moi znajomi zgubili się

Pro-shair me po-moots? /Mo-yah tsoor-kah zgoo-bee-wah sheh /Mooy sen zgoo-beew sheh /Mooy znay-omee zgoo-beew sheh/Mo-yee znay-omee zgoo-bee-leeh sheh

Please go away!/Leave me alone
Proszę odejść!/Proszę mnie zostawić w spokoju
Pro-shair o-dey-shch!/Pro-shair mnyeh zo-sta-veech v spo-ko-yoo

I'm sorry
Przepraszam
Pshe-pra-sham

I want to contact the British/American/Canadian/ Irish/Australian/New Zealand/South African Consulate
Chciałbym się skontaktować z Konsulatem Brytyjskim/ Amerykańskim/Kanadyjskim/ Irlandzkim/Australijskim/ Nowozelandzkim/RPA
Hcha-wbem sheh skon-tak-toh-vach s Kon-soo-la-tem Bre-tey-skem/ Ame-re-kan-skem/Ka-na-dey-skem/ Eer-land-skem/Aus-tra-leey-skem/ No-vo-ze-land-skem/Air-Pey-Ah

I'm ill/we're ill/he is ill/she is ill/they are ill
Jestem chory/chora (fem.)/ jesteśmy chorzy/ona jest chora/on jest chory/oni są chorzy
Yestem ho-re /ho-rah./ye-ste-shme ho-je/onah yest ho-rah/on yest ho-re/onee soh ho-je

I'm lost/we're lost/he is lost/she is lost/they are lost
Zgubiłem/zgubiłam (fem.) się/ zgubiliśmy się/ona zgubiła się/ on zgubił się/oni zgubili się
Zgoo-bee-wem /zgoo-bee-wam sheh/zgoo-bee-lee-shme sheh/onah zgoo-bee-wa sheh/on zgoo-beew sheh/onee zgoo-bee-lee sheh

I'm injured/we're injured/he is injured/she is injured/they are injured
Jestem ranny/ranna (fem.)/ jesteśmy ranni/on jest ranny/ ona jest ranna/oni są ranni
Yestem ran-ne/ran-nah/ye-ste-shme ran-nee/onah yest ran-nah/on yest ran-ne/onee soh ran-nee

PORTUGUESE

INTRODUCTION

Portuguese is a descendant of Latin, like Italian, Spanish and French, and a knowledge of any of these other languages will help you to understand a lot of written Portuguese. Spoken Portuguese, however, can be quite difficult for a beginner to comprehend and to speak, and you may need to ask to have things written down for you more often than in other Western European countries. If you have to resort to speaking a second language, try English or even French rather than Spanish.

Addresses for Travel and Tourist Information

Australia: *Consulate-General,* 30 Clarence St, Level 9, Sydney, NSW 2000; tel: (02) 9262 2199; fax: (02) 9262 5991.

UK: *Portuguese Tourism Office,* Portuguese Embassy, 11 Belgrave Sq., London SW1X 8PP; tel: (020) 7201 6633 (brochure line 0845 355 1212); fax: (020) 7201 6633.

USA: *Portuguese National Tourist Office,* 590 Fifth Ave, New York, NY 10036; tel: (800) PORTUGAL or (212) 354 4403.

Official tourism website: www.portugalinsite.com.

Portugal Facts

CAPITAL: Lisbon, Lisboa
CURRENCY: Euro (€). €1 = 100 cents.
OPENING HOURS: Banks: Mon–Fri 0830–1500. Shops: Mon–Fri 0900–1300, 1500–1900; Sat 0900–1300; shopping centres every day 1000–2300. Museums: generally 1000–1230, 1400–1700, closed Monday.
TELEPHONES: To dial in, +351. Outgoing, 00 plus the country code. Police, Fire, Ambulance, all 115 (112 in Madeira).
PUBLIC HOLIDAYS: 1 Jan; Good Friday; 25 Apr; 1 May; Corpus Christi (May/Jun); 15 Aug; 5 Oct; 1 Nov; 1, 8, 25 Dec.

Technical Language Hints

The most noticeable characteristics of Portuguese are the many diphthongs and nasal sounds. Although they are not difficult for an English speaker to pronounce, they can be intimidating when you hear them spoken by a Portuguese speaker at speed. Some characters have more than one pronunciation, though in practice you soon become familiar with

these: e.g. x is normally like English sh, as in peixe (fish), but sometimes it is like the English x, as in táxi (taxi), sometimes an s sound, as in próximo (next) or even a z sound, as in exame (exam).

ESSENTIALS

Alphabet and Pronunciation

	Name	Pronounced
A a	*ah*	**long a as in father; short a is a neutral sound like the a of about**
B b	*beh*	**like English b**
C c	*she*	**hard c, as in card, before a, o and u; before e and i like s, as in cede; ch is pronounced sh, like the ch of charade**
Ç ç		**like s, as in cede**
D d	*deh*	**like English d**
E e	*e*	**generally like short e of get; sometimes (including when written as ê) long e as in hey; when not stressed, er sound like the a of about; at the start of a word, short i sound as in sit**
F f	*effi*	**like English f**
G g	*jeh*	**hard g, as in go, before a, o and u; zh, like the s in pleasure, before e or i**
H h	*agah*	**not pronounced**
I i	*ee*	**long ee sound like the i of machine, or short i as in sit**
J j	*jota*	**zh, like the s in pleasure**
K k	*kahpa*	**in foreign words only**
L l	*elli*	**like English l; lh pronounced ly, like the ll in million**
M m	*emmi*	**at the start of a word or between vowels, like English m; at the end of words or before a consonant, m is not pronounced but makes the preceding vowel a nasal sound**
N n	*enni*	**at the start of a word or between vowels, like English n; before a consonant, n is not pronounced but makes the preceding vowel a nasal sound; nh is an ny sound, as in onion**
O o	*o*	**short o as in got or (including when in combination with u, ou) long oh as in boat; when not stressed, oo as in foot**

P p	*peh*	**like English p**
Q q	*keh*	**like English k**
R r	*erre*	**strongly trilled, as in Scottish**
S s	*essi*	**at the start of a word or after a consonant, hard s as in sit; between vowels, z sound like s of ease; at end of word and before some consonants, sh as in shut; before most consonants, zh sound like the s of pleasure**
T t	*tey*	**like English t**
U u	*oo*	**usually long oo as in zoo**
V v	*veh*	**like English v**
W w	*veh dooplo*	**in foreign words only**
X x	*sheesh*	**usually like sh in shut; some times like the English x; ex- is pronounced ez**
Y y	*eepselohn*	**in foreign words only**
Z z	*zeh*	**at the start of a word or between vowels, like English z; at end of word and before some consonants, sh as in shut; before most consonants, zh sound like the s of pleasure**

Basic Words and Phrases

Yes Sim *Seem*	**No** Não *Nown*
Please Por favor *Poor favohr*	**Thank you** Obrigado/a *Ohbreegahdoo/a*
Hello Olá *Ohlah*	**Goodbye** Adeus *Adayoosh*
Excuse me Com licença *Cong lisensah*	**Sorry** Desculpe *Dishkoolper*
How Como *Kohmoo*	**When** Quando *Kkwahndoo*
Why Porquê *Poorkay*	**What** O que *Oo ki*
Who Quem *Kerng*	
That's O.K. Está bem *Istah bayng*	**Perhaps** Talvez *Tahlvaysh*
To Para *Para*	**From** De *Di*
Here Aqui *Akee*	**There** Ali *Alee*
I don't understand Não entendo *Nown ayngtayngdoo*	

I don't speak Portuguese
Não sei falar Português
Nown say falahr Portoogehsh

Do you speak English?
Fala Inglês?
Fahla eenglaysh?

Can you please write it down?
Por favor, pode escrever isso?
Poor favohr pohd ishkrivayr eessoo?

Please can you speak more slowly?
Por favor, pode falar mais devagar?
Poor favohr, pohd falahr myish devagahr?

Greetings

Good morning/good afternoon/good evening/ goodnight
Bom dia/boa tarde/boa noite/boa noite
Bohm deea/boha tahrd/boha noyt

Pleased to meet you
Muito prazer
Muhingtoo prazayr

How are you?
Como está?
Kohmoo istah?

I am well thank you. And you?
Bem, obrigado. E você?
Bayng ohbreegahdoo. Ee vohsay?

My name is ...
Chamo-me ...
Shamoo-mi ...

This is my friend/boyfriend/ girlfriend/husband/wife/ brother/sister
Este é o meu/minha amigo/ amiga/namorado/namorada/ marido/mulher/irmão/irmã
Aysht e oo mayoo/meenya amighoo/amigha/namoorahdoo/namoorahda/mareedoo/moolyer/ eermowng/eermang

Where are you travelling to?
Para onde vai viajar?
Para ohngdee va'ee veeazhahr?

I am/we are going to ...
Vou/vamos para ...
Voh/vamoosh para ...

How long are you travelling for?
Por quanto tempo vai viajar?
Porr kwantoo tempo vay viazhar?

Where do you come from?
De onde é?
Di ohngd eh?

I am/we are from ... Australia/Britain/Canada/ America/New Zealand
Sou/somos de ... Austrália/ Grã-Bretanha/Canadá/América/ Nova Zelândia
Soh/sohmoosh di ... owstrahleea/ grang-britanya/kanadah/amehreeka/ nohva zelangdeea

We are on holiday
Estamos de férias
Ishtahmoos di fehreeas

This is our first visit here
Esta é a nossa primeira visita aqui
Ehshta e er nossa preemehrah visita ahkee

ESSENTIALS

How old are you?
Quantos anos tem?
Kwahntooss ahnoosh tehng?

I am ... years old
Tenho ... anos
Tehnyoo ... ahnoosh

I am a business person/ doctor/journalist/manual worker/administrator/ scientist/student/teacher
Sou um homem de negócios/ médico/jornalista/operário/ administrador/cientista/ estudante/professor
Soh oong omeng di nergossyoosh/ mehdikoo/zhoornalishta/operahree-oo/admeeneeshtradohr/see-enteesta/ishtoodante/professohr

I am waiting for my husband/ wife/boyfriend/girlfriend
Estou à espera do meu/minha marido/mulher/namorado/ namorada
Ishtoh ah ishpehra doo mayoo/ meenyia mareedoo/moolyer/ namoorahdoo/namoorahda

Would you like/may I have a cigarette?
Quer um cigarro/dá-me um cigarro?
Ker oong seegahrro/dah-mi oong seegahroo?

Do you mind if I smoke?
Importa-se se eu fumar?
Eemporta-si see ayoo foomahr?

Do you have a light?
Tem lume?
Tayng loome?

Days

Monday
Segunda-feira
Sigoongda-fayra

Tuesday
Terça-feira
Tayrsa-fayra

Wednesday
Quarta-feira
Kwahrta-fayra

Thursday
Quinta-feira
Keengta-fayra

Friday
Sexta-feira
Sayshta-fayra

Saturday
Sábado
Sahbadoo

Sunday
Domingo
Doomeengoo

Morning
Manhã
Manyang

Afternoon/Evening/Night
Tarde/Noite/Noite
Tahrd/Noyt/Noyt

Yesterday/Today/Tomorrow
Ontem/Hoje/Amanhã
Ohngtayng/Ohzhay/Ahmanyang

Numbers

Zero
Zero
Zeroo

One
Um
Oong

Two
Dois
Doysh

Three
Três
Traysh

Four
Quatro
Kwahtroo

Five
Cinco
Seengkoo

Six
Seis
Saysh

Seven
Sete
Set

Eight
Oito
Oytoo

Nine
Nove
Nov

Ten
Dez
Desh

Eleven
Onze
Ohngz

Twelve
Doze
Dohz

Thirteen
Treze
Trayz

Fourteen
Catorze
Katohrz

Fifteen
Quinze
Keengz

Sixteen
Dezasseis
Dizasaysh

Seventeen
Dezassete
Dizaset

Eighteen
Dezoito
Dizoytoo

Nineteen
Dezanove
Dizanov

Twenty
Vinte
Veengt

Twenty-one
Vinte e um
Veengt ee oong

Twenty-two
Vinte e dois
Veengt ee doysh

Thirty
Trinta
Treengta

Forty
Quarenta
Kwarayngta

Fifty
Cinquenta
Seengkwayngta

Sixty
Sessenta
Sisayngta

Seventy
Setenta
Sitayngta

Eighty
Oitenta
Oytayngta

Ninety
Noventa
Noovayngta

One hundred
Cem
Sayng

Five hundred
Quinhentos
Keenyengtoos

One thousand
Mil
Meel

One million
Um milhão
Oong meelyowng

Time

What time is it?
Que horas são?
Ki orash sowng?

It is ...
É/São ...
Eh/Sowng ...

9.00
Nove horas
Nov orash

9.05
Nove e cinco
Nov ee seengkoo

9.15
Nove e um quarto
Nov ee oong kwahrtoo

9.20
Nove e vinte
Nov ee veengt

9.30
Nove e meia
Nov ee maya

9.35
Nove e trinta e cinco
Nov ee treengta ee seengkoo

9.40
Nove e quarenta
Nov ee kwarayngta

9.45
Nove e quarenta e cinco
Nov ee kwarayngta ee seengkoo

9.50
Nove e cinquenta
Nov ee seengkwayngta

9.55
Nove e cinquenta e cinco
Nov ee seengkwaynta ee seengkoo

12.00/Midday/Midnight
Doze horas/Meio dia/Meia noite
Dohzi orash/mayoo-deea/maya-noyt

Money

I would like to change these traveller's cheques/this currency
Queria trocar estes cheques de viagem/estas divisas
Kireea trookahr aystsh shehkish di veeazhayng/ehshtash deeveezash

How much commission do you charge? (What is the service charge?)
Que comissão cobra?
Ke coomeessowng kohbra?

Can I obtain money with my Mastercard?
Posso levantar dinheiro com o meu Mastercard?
Possoo levangtahr deenyayroo kohm oo mayo mahstercahrd?

Where is the nearest ATM?
Onde fica a caixa multibanco mais próxima?
Awngder feeka ah kysha moltibahngkoo mysh prossima?

My name is ... Some money has been wired to here for me to collect
Chamo-me ... Enviaram algum dinheiro para aqui para eu levantar
Shamoo-mi ... Enveearahng algoong dinyehroo para erkee para eh-oo lervangtahr

ARRIVING AND DEPARTING

Airport

Excuse me, where is the check-in desk for ...?
Desculpe, onde é o balcão de check-in da ...?
Dishkoolp, ohngdee eh oo bahlkowngdi check-een da ...?

What is the boarding gate/time for my flight?
Qual é a porta/hora para o meu voo?
Kwal e a porta/ora para oo mayo vo'oo?

How long is the delay likely to be?
De quanto será o atraso?
Di kwanto sirah oo atrahzoo?

Where is the duty-free shop?
Onde é a loja duty-free?
Ohngdee eh a lohzha duty-free?

Which way is the luggage reclaim?
Onde é a recolha de bagagem?
Ohngdee eh a rrecohlya di bagahzhayng?

I have lost my luggage. Please can you help?
Perdi as minhas malas. Pode ajudar-me?
Perdee as meenyas mahlas. Pohdee ahzhoodar-mi?

I am flying to ...
Vou de avião para ...
Voh di ervyahng para ...

Where is the bus for the city centre (downtown)?
Onde posso apanhar o autocarro para o centro da cidade?
Ohngd possoo apanyar oo owtohk-ahrroo para o sayngtroo da seedahdi?

Trains and Boats

Where is the ticket office/ information desk?
Onde é a bilheteira/o balcão de informações?
Ohngdee eh a beelyaytayra/oo bahlkowng di eenfoormasoyesh?

Which platform does the train/speedboat/ferry to ... depart from?
De que plataforma partirá o combóio/barco/ferry para ...?
Di ke plataforma pahrtirah oo kohmboyoo/barkoo/ferry para ...?

Where is platform ...?
Onde é a linha ...?
ohngdee eh a leenya ...?

When is the next train/boat to ...?
Quando é o próximo combóio/barco para ...?
Kwandoo eh oo prohseemoo kohmboyoo/barkoo para ...?

Is there a later train/boat to ...?
Há algum combóio/barco mais tarde para ...?
Ah algoong kohmboyoo/barkoo my-ish tahrd para ...?

Notices and Signs

Carruagem-Restaurante
Karrooahzhayng rishtowrahnt
Buffet (Dining) car

Autocarro
Owtokahrroo
Bus

Água potável/não potável
Ahgwa pootahvel/nown pootahvel
Drinking/non-drinking water

Entrada
Entrahda
Entrance

Saída
Saihda
Exit

Hospital
Ohshpitahl
Hospital

Informações
Eenfoormasoyesh
Information

Recolha de Bagagem
Rrecohliya do bagahzhayng
Left luggage (Baggage claim)

Cacifos de bagagem
Kaseefoosh di bagahzhayng
Luggage lockers

Correio
Koorrayoo
Post office

Linha
Leenya
Platform

Estação de Caminho de Ferro
Ishtasowng di kamihnyo di fehrroo
Railway (Railroad) station

Aeroporto
Aehrohportoo
Airport

Posto da polícia
Pohshtoo da pooleeseea
Police station

Porto
Porto
Port

Restaurante
Ristowrangt
Restaurant

Fumadores/Não fumadores
Foomadohrsh/nown-foomadohrsh
Smoking/non-smoking

Telefone
Tilifohne
Telephone

Bilheteira
Beelyaytayra
Ticket Office

Balcão de check-in
Bahlkowng di check-een
Check-in Desk

Horário
Orahreoo
Timetable (Schedule)

Lavabos
Lavahboosh
Toilets (Restrooms)

Senhoras/Homens
(Cavalheiros)
Sinyohrash/Omayngsh
(Kavalyayroosh)
Ladies/Gentlemen

Metropolitano
Metropooleetahnoo
Underground (Subway)

Sala de espera
Sahla di ishpehra
Waiting Room

Buying a Ticket

I would like a first-class/ second-class single (one-way)/return (round-trip) ticket to ...
Queria um bilhete de primeira classe/segunda classe/simples/ida e volta para ...
Kireea oong beelyayt di preemayra/sigoonda klahs/seem-plish/eeda ee vohlta para ...

Is it an express (fast) train/bus?
Aquele comboio/autocarro é um expresso?
Erkehleh kohmboyoo/owtohkahroo eh oong ezpressoo?

Is my rail pass valid on this train/ferry/bus?
A minha assinatura é válida para este combóio/barco/autocarro?
A meenya aseenatoora eh vahleeda para eshte lohmboyoo/bahrkoo/ owtohkahrroo?

I would like an aisle/window seat
Queria um lugar no corredor/ na janela
Kireea oong loogahr noo korridohr/ na zhanehla

No smoking/smoking, please
Por favor, não fumador/fumador
Poor favohr, nown foomadohr/ foomadohr

We would like to sit together
Queríamos lugares juntos
Kireeamoosh loogahrsh zhoongtoosh

I would like to make a seat reservation
Queria marcar um lugar
Kireea marcahr oong loogahr

I would like to reserve a couchette/sleeper for one person/two people/for my family
Queria marcar uma couchette/ cama para uma pessoa/duas pessoas/para a minha família
Kireea marcahr ooma koooshet/ kama para ooma pesoha/dooash pesohash/para a meenya fameehleea

I would like to reserve a cabin
Queria marcar uma cabina
Kireea markahr ooma kahbeena

Timetables (Schedules)

Chegada
Shigahda
Arrive

Com paragem em ...
Kohng parahzhayng ayng ...
Calls (Stops) at ...

Serviço de Restaurante
Serveehsoo di rishtowrangt
Catering service

Mudar em ...
Moodahr ayng ...
Change at ...

Ligação/Via
Leegasowng/Veeah
Connection/Via

Todos os dias
Tohdoosh oosh deeash
Daily

De 40 em 40 minutos
Di 40 ayng 40 meenootoosh
Every 40 minutes

Primeira Classe
Preemayra klahs
First class

De hora a hora
Di ora a ora
Hourly

Recomenda-se marcação de lugares
Rrikoomaynda-si markasowng si loogahrsh
Seat reservations are recommended

Segunda classe
Sigoonda klahs
Second Class

Suplemento Pagável
Sooplimayngtoo pagahvel
Supplement Payable

Luggage

How much will it cost to send (ship) my luggage in advance?
Quanto custa mandar a minha bagagem primeiro?
Kwantoo kooshta mandahr a meenya bagahzhayng preemayuroo?

Where is the left luggage (baggage claim) office?
Onde é o escritório de recolha de bagagem?
Ohngdee eh oo ishkreetohreeoo di rricohliyadi bagahzhayng?

What time do you open/close?
A que horas abre/fecha?
A ke orash ahbre/fesha?

Where are the luggage trolleys (carts)?
Onde estão os carrinhos?
Ohngdee ishtowng oos karreenyoosh ?

Where are the lockers?
Onde são os cacifos?
Ohngd sowng oos kaseefoosh?

I have lost my locker key
Perdi a chave do meu cacifo
Perdee a shahve doo mayo kaseefoo

On Board

Is this seat taken?
Este lugar está ocupado?
Aysht loogahr istah ohkoopahdoo?

Excuse me, you are sitting in my reserved seat
Desculpe, está sentado no meu lugar marcado
Dishkoolp, istah sayntahdoo noo mayo loogahr markahdoo

Which station is this?
Que estação é esta?
Ki ishtasowng eh ehshta?

What time is this train/bus/ferry/flight due to arrive/depart?
A que horas deve chegar/partir este combóio/autocarro/barco/voo?
A ke orash dehv shigahr/parteer aysht kohngboyoo/owtohkahrro/bahrkoo/vo'oo?

Travelling with Children

Do you have a high chair/ babysitting service/cot?
Tem uma cadeira alta/serviço de babysitting/cama de bébé?
Tayng ooma kadayra ahlta/ sirveessoodi babysitting/kama di behbeh?

Where is the nursery/ playroom?
Onde é a creche/infantário?
Ohngd e er kresh/eengfantahreeoo

Where can I warm the baby's bottle?
Onde posso aquecer o biberon do bébé?
Ohngd possoo akesayr oo beeberohng doo behbeh?

Customs and Passports

Os passaportes, por favor!
Oosh pahsaportsh poor favohr!
Passports, please!

I have nothing to declare. I have wine/spirits (alcohol)/ tobacco to declare
Não tenho nada a declarar. Tenho/vinho/bebidas alcoólicas/ tabaco a declarar
Nown taynyoo nahda a deklarahr. Taynyoo nahda/veenyo/bibeedash ahlcohleecash/tabahkoo a deklarahr

I will be staying for ... days/weeks/months.
Vou ficar durante ... dias/ semanas/meses.
Voh feecahr doorangt ... deeash/simahnash/mehzesh

SIGHTSEEING

Asking the Way

Excuse me, do you speak English?
Desculpe, fala Inglês?
Dishkoolp, fahla eenglays?

Excuse me, can you help me please?
Por favor, será que poderia ajudar-me?
Poor favohr, serah ki pohdereea ahzhoodar-mi?

Where is the Tourist Information Office?
Onde é o Turismo?
Ohngdee eh oo tooreeshmoo?

Excuse me, is this the right way to ...?
Desculpe é este o caminho certo para ...?
Dishkoolp, eh aysht oo kameenyo sehrtoo para ...?

... the cathedral/the Tourist Information Office/the castle/ the old town
... a catedral/os serviços de informações turísticas (o turismo)/o castelo/a cidade velha
... er katidrahl/oos sirveessoos de eemfoormasoyesh tooreehshteekash (oo tooreesmoo)/oo kastehloo/er seedahd vehlya

Can you tell me the way to the railway (railroad) station/ bus station/taxi rank (stand)/ city centre (downtown)/ beach?
Pode-me indicar o caminho para a estação de caminho de ferro

estação de autocarros/a paragem de táxis/o centro da cidade/a praia?
Podd-mi eendeecahr oo kameenyoo para er ishtasowng de kameenyo do fehrro ishtasowng di owtohkahrrosh/er parahzhayng de tahkseesh/oo sayntroo da seedahd/er prahya?

Primeira/segunda à esquerda/à direita/sempre em frente
Premayra/sigoonda ah ishkehrda/ah deerayta/sayngpri ayng fraynti
First/second left/right/ straight ahead

Na esquina/Nos semáforos
Na ishkeener/Nohsh sermahforoosh
At the corner/At the traffic lights

Where is the nearest police station/post office?
Onde é o posto da polícia/o c orreio?
Ohngdee eh oo pohshtoo da pooleesseea/oo koorrayoo?

Is it near/far?
É perto/longe?
Eh pehrtoo/lohnzhi?

Do I need to take a taxi/catch a bus?
Preciso de apanhar um táxi/um autocarro?
Preseezoo di apanyahr oong tahksee/oong owtohkahrroo?

Do you have a map?
Tem um mapa?
Tehng oong mapa?

Can you point to it on my map?
Pode indicá-lo no meu mapa?
Pohd eendeecahloo noo mayo mahpa?

Thank you for your help
Obrigado pela sua ajuda
Ohbreegahdoo pehla sooa azhooda

How do I reach the motorway/main road?
Como vou para a autoestrada/estrada principal?
Kohngoo voh para a owtoishtrahda/ishtrahda preengseepahl?

I think I have taken the wrong turning
Acho que virei no sítio errado
Ahshoo ki veeray noo seeteeoo irradoo

I am looking for this address
Estou à procura desta morada
Ishtoh ah prohkoora deshta moorahda

I am looking for the ... hotel
Estou à procura do hotel ...
Ishtou ah prokoora doo otel ...

How far is it to ... from here?
A que distância daqui fica ...?
A ki deeshtangseea dakee feeka ...?

Continue a direito por ... quilómetros
Kongteenooee a deeraytoo poor ... keelohmetrosh
Carry straight on for ... kilometres

Vire na próxima à direita/esquerda
Veer na prohseema ah deerayta/ishkayrda

Take the next turning on the right/left

Vire à direita/esquerda no próximo cruzamento/semáforo
veer ah deerayta/ishkayrda noo prohseemoo kroozamengtoo/simah-fooroo
Turn right/left at the next crossroads/traffic lights

Vai na direcção errada
Va'ee na deeresowng irrahda
You are going in the wrong direction

Where is the cathedral/church/museum/pharmacy?
Onde é a catedral/igreja/museu/farmácia?
Ohngdee eh er katidrahl/eegrayzha/moosayo/fahrmahrseeah?

How much is the admission (entrance) charge?
Qual é o preço da entrada?
Kwal eh oo preso do ayntrahda?

Is there a discount for children/students/senior citizens?
Há desconto para crianças/estudantes/pessoas da terceira idade?
Ah dishkohngtoo para kreeangsash/ishtoodangtish/pisoahsh da tersayra eedahd?

What time does the next guided tour (in English) start?
A que horas começa a próxima visita guiada (in Inglês)?
Er ki orash koomehsa er prohseema veezeeta gueeahda (in eenglaysh)?

One/two adults/children, please
Um/dois adultos, uma/duas crianças, por favor
Oong/doysh adooltoosh, ooma/dooash kreeangsash poor favohr

May I take photographs here?
Posso tirar fotografias aqui?
Possoo teerahr footoografeeash akee?

At the Tourist Office

Do you have a map of the town/area?
Tem um mapa da cidade/zona?
Tayng oong mahpa da seedahde/zohna?

Do you have a list of accommodation?
Tem uma lista de alojamentos?
Tayng ooma leeshta di aloozhamayntoosh?

Can I reserve accommodation?
Posso fazer marcação de alojamento aqui?
Possoo fazayr markasowng de aloozhamayntoo akee?

ACCOMMODATION

Hotels

I have a reservation in the name of ...
Tenho uma marcação em nome de ...
Taynyo ooma markasowng ayng nohmi di ...

I wrote to/faxed/telephoned you last month/last week
Escrevi/mandei um fax/telefonei no mês passado/na semana passada
Ishkrevee/manday oong fahks/ tilifoonay noo mays pasahdoo/na simahna pasahda

Do you have any rooms free?
Tem quartos vagos?
Tayng kwahrtoosh vahgoosh?

I would like to reserve a single/double room with/ without a bath/shower
Queria marcar um quarto para uma pessoa/para duas pessoas com/sem banho/chuveiro.
Kireea marcahr oong kwahrtoo para ooma pesoha/para dooash pesoash cohng/sehng banyoo/chooveyroh

I would like bed/breakfast/ (room and) full board
Queria cama e pequeno almoço/pensão completa
Kireea kam ee pikayno ahlmohso/pengsowng komplehta

How much is it per night?
Quanto custa por noite?
Kwantoo koosta poor noyt?

Is breakfast included?
O pequeno almoço está incluído?
Oo pikaynoo ahlmohsoo istah eenklooeedoo?

Do you have any cheaper rooms?
Tem quartos mais baratos?
Tayng kwartoosh myish barahtoosh?

I would like to see/take the room
Queria de ver/ficar com o quarto
Kireea di vehr/feekar oo kwahrtoo

I would like to stay for ... nights
Queria ficar por ... noites
Kireea ficahr poor ... noytish

The shower/light/tap doesn't work
O chuveiro/a luz/a torneira não funciona
Oo shoovayroo/er loosh/er toornayra nown foongsyona

At what time/where is breakfast served?
A que horas/onde é servido o pequeno almoço?
Er ke orash/oongdeeh eh sirveedo oo pikaynoo ahlmossoo?

What time do I have to check out?
A que horas tenho de deixar o quarto?
A ke orash taynyo di dayshahr oo kwahrto?

Can I have the key to room number ...?
Pode-me dar a chave do quarto número ...?
Pohdi-mi dahr er shahv doo kwahrtoo noomiroo ...?

My room number is ...
O número do meu quarto é ...
Oo noomiroo doo mayo kwahrto eh ...

My room is not satisfactory/ not clean enough/too noisy.

Please can I change rooms?
O meu quarto não é do meu agrado/não está bem limpo/tem muito barulho. Posso mudar de quarto, por favor?
Oo meyoo kwahrtoo nowng eh doo meyoo agrahdoo/nowng ishta behng leengpoo/tehng moongtoo baroolyoo. Possoo moodar di kwahrtoo, poor favohr?

Where is the bathroom?
Onde fica a casa de banho?
Awngder feeka ah caza di banyoo?

Do you have a safe for valuables?
Tem um cofre para depositar valores?
Tehng oong koffrer para derpoozitahr verlohres?

Is there a laundry/do you wash clothes?
Têm lavandaria/lavam a roupa?
Tehng lervahngdereea/lavang ah rohpa?

I would like an air-conditioned room
Queria de um quarto com ar condicionado
Kireea di oong kwahrtoo kawng ahr kawngdeesyoonahdoo

Do you accept traveller's cheques/credit cards?
Aceita cheques de viagem/cartões de crédito?
Asayta shehkiesh di veeahzhayng/kartoyesh di kredeetoo?

May I have the bill please?
Pode-me dar a conta, por favor?
Pohd-mi dahr er kohngta, poor favohr?

Excuse me, I think there is a mistake in this bill
Desculpe, acho que há um erro nesta conta
Dishkoolp, ahshoo ke ah oong ayrroo na kohngta

Youth Hostels

How much is a dormitory bed per night?
Quanto é uma cama num dormitório por noite?
Kwantoo eh ooma kama noong dormeetohreeoo poor noyt?

I am/am not an HI member.
Sou/não sou membro do HI
Soh/nown soh mayngbroo doo agah ee

May I use my own sleeping bag?
Posso usar o meu saco de dormir?
Possoo oozahr oo mayu sahkoo di dormeer?

What time do you lock the doors at night?
A que horas fecham as portas à noite?
Er ki orash fayshowm as portash ah noyt?

Camping

May I camp for the night/two nights?
Posso acampar aqui esta noite/por duas noites?
Posso akampahr akee eshta noyt/poor dooash noytsh?

Where can I pitch my tent?
Onde posso armar a minha tenda?
Ohngd possoo ahrmahr er meenya tayngda?

How much does it cost for one night/week?
Quanto custa por uma noite/uma semana?
Kwantoo kooshta poor ooma noyt/ooma simana?

Where are the washing facilities?
Onde são as lavandarias?
Ohngd sowng ash lavandariash?

Is there a restaurant/ supermarket/swimming pool on site/nearby?
Há aqui/perto um restaurante/supermercado/uma piscina?
Ah akee pehrtoo oong ristowrangt/soopermercahdoo/ooma peeshseena?

Do you have a safety deposit box?
Tem cofre para guardar valores?
Tayng kohfr para gwardahr valohrsh?

EATING AND DRINKING

Cafés and Bars

I would like a cup of/two cups of/another coffee/tea
Queria uma chávena de/duas chávenas de/outro café/chá
Kireea ooma shahvna di/dooash shahvnash di ohtroo kafeh/shah

With/without milk/sugar
Com/sem leite/açúcar
Kohng/sayng layt/asookar

I would like a bottle/glass/ two glasses of mineral water/ red wine/white wine, please
Queria uma garrafa/um copo/dois copos/de água mineral/vinho tinto/vinho branco, por favor
Kireea ooma garrahfa/oong kohpoo/doysh kopoosh/di ahgwa meenirahl/veenyo teengto/veenyo brahngkoo poor favohr

I would like a beer/two beers, please
Queria uma cerveja/duas cervejas, por favor
Kireea ooma servayzha/dooash servaizhash, poor favohr

Please may I have some ice?
Pode-me dar gelo?
Pohd-mi dahr zhayloo?

Do you have any matches/ cigarettes/cigars?
Tem fósforos/cigarros/charutos?
Tayng fohshfooroosh/seegahrroosh/ sharootoosh?

Restaurants

Can you recommend a good/ cheap restaurant in this area?
Pode recomendar um restaurante bom/económico nesta área?
Pohd rrikoomayndahr oong ristowrangt bohm/eekinohmeekoo nehshta ahreea?

I would like a table for ... people
Queria uma mesa para ... pessoas
Kireea ooma mehza para ... pesoash

Do you have a non-smoking area?
Tem uma área de não fumadores?
Tayng ooma ahreea di nown foomadohrsh?

Waiter/Waitress!
Faz favor!
Fash favohr!

Excuse me, please may we order?
Podemos pedir, faz favor?
Poddehmoosh pedeer, fash favohr!

Do you have a set menu/ children's menu/wine list ... in English?
Tem uma ementa turística/ ementa para crianças/carta de vinhos ... em Inglês?
Tayng oom eemaynta tooreehshtee-ka para kreeangsash/kahrta di veenyoosh ... eng eenglaysh?

Do you have any vegetarian dishes?
Tem pratos vegetarianos, por favor?
Tayng prahtoosh vezhetareeah-noosh, poor favohr?

Do you have any local specialities?
Há algumas especialidades locais?
Ah ahlgoomash ishpiseealeedahdsh lookeyish?

Are vegetables included?
Os legumes estão incluídos?
Oosh ligoomish ishtowng eenklooihdoosh?

Could I have it well-cooked/ medium/rare please?
Posso escolher bem passado/ médio/mal passado, por favor?
Possoo ishkoolyer bayng pasah-doo/mahl pasahdoo, poor favohr?

What does this dish consist of?
De que consiste este prato?
Di ki konseesht aysht prahtoo?

I am a vegetarian. Does this contain meat?
Sou vegetariano. Isto tem carne?
Soh vezhetahreeahnoo. Ishtoo tehng kahrni?

I do not eat nuts/dairy products/meat/fish
Não como nozes/produtos lácteos/carne/peixe
Nawng coomoo nozesh/prodootoosh lacteyoosh/kahrni/pehsh

Not (very) spicy please
Sem (muito) picante se faz favor
Sehng (moongtoo) pikanter se fash favohr

I would like the set menu, please
Queria a ementa turística, por favor
Kireea er eemengta toorihshteeca, poor favohr

We have not been served yet
Ainda não fomos servidos
Aeehnda nown fohmoosh serveedosh

Please bring a plate/knife/fork
Traga-me um prato/faca/garfo, por favor
Trahger-mi oong prahtoo/fahker/gahrfoo, poor favohr

Excuse me, this is not what I ordered
Desculpe, não foi isto que encomendei
Dishkoolp, nown fohee eeshtoo ki inkoomaynday

May I have some/more bread/water/coffee/tea?
Pode-me dar pão/mais pão/água/café/chá?
Pohde-mi dahr myish powng/ahgwa/cafeh/shah

May I have the bill, please?
Pode-me dar a conta, por favor?
Pohd-mi dahr er kohngta, poor favohr?

Does this bill include service?
A conta inclui serviço?
Er kohngta eengklooee sirveesso?

Do you accept traveller's cheques/Mastercard/US dollars?
Aceita cheques de viagem/Mastercard/Dólares americanos?
Asayta shehkish di veeahzhayng/mahshtehrkahrd/dohlarsh amireekahnoosh?

Can I have a receipt, please?
Pode-me dar um recibo, por favor?
Pohd-mi dahr oong rriseeboo, poor favohr?

Where is the toilet (restroom), please?
Por favor, onde são os lavabos?
Poor favohr, ohngdee sowng oos lavahboosh?

On the Menu

Pequeno-almoço/Almoço/Jantar
Pikayno-ahlmohsoo/Ahlmohsoo/Zhahngtahr
Breakfast/Lunch/Dinner

Entradas *Intrahdash* **First courses**	Sopas *Sohpash* **Soups**

Pratos principais
Prahtoosh preengseepaheesh
Main courses

Pratos de peixe
Prahtoosh di paysh
Fish dishes

Pratos de carne
Prahtoosh di kahrni
Meat dishes

Carne de vaca *Karni di vahka* **Beef**	Bife *Beefer* **Steak**
Carne de porco *Karni di pohrkoo* **Pork**	Vitela *Vitehla* **Veal**
Frango *Frahngoo* **Chicken**	Borrego *Borrehgoo* **Lamb**

Fiambre
Feeyawngbrer
Ham

Pratos vegetarianos
Prahtoosh vizhitareeanoosh
Vegetarian dishes

Legumes
Ligoomish
Vegetables

Batatas fritas
Bertahtersh freetersh
Chips (french fries)

Batatas cozidas/salteadas/puré
Bertahtershkoozeedersh/ salteyahderspooreh
Boiled/sauté/mashed potatoes

Arroz
Arrohsh
Rice

Queijo
Kayzhoo
Cheese

Sobremesas
Kohbrimehzash
Desserts

Gelado
Zhelahdoo
Ice cream

Bolos
Bohloosh
Cakes

Pastéis
Pahshtehsh
Pastries

Fruta
Frooter
Fruit

Pão
Pahng
Bread

Baguetes
Bergehtesh
Rolls

Tosta
Tohshta
Toast

Manteiga
Mahngtehga
Butter

Sal/pimenta
Sahl/pimehngta
Salt/pepper

Açúcar
Ersooker
Sugar

Menu fixo
Mernoo feeshoo
Set menu

Especialidades
Ishpiseealeedahdsh
Specialities

Especialidades locais
Ishpiseealeedahdesh lokysh
Local specialities

Carta de vinhos
Kahrta di veenyoosh
Wine list

Vinhos tintos
Veenyoosh teengtoosh
Red wines

Vinhos brancos
Veenyoosh brahngkoosh
White wines

Vinhos rosé
Veenyoosh rohzeh
Rosé wines

Espumantes
Ishpoomahngtesh
Sparkling wines

Cerveja
Sairvhezha
Beer

Cerveja de garrafa/Cerveja de pressão
Sairvhezha di gerrahfa/Sairvhezha di pressahng
Bottled beer/draught (draft) beer

Bebidas sem álcool
Bebeedash sehng alcoh-ol
Non-alcoholic drinks

Água mineral
Ahgwa meenerahl
Mineral water

Sumos de fruta
Soomoos de frooter
Fruit juices

Sumo de laranja
Soomoo di larrahngzha
Orange juice

Limonada *Limoonahda* **Lemonade**	Gelo *Zhehloo* **Ice**

Café com leite/café de saco/expresso
Kerfeh cawng lehter/kerfeh di sahkoo/expressoo
White coffee/black coffee/ espresso coffee

Chá com leite/com limão
Shah cawng lehter/cawng leem ahng
Tea with milk/with lemon

Leite com chocolate *Leyteh cong chocolahteh* **Chocolate (drink)**	Leite *Lehter* **Milk**

Snacks/Refeições ligeiras
Snacks/Refehsohngsh lizheherash
Snacks/Light meals

Saladas *Serlahdash* **Salads**	Sanduíches *Sandweeshesh* **Sandwiches**

Ovos *Ovoosh* **Eggs**	Salsichas *Salseechash* **Sausage**

Ovos cozidos/fritos/mexidos
Ovoosh cozeedoosh/freetoosh/ mershhedoosh
Boiled/fried/scrambled eggs

Typical Local Dishes

Bacalhau à Brás
Berkerlyow ah brahs
Dried, salted cod, onions and potatoes cooked in egg

Bife na frigideira
Beefer ner frizhidehrer
Steak fried in butter with wine and garlic

Arroz de frango
Arrohsh di frahngoo
Casserole of chicken, white wine, ham and rice

Pudim flan
Poodeeng flahng
Custard and caramel pudding

GETTING AROUND

Public Transport

Where is the bus stop/coach station/nearest metro (subway) station?
Onde é a paragem do autocarro/garagem das camionetas/a estação de metro mais próxima?
Ohngdee eh er parahzhayng doo owtohkahrroo/garahzhayng das kameeonehtash/er ishtasowng di

mehtroo myish prohseema?

When is the next/last bus to ...?
Quando sai o próximo/último autocarro para ...?
Kwandoo sahee oo prohseemoo owtohkahrroo para ...?

How much is the fare to the city centre (downtown)/ railway (railroad) station/ airport?
Quanto é o bilhete para o centro da cidade/estação de caminho de ferro/aeroporto?
Kwantoo eh oo beelyayte para oo sengtroo da seedahdi/ishtasowng di kaminyoo di fehrroo/aehrohportoo?

Will you tell me when to get off?
Diz-me quando devo sair?
Deesh-mi kwandoo dehvoo saeehr?

Does this bus go to ...?
Este autocarro vai para ...?
Aysht owtohkahrroo va'ee para ...?

Which number bus goes to ...?
Qual é o número do autocarro que vai para ...?
Kwal eh oo noomiroo doo owtohkahrroo ki va'ee para ...?

May I have a single (one-way)/return (round-trip)/day ticket/book of tickets?
Pode-me dar um bilhete simples/ ida e volta/diário/caderneta de bilhetes?
Pohd-mi dahr oong beelyayt seemplish/eeda ee vohlta/deeahree-oo/kadirnayta di beelyaytsh?

Taxis (Táxi)

I would like to go to ... How much will it cost?
Queria ir para ... Quanto custa?
Kireea eer para ... Kwngtoo kooshta?

Please may I stop here
Pare aqui, por favor
Pahr akee, poor favohr

I would like to order a taxi today/tomorrow/at 2pm to go from ... to ...
Queria um táxi para hoje/ amanhã/às duas da tarde para ir de ... para ...
Kireea oong tahksee para ohzhay/ahmanyang/ahsh dooash da tahrd para eer de ... para ...

Entertainment

Can you recommend a good bar/nightclub?
Pode recomendar um bom bar/discoteca?
Pohd rrikoomayngdahr oong bohm bahre/discotehkah?

Do you know what is on at the cinema (playing at the movies)/theatre at the moment?
Sabe o que vai no cinema/teatro de momento?
Sahb oo ke va'ee noo seenayma/ teeahtroo do momayngtoo?

I would like to book (purchase) ... tickets for the matinee/evening performance on Monday
Queria comprar . . . bilhetes para a sessão da tarde/noite,

segunda-feira
Kireea komprahr . . . beelyaytsh para er sessowngda tahrd/noyt, sigoonda-fayra

What time does the film/ performance start?
A que horas começa o filme/a sessão?
Er ki orash koomehsa oo film/er sesowng?

COMMUNICATIONS

Post

How much will it cost to send a letter/postcard/this package to Britain/Ireland/ America/Canada/Australia/ New Zealand?
Quanto custa mandar uma carta/postal/este pacote para Grã-Bretanha/Irlanda/América/ Canadá/Austrália/Nova Zelândia?
Kwantoo kooshta mandahr ooma kahrta/pooshtahl/esht pakoht para grang-britanya/eerlangda/ amehreeka/kanadah/owstrahleea/no hva zelangdeea?

I would like one stamp/two stamps
Queria um selo/dois selos
Kireea oong saylo/doysh sayllosh

I'd like ... stamps for postcards to send abroad, please
Queria ... selos para postais para o estrangeiro, por favor
Kireea ... sayloosh para pooshtiysh para o ishtrangzhayroo, poor favohr

Phones

I would like to make a telephone call/reverse the charges to (make a collect call to) ...
Queria fazer uma chamada/a pagar por quem recebe ...
Kireea fazayr ooma shamahda/er pagahr poor kayng ressebe ...

Which coins do I need for the telephone?
Que moedas preciso para telefonar?
Ki mwedash preseezoo para tilifoonahr?

The line is engaged (busy)
A linha está impedida
A leenya istah eempideeda

The number is ...
O número é ...
Oo noomiroo e ...

Hello, this is ...
Está, aqui fala ...
Ishtah, akee fahla ...

Please may I speak to ...?
Posso falar com ...?
Possoo falahr kom ...?

He/she is not in at the moment. Please can you call back?
Não está neste momento. Pode tornar a chamar?
Nown ishtah nayshte moomayntoo. Pohd toornahr a shamahr?

SHOPPING

Shops

Livraria/Papelaria
Leevrareea/Papilareea
Bookshop/Stationery

Joalharia/Presentes
Zhooalyareea/Prizayntsh
Jeweller/Gifts

Sapatos
Sapahtoosh
Shoes

Ferragens
Ferrahzhayngsh
Hardware

Cabeleireiro
(de homens)/(de senhoras)
Kabilayrayroo
(di ohmayns)/(di sinyorash)
Hairdresser
(men's)/(women's)

Padaria
Padareea
Baker

Supermercado
Soopermercahdoo
Supermarket

Fotografia
Footoografeea
Photo shop

Agente de Viagens
Azhayngt di veeahzhayngsh
Travel agent

Farmácia
Fahrmahseeah
Pharmacy

In the Shops

What time do the shops open/close?
A que horas abrem/fecham as lojas?
A kee orah abrayng/fayshown ash lohzhash?

Where is the nearest market?
Onde é o mercado mais próximo?
Ohngdee eh oo mercahdoo myish prohseemoo?

Can you show me the one in the window/this one?
Pode mostrar-me aquele na janela/este?
Pohd mooshtrahr-mi akehle na zhanehla/aysht?

Can I try this on?
Posso provar este?
Possoo proovahr aysht?

What size is this?
Que tamanho (número) é este?
Ki tamanyo (noomiroo) eh ayst?

This is too large/too small/ too expensive. Do you have any others?
Este é muito grande/muito pequeno/muito caro. Tem outros?
Aysht eh muingtoo grangdi/muingtoo pikaynoo/muingtoo kahroo. Tayng ohtroosh?

My size is ...
O meu tamanho (número) é ...
Oo mayo tamanyo (noomiroo) eh ...

Where is the changing room/children's/cosmetic/ladieswear/menswear/food department?
Onde é o gabinete de prova/secção infantil/cosmética/roupa de senhora/roupa de homem/secção de alimentos?
Ohngdee eh oo gabeeneht di prohva/sehksowng eengfangteel/koosmehteeca/rohpa di sinyora/rohpa di omayng/seksowng di aleemayngtoosh?

I would like ... a quarter of a kilo/half a kilo/a kilo of bread/butter/cheese/ham/tomatoes
Queria duzentos ... e cinquenta gramas/meio quilo/um quilo de pão/manteiga/queijo/fiambre/tomate
Kireea doozayntoosh ... ee seengkwayngta gramash/mayoo keeloo/oong keeloo di powng/mang-tayga/kayzhoo/feeangbri/toomaht

How much is this?
Quanto custa isto?
Kwantoo kooshta eeshtoo?

I'll take this one, thank you
Levo este, obrigado
Lehvoo aysht, ohbreegahdoo

Do you have a carrier (shopping) bag?
Tem um saco de plástico com pegas?
Tayng oong sahkoo di plahshteekoo kohng pehgash?

Do you have anything cheaper/larger/smaller/of better quality?
Tem alguma coisa mais barata/maior/mais pequena/de melhor qualidade?
Tayngahlgooma kohyza myish barahta/mahyohr/myish peekayna/do melior kwaleedahd?

I would like a film for this camera
Queria um rolo para esta máquina
Kireea oongrohloo para ehshta mahkeena

I would like some batteries, the same size as this old one
Queria umas pilhas do mesmo tamanho que esta
Kireea oomash peelyash doo maysmoo tamahnyo ki ehshta

Would you mind wrapping this for me, please?
Importa-se de me embrulhar isto, por favor?
Eemporta-si di mi aymbroolyahr eeshtoo, poor favohr?

Sorry, but you seem to have given me the wrong change
Desculpe mas parece que me deu o troco errado
Dishkoolp maysh parehse ki mi dayoo oo trohcoo eerrahdoo

MOTORING

Car Hire (Rental)

I have ordered (rented) a car in the name of ...
Reservei um carro em nome de ...
Rrizervay oongkahrrooay nohmdi ...

How much does it cost to hire (rent) a car for one day/ two days/a week?
Quanto custa alugar um carro por um dia/dois dias/uma semana?
Kwantoo kooshta aloogahr oong kahrroo poor oong deea/doysh deeash/ooma simahna?

Is the tank already full of petrol (gas)?
O depósito já está cheio de gasolina?
Oo depohzeetoo zhah ishtah shayoo di gazooleena?

Is insurance and tax included? How much is the deposit?
O seguro e o imposto estão incluídos? Quanto é o depósito?
Oosigooro ee oo eempohshtoo ishtowng eenklooeehdoosh? Kwantoo eh oo depohzeetoo?

By what time must I return the car?
A que horas devo devolver o carro?
A ki orash devoo divolvehr oo kahrroo?

I would like a small/large family/sports car with a radio/cassette player
Queria um carro pequeno/grande familiar/esporte com rádio/leitor de cassettes
Kireea oong kahrroo pikayni/ grahndeh fameeleeahr/espoorteh kohng rahdeeoo/laytohr do casehtsh

Do you have a road map?
Tem um mapa das estradas?
Tayng oong mahpa dash ishtradash?

Parking

How long can I park here?
Por quanto tempo posso estacionar aqui?
Poor kwantoo taympoo possoo ishtaseeoonahr akee?

Is there a car park near here?
Há um parque de estacionamento aqui perto?
Ah oong pahrki di ishtaseeoonamayngtoo akee pehrtoo?

At what time does this car park close?
A que horas fecha este parque de estacionamento?
A ki orash faysha aysht pahrk di ishtaseeoonamayngtoo?

Signs and Notices

Via única
Veea oohneeka
One way

Entrada proibida
Ayntrahda proeebeeda
No entry

Estacionamento proibido
Ishtaseeoonamayngto proeebeedoo
No parking

Desvio
Dishveeoo
Detour (diversion)

Pare!
Pahreh!
Stop!

Dê passagem
Deh passahzhayng
Give way (yield)

Estrada escorregadia
Ishtrahda iskorregadeea
Slippery road

Ultrapassagem proibida
Ultrapassahzhayng proeebeeda
No overtaking

Perigo!
Perreegoo!
Danger!

At the Filling Station
(Posto de abastecimento)

Unleaded (lead-free)/ standard/premium/diesel
Sem chumbo/normal/super/ gasóleo
Sayng shoongboo/normahl/sooper/ gahzohleyoo

Fill the tank please
Encha o depósito por favor
Ayngsha oo depohzeetoo poor favohr

Do you have a road map?
Tem um mapa das estradas?
Tayng oong mahpa dash ishtradash?

How much is the car wash?
Quanto é a lavagem do carro?
Kwanto eh a lavazhayng doo kahrroo?

Breakdowns

I've had a breakdown at ...
Tive uma avaria em ...
Teev ooma avareea ayng ...

I am a member of the ... [motoring organisation]
Sou membro da ...
Soh membroo dah ...

I am on the road from ... to ...
Estou na estrada de ... para ...
Ishtoh na ishtrahda di ... para ...

I can't move the car. Can you send a tow-truck?
Não posso mover o carro. Pode mandar um reboque?
Nown possoo moovehr oo kahrroo. Pohd mandahr oong ribok?

I have a flat tyre
Tenho um pneu furado
Tayngoo oong pnayoo foorahdoo

The windscreen (windshield) has smashed/cracked
O pára-brisas estilhaçou-se/ rachou
Oo pahra-breezash isteelyasoh-si/ rrashoh.

There is something wrong with the engine/brakes/ lights/steering/gearbox/ clutch/exhaust
Qualquer coisa está mal com o motor/os travões/os faróis/o volante/a caixa de velocidades/ a embraiagem/o tubo de escape
Kwalkehr kohiza ishtah mahl kohng oo mootohr/oosh travoyesh/oosh faroysh/oo voolangt/a kaisha dash vilooseedahdish/a aymbriyahzhayng oo tayoobayo daye essayahpaye

It's overheating
Está a aquecer demais
Istah a akehser demaish

It won't start
Não arranca
Nown arrangka

Where can I get it repaired?
Onde posso mandá-lo arranjar?
Ohngd possoo mandahloo arrangzhahr?

Can you take me there?
Pode-me levar lá?
Pohdmi livahr lah?

Will it take long to fix?
Leva muito tempo a arranjar?
Lehva muingtoo tayngpoo a arrangzhahr?

How much will it cost?
Quanto vai custar?
Kwantoo va'ee kooshtahr?

Please can you pick me up/give me a lift?
Pode levar-me/dar-me boleia?
Pohdd lehvahr-mi/dahr-mi booleya?

Accidents and Traffic Offences (Violations)

Can you help me? There has been an accident
Pode-me ajudar? Houve um acidente
Pohdmi azhoodahr? Ohv oong aseedayngt

Please call the police/an ambulance
Por favor chame a polícia/uma ambulância
Poor favohr, shahm a pooleesya/ ooma angboolansya

Is anyone hurt?
Há alguém ferido?
Ah ahlguayng fereedoo?

I'm sorry, I didn't see the sign
Desculpe, não vi o sinal
Dishkoolp nown vee oo seenahl

Must I pay a fine? How much?
Tenho de pagar uma multa? De quanto?
Taynyoo di pagahr ooma moolta? Di kwantoo?

Mostre-me os seus documentos.
Mohshtrimi oosh sayosh dokoomayngtoosh
Show me your documents

HEALTH

Pharmacy (Farmácia)

Do you have anything for a stomach ache/headache/sore throat/toothache?
Tem qualquer coisa para dores de estômago/dores de cabeça/dores de garganta/dores de dentes?
Tayng kwalkehr kohiza para dohrish di ishtohmago/dohrish di kabehsa/dorish do gargangta/dorish di dengtish?

I need something for diarrhoea/constipation/ a cold/a cough/insect bites/sunburn/travel (motion) sickness
Preciso de alguma coisa contra diarreia/prisão de ventre/uma constipação/tosse/picadas de insectos/queimaduras do sol/enjoo
Preseezoo di ahlgooma kohiza kongtra deearraya/preezowng di ventre/ooma konshteepasowng/ tohs/peekahdash do eensetoosh/ kaymadoorash doo sohl/ingzho'oo

How much/how many do I take?
Quanto/quantos devo tomar?
Kwantoo/kwantoosh dayvoo toomahr?

How often do I take it/them?
Quantas vezes devo tomar isto?
Kwantash vehzesh dayvoo toomahr ishto?

I am/he is/she is taking this medication
Estou/ele está/ela está a tomar este medicamento
Ishtoh/ishtah a toomahr aysht medeekamayngtoo

How much does it cost?
Quanto custa?
Kwantoo kooshta?

Can you recommend a good doctor/dentist?
Pode recomendar um bom médico/dentista?
Pohd rrikoomayngdahr oong bohm mehdeekoo/dayngteeshta?

Is it suitable for children?
É bom para crianças?
Eh bohm para kreeansash?

Doctor (Médico)

I have a pain here/in my arm/ leg/chest/stomach
Tenho uma dor aqui/no braço/na perna/no peito/no estômago
Taynyoo ooma dohr akee noo brahsoo/na perna/noo ishtohmagoo

Please call a doctor, this is an emergency
Por favor, chame um médico, é uma emergência
Poor favohr sahmi oong mehdeekoo, eh ooma imerzhayngseea

I would like to make an appointment to see the doctor
Queria marcar uma consulta para um médico
Kireea markahr ooma kongsoolta para oong mehdeekoo

I am diabetic/pregnant
Sou diabético(a)/estou grávida
Soh deeabehteekoo(a)/ishtoh grahveeda

I need a prescription for ...
Preciso de uma receita para ...
Priseezoo di ooma rresayta para ...

Can you give me something to ease the pain?
Pode-me dar alguma coisa para as dores?
Pod-mi dahr ahlgwma kohiza para as dohrish?

I am/he is/she is allergic to penicillin
Sou/ele é/ela é/alérgico/alérgica à penicilina
Soh/ili eh/ehla eh/alehrzheekoo/ alehrzheeka ah peneeseeleena

Isso faz doer?
Eesso fahsh dooayr?
Does this hurt?

Você/ele/ela deve ir para o hospital
Vooseh/elleh/ellah dev eer para oo ohspeetahl
You/he/she must go to hospital

Tome isto uma vez/duas vezes/três vezes ao dia
Tohmi ishtoo ooma vays/dooash vayzish/traysh vayzish ow deea
Take these once/twice/three times a day

I am/he is/she is taking this medication
Estou/ele está/ela está a tomar este medicamento
Ishtoh/ishtah a toomahr aysht medeekamayngtoo

I have medical insurance
Tenho seguro médico
Taynyo sigooroo mehdeekoo

Dentist (Dentista)

I have toothache
Tenho uma dor de dente.
Taynyo ooma dohr do daynteesh

My filling has come out
O meu chumbo caiu
Oo mayo shoongboo kaeehoo

I do/do not want to have an injection first
Quero/não quero levar uma injecçãao primeiro
Kehroo/nown kehroo levahr ooma eenzhehsowng preemayroo

EMERGENCIES

Help!
Socorro!
Sookohrroo!

Fire!
Fogo!
Fohgoo!

Stop!
Pare!
Pahreh!

Call an ambulance/a doctor/ the police/the fire brigade!
Chame uma ambulância/um médico/a polícia/os bombeiros!
Shami ooma angboolangsya/oong medeekoo/a pooleesseeya/oosh bombehroosh!

Please may I use a telephone?
Posso usar um telefone, por favor?
Posoo uzahr oong telefonner, poor favohr?

I have had my traveller's cheques/creditcardshandbag/ rucksack/luggage/wallet/ passport/mobile phone stolen
Roubaram-me os meus cheques de viagem/cartões de crédito/a minha bolsa/mala de mão/a minha mochila/bagagem/carteira/ o passaporte/telemóvel.
Rrohbahrowm-mi oosh mayos shehkish di veeahzhayng/kartoyesh di kredeetoo/a meenya bohlsa/mahla di mowng/a meenya moosheela/bagahzhayng/kartayra/ oo pahssaport/telemohvel.

May I please have a copy of the report for my insurance claim?
Posso ficar com uma cópia do relatório para entregar à minha companhia seguradora?
Possoo feekahr cawng oomer kopeeya doo rerlertohrioo para entrehgahr ah meenya cawngpany-eea sigooradohra?

Can you help me? I have lost my daughter/son/my companion(s)
Pode ajudar-me? Perdi a minha filha/o meu filho/meu(s) companheiro(s)
Pohdee azhoodahr-mi? Perdee a meenya feelya/oo mayo feelyoo/ meyoo(sh) companyehroo(sh)

Please go away/leave me alone
Por favor, vá-se embora/ deixe-me em paz
Poor favohr, vah-see ayngbohra/daysh-mi ayng pahsh

I'm sorry
Desculpe
Dishkoolp

I want to contact the British/ American/Canadian/Irish/ Australian/New Zealand/ South African Consulate
Quero contactar o Consulado Britânico/Americano/Canadiano/ Irlandês/Australiano/da Nova Zelândia/Sul Africano
Keroo kohntaktahr oo Konsoolahdoo Breetahngeekoo/Amireekanoo/ Kanadeeanoo/Eerlahngdays/ Owshtraleeanoo/da Nohva Zeelangdeea/Soolafreekanoo

I'm/he is/she is ill/lost/injured
Estou/ele está/ela está doente/perdido/ferido
Ishtoh/ehleh/ehla ishta dwehteh/pehrdeedoo/ferreedoo

We are/they are/ill/ lost/injured
Estamos/eles estão/doentes/ perdidos/feridos
Ishtahmossh/ehlesh ishtawng/ dwehtehsh/pehrdeedoosh/ ferreedoosh

ROMANIAN

INTRODUCTION

Alone among the languages of Eastern Europe, Romanian is a Romance tongue, descended from Latin and therefore a distant cousin of French, Italian, Spanish and Portuguese. This is of more than academic interest, since the basic meaning of many words in written Romanian can be understood by someone with a knowledge of one of these other languages. Spoken Romanian is reminiscent of French, which is the most likely second language you will encounter, at least among older and better-educated Romanians. In some regions of the country Hungarian or German will be understood.

Addresses for Travel and Tourist Information

Australia: *Embassy,* 4 Dalman Crescent, O'Malley, Canberra, ACT 2606; tel: (02) 6286 2343; fax: (02) 6286 2433.

UK: *Romanian Tourist Office,* 22 New Cavendish St, London WIM 7LH; tel: (020) 7224 3692; fax: (020) 7935 6435.

USA: *Romanian Tourist Office,* 355 Lexington Ave, 19th Floor, New York, NY 10017; tel: (212) 545 8484; fax: (212) 251 0429.

Official tourism websites: www.VisitRomania.com (UK); www.RomaniaTourism.com (USA).

Romania Facts

CAPITAL: Bucharest, Bucureşti (pronounced Boocooreshti)
CURRENCY: Leu (plural Lei). 1 Leu = 100 bani.
OPENING HOURS: Banks: Mon–Thur 0800–1600, Fri 0800–1300. Shops: Mon–Fri 0700–1900, Sat 0700–1400. Some shops open 24 hrs including Sundays. Museums: Tues–Sun 1000–1800.
TELEPHONES: To dial in, + 40. Outgoing, 00 plus the country code. Police, 955. Fire, 981. Medical emergency, 961. (These numbers are being replaced by a single number for all emergencies, 112.)
PUBLIC HOLIDAYS: 1, 2 Jan; Orthodox Easter Monday (Apr/May); 1 May; 1, 25, 26 Dec.

Technical Language Hints

There are three grammatical genders, masculine, feminine, and neutral (masculine in the singular and feminine in the plural).

Consonant clusters in Romanian occur at the beginning of syllables, which is again unusual among Romance languages.

Stress can occur on any syllable, but be careful to follow the phonetics accurately, as varying the stressed syllable can change meaning.

ESSENTIALS

Alphabet and Pronunciation

	Name	Pronounced
A a	*ah*	**long a as in father**
Ă ă		**neutral sound like the o in other**
Â â		**no equivalent in English**
B b	*beh*	**b as in bed**
C c	*cheh*	**k as in keep or ch as in check**
D d	*deh*	**d as in delta**
E e	*eh*	**short e as in bell or eh sound as in way**
F f	*eff*	**f as in far**
G g	*djeh*	**j sound as in gesture**
H h	*hash*	**aspirated h as in Scottish loch**
I i	ee	**i as in pit**
Î î		**no equivalent in English**
J j	*zheu*	**soft zh like the s of pleasure**
K k	*kah*	**k as in keep**
L l	*ell*	**l as in elf**
M m	*em*	**m as in mother**
N n	*en*	**n as in no**
O o	*oh*	**o as in old**
P p	*peh*	**p as in pelt**
Q q	*kew*	**like the qu of queen**
R r	*air*	**r as in rock**
S s	*ess*	**s as in sit**
Ş ş		**sh as in shelf**
T t	*teh*	**t as in tick**
Ţ ţ		**ts as in hats**
U u	*oo*	**oo as in boot**
V v	*veh*	**v as in velvet**
W w	*doobl-ooveh*	**w as in wet**
X x	*icks*	**x as in fix**
Y y	*eegrek*	**y as in yellow**
Z z	*zed*	**z as in zoo**

Basic Words and Phrases

Yes
Da
Dah

No
Nu
Noo

ESSENTIALS

ROMANIAN

Please
Vă rog
Vah rohg

Thank you
Mulţumesc
Mooltzoomesc

Hello
Bună ziua
Boonah zeeooa

Goodbye
La revedere
La revedereh

Excuse me
Scuzaţi-mă
Scoozatz-mah

Sorry
Pardon
Pardon

How
Cum
Coom

When
Când
Cund

Why
De ce
Deh cheh

What
Ce
Cheh

Who
Cine
Cheene

That's O.K.
E în regulă
Eh an rehgoolah

Perhaps
Poate
Pwahteh

To
Către
Cahtreh

From
De la
Deh lah

Here
Aici
Aich

There
Acolo
Acohlo

I don't understand
Nu înţeleg
Noo untzehleg

I don't speak Romanian
Nu înţeleg românește
Noo untzeleg romaneshteh

Do you speak English?
Vorbiţi englezeşte?
Vorbeetz englezeshteh?

Can you please write it down?
Scrieţi, vă rog?
Screeyetz, vah rohg?

Please can you speak more slowly
Vorbiţi mai rar, vă rog
Vobeetz my rar, vah rohg

Greetings

Good morning/ Good afternoon/ Good evening/Good night
Bună dimineaţa/Bună ziua/ Bună seara/Noapte bună
Boonah deemeeneyatza/Boonah zeeooa/Boonah sara/Nwapteh boonah

Pleased to meet you
Mă bucur de cunoştinţă
Mah boocoor deh coonoshteentzah

How are you?
Ce mai faceţi?
Cheh my fachetz?

I am well, thank you, and you?
Bine, mulţumesc. Şi dumneavoastră?
Beeneh, mooltzoomesc. She doomneyahvwastrah?

My name is ...
Mă numesc...
Mah noomesc ...

This is a male (female) friend/this is my boyfriend/girlfriend/husband/wife/brother/sister
Acesta (aceasta) este un prieten (o prietenă)/acesta (aceasta) este prietenul (prietena)/soţul/soţia/fratele/sora mea (meu)
Achesta (acheyasta) esteh oon pree-eten (oh pree-etenah) … achesta (acheyasta) esteh pree- etenool (pree-etenah) sotzo-ol/sotzeya/frateleh/sora meha (meyoo)

Where are you travelling to?
Unde călătoriţi?
Oondeh cahlahtoreetz?

I am/we are going to …
Merg/mergem la ...
Merg/merdjehm lah …

How long are you travelling for?
Cât timp va dura călătoria?
Cuht teemp vah doorah cahlahtoreeya?

Where do you come from?
De unde sunteţi?
Deh oondeh soontetz?

I am/we are from … Australia/Britain/Canada/America
Eu sunt/noi suntem din ... Australia/Marea Britanie/Canada/America
Eoo soont/noy soontem deen … Aoostraleyah/Mareya/Breetaneeye/Canadah/Amereecah

We are on holiday
Suntem în concediu
Soontem un conchedeeyoo

This is our first visit here
Este prima noastră vizită aici
Esteh preemah nwastrah veezeetah aich

How old are you?
Câţi ani aveţi?
Cutz ahny avetz?

I am … years old
Am ... ani
Am … ahny

I am a business person/doctor/journalist/manual worker/administrator/scientist/student/teacher
Sunt om de afaceri/doctor/ziarist/muncitor/administrator/om de ştiinţă/student/profesor
Soont ohm deh afachery/doctor/zeeyareest/moonchee-tor/administratohr/ohm deh shteentzah/student/profesor

I am waiting for my husband/wife/boyfriend/girlfriend
Il (o) aştept pe soţul/soţia/prietenul/prietena mea (meu)
Ul (oh) ashtept peh sotzool/sotzeeya/pree-etenool/pree-etenah meha

Would you like/may al have a cigarette?
Doriţi/Îmi puteţi da o ţigară?
Doreetz/Um pootezi dah oh tzee-garah?

Do you mind if I smoke?
Vă deranjează dacă fumez?
Vah deranjeyazah dacah foomez?

Do you have a light?
Aveți un foc?
Avetz oon fohc?

Days

Monday
Luni
Loony

Tuesday
Marți
Marti

Wednesday
Miercuri
Me-ehrcooree

Thursday
Joi
Zhoy

Friday
Vineri
Vinehry

Saturday
Sâmbătă
Sumbahtah

Sunday
Duminică
Doomeeneeka

Morning
Dimineața
Deemeeneyatzah

Afternoon/Evening/Night
După amiaza/Seara/Noapte
Doopah ameyazah/Sara/Nwapteh

Yesterday
Ieri
Yeree

Today
Azi
Ahzee

Tomorrow
Mâine
Mu-yneh

Numbers

Zero
Zero
Zehro

One
Unu
Oonoo

Two
Doi
Doy

Three
Trei
Tray

Four
Patru
Patroo

Five
Cinci
Chinc

Six
Şase
Shaseh

Seven
Şapte
Shapteh

Eight
Opt
Opt

Nine
Nouă
Nowah

Ten
Zece
Zecheh

Eleven
Unsprezece
Oonsprezeche

Twelve
Doisprezece
Doysprezecheh

Thirteen
Treisprezece
Traysprezecheh

Fourteen
Paisprezece
Pie-sprezeche

Fifteen
Cincisprezece
Chinchsprezecheh

Sixteen
Şaisprezece
Shy-sprezecheh

Seventeen
Şaptesprezece
Shaptesprezecheh

Eighteen
Optsprezece
Optsprezecheh

Nineteen
Nouăsprezece
Nowahsprezecheh

Twenty
Douăzeci
Dowahzech

Twenty-one
Douăzeci şi unu
Dowahzech she oonoo

Twenty-two
Douăzeci şi doi
Dowahzech she doy

Thirty
Treizeci
Trayzech

Forty
Patruzeci
Patroozech

Fifty
Cincizeci
Chinchzech

Sixty
Şaizeci
Shy-zech

Seventy
Şaptezeci
Shaptezech

Eighty
Optzeci
Optzech

Ninety
Nouăzeci
Nowahzech

One hundred
O sută
Oh sooter

Five hundred
Cinci sute
Chinch sooteh

One thousand
O mie
Oh meeyeh

One million
Un milion
Oon milion

Time

What time is it?
Cât este ceasul?
Cuht esteh cheyasool?

It is ...
Este ora ...
Esteh orah ...

9.00
Nouă
Nowoa

9.05
Nouă şi cinci
Nowa she chinch

9.15
Nouă şi un sfert
Nowa she oon sfehrt

9.20
Nouă şi douăzeci
Nowa she dowahzech

9.30
Nouă şi jumătate
Nowa she joomahtateh

9.35
Nouă şi treizeci şi cinci
Zecheh she treyzech she chinch

9.40
Nouă şi patruzeci
Zecheh she patroozech

9.45
Nouă şi patruzeci şi cinci
Zecheh she patroozech she chinc

9.50
Nouă şi cincizeci
Zecheh she chinchzech

9.55
Nouă şi cincizeci şi cinci
Zecheh she chinchzech she chinc

12.00/Midday/Midnight
Ora douăsprezece/Amiază/ Miezul nopţii
Orah dowahsprezecheh/ Amiazah/Mee-ehzool noptzee

Money

I would like to change these traveller's cheques/this currency
Vreau să schimb aceste cecuri de călătorie/valuta aceasta
Vreyahoo sah skimb achesteh checooree de kerlertoreeyeh/valoota acheyasta

How much commission do you charge? (What is the service charge?)
Cât este comisionul?
Cuht esteh comeeseeohnool?

Can I obtain money with my Mastercard?
Pot să obţin bani cu Mastercard?
Pot sah obtzeen banee coo Mastercard?

Where is the nearest ATM?
Unde este cel mai apropiat ATM?
Oondeh esteh chehl mahy apropyat ATM?

My name is … Some money has been wired to here for me to collect
Numele meu este … Mi s-au trimis nişte bani aici
Noomele meoo esteh … Mee saoo trymys nyshteh bany aychy

ARRIVING AND DEPARTING

Airport

Excuse me, where is the check-in desk for … airline?
Scuzaţi-mă, unde este ghişeul check-in pentru linia aeriană ...?
Scoozatz-mah, oondeh esteh gishehool check-in pentroo liniah ayereeanah …?

What is the boarding gate/time for my flight?
Care este poarta/ora de îmbarcare pentru cursa mea?
Careh esteh pwartah/orah deh uhmbarcareh pentroo coorsa meya?

How long is the delay likely to be?
Cam cât o să dureze întârzierea?
Cam cuht oh sah doorezeh untuhrzeeyereya?

Where is the duty-free shop?
Unde este magazinul „duty free"?
Oonde esteh magazeenool deh duty-free?

Which way is the baggage reclaim?
De unde se ridică bagajele?
Deh oonde she ridiker bagazheleh?

I have lost my luggage. Please can you help?
Mi-am pierdut bagajul. Mă puteţi ajuta, vă rog?
Mee-am pee-erdoot bagazhool. Mah pootetz ajootah, vah rohg?

I am flying to …
Merg cu avionul la ...
Merg coo aveeohnool lah …

Where is the bus for the city centre?
Unde este autobuzul pentru centrul oraşului?
Oondeh esteh aootoboozool pentroo chentrool orashoolooi?

Trains and Boats

Where is the ticket office/information desk?
Unde este ghişeul de bilete/biroul de informaţii?
Oondeh esteh gishehool deh bileteh/birohool de infor matzee?

Which platform does the train/speedboat/ferry to ... depart from?
De la ce peron pleacă trenul/vaporul/feribotul?
Deh lah cheh pehron pleyacah trenool/vaporool/feribotool?

Where is platform ... ?
Unde este peronul ... ?
Oondeh esteh pehronool ...?

When is the next train/boat to ...?
Când este următorul tren/vapor spre ...?
Cund esteh oormahtorool tren/vapor spre ...?

Is there a later train/boat to ...?
Este un tren/vapor mai târziu?
Esteh oon tren/vapor my turzeeyoo?

Notices and Signs

Vagon restaurant
Vagon restaoorant
Buffet (Dining) car

Autobuz
Aootobooz
Bus

Apă potabilă/nepotabilă
Apah potabilah/nepotabilah
Drinking/non-drinking water

Intrare
Intrareh
Entrance

Ieşire
Yehsheereh
Exit

Spital
Spital
Hospital

Informaţii
Informatzee
Information

Biroul de bagaje
Birohool de bagazhe
Left luggage (Baggage claim)

Dulăpioare pentru bagaje
Doolahpeeyowareh pentroo bagazhe
Luggage lockers

Oficiul poştal
Ofeecheeool poshtal
Post office

Peron
Perohn
Platform

Gară
Garah
Railway (Railroad) station

Aeroport
Aeroport
Airport

Circa de poliţie
Chircah deh politzye
Police station

ROMANIAN

Port
Port
Port

Restaurant
Restaoorant
Restaurant

Fumători/Nefumători
Foomahtoree/Nefoomahtoree
Smoking/Non smoking

Telefon
Telephon
Telephone

Ghişeu de bilete
Gishehoo deh bileteh
Ticket office

Ghişeu check-in
Gishehoo check-in
Check-in desk

Orar
Orar
Timetable (Schedule)

Toalete
Twaleteh
Toilets

Femei/Bărbaţi
Femay/Bahrbatz
Ladies/Gentlemen

Metrou
Metro
Underground (Subway)

Sala de aşteptare
Salah de ashteptareh
Waiting room

Buying a Ticket

I would like a first-class/second-class/third-class/single (one-way)/return (round trip) ticket to ...
Un bilet clasa întâi/clasa a doua/clasa a treia dus/dus întors până la ...
Oon bilet clasah untuy/clasah ah dowa/clasah ah tray-ah doos/untors punah lah ...

Is it an express (fast) train/bus?
Este un tren/autobuz express?
Esteh oon tren/aootobooz express?

Is my rail pass valid on this train/ferry/bus?
Este valabil abonamentul meu de tren pentru trenul/feribot-ul/autobuzul acesta?
Esteh valabil abonamentool meyoo deh tren pentroo trenool/feree-botool/aootoboozool achestah?

I would like an aisle/window seat
Doresc un loc lângă coridor/la fereastră
Doresc oon loc lungah coridor/lah ferehastrah

No smoking/smoking please
Nefumători/fumători, vă rog
Nefoomahtoree/foomahtoree, vah rohg

We would like to sit together
Dorim să stăm împreună
Dorim sah stahm umpreoonah

I would like to make a seat reservation

Doresc să rezerv un loc
Doresc sah rezerv oon loc

I would like to reserve a couchette/sleeper for one person/two people/my family
Doresc să rezerv o cuşetă pentru o persoană/două persoane/familia mea
Doresc sah rezerv oh coshetah pentroo oh perswanah/dowoah perswaneh/fameeleeya meya

I would like to reserve a cabin
Doresc să rezerv o cabină
Doresc sah rezerv oh cabeenah

Timetables (Schedules)

Soseşte
Soseshteh
Arrives

Opreşte la
Opresheteh lah
Calls (stops) at

Bufet - Restaurant
Boofet Restaoorant
Catering service

Cu schimbare la
Coo skeembareh lah
Change at

Legătură/Prin
Legahtoorah/Prin
Connection/Via

Zilnic
Zilnic
Daily

La fiecare 40 de minute
Lah fiehcareh 40 deh minooteh
Every 40 minutes

Clasa întâi
Clasah untuy
First class

La fiecare oră
Lah fiehcareh orah
Hourly

Se recomandă să rezervaţi locuri
Se recomandah sah rezervatz locooree
Seat reservations are recommended

Clasa a doua
Clasah ah dowah
Second class

Se plăteşte supliment
Seh plahteshteh soopliment
Supplement payable

Luggage

How much will it cost to send (ship) my luggage in advance?
Cât costă să trimit bagajul în avans?
Cuht costah sah trimit bagazhool uhn avans?

Where is the left luggage (baggage claim) office?
Unde este biroul de bagaje?
Oonde esteh birohool deh bagazheh?

ROMANIAN

What time do you open/close?
La ce oră deschideți/închideți?
Lah cheh orah deskidetz/unkidetz?

Where are the luggage trolleys (carts)?
Unde sunt cărucioarele de bagaje?
Oondeh sunt cahroochiwareleh deh bagazheh?

Where are the lockers?
Unde sunt dulăpioarele de bagaje?
Oonde sunt doolahpeewareleh de bagezheh?

I have lost my locker key
Am pierdut cheia de la dulăpior
Am piehrdoot kaya deh lah doolahpeeor

On Board

Is this seat free?
E liber locul acesta?
Eh liber locool achestah?

Excuse me, you are sitting in my reserved seat
Scuzați-mă, dar stați pe locul meu rezervat
Scoozatz-mah, dar statz pe locool meyoo rezervat

Which station is this?
La ce gară ne aflăm?
Lah cheh garah neh aflahm?

What time is this train/bus ferry/flight due to arrive/depart?
La ce oră urmează să sosească/plece trenul/autobuzul/feribotul/avionul acesta?
Lah cheh orah oormeyazah sah soseyascah/plecheh/aootoboozool/feribotool/avionool achestah?

Travelling with Children

Do you have a high chair/babysitting service/cot?
Aveți un scaun pentru copil/serviciu de babysitting/pătuț pentru copil?
Avetz oon scaoon pentroo copil/servicheeoo deh baby sittining/pahtootz pentroo copil?

Where is the nursery/playroom?
Unde e camera copilului/camera de joacă?
Oonde e camera copiloolooi/camerah deh zhoacah?

Where can I warm the baby's bottle?
Unde pot să încălzesc biberonul copilului?
Oondeh pot sah uncahlzesc biberonool copiloolooi?

Customs and Passports

Pașapoartele, vă rog!
Pashapoarteleh, vah rohg!
Passports please!

I have nothing/wine/spirits (alcohol) tobacco to declare
Nu am nimic/vin/alcool/tutun de declarat
Noo am neemeek/veen/alcol/tootoon deh declarat

I will be staying for ... days/weeks/months
Voi sta ... zile/săptămâni/luni
Voy stah ... zeele/sahptahmuny/loony

SIGHTSEEING

Asking the Way

Excuse me, do you speak English?
Scuzaţi-mă, vorbiţi engleză?
Scoozatz-mah, vorbitz englehzah?

Excuse me, can you help me please?
Scuzaţi-mă, mă puteţi ajuta vă rog?
Scoozatz-mah, mah pootetz azhootah vah rohg?

Where is the Tourist Information Office?
Unde este Biroul de Informaţii Turistice?
Oondeh esteh Birohool deh Informatzee Tooristicheh?

Excuse me, is this the right way to ... ?
Scuzaţi-mă, acesta este drumul spre ... ?
Scoozatz-mah, achestah esteh droomool spreh ...?

... the cathedral/the Tourist Office/the castle/the old town
... catedrala/Biroul de Turism/castelul/oraşul vechi
... catedralah/Birohool deh Toorism/castelool/orashool veki

Can you tell me the way to the railway station/bus station/taxi rank/city centre/beach?
Puteţi să-mi spuneţi cum să ajung la gară/staţia de auto-buz/staţia de taxi/centru/plajă?
Pootetz sah-me spoonetz coom sah azhoong lah garah/statzia deh aootobooz/statzia deh taxi/chen-troo/plazhah?

Prima/a doua/stânga/dreapta/drept înainte
Preema/a dowah/stungah/dreyaptah/drept unainteh
First/second/left/right/straight ahead

La colţ/La semafor
Lah coltz/lah semafor
At the corner/At the traffic lights

Where is the nearest police station/post office?
Unde este cea mai apropiată circă de poliţie/cel mai apropiat oficiu poştal?
Oonde esteh cheah my apropiatah chircah deh politzye/chel my apropi-at ofeecheeoo poshtal?

Is it near/far?
Este aproape/departe?
Esteh aprwapeh/departeh?

Do I need to take a taxi/catch a bus?
Este nevoie să iau un taxi/auto-buzul?
Esteh nevoyeh sah iaw oon taxi/aootobooz?

Do you have a map?
Aveţi o hartă?
Avetz o hartah?

Can you point to it on my map?
Puteți să-mi arătați pe hartă?
Pootetz sah-mee arahtatz pe hartah?

Thank you for your help
Mulțumesc pentru ajutor
Mooltzoomesc pentroo azhootor

How do I reach the motorway/main road?
Cum ajung la autostradă/ drumul principal?
Coom azhoong lah aootostradah/droomool princhipal?

I think I have taken the wrong turning
Cred că am greşit drumul
Cred cah am greshit droomool

I am looking for this address
Caut adresa aceasta
Caoot adresah acheyastah

I am looking for the ... hotel
Caut hotelul ....
Caoot hotelool ....

How far is it to ... from here?
Cât de departe este de aici până la ...
Cuht deh departeh esteh deh aich punah la ...

Continuați drept înainte încă ... kilometri
Continooatz drept unainteh uncah ... kilometree
Carry straight on for ... kilometres

Faceți prima la dreapta/stânga
Fachetz primah la dreaptah/stunga

Take the next turning on the right/left

La prima intersecție/primul semafor luați-o la dreapta/ stânga
Lah primah intersectzieh/primool semafor/looatz-oh lah dreaptah/stungah
Turn right/left at the next crossroads/traffic lights

Mergeți în direcție greşită
Merdjetz un directzieh greshitah
You are going in the wrong direction

Where is the cathedral/ church/museum/pharmacy?
Unde este catedrala/ biserica/muzel/farmacie?
Oondeh esteh catedrahla/bisehrica/ moozeul/farmachye?

How much is the admission/entrance charge?
Cât costă intrarea?
Cuht costah intrareyah?

Is there a discount for children/students/senior citizens?
Există reducere pentru copii/studenți/persoane în vârstă?
Existah redoochereh pentroo copee/stoodentz/perswaneh un vurstah?

What time does the next guided tour (in English) start?
La ce oră începe următorul tur cu ghid (în engleză)?
Lah cheh orah unchepeh oormahtorool toor coo gid (un englehzah)?

One/two adults/children please
Un/doi adulți/copii, vă rog
Oon/doy adooltz/copee, vah rohg

May I take photographs here?
Am voie să fac poze aici?
Am voyeh sah fahc pozeh aich?

At the Tourist Office

Do you have a map of the town/area?
Aveți o hartă a orașului/regiunii?
Avetz oh hartah a orashoolooi/redjeeoonee?

Do you have a list of accommodation?
Aveți o listă cu locuri disponibile?
Avetz o listah coo locoori deesponeebeelee?

Can I reserve accommodation?
Pot să rezerv cazarea?
Pot sah rezerv cazareya?

ACCOMMODATION

Hotels

I have a reservation in the name of ...
Am făcut o rezervare pe numele de ...
Am fahcoot oh rezervare peh noomeleh deh ...

I wrote to/faxed/telephoned you last month/last week
V-am scris/trimis un fax/telefonat/luna trecută/săptămâna trecută
V-am screes/treemees oon fax/telephonat/loonah trecootah/sahptahmunah trecootah

Do you have any rooms free?
Aveți camere libere?
Avetz camereh leebereh?

I would like to reserve a single/double room with/without a bath/shower
Doresc să rezerv o cameră pentru o persoană/două persoane cu/fără baie/duș
Doresc sah rezerv oh camerah pentroo oh perswanah/dowah perswaneh coo/fahrah baeeyeh/doosh

I would like bed/breakfast (room and) full board
Doresc o cameră cu micul dejun/pensiune
Doresc oh camerah coo meecool dezhoon/penseeooneh

How much is it per night?
Cât costă pe noapte?
Cuht costah peh nowapteh?

Is breakfast included?
Este inclus micul dejun?
Esteh incloos meecool dezhoon?

Do you have any cheaper rooms?
Aveți camere mai ieftine?
Avetz camereh my yehfteeneh?

I would like to see/take the room
Doresc să văd/închiriez camera
Doresc sah vahd/unkeeryez camerah

I would like to stay for ... nights
Doresc să stau .... nopți
Doresc sah staoo … noptz

The shower/light/tap/hot water doesn't work
Nu merge duşul/lumina/robinetul/apa fierbinte
Noo merdje dooshool/loominah/robeenetool/apa fierbinteh

At what time/where is breakfast served?
La ce oră/unde se serveşte micul dejun?
Lah cheh orah/oondeh se serveshteh meecool dezhoon?

What time do I have to check out?
Când trebuie să eliberez camera?
Cund trebooyeh sah eleeberez camerah?

Can I have the key to room number ...?
Doresc cheia de la camera numărul ...?
Doresc kaya deh lah camerah noomahrool ...?

My room number is ...
Stau la camera numărul ...
Stau lah camerah noomahrool ...

My room is not satisfactory/not clean enough/too noisy. Please can I change rooms?
Camera mea nu este satisfăcătoare/curată/e prea zgomotoasă. Vă rog, pot să schimb camera?
Camerah meya noo esteh sateesfahcahtoareh/cooratah/eh preah zgomotwasah. Vah rohg, pot sah skimb camerah?

Where is the bathroom?
Unde este baia?
Oonde esteh ba-ya?

Do you have a safe for valuables?
Aveți un seif pentru lucruri de valoare?
Avetz oon sayph pentroo loocroory deh valowareh?

Is there a laundry/do you wash clothes?
Aveți o spălătorie/primiți haine la spălat?
Avetz oh spahlahtoreeye/preemeetz roofeh lah spahlat?

I would like an air-conditioned room
Doresc o cameră cu aer condiționat
Doresc oh camerah coo aer conditzonat

Do you accept traveller's cheques/credit cards?
Acceptați cecuri de călătorie/cărți de credit?
Akcheptatz checoory de kerlertoreeyeh/cahrtz deh credit?

May I have the bill please?
Îmi puteți da nota de plată?
Umy pootetz dah notah deh platah?

Excuse me, I think there may be a mistake in this bill
Scuzați-mă, cred că e o greşeală în nota de plată
Scoozatz-mah, cred cah eh oh gresheyalah um notah deh platah

Youth Hostels

How much is a dormitory bed per night?
Cât costă un pat pe noapte în dormitorul comun?
Cuht costah oon pat peh nowapteh un dormeetorool comoon?

I am/am not an HI member
Sunt/nu sunt membru în HI
Soont/noo soont membroo HI

May I use my own sleeping bag?
Pot să folosesc sacul meu de dormit?
Pot sah folosesc sacool meyoo deh dormeet?

What time do you lock the doors at night?
La ce oră se încuie uşa seara?
Lah cheh orah se unkooye oosha sara?

Camping

May I camp for the night/two nights?
Pot să pun cortul pentru noaptea asta/două nopți?
Pot sah poon cortool pentroo nwapteah astah/dowoah noptz?

Where can I pitch my tent?
Unde pot să pun cortul?
Oondeh pot sah poon cortool?

How much does it cost for one night/week?
Cât costă pe noapte/săptămână?
Cuht costah peh nwapteh/sahptahmunah?

Where are the washing facilities?
Unde sunt lavabourile?
Oonde sunt lavaboureeleh?

Is there a restaurant/supermarket/swimming pool on site/nearby?
Este un restaurant/magazin alimentar/bazin de înot aici/în apropiere?
Esteh oon restaoorant/magazeen aleementar/bazeen deh unot aich/un apropiereh?

Do you have a safety deposit box?
Unde pot fi păstrate lucrurile de valoare?
Ondeh pot fi pahstrate loocrooreeleh deh valwareh?

EATING AND DRINKING

Cafés and Bars

I would like a cup of/two cups of/another coffee/tea
Mai doresc o ceaşcă/două ceşti de cafea/ceai
My doresc oh cheyashcah/dowoah cheshty deh cafeya/cheyai

With/without milk/sugar
Cu/fără lapte/zahăr
Coo/fahrah lapteh/zahahr

I would like a bottle/glass/two glasses of mineral water/red wine/white wine, please
Doresc o sticlă/un pahar/două pahare de apă minerală/vin roşu/vin alb, vă rog
Doresc oh steeclah/oon pahar/dowah pahare deh apah meeneralah/veen roshoo/veen alb, vah rohg

I would like a beer/two beers, please
Doresc o bere/două beri, vă rog
Doresc oh bereh, dowah beree, vah rohg

Please, may I have some ice?
Gheaţă, vă rog?
Gheyatzah, vah rohg?

Do you have any matches/cigarettes/cigars?
Aveţi chibrituri/ţigări/trabucuri?
Avetz keebreetooree/tzigahree/tra-bookoori?

Restaurants

Can you recommend a good/cheap restaurant in this area?
Îmi puteţi recomanda un restaurant bun/ieftin în zona asta?
Umi pootetz recomandah oon restaoorant boon/yefteen un zona asta?

I would like a table for ... people
Doresc o masă pentru .... persoane
Doresc oh masah pentroo .... perswaneh

Do you have a non-smoking area?
Aveţi locuri pentru nefumători?
Avetz locooree pentroo nefoomah-toree?

Waiter/Waitress!
Chelner/Chelneriţă!
Kelner/Kelnehritsa!

Excuse me, please may we order?
Scuzaţi-mă, putem să comandăm?
Scoozatz-mah, pootem sah comandahm?

Do you have a set menu/ children's menu/wine list ... in English?
Aveţi un meniu fix/un menu pentru copii/o listă de vinuri ... în engleză?
Avetz oon menyoo fix/oon mehnoo pentroo copii/o listah deh veenooree ... un englehzah?

Do you have any vegetarian dishes?
Aveţi mâncăruri pentu vegetarieni?
Avetz muncuroori pentroo vegetaryehnee?

Do you have any local specialities?
Aveţi specialităţi locale?
Avetz spechialitahtz lokahleh?

Are vegetables included?
Sunt incluse legumele?
Sunt inclooseh legoomeleh?

Could I have it well-cooked/medium/rare please?
Doresc carnea bine prăjită/nu foarte prăjită/în sânge?
Doresc carneya beeneh prahzheetah/noo fwarteh prahzheetah/un sundjeh?

What does this dish consist of?
Din ce constă felul acesta de mâncare?
Deen cheh constah felool achesta deh muncareh?

I am a vegetarian. Does this contain meat?
Sunt vegetarian. Conține carne?
Soont vegetaryan. Kontzyneh carneh?

I do not eat nuts/dairy products/meat/fish
Nu mănânc nuci/produse lactate/carne/peşte
Noo mahnunc noochi/prodooseh lactateh/carneh/pehshteh

Not (very) spicy please
Nu (foarte) condimentat, vă rog
Noo (fwarteh) condeementat, vah rohg

I would like the set menu, please
Doresc meniul fix, vă rog
Doresc menyool fix, vah rohg

We have not been served yet
N-am fost serviți încă
Nam fost serveetz uncah

Please bring a plate/knife/fork
Vă rog să aduceți o farfurie/un cuțit/o furculiță
Vah rog sah adoocetzy oh farfooryeh/oon cootzyt/o foorkoolitzah

Excuse me, this is not what I ordered
Scuzați-mă, eu nu am comandat asta
Scoozatz-mah, eoo noo am comandat asta

May I have some/more bread/water/coffee/tea?
Îmi mai puteți da pâine/apă/cafea/ceai?
Umi my pootetz dah puyneh/apah/cafeya/cheyai?

May I have the bill please?
Nota de plată, vă rog?
Notah deh platah, vah rohg?

Does this bill include service?
Nota de plată include bacşişul?
Notah deh platah incloodeh bakshishool?

Do you accept traveller's cheques/Mastercard/US dollars?
Acceptați cecuri de călătorie/Mastercard/dolari americani?
Akcheptatz checooree de kerlertoreeyeh/Mastercard/dolaree americanee?

Can I have a receipt please?
Îmi puteți da o chitanță, vă rog?
Umi pootetz dah o kitantzah, vah rohg?

Where is the toilet (rest room) please?
Unde este toaleta, vă rog?
Oondeh este twaleta, vah rohg?

On the Menu

Mic dejun/Prânz/Cină
Mik dejoon/Prunz/Chynah
Breakfast/Lunch/Dinner

Felul întâi
Felool untuy
First Courses

Supe
Soopeh
Soups

Felul doi
Felool doy
Main Courses

Mâncăruri cu peşte
Muncahrooree coo pehshteh
Fish dishes

Mâncăruri cu carne
Muncahrooree coo carneh
Meat Dishes

Carne de vacă
Karneh deh vakah
Beef

Friptură
Friptoorah
Steak

Carne de porc
Karneh deh pork
Pork

Carne de viţel
Karneh deh vitzel
Veal

Carne de pui
Karneh deh pooy
Chicken

Carne de miel
Karneh deh myehl
Lamb

Şuncă
Shooncah
Ham

Mâncăruri vegetariene
Muncahrooree vedjetarieneh
Vegetarian Dishes

Legume
Lehgoomeh
Vegetables

Cartofi prăjiţi
Kartofy prahdjitzi
Chips (french fries)

Cartofi natur/sauté/piure
Kartofy natoor/sohteh/pyooreh
Boiled/sauté/mashed potatoes

Orez
Ohrehz
Rice

Deserturi
Desertooree
Desserts

Îngheţată
Ungetzatah
Ice cream

Fursecuri
Foorsehkoory
Cakes

Clătite
Klahtyteh
Pastries

Fructe
Froocteh
Fruit

Pâine
Punyneh
Bread

Ruladă
Roolahduh
Rolls

Pâine prăjită
Punyneh prahdjitah
Toast

Unt
Oont
Butter

Sare/piper
Sareh/pypehr
Salt/pepper

Zahăr
Zahahr
Sugar

Specialităţi
Spechialeetahtz
Specialities

Specialităţi locale
Spechalytahtzy localeh
Local specialities

Meniu fix
Menyu fix
Set menu

Lista de vinuri
Listah deh vynoory
Wine list

Vinuri roşii
Vynoory roshy
Red wines

Vinuri albe
Vynoory albeh
White wines

Vinuri rosé
Vynoory rohzeh
Rosé wines

Vinuri spumoase
Vynoory spoomoahseh
Sparkling wines

Bere
Behreh
Beer

Bere îmbuteliată/halbă
Behreh unmbootehlyatah/halbah
Bottled/Draught (draft) beer

Băuturi nealcoolice
Bahootoory nehalkoliche
Non-alcoholic drinks

Apă minerală
Apah mineralah
Mineral water

Sucuri de fructe
Sookoory de frookteh
Fruit juices

Suc de portocale
Sook de portokaleh
Orange juice

Limonadă
Lymonadah
Lemonade

Gheaţă
Geahtzah
Ice

Cafea cu lapte/cafea simplă/esspresso
Cafeah coo lapteh/cafeah symplah/esspresso
White coffee/black coffee/espresso coffee

Ceai cu lapte/cu lămâie
Cheay coo lapteh/coo lahmunyeh
Tea with milk/with lemon

Ciocolată lichidă
chyocolaatah liquidah
Chocolate (drink)

Lapte
Lapteh
Milk

Gustări/Mâncăruri uşoare
Goostahri/Muncahroory ushooahreh
Snacks/Light meals

Salate
Salateh
Salads

Sandvişuri
Sandvishoori
Sandwiches

Ouă
Oh-uah
Eggs

Ouă fierte/ochiuri/omletă
Oh-uah fyerteh/okyoory/omletah
Boiled/fried/scrambled eggs

Typical Local Dishes

Ciorbă de perişoare
Cheeorbah deh pereeshoareh
Meatball Soup (sour soup with tomato and meat-balls)

Sarmale
Sarmaleh
Stuffed Cabbage Leaves (cabbage leaves stuffed with a mixture of pork mince and rice, in sauce)

Mititei
Meeteetei
Grilled Minced Meat Rolls (spicy meat and garlic rolls)

Borş de miel
Borsh deh miehl
Sour Lamb Soup

Musaca
Moosacah
Minced Meat Pie (layers of potato slices, minced meat and vegetables)

Ardei umpluţi
Ardei oomplootz
Stuffed Peppers (large peppers stuffed with rice, vegetables and/or minced meat, in sauce)

Mămăliguţă
Mahmahleegootzah
Maize Polenta (traditional Romanian dish, can be served as a starter, with yoghurt or sour cream, or on its own as an accompaniment to 'sarmale')

GETTING AROUND

Public Transport

Where is the bus stop/coach stop/nearest metro station?
Unde este staţia de autobuz/autocar/cea mai apropiată staţie de metro?
Oondeh esteh statzia deh aooto-booz/aootocar/cheya my apropiatah statzyeh deh metro?

When is the next/last bus to ...?
Când este următorul/ultimul autobuz spre ... ?
Cund esteh oormahtorool/ooltimool aootobooz spreh ...?

How much is the fare to the city centre (downtown)/ railway station/airport?
Cât este biletul până în centru/la gară/aeroport?
Cuht esteh beeletool punah un chentroo/lah garah/aeroport?

Will you tell me when to get off?
Îmi puteți spune unde să cobor?
Umi pootetz spooneh oondeh sah cobor?

Does this bus go to...?
Autobuzul acesta merge la ...?
Aootoboozool achesta merdje lah.. ?

Which number bus goes to ...?
Ce autobuz merge la ...?
Cheh aootobooz merdje lah ...?

May I have a single (one-way)/return (round-trip)/day ticket/book of tickets?
Doresc un bilet dus/ dus - întors/abonament pe o zi/carnet de bilete?
Doresc oon bilet doos/doos - untors/abonament peh oh zee/ carnet deh bileteh?

Taxis (Taxiuri)

I would like to go to ... How much will it cost?
Doresc să merg la ... Cât costă?
Doresc sah merg lah ... Cuht costah?

Please may I stop here?
Vă rog, ne putem opri aici?
Vah rohg, neh pootem opree aich?

I would like to order a taxi today/tomorrow at 2pm to go from ... to ...
Doresc să comand un taxi pentru astăzi/mâine la ora 2 după amiază, de la ...... pâna la ....
Doresc sah comand oon taxi pentroo astahzee/muyeeneh lah orah dowah doopah ameeazah, deh lah ... punah lah ...

Entertainment

Can you recommend a good bar/night club?
Puteți să îmi recomandați un bar/club bun de noapte?
Pootetz sah umi recomandatz oon bar/cloob boon deh nwapteh?

Do you know what is on at the cinema (playing at the movies)/theatre at the moment?
Știți ce se joacă acum la cinema/teatru?
Shteetz cheh se zhoacah acoom lah cheenemah/teyatroo?

I would like to book (purchase) ... tickets for the matinee/evening performance on Monday
Doresc să rezerv (cumpăr) bilete pentru luni, la matineu/spectacolul de seară
Doresc sah rezerv (coompahr) beeleteh pentroo loony, lah mateeneyoo/spectacolool deh sara

What time does the film/ performance start?
La ce oră începe filmul/ spectacolul?
Lah cheh orah unchepeh filmool/spectacolool?

COMMUNICATIONS

Post

How much will it cost to send a letter/postcard/this package to Britain/Ireland/ America/Canada/Australia/ New Zealand?
Cât costă să trimit o scrisoare/vedere/un pachet în Marea Britanie/Irlanda/ America/Canada/Austrialia/ Noua Zeelandă?
Cuht costah sah treemeet oh screesoareh/vedereh/oon paket un Mareya Breetanyeh/Irlanda/ Amereecah/Canadah/Aoostrayleeah/ Nowa Zeehlandah?

I would like one stamp/two stamps
Doresc un timbru/două timbre.
Doresc oon teembroo/dowah teembreh

I'd like ... stamps for postcards to send abroad, please
Doresc ... timbre de străinătate pentru vederi, vă rog
Doresc …teembreh deh straheenahtateh pentroo vederee, vah rohg

Phones

I would like to make a telephone call/reverse the charges to (make a collect call to)...
Doresc să dau un telefon/ cu taxă inversă la ...
Doresc sah daoo oon telephon/coo taxah inversah lah …

What coins do I need for the telephone?
Ce monezi îmi trebuie pentru telefon?
Cheh monezee umy trebooye pentroo telephon?

The line is engaged (busy)
E ocupat
E ocoopat

The number is ...
Numărul este ...
Noomahrool esteh …

Hello, this is ...
Alo, ...la telefon.
Alo,… lah telephon.

Please may I speak to ...?
Pot să vorbesc cu ..., vă rog?
Pot sah vorbesc coo ... vah rohg?

He/she is not in at the moment. Please can you call back?
El/ea nu este aici. Telefonați mai târziu, vă rog?
El/ea noo esteh aich. Telefonatsi my turzeeyoo, vah rohg?

SHOPPING

Shops

Librărie/Papetărie
Leebrahryeh
Bookshop/Stationery

Bijuterii/Cadouri
Beedjooteree/Cadowree
Jeweller/Gifts

Încălţăminte
Uncahltzahmeenteh
Shoes

Confecţii
Confectzee
Clothes

Spălătorie
Spahlahtoryeh
Laundry

Articole de menaj
Arteecoleh deh menadj
Hardware

Coafor
Cwafor
Hairdresser

Brutărie
Brootahryeh
Baker

Supermarket
Soopermarkeet
Supermarket

Magazin foto
Magazeen photo
Photo shop

Agenţie de voiaj
Adjentzyeh deh voyadj
Travel agent

Farmacie
Farmachye
Pharmacy

In the Shops

What time do the shops open/close?
La ce oră se deschid/închid magazinele?
Lah cheh orah she deskid/unkid magazeeneleh?

Where is the nearest market?
Unde e cea mai apropiată piaţă?
Oondeh eh chyea my apropiatah piatzah?

Can you show me the one in the window/this one?
Puteţi să mi-o arătaţi pe cea din vitrină/cel din vitrină/ aceasta (acesta)?
Pootetz sah mee-oh arahtatz peh cheah deen veetreenah/chel deen veetreenah/achesta (acheyasta)?

Can I try this on?
Pot să o (îl) probez?
Pot sah oh (ul) probez?

What size is this?
Ce mărime e aceasta (acesta)?
Cheh mahreemeh eh acheyasta (achesta)?

This is too large/too

small/too expensive. Do you have any others?
Acesta (acesta) e prea mare/prea mic (mică)/prea scump (scumpă). Mai aveţi şi altele?
Achesta (acheyasta) eh preya mareh/preha meec (meecah)/preha scoomp (scoompah). My avetz she alteleh?

My size is ...
Am mărimea ...
Am mahreemeya ...

Where is the changing room/children's/cosmetic/ladieswear/menswear/food department?
Unde este camera de probă/departamentul pentru copii/cosmetice/femei/bărbaţi/raionul alimentar?
Oondeh esteh camerah deh probah/departamentool pentroo copee/cosmeteecheh/femay/bahrbatz/raionool aleementar?

I would like ... a quarter of a kilo/half a kilo/a kilo of bread/butter/ham/this fruit
Doresc ... un sfert de kilogram/o jumătate de kilogram/un kilogram de pâine/unt/şuncă/din fructele acestea
Doresc ... oon sfert deh kilogram/oh zhoomahtateh deh kilogram/oon kilogram deh puyneh/oont/shooncah/deen froocteleh achestea

How much is this?
Cât costă?
Cuht costah?

I'll take this one, thank you
O iau pe aceasta, mulţumesc
Oh iaoo peh acheyasta, mooltzoomesc

Do you have a carrier (shopping) bag?
Aveţi o pungă de plastic?
Avetz oh pungah deh plastic?

Do you have anything cheaper/larger/smaller/of better quality?
Aveţi ceva mai ieftin/mare/mic (mică)/de calitate mai bună?
Avetz cheva my yefteen/mareh/meec (meecah)/deh caleetateh my boonah?

I would like a film/to develop this film for this camera
Doresc un film/să developez filmul acesta pentru acest aparat
Doresc oon film/sah developez filmool achesta pentroo achest aparat

I would like some batteries, the same size as this old one
Doresc nişte baterii, de aceeaşi mărime ca aceasta
Doresc neeshteh bateree, deh acheyash mahreemeh ka acheyasta

Would you mind wrapping this for me, please?
Vreţi să mi-l (mi-o) împachetaţi, vă rog?
Vretz sah mee-l (mee-o) umpahetatz, vah rohg?

Sorry, but you seem to have given me the wrong change
Îmi pare rău, dar se pare că mi-aţi dat restul greşit
Umi pareh row, dar se pareh cah mee-atz dat restool greshit

MOTORING

Car Hire (Rental)

I have ordered (rented) a car in the name of ...
Am comandat (închiriat) o maşină pe numele de ...
Am comandat (ernchiriat) oh masheenah peh noomeleh deh ....

How much does it cost to hire (rent) a car for one day/two days/a week?
Cât costă să închiriez o maşină pentru o zi/două zile/o săptămână?
Cuht costah sah unkiriez oh masheenah pentroo oh zee/dowah zeeleh/oh sahptahmunah?

Is the tank already full of petrol (gas)?
E plin rezervorul cu benzină/motorină?
E pleen rezervorool coo benzeenah/motoreenah?

Is insurance and tax included? How much is the deposit?
E inclusă asigurarea şi taxa? Cât este depozitul?
E incloosah aseegoorareya she taxa? Cuht esteh depozeetool?

By what time must I return the car?
La ce oră trebuie să aduc maşina înapoi?
Lah cheh orah trebooyeh sah adook masheena unapoy?

I would like a small/large/family/sports car with a radio/cassette
Doresc o maşină mică/mare/de familie/sport cu radio/casetofon
Doresc oh masheenah meecah/mareh/deh fameelyeh/sport coo radio/casetophon

Do you have a road map?
Aveţi o hartă rutieră?
Avetz oh hartah rootyehrah?

Parking

How long can I park here?
Cât timp pot să parchez aici?
Cuht teemp pot sah parkez aich?

Is there a car park near here?
E o parcare în apropiere?
E oh parcare un apropyehreh?

At what time does this car park close?
La ce oră se închide parcarea?
Lah cheh orah se unkideh parcareya?

Signs and Notices

Sens unic
Sens ooneec
One way

Intrarea interzisă
Intrareya interzeesah
No entry

Parcarea interzisă
Parcareya interzeesah
No parking

Detur
Detoor
Detour (Diversion)

Stop
Stop
Stop

Acordați prioritate
Acordatz preeoreetateh.
Give way (Yield)

Drum alunecos
Droom aloonecos.
Slippery road

Depăşirea interzisă
Depahshireya interzeesah.
No overtaking

Pericol!
Pereecol!
Danger!

At the Filling Station (La Benzinărie)

Unleaded (lead free)/ standard/premium/diesel
Fără plumb/standard/ premium/diesel
Fahrah ploomb/standard/ premyoom/deezel

Fill the tank please
Umpleți rezervorul, vă rog
Oompletz rezervorool, vah rohg

Do you have a road map?
Aveți o hartă rutieră?
Avetz oh hartah rootyehrah?

How much is the car wash?
Cât costă un spălat de maşină?
Cuht costah oon spahlat deh masheenah?

Breakdowns

I've had a breakdown at ...
Am făcut pană la ...
Am fahkoot panah lah ...

I am a member of the ... [motoring organisation]
Sunt un membru al...
Soont oon membroo al ...

I am on the road from... to ...
Sunt pe drumul de la ... la ...
Soont peh droomool deh lah.. lah ...

I can't move the car. Can you send a tow truck?
Nu pot să mişc maşina. Puteți trimite o maşină să mă remorcheze?
Noo pot sah meeshk masheena. Pootetz treemeeteh oh masheenah sah mah remorkezeh?

I have a flat tyre
Am făcut pană de cauciuc
Am fahkoot panah deh cowchyooc

The windscreen (windshield) has smashed/cracked
S-a spart/crăpat parbrizul
S-a spart/crahpat parbreezool

There is something wrong with the engine/brakes/ lights/steering/gearbox/ clutch/exhaust
E o problemă cu motorul/ frânele/farurile/volanul/cutia de viteze/ambreiajul/țeava de eşapament

E oh problemah coo motorool/ fruneleh/farooreeleh/volanool/cootya deh veetezeh/ambrehyazhool/tzeya-va deh eshapament

It's overheating
Se încălzeşte prea tare
Se uncahlzeshteh preya tareh

It won't start
Nu porneşte
Noo porneshteh

Where can I get it repaired?
Unde pot să o repar?
Ondeh pot sah oh repar?

Can you take me there?
Mă puteţi duce acolo?
Mah pootetz doocheh acoloh?

Will it take long to fix?
O să dureze mult reparaţia?
Osah doorezeh moolt reparatzya?

How much will it cost?
Cât o să coste?
Cuht oh sah costeh?

Please can you pick me up/give me a lift?
Vă rog, mă puteţi lua/duce cu maşina?
Vah rohg, mah pootetz doocheh coo masheenah?

Accidents and Traffic Offences (Violations)

Can you help me? There has been an accident
Vreţi să mă ajutaţi vă rog? Am avut un accident
Vretz sah mah azhootatz vah rohg? Am avoot oon akcheedent

Please call the police/an ambulance
Chemaţi vă rog poliţia/salvarea
Kehmatz vah rohg poleetzia/ salvareya

Is anyone hurt?
Sunt răniţi?
Sunt rahneetz?

Sorry, I didn't see the sign
Îmi pare rău, nu am văzut tăbliţa indicatoare
Umi pareh row, noo am vahzoot tahbleetza indicatwareh

Must I pay a fine? How much?
Trebuie să plătesc amendă? Cât?
Trebooych sah plahtesc amendah? Cuht?

Arătaţi-mi actele
Arahtatz-me acteleh
Show me your documents

HEALTH

Pharmacy (Farmacie)

Do you have anything for a stomach ache/headache/sore throat/toothache?
Aveţi ceva pentru durere de stomac/cap/usturime de gât/dinţi?
Avetz cheva pentroo doorereh deh stomac/cap/oostooreemeh deh guht/deentz?

HEALTH

ROMANIAN

I need something for diarrhoea/constipation/ a cold/a cough/insect bites/sunburn/travel (motion) sickness
Am nevoie de ceva pentru diaree/constipație/răceală/ tuse/muşcătură de insecte/ arsură de soare/rău de maşină
Am nevoye deh chevah pentroo dyaryeh/consteepatzye/rahcheyalah/ mooshcahtoorah deh insecteh/ arsoorah deh sohareh/row deh masheenah

How much/how many do I take?
Cât/câte să iau?
Cuht/cuhteh sah iaoo?

I am taking anti-malaria tablets/these pills
Iau tablete anti-malarie/ pastilele acestea
Iaoo tableteh antee - malaryeh/ pasteeleleh achestea

How often do I take it/them?
De câte ori o/le iau?
Deh cuhteh ory oh/leh iaoo?

I am/he is/she is taking this medication
Eu iau/el/ea ia medicamentele acestea
Eoo iaoo/el/ea ia medeecamenteleh achestea

How much does it cost?
Cât costă?
Cuht costah?

Can you recommend a good doctor/dentist?
Puteți recomanda un doctor/dentist bun?
Pootetz recomanda oon doctor/ dentist boon?

Is it suitable for children?
E bun pentru copii?
Eh boon pentroo copee?

Doctor (Doctor)

I have a pain here/in my arm/leg/chest/stomach
Mă doare aici/brațul/ piciorul/pieptul/stomacul
Mah doareh aich/bratzool pee-chiorool/pee-eptool/stomacool

Please call a doctor, this is an emergency
Vă rog să chemați un doctor de urgență
Vah rohg sah kematz oon doctor deh oordjentzah

I would like to make an appointment to see the doctor
Doresc să fac programare la doctor
Doresc sah fahc oh programareh lah doctol

I am diabetic/pregnant
Am diabet/sunt gravidă
Am deyabet/soont gravidah

I need a prescription for ...
Am nevoie de o rețetă pentru ...
Am nevoyeh deh oh retzetah pentroo ...

Can you give me something to ease the pain?
Îmi puteți da ceva pentru durere?
Umi pootetz dah cheva pentroo doorereh?

I am/he is/she is allergic to penicillin
Eu sunt/el/ea este alergică la penicilină
Eoo soont/el/ea esteh alerdjeecah la penichilinah

Doare aici?
Doareh aich?
Does this hurt?

Dumneavoastră trebuie să mergeți/el/ea trebuie să meargă la spital
Doomneyavwastrah trebooyeh sah mergetz/el/ea/trebooyeh sah meargah lah spital
You must/he must/she must go to hospital

Luați astea o dată/de două/de trei ori pe zi
Looatz asteya oh datah/deh dowah/deh tray oree peh zee
Take these once/twice/three times a day

I am/he is/she is taking this medication
Eu iau/el/ea ia medicamentele acestea
Eoo iaoo/el/ea ia medeecamenteleh achestea

I have medical insurance
Am asigurare medicală
Am aseegoorareh medicalah

Dentist (Dentist)

I have toothache/my filling has come out
Mă doare o măsea/a căzut plomba
Mah dwareh oh mahseya/a cahzoot plombah

I do/do not want to have an injection
Vreau/nu vreau injecție
Vrehaoo/noo vrehaoo injectzyeh

EMERGENCIES

Help!
Ajutor!
Ajootor!

Fire!
Foc!
Fohc!

Stop
Stop!
Stop!

Call an ambulance/ a doctor/the police/the fire brigade!
Chemați salvarea/doctorul/ poliția/pompierii!
Kematz salvareya/doctorool/poleet-zya/pompee-eree!

Please may I use a telephone?
Vă rog, pot să folosesc telefonul?
Vah rohg, pot sah folosesc telephonool?

I have had my traveller's cheques/credit cards/ handbag/rucksack/luggage/ wallet/passport/mobile phone stolen
Mi s-au furat cecurile de călă-torie/cărțile de credit/geanta/ rucsacul/bagajul/portofelul/ paşaportul/telefonul mobil
Me s-aw foorat checooreele de kerlertoreeyeh/cahrtzeeleh deh credeet/roocsacool/bagazhool /portofelool/pashaportul/telefonul mobyl

May I please have a copy of the report for my insurance claim?
Îmi dați vă rog o copie a raportului pentru cererea mea de asigurare?
Unmy datzy vah rog oh kopye ah rahportoolooy pentroo cherereah meah deh asygoorare?

Can you help me I have lost my daughter/son/my companion(s)?
Mă puteți ajuta, mi-am pierdut fiica/fiul/însoțitorul (însoțitorii)?
Mah pootetz ajoota, me-am pee-ehrdoot feeca/feeool/unsotzeetorool (unsotzeetoree)?

Please go away/leave me alone
Vă rog să plecați/lăsați-mă în pace
Vah rohg sah plecatz/lahsatz-mah uhn pacheh

I'm sorry
Îmi pare rău
Umi pareh row

I want to contact the British/American/Canadian/ Irish/Australian/New Zealand/South African consulate
Vreau să contactez Consulatul Marii Britanii/American/ Canadian/Irlandez/Australian/ Noii Zeelande/Africii de Sud
Vreaoo sah contactez Consoolatool Maree-ee Britanee-ee/Amereecan/Canadeean/Irlandez/ Aoostraleean/No-ee-ee Zehlandeh/Africhee-ee deh Sood

I'm ill/injured/lost
Sunt bolnav/lovit/m-am rătăcit
Soont bolnav/lovit/m-am rahtahcheet

We're ill/injured/lost
Suntem bolnavi/loviți/ne-am rătăcit
Soontem bolnavee/lovitz/ne-am rahrahcheet

He is ill/injured/lost
El este bolnav/lovit/s-a rătăcit
El esteh bolnav/lovit/s-a rahtahcheet

She is ill/injured/lost
Ea este bolnavă/lovită/s-a rătăcit
Ea esteh bolnavah/lovitah/s-a rahtahcheet

They are/ill/injured/lost
Ei sunt bolnavi/loviți/s-au rătăcit
Ey sunt bolnavee/lovitz/s-aoo rahtahcheet

SPANISH

INTRODUCTION

Castilian Spanish, the official form of the language, is spoken all over Spain. Some regions also have their own official languages: Catalan in Catalonia and the Balearic Islands, Galego in Galicia and Basque in parts of the north-east. These are separate languages and not dialects of Spanish. In the popular tourist areas English is widely understood.

If using a Spanish dictionary, phone directory or other alphabetical listing, remember that words beginning with 'ch' come after all the other 'c's, and words starting with 'll' after all the other 'l's.

Addresses for Travel and Tourist Information

Australia: *Embassy,* 15 Arkana St, Yarralumla, ACT 2600; tel: (02) 6273 3555; fax: (02) 6273 3918.

South Africa: *Embassy,* 169 Pine St, Arcadia, Pretoria 0083; tel: (12) 344 3875; fax: (12) 343 4891.

UK: *Spanish National Tourist Office,* 2nd Floor, 79 New Cavendish St, London W1W 6XB; tel: (020) 7486 8077; fax: (020) 7486 8034.

USA: *Tourist Office of Spain,* 665 Fifth Ave, New York, NY 10022; tel: (212) 759 8822. *Tourist Office of Spain,* 8383 Wilshire Blvd, #960, Beverly Hills, CA 90211; tel: (213) 658 7188.

Official tourism website: www.spain.info.

Spain Facts

CAPITAL: Madrid
CURRENCY: Euro (€) €1 = 100 cents.
OPENING HOURS: Banks: Mon–Fri 0800–1400; some banks also open Sat 0900–1300. Shops: Mon–Sat 0930–1400, 1700–2000. Large shops may be open 1000–2100. Museums: Tues–Sat, times vary; Sun morning; closed on public holidays.
TELEPHONES: To dial in, + 34. Outgoing, 00 plus the country code. Police, 091 (major incidents), 092 (cities), 062 (smaller places). Fire, 080. Ambulance, 061. There is also a general emergency number, 112.
PUBLIC HOLIDAYS: 1, 6 Jan; Maundy Thursday, Good Friday and Easter Monday; 1 May; 1 Aug; 12 Oct; 1 Nov; 6, 8, 25 Dec.

Technical Language Hints

Two Spanish sounds which can cause English speakers difficulty are the very trilled r and s, which before some consonants has a sh sound, e.g. mismo, *mishmo*, 'same'.

ESSENTIALS

Alphabet and Pronunciation

	Name	Pronounced
A a	*a*	**ah, like the vowel sound of cart**
B b	*be*	**like English b; between vowels, a sound between b and v**
C c	*ce*	**hard c as in can; but before e and i, th as in thin;**
D d	*de*	**like English d; but between vowels and at end of words, th as in those**
E e	*e*	**long eh as in hey**
F f	*effeh*	**like English f**
G g	*ge*	**like g in go; but before e and i, kh sound as in Scottish loch; between vowels a weak er gh sound**
H h	*atchey*	**not pronounced in Spanish**
I i	*ee lateena*	**ee sound as in machine**
J j	*hota*	**kh sound as in Scottish loch**
K k	*ka*	**like English k**
L l	*elleh*	**like English l**
Ll ll	*ellyeh*	**ly as in million**
M m	*emmeh*	**like English m**
N n	*enneh*	**like English n**
Ñ ñ	*enyeh*	**ny as in onion**
O o	*o*	**short o as in got; long o an oh sound as in soap**
P p	*pe*	**like English p**
Q q	*koo*	**qu always a k sound**
R r	*ereh*	**a trilled r like the Scottish r**
Rr rr	*erreh*	**even more strongly trilled r**
S s	*esseh*	**like the s in sit**
T t	*te*	**like English t**
U u	*oo*	**long oo sound as in cool**
V v	*oobeh*	**at beginning of words like b in bad; when between vowels, more like English v**
W w	*oobeh dobleh*	**only in foreign words**
X x	*ekees*	**like English x**
Y y	*ee gree-ehga*	**when alone or at the end of words, an ee sound as in party**
Z z	*thehta*	**like th in thin**

SPANISH

ESSENTIALS

SPANISH

Basic Words & Phrases

Yes
Si
Si

No
No
Noh

Please
Por favor
Por fabor

Thank you
Gracias
Gratheeas

Hello
Hola
Ola

Goodbye
Adiós
Adeeos.

Excuse me
Disculpe
Deeskoolpeh

Sorry
Perdón
Pairdohn

How
Cómo
Como

When
Cuándo
Cwandoe

What
Qué
Kay

Why
Por qué
Porkay

Who
Quién
Keeyen

That's O.K.
De acuerdo
Dey acwerdo

Perhaps
Quizá
Keetha

To
A
A

From
Desde/de
Desdey/dey

Here
Aquí
Akee

There
Allí
Ayee

I don't understand
No entiendo
Noh enteeyendo

I don't speak Spanish
No hablo español
Noh ahblo espanyol

Do you speak English?
¿Habla usted inglés?
¿Ahbla oosteth eengless?

Can you please write it down?
¿Lo puede escribir, por favor?
¿Lo pwedeh escreebeer, porr fabor?

Please can you speak more slowly?
¿Quiere usted hablar más despacio?
¿Keyerehh oosteth ablar mas despathio?

Greetings

Good morning/good afternoon/good evening/goodnight
Buenos días/buenas tardes/buenas noches
Bwenos dee-ahs/bwenas tarrdess/bwenas notchess

Pleased to meet you
Encantado de conocerle
Encantadoe dey conotherle

How are you?
¿Cómo está usted?
¿Como esta oosteth?

I am well thank you. And you?
Bien, gracias. ¿Y usted?
Beeyen, grathias. ¿Ee oosteth?

My name is ...
Me llamo ...
Meh lliamo ...

This is my friend/boyfriend/girlfriend/husband/wife/brother/sister
Este es mi amigo/novio/novia/marido/esposa/hermano/hermana
Este es mee ameego/nobeeo/nobeea/mareedo/esposa/ermano/er mana

Where are you travelling to?
¿A dónde viaja?
¿A donde beeaha?

I am/we are going to ...
Voy/vamos a ...
Boy/bamos a ...

How long are you travelling for?
¿Cuánto tiempo van a viajar?
¿Cwantoe teaempo ban a beahar?

Where do you come from?
¿De dónde es usted?
¿Dey donde es oosteth?

I am/we are from ... Australia/Britain/Canada/America
Soy/somos de ... Australia/Bretaña/Canadá/América
Soy/somos de ... Awstralea/Bretannia/Canada/Amereeca

We are on holiday
Estamos de vacación
Estamos deh bakathion

This is our first visit here
Es la primera vez que venimos aquí
Es la preemera beth keh benimos akee

How old are you?
¿Qué edad tiene?
¿Keh ethath teeyene?

I am ... years old
Tengo ... años
Tengoh ... anyohs

I am a business person/doctor/journalist/manual worker/administrator/scientist/student/teacher
Soy empresario/médico/periodista/obrero/administrador/científico/estudiante/professor
Soy emprehsahreeoh/mehdicoh/perodeesta/obrehroh/administrah-dor/thee-enteeficoh/estoodianteh/professor

I am waiting for my husband/wife/boyfriend/girlfriend
Estoy esperando a mi marido/mujer/novio/novia
Estoy esperando a mee mareedo/mooher/nobyoh/nobya

Would you like/may I have a cigarette?
¿Quiere un cigarrillo/me da un cigarrillo?
¿Keyerey oon theegarrellio/mey da oon theegarrellio?

Do you mind if I smoke?
¿Le molesta si fumo?
¿Ley molesta see foomo?

Do you have a light?
¿Tiene fuego?
¿Teeyene fwego?

ESSENTIALS

SPANISH

Days

Monday
Lunes
Loones

Tuesday
Martes
Martes

Wednesday
Miércoles
Meeyercoles

Thursday
Jueves
Hooebes

Friday
Viernes
Beeyernes

Saturday
Sábado
Sabadoe

Sunday
Domingo
Domeengo

Morning
Mañana
Manyana

Afternoon/Evening/Night
Tarde/Noche/Noche
Tardey/Nochey/Nochey

Yesterday/Today/Tomorrow
Ayer/Hoy/Mañana
Ayer/Oy/Manyana

Numbers

Zero
Cero
Theroe

One
Uno
Oono

Two
Dos
Dos

Three
Tres
Tres

Four
Cuatro
Cwatro

Five
Cinco
Thinco

Six
Seis
Seys

Seven
Siete
Seeyetey

Eight
Ocho
Ocho

Nine
Nueve
Nwebey

Ten
Diez
Deeyeth

Eleven
Once
Onthey

Twelve
Doce
Dothey

Thirteen
Trece
Trethey

Fourteen
Catorce
Catorthey

Fifteen
Quince
Keeyenthe

Sixteen
Dieciséis
Deeyetheeseys

Seventeen
Diecisiete
Deeyethee-seeyetey

Eighteen
Dieciocho
Deeyetheoocho

Nineteen
Diecinueve
Deeyethee -nwebey

Twenty
Veinte
Beintey

Twenty-one
Veintiuno
Beinteoono

Twenty-two
Veintidós
Beintedos

Thirty
Treinta
Treinta

Forty
Cuarenta
Cwarenta

Fifty
Cincuenta
Thincwenta

Sixty
Sesenta
Sesenta

Seventy
Setenta
Setenta

Eighty
Ochenta
Ochenta

Ninety
Noventa
Nobenta

One hundred
Cien
Thien

Five hundred
Quinientos
Keyneeyentos

One thousand
Mil
Mil

One million
Un millón
Oon mellion

Time

What time is it?
¿Qué hora es?
¿Kay ora es?

It is ...
Son las ...
Son las ...

9.00
Nueve
Nwebey

9.05
Nueve y cinco
Nwebey ee thinco

9.15
Nueve y cuarto
Nwebey ee quarto

9.20
Nueve y veinte
Nwebey ee beinte

9.30
Nueve y media
Nwebey ee medeea

9.35
Diez menos veinticinco
Deeyeth menos beinteethinco

9.40
Diez menos veinte
Deeyeth menos beinte

9.45
Diez menos cuarto
Deeyeth menos quarto

9.50
Diez menos diez
Deeyeth menos deeyeth

9.55
Diez menos cinco
Deeyeth menos thinco

12.00/Midday/Midnight
Las doce/Mediodía/Medianoche
Las dothe/medeeodeea/ medeeanoche

Money

I would like to change these traveller's cheques/this currency
Quisiera cambiar estos cheques de viaje/dinero
Keyseeeyera canbeear estos chekes de beeahe/denero

How much commission do you charge (What is the service charge)?
¿Qué comisión recargan?
¿Kay comeeseeon recargan?

Can I obtain money with my Mastercard?
¿Puedo sacar dinero con la tarjeta Mastercard?
¿Pwedo sacar deenero con la tarheta Mastercard?

Where is the nearest ATM?
¿Dónde está el cajero automático más cercano?
¿Dondeh estah el cakhehroh awtomaticoh mahs thercahnoh?

My name is ... Some money has been wired to here for me to collect
Me llamo ... Me han enviado dinero aquí para que lo recoja
Meh lyahmoh ... Meh han enviahdoh dinehroh akee para keh loh recokhah

ARRIVING AND DEPARTING

Airport

Excuse me, where is the check-in desk for ... airline?
¿Perdone, dónde está la facturación de la línea ...?
¿Perdoneh, dondeh estah el mostrador deh faktoorathion deh la leenya ...?

What is the boarding gate/time for my flight?
¿Por qué puerta/a qué hora sale mi vuelo?
¿Porr keh pwerta/ah keh ora saleh mee bwehlo?

How long is the delay likely to be?
¿Cuánto lleva de retraso, aproximadamente?
¿Kwanto llieba deh rehtraso, aproksimadamenteh?

Where is the duty-free shop?
¿Dónde está el duty free?
¿Dondeh esta el duty free?

Which way is the luggage reclaim?
¿Por dónde se va a la recogida de equipajes?
¿Porr dondeh seh ba ah rekoheeda deh ekeypahess?

I have lost my luggage. Please can you help?
He perdido mi equipaje. ¿Puede ayudarme, por favor?
Eh pehrdeedoh mee ekeepahkheh. ¿Pwehdeh ayoodarmeh, porr fabor?

I am flying to ...
Vuelo a ...
Bwehlo a ...

Where is the bus for the city centre (downtown)?
¿De dónde sale el autobús al centro?
¿Deh dondeh saleh el outoboos al thentro?

Trains and Boats

Where is the ticket office/information desk?
¿Dónde está la taquilla de billetes/la ventanilla de información?
¿Donde estaa la taakeellia dey beellietes/la bentaaneellia dey informatheeon?

Which platform does the train/speedboat/ferry to ... depart from?
¿De qué vía/muelle sale el tren/la lancha motora/el transbordador para ...?
¿Deh keh beea/mooelyeh sale el tren/la lancha mohtora/el transbordahdor para ...?

Where is platform ...?
¿Dónde está el andén ...?
¿Donde esta el anden ...?

When is the next train/boat to ...?

¿Cuéndo sale el próximo tren/barco a ...?
¿Kwando sale el proxeemo tren/barrco a ...?

Is there a later train/boat to ...?
¿Hay un tren/barco posterior a ...?
¿Eye un tren/barrco possterior a ...?

Notices and Signs

Coche restaurante
Koche restaoorante
Buffet (Dining) car

Autobús
Awtoeboos
Bus

Agua potable/Agua no potable
Agwa potable/agwa no potable
Drinking/non-drinking water

Entrada
Entrada
Entrance

Salida
Saleeda
Exit

Hospital
Ohspeetahl
Hospital

Información
Informatheeon
Information

Consigna
Consigna
Left luggage (Baggage claim)

Consigna automática
Consigna awtomateeka
Luggage lockers

Oficina de Correos
Ofeetheena de korreos
Post office

Vía
Veea
Platform

Estación de trenes
Estatheeon de tren
Railway (Railroad) station

Aeropuerto
Aehropwerto
Airport

Comisaría de policía
Comissarreeah deh politheeah
Police station

Puerto
Pwerto
Port

Restaurante
Restaoorante
Restaurant

Fumadores/No fumadores
Foomadoores/no foomadoores
Smoking/non-smoking

Teléfono
Telephono
Telephone

ARRIVING AND DEPARTING

Taquilla de billetes
Takeellia de beellietes
Ticket office

Facturación
Faktoorathion
Check-in desk

Horario
Orareeo
Timetable (Schedule)

Servicios
Serbeetheeos
Toilets (Restrooms)

Señoras/Caballeros
Senyoras/Kaballieros
Ladies/Gentlemen

Metro
Metro
Underground (Subway)

Sala de espera
Sala de espera
Waiting room

Buying a Ticket

I would like a first-class/second-class single (one-way)/return (round-trip) ticket to ...
Quisiera un billete de primera clase/de segunda clase/de ida/de ida y vuelta a ...
Keyseeyera oon beelliete de premera clase/dey segoonda clase/dey eeda/dey eeda ee bwelta a ...

Is it an express (fast) train/bus?
¿Es un tren/autobús express?
¿Es oon tren/awtohboos express?

Is my rail pass valid on this train/ferry/bus?
¿Puedo usar mi pase en este tren/ferry/autobús?
¿Pwedo usar mee pasey en esteh tren/ferry/outoboos?

I would like an aisle/window seat
Me gustaría un asiento junto al pasillo/de ventanilla
Me goosetareea oon aseeyento hoontoe al paseellio/de bentaneellya

No smoking/smoking please
No fumadores/fumadores por favor
No foomadoores/foomadoores por farbor

We would like to sit together
Nos gustaría sentarnos juntos
Nos goosetareea sentarnos hoontos

I would like to make a seat reservation
Quisiera reservar una plaza
Keyseeyera rehzerbar oona platha

I would like to reserve a couchette/sleeper for one person/two people/for my family
Quisiera hacer una reserva en el coche-literas/coche-camas para una persona/dos personas/mi familia
Keyseeyera ather oona resserba en el koche-literas/koche-kama para oona persawna/dos persawnas/mee fameleeya

I would like to reserve a cabin
Quisiera reservar un camarote
Keyseeyera rehzerbar oon kamarote

Timetables (Schedules)

Llegada
Yeygada
Arrive

Para en
Para en
Calls (stops) at

Servicio de restauración
Serbeetheeo dey restawratheeon
Catering service

Transbordo en
Transbordoe en
Change at

Correspondencia/Por
Correespondenthia/Beea
Connection/Via

Diario
Deeareeo
Daily

Cada 40 minutos
Kada cwarenta menootos
Every 40 minutes

Primera clase
Preemera clase
First class

Cada hora
Kada ora
Hourly

Se recomienda reservar plaza
Se rekomeenda reserbar platha
Seat reservations are recommended

Segunda clase
Segoonda clase
Second class

Hay que pagar suplemento
Eye ke pagar sueplemento
Supplement payable

Luggage

How much will it cost to send (ship) my luggage in advance?
¿Cuánto costaría enviar mi equipaje por adelantado?
¿Cwantoe costareea enbeear mee ekeypahe por adelantado?

Where is the left luggage (baggage claim) office?
¿Dónde está la consigna?
¿Donde esta la consinya?

What time do you open/close?
¿A qué hora abren/cierran?
¿A kay ora abren/theeyeran?

Where are the luggage trolleys (carts)?
¿Dónde están las carretillas para el equipaje?
¿Donde estan lahs karretillias para el ekeypahe?

SPANISH

ARRIVING AND DEPARTING

S P A N I S H

Where are the lockers?
¿Dónde está la consigna automática?
¿Dondeh esta la konseegna awtoematika?

I have lost my locker key
He perdido la llave de la consigna automática
Ey perdeedo la lliabe de la consigna awtoematecar

On Board

Is this seat free?
¿Está libre este asiento?
¿Esta leebre este aseeyento?

Excuse me, you are sitting in my reserved seat
Perdone, pero se ha sentado en mi asiento reservado
Perdone pero sey a sentado en mee aseeyento resserbado

Which station is this?
¿Qué estación es esta?
¿Kay estatheeon es esta?

What time is this train/bus/ferry/flight due to arrive/depart?
¿A qué hora sale/llega este tren/autobús/vuelo?
¿Ah keh ora saleh/lliega esteh tren/outoboos/bwelo?

Travelling with Children

Do you have a high chair/babysitting service/cot?
¿Tienen sillas para bebés/servicio de kanguro/cuna?
¿Teeyenen seellias para bebes/serbeetheeo de cangooro/coona?

Where is the nursery/playroom?
¿Dónde está la guardería/el cuarto de niños?
¿Donde esta la gwardereea/el kwarto de neenyos?

Where can I warm the baby's bottle?
¿Dónde puedo calentar el biberón?
¿Donde pwedo calentar el beeberron?

Customs and Passports

¡Los pasaportes, por favor!
¡Los pasaportes por farbor!
Passports, please!

I have nothing to declare. I have wine/spirits (alcohol)/tobacco to declare
No tengo nada que declarar. Tengo vino/licores/tabaco que declarar
No tengo nada kay declarar. Tengo beeno/leekores/tabaco kay declarar.

I shall be staying for ... days/weeks/months
Me quedaré ... días/semanas/meses
Mey keydarey ... deeas/semanas/messes

SIGHTSEEING

Asking the Way

Excuse me, do you speak English?
Perdone, ¿habla usted inglés?
Perdoene, ¿abla oosteth ingles?

Excuse me, can you help me please?
Disculpe, ¿puede ayudarme, por favor?
Deeskoolpeh, ¿pwehdeh ayoodarmeh, porr fabor?

Where is the Tourist Information Office?
¿Dónde está la oficina de información y turismo?
¿Donde esta la ofeetheena de informatheeon ee toorismo?

Excuse me, is this the right way to ...?
Perdone, ¿por aquí se va a ...?
Perdoneh, ¿porr akee seh bah ah ...?

... the cathedral/the tourist information office/the castle/the old town
... la catedral/oficina de turísmo/el castillo/el casco antiguo
... la katehdral/offeetheena deh toorismoe/el kasteellio/el kasko antigwo

Can you tell me the way to the railway (railroad) station/bus station/taxi rank (stand)/city centre (downtown)/beach?
¿Puede decirme cómo se va a la estación de trenes/estación de autobuses/parada de taxis/al centro de la ciudad/a la playa?
¿Pwede detheerme como sey ba a la estatheeon de trenes/estatheeon dey awtoebooses/parada de taxsis/al thentroe de la theeoodath/a la playa?

Primera/segunda a la izquierda/derecha/todo seguido
Preemera/segoonda a la eethkeyerda/derecha/toedoe segeedoe
First/second left/right/straight ahead

En la esquina/en el semáforo
En la eskeena/en el sehmahforoh
At the corner/at the traffic lights

Where is the nearest police station/post office?
¿Dónde está la comisaría de policía/la oficina de correos?
¿Donde esta la comeesarea dey poleetheea/la ofeetheena dey coreos?

Is it near/far?
¿Está cerca/lejos?
¿Esta thairka/lekhohs?

Do I need to take a taxi/catch a bus?
¿Necesito coger un taxi/un autobús?
¿Netheeseeto coher oon taxsee/oon aootoeboos?

Do you have a map?
¿Tiene un mapa?
¿Teeyene oon mapa?

Can you point to it on my map?
¿Puede señalármelo en el mapa?
¿Pwede senyarlarmeloe en el mapa?

SPANISH

SIGHTSEEING

SPANISH

Thank you for your help
Muchas gracias por su ayuda
Moochas gratheeas poor soo ayuda

How do I reach the motorway/main road?
¿Por dónde se va a la autopista/carretera principal?
¿Porr dondeh seh ba a la out-opeesta/karretehrra printhipal?

I think I have taken the wrong turning
Creo que me he equivocado de camino
Kreoh keh meh eh ekeebokado deh kameeno

I am looking for this address
Busco esta dirección
Boosko esta deerekthion

I am looking for the ... hotel
Busco el hotel ...
Boosko el ohtel ...

How far is it to ... from here?
¿ ... queda muy lejos de aquí?
¿ ... kayda mooy lehos deh akee?

Siga derecho unos ...kilómetros
Seega deretcho oonos ...keelometros
Carry straight on for ... kilometres

La próxima a la derecha/izquierda
La proksima a la deretcha/eethkyerda
Take the next turning on the right/left

Tire a la derecha/izquierda en el próximo cruce/semáforo.
Teereh a la deretcha/eethkyerda en el proksimo crootheh/sehmaforo
Turn right/left at the next crossroads/traffic lights

No se va por ahí
Noh seh ba porr ah-ee
You are going in the wrong direction

Where is the cathedral/church/museum/pharmacy?
¿Dónde está la catedral/la iglesia/el museo/farmacia?
¿Donde esta la catedral/la igleeseea/el mooseo/farmaseeah?

How much is the admission/entrance charge?
¿Cuánto cuesta la entrada?
¿Cwantoe cwesta la entrada?

Is there a discount for children/students/senior citizens?
¿Tienen descuento los niños/los estudiantes/los jubilados?
¿Teeyenen descwento los neenyos/los estoodeeantes/los hubeelados?

What time does the next guided tour (in English) start?
¿A qué hora empieza la siguiente visita guiada?
¿A kay ora enpeeyetha la seegeeyente veezeeta geeahdah?

One/two adults/children please
Uno/dos adultos/niños por favor
Oonoh/dos adooltos/neenios porfarbor

May I take photographs here?
¿Puedo sacar fotos?
¿Pwedo sakar fotos?

At the Tourist Office

Do you have a map of the town/area?
¿Tiene un mapa de la ciudad/de la zona?
¿Teeyene oon mapa de la theeoodath/de la thona?

Do you have a list of accommodation?
¿Tiene una lista de hoteles?
¿Teeyene oona leesta deh oteles?

Can I reserve accommodation?
¿Puedo reservar alojamiento aquí?
¿Pwedo reserbar alohameeyento akee?

ACCOMMODATION

Hotels

I have a reservation in the name of ...
Tengo una reserva a nombre de ...
Tengo oona resserba a nonbre dey ...

I wrote to/faxed/telephoned you last month/last week
El mes pasado/la semana pasada les escribí/envié un fax/llamé por teléfono
El mes passado/la sehmanna passada les eskreebee/embeeyeh oon faks/lliameh porr tehlehfono

Do you have any rooms free?
¿Tienen habitaciones?
¿Teeyenen abeetathiones?

I would like to reserve a single/double room with/without a bath/shower
Quisiera reservar una habitación individual/doble con/sin baño/ducha
Keyseeyera resserbar oona abeetatheeon indeebeedooal/doeble con/sin banyo/doocha

I would like bed/breakfast/(room and) full board
Me gustaría cama y desayuno/pensión completa
Mey goosetareea kama ee desayuno/penseeon conpleta

How much is it per night?
¿Cuánto cuesta por noche?
¿Cwantoe cwesta por noche?

Is breakfast included?
¿Está el desayuno incluido?
¿Esta el desayoonoh inclueedo?

Do you have any cheaper rooms?
¿Tienen habitaciones más baratas?
¿Teeyenen abeetatheeones mass baratas?

I would like to see/take the room
Quisiera ver/que me dieran una habitación
Keeseeyehra behr/keh me deeran oona abitathiohn

I would like to stay for ... nights
Quisiera quedarme ...noches
Keyseeyera keydarme ...noches

SPANISH

The shower/light/tap doesn't work
La ducha/luz/el grifo no funciona
La dootcha/looth/el greefoh noh foonthiona

At what time/where is breakfast served?
¿A qué hora/dónde se sirve el desayuno?
¿A kay ora/donde sey seervey el desayoono?

What time do I have to check-out?
¿A qué hora debo desalojar la habitación?
¿A kay ora debo desalohar la abeetatheeon?

Can I have the key to room number ...?
¿Me quiere dar la llave de la habitación número ...?
Meh keyereh dahrr la lliabeh deh la abeetathion noomero ...?

My room number is ...
Mi habitación es el número ...
Me abeetatheeon es el noomero ...

My room is not satisfactory/not clean enough/too noisy. Please can I change rooms?
Mi habitación no me satisface/no está lo bastante limpia/es demasiado ruidosa. ¿Puedo cambiar de habitación, por favor?
Mee abitathiohn noh me satisfahtheh/noh esta loh bastante limpia/es demaseeahdoh rooeedohsa. ¿Pwehdeh cambeeahrr de abitathiohn, porr fabor?

Where is the bathroom?
¿Dónde está el cuarto de baño?
¿Donde esta el kwartoh de banyoh?

Do you have a safe for valuables?
¿Tiene una caja fuerte para los objetos de valor?
¿Teeyene oona cakha fooehrte para lohs obkhehtohs de balor?

Is there a laundry/do you wash clothes?
¿Hay una lavandería?/¿Lavan la ropa?
¿Eye oona lavandereea?/¿Lavan la rohpa?

I would like an air-conditioned room
Me gustaría tener una habitación con aire acondicionado
Me goostareea tenehr oona abitathiohn con a-eereh acondeetheeonahdoh

Do you accept traveller's cheques/credit cards?
¿Aceptan cheques de viaje/tarjetas de crédito?
¿Atheptan tchekes deh biaheh/tarhetas deh credeeto?

May I have the bill please?
¿Por favor me da la cuenta?
¿Por farbor meh da la cwenta?

Excuse me, I think there may be a mistake in this bill
Oiga, me parece que la cuenta está mal
Oyga, meh parethe keh la kwenta esta mal

Youth Hostels

How much is a dormitory bed per night?
¿Cuánto cuesta una cama por noche?
¿Cwantoe cwesta oona kama por noche?

I am/am not an HI member
Soy/no soy miembro de HI
Soy/no soy meeyembro dey hachey ee

May I use my own sleeping bag?
¿Puedo utilizar mi propio saco de dormir?
¿Pwedo ooteeleethar mee propeeo saco de dormeer?

What time do you lock the doors at night?
¿A qué hora cierran por la noche?
¿A kay ora theeyerran por la noche?

Camping

May I camp here for the night/two nights?
¿Puedo acampar aquí esta noche/dos noches?
¿Pwedo acanpar akee esta noche/dos noches?

Where can I pitch my tent?
¿Dónde puedo montar la tienda?
¿Donde pwedo montar la teeyenda?

How much does it cost for one night/week?
¿Cuánto cuesta por noche/semana?
¿Cwantoee cwesta por noche/semana?

Where are the washing facilities?
¿Dónde están los aseos?
¿Donde estan los aseos?

Is there a restaurant/supermarket/swimming pool on site/nearby?
¿Hay algún restaurante/supermercado/alguna piscina por aquí/cerca?
¿Eye algoon restawrante/sueperme-rkadoe/algoona pistheena por akee/therca?

Do you have a safety deposit box?
¿Tienen caja fuerte?
¿Teeyenen kaha fwerte?

EATING AND DRINKING

Cafés and Bars

I would like a cup of/two cups of/another coffee/tea
Quisiera una taza de/dos tazas de/otra taza de café/té
Keyseeyera oona tatha dey/dos tathas/otra tatha dey kafey/te

With/without milk/sugar
Con/sin leche/azúcar
Con/seen leche/athoocar

I would like a bottle/glass/ two glasses of mineral water/ red wine/white wine, please
Quisiera una botella/un vaso/dos vasos de agua mineral/de vino tinto/de vino blanco, por favor
Keyseeyera oona botellia/oon baso/dos basos dey agwa meneral/dey beeno tintoe/dey beeno blanco, por farbor

I would like a beer/two beers, please
Quisiera una cerveza/dos cervezas, por favor
Keyseeyera oona therbeytha/dos therbeythas, por farbor

Please may I have some ice?
¿Pueden ponerme hielo?
¿Pweden ponerme eeyelloe?

Do you have any matches/ cigarettes/cigars?
¿Tienen cerillas/cigarrillos/puros?
¿Teeyenen thereellias/theegarrel-lios/pooros?

Restaurants

Can you recommend a good/ cheap restaurant in this area?
¿Puede recomendarme un buen/ restaurante barato en la zona?
¿Pwede recomendarme oon bwen/ restawrante barato en la thona?

I would like a table for ... people
Quisiera una mesa para ... personas
Keyseeyera oona mesa para ... personas

Do you have a non-smoking area?
¿Tiene una zona reservada para no fumadores?
¿Teeyene oona thona rehzerbada para noh foomadores?

Waiter/Waitress!
¡Camarero/Camarera!
¡Camareroe/Camarera!

Excuse me, please may we order?
¿Disculpe, puedo pedir, por favor?
¿Deeskoolpeh, pwedoh pedeer, por fabor?

Do you have a set menu/ children's menu/wine list (in English)?
¿Tienen menú del día/menú para niños/la carta de vinos (in inglés)?
¿Teeyenen menoo del deea/menoo para neenios/la carta dey beenos (en ingles)?

Do you have any vegetarian dishes, please?
¿Dan comidas vegetarianas, por favor?
¿Dan comeedas behetareanas, por farbor?

Do you have any local specialities?
¿Tienen especialidades del lugar?
¿Teeyenen espethialeedades del loogar?

Are vegetables included?
¿Están incluidas las verduras?
¿Estan eenklooeedas las berdooras?

Could I have it well-cooked/ medium/rare please?
¿Por favor, la carne bien cocida/al

punto/roja?
¿Porr fabor, la kahrrne beeyen kotheeda/al poontoh/roha?

What does this dish consist of?
¿Qué contiene este plato?
¿Kay conteeyene este platoe?

I am a vegetarian. Does this contain meat?
Soy vegetariano. ¿Tiene carne este plato?
Soy begetahreeahnoh. ¿Teeyene carneh esteh plahtoh?

I do not eat nuts/dairy products/meat/fish
No como frutos secos/productos lácteos/carne/pescado
Noh como frootohs secohs/produc-tohs lacteh-ohs/carrne/pescahdoh

Not (very) spicy, please
No (muy) sazonado, por favor
Noh (mooee) sathonahdoh, porr fabor

I would like the set menu, please
Quisiera el menú del día, por favor
Keyseeyera el menoo del deea, por farbor

We are still waiting to be served
Todavía no nos han servido
Toedabeea no nos an serbeedoe

Please bring a plate/knife/ fork
Por favor, tráigame un plato/ cuchillo/tenedor
Porr fabor, traeegameh onn plahtoh/coocheelyoh/tenedor

Excuse me, this is not what I ordered
Perdone, no he pedido esto
Perdoneh, noh eh pedeedo esto

May I have some/more bread/water/coffee/tea?
¿Podría traerme/más pan/agua/café/té?
¿Pordreea trayerme/mass pan/agwa/kafey/te?

May I have the bill, please?
¿Podría traerme la cuenta por favor?
¿Pordreea trayerme la cwenta por farbor?

Does this bill include service?
¿Está incluido el servicio en la cuenta?
¿Esta inclueedoe el serbeetheeo en la cwenta?

Do you accept traveller's cheques/Mastercard/US dollars?
¿Aceptan cheques de viaje/ Mastercard/dólares americanos?
¿Atheptan chekes de beeahe/ Mastercard/doelares amereecarnos?

Can I have a receipt, please?
¿Me quiere dar un recibo, por favor?
¿Meh keyereh dahrr oon resgwardo, por fabor?

Where is the toilet (restroom), please?
¿Dónde están los servicios, por favor?
¿Donde estan los serbeetheeos, por fabor?

SPANISH

SPANISH

On the Menu

Desayuno/Almuerzo/Cena
Dehsayoonoh/Almwerhthoh/Cehna
Breakfast/Lunch/Dinner

Entradas
Entradas
First courses

Sopas
Sohpas
Soups

Platos principales
Platos preentheepales
Main courses

Pescados
Peskados
Fish dishes

Carnes
Kahrrnes
Meat dishes

Carne de vaca
Karrneh de baca
Beef

Bistec
Beestec
Steak

Cerdo
Thehrdoh
Pork

Ternera
Tehrnehrah
Veal

Pollo
Polyoh
Chicken

Cordero
Cordehroh
Lamb

Jamón
Khahmohn
Ham

Platos vegetarianos
Platos behetaryanos
Vegetarian dishes

Verduras
Behrdoorahs
Vegetables

Patatas fritas
Patahtahs freetahs
Chips (french fries)

Patatas cocidas/salteadas/puré de patatas
Patahtahs cotheedahs/salteh-ahdahs/pooreh de patahtahs
Boiled/sauté/mashed potatoes

Arroz
Arroth
Rice

Queso
Kehso
Cheese

Postres
Postres
Desserts

Helado
Elahdoh
Ice cream

Pasteles
Pastehles
Cakes

Bollos
Bolyohs
Pastries

Fruta
Frootah
Fruit

Pan
Pahn
Bread

Rollos
Rolyohs
Rolls

Tostada
Tostahdah
Toast

Mantequilla
Mantehkeelyah
Butter

Sal/pimiento
Sal/peemee-entoh
Salt/pepper

Azúcar
Athookarr
Sugar

Especialidades
Espetheealeedades
Specialities

Especialidades locales
Espethialithadehs locahlehs
Local specialities

Menú establecido
Menoo establetheedoh
Set menu

Carta de vinos
Carta de beenohs
Wine list

Vinos tintos
Beenohs tintohs
Red wines

Vinos blancos
Beenohs blancohs
White wines

Vinos rosados
Beenohs rohsahdohs
Rosé wines

Vinos espumosos
Beenohs espoomohsohs
Sparkling wines

Cerveza
Thehrvehtha
Beer

Cerveza en botella/
Cerveza de barril
Thehrvehtha en botehlyah/
Thehrvehtha de barreel
Bottled beer/Draught (draft) beer

Bebidas sin alcohol
Bevidahs sin alcohol
Non-alcoholic drinks

Agua mineral
Agwa meenerahl
Mineral water

Zumos de frutas
Thoomohs de frootahs
Fruit juices

Zumo de naranja
Thoomo de narankhah
Orange juice

Limonada
Limohnahda
Lemonade

Hielo
Yehloh
Ice

Café con leche/solo/expreso
Cafeh con lecheh/sohloh/expresso
White coffee/black coffee/espresso coffee

Té con leche/con limón
The con lecheh/con leemohn
Tea with milk/with lemon

Chocolate a la taza
Chocolahteh a la tahthah
Chocolate (drink)

Leche
Lecheh
Milk

Tentempiés/Comidas ligeras
Tentempee-ehs/Comeedahs likherahs
Snacks/Light meals

Ensaladas
Ensalahdahs
Salads

Sandwiches
Sandwiches
Sandwiches

Huevos
Wehvohs
Eggs

Salchicha
Salcheechah
Sausage

Huevos cocidos/fritos/revueltos
Wehvohs cotheedohs/freetohs/revweltohs
Boiled/fried/scrambled eggs

Typical local dishes

Spanish Chorizo
Choh-reethoh
Spicy sausage served as an appetiser

Empanadillas
Ehmpahnah-deelyas
Savoury filled pastries

Gazpacho
Gahth-pah-choh
Chilled tomato and pepper soup

Paella valenciana
Pahella bahlehn-thee-ahnah
Rice with chicken and seafood

Zarzuela
Thahr-thweh-lah
Spicy seafood stew

Cocido madrileño
Kotheedoh mahdri-lehn-yoh
Rich hotpot of mixed meats

GETTING AROUND

Public Transport

Where is the bus stop/coach station/nearest metro station?
¿Dónde está la parada de autobuses/la estación de autobuses/la estación de metro más cercana?
¿Donde esta la parrada dey awtoebooses/la estatheeon dey awtoebooses/la estatheeon dey metro mass thercana?

When is the next/last bus to ...?
¿A qué hora sale el próximo autobús/el último autobús para ...?
¿A kay ora sale el proxseemo awtoeboos/el ultimo awtoeboos para ...?

How much is the fare to the city centre (downtown)/railway (railroad) station/airport?
¿Cuánto cuesta el billete hasta el centro/la estación de trenes/el aeropuerto?
¿Cwantoe cwesta el beelliete asta el thentro/la estatheeon de trenes/el aeropwerto?

Will you tell me when to get off?
¿Podría decirme cuando tendré que bajar?
¿Poordreea detheerme cwandoe tendray kay bahar?

Does this bus go to ...?
¿Es este el autobús de ...?
¿Es este el awtoeboos de ...?

Which number bus goes to ...?
¿Cuál es el número del autobús que va a ...?
¿Cwal es el noomero del awtoeboos kay ba a ...?

May I have a single (one-way)/return (round-trip)/day ticket/book of tickets?
¿Quisiera un billete de ida/de ida y vuelta/de día/tarjeta?
¿Keyseeyera oon beelliete dey eeda/dey eda ee bwelta/dey dea/tarheyta?

Taxis (Taxi)

I would like to go to ... How much will it cost?
Quisiera ir a ... ¿Cuánto me costaría?
Keyseeyera eer a ... ¿Cwantoe me costarea?

Please may I stop here?
Por favor pare aquí
Por farbor parey akee

I would like to order a taxi today/tomorrow at 2pm to go from ... to ...
Quisiera reservar un taxi para hoy/mañana/a las dos de la tarde para ir de ... a ...
Keyseeyera resserbar oon taxsee para oy/manyana/a las dos de la tarde para eer dey ... a ...

Entertainment

Can you recommend a good bar/nightclub?
¿Puede recomendarme un bar bueno/una discoteca buena?
¿Pwede recomendarme oon bar bweno/oona discoteca bwena?

Do you know what is on at the cinema (playing at the movies)/theatre at the moment?
¿Sabe lo que están dando en el cine/en el teatro en estos momentos?
¿Sabe lo key estan dando en el theenne/en el tayatro en estos momentos?

I would like to book (purchase) ... tickets for the matinee/evening performance on Monday
Quisiera reservar ... entradas para la sesión de tarde/de noche del lunes
Keyseeyera resserbar ... entradas para la seseeon dey tarde dey noche del loones

What time does the film/ performance start?
¿A qué hora empieza la sesión/la función?
¿A key ora enpeeyetha la seseeon/la foontheeon?

S P A N I S H

COMMUNICATIONS

Post

How much will it cost to send a letter/postcard/this package to Britain/Ireland/ America/Canada/Australia/ New Zealand?
¿Cuánto cuesta enviar esta carta/postal/paquete a Gran Bretaña/Irlanda/América/Canadá/ Australia/Nueva Zelanda?
¿Cwantoe cwesta enbeear esta carta/pohstal/pakete a gran bretannia/eerlandda/amereeca/canada/ awstralea/nweyba theylanda?

I would like one stamp/two stamps
Quisiera un sello/dos sellos
Keyseeyera oon sellio/dos sellios

I'd like ... stamps for postcards to send abroad, please
Quisiera ... sellos para postales al extranjero, por favor
Keysyera ... sellios para postales al estranhero, porr fabor

Phones

I would like to make a telephone call/reverse the charges to (make a collect call to) ...
Quisiera llamar por teléfono/ llamar a cobro revertido a ...
Keyseeyera lliamar por telephono/ lliamar a cobro rebertedo a ...

Which coins do I need for the telephone?
¿Qué monedas necesito para el teléfono?
¿Kay monehdas netheseeto para el telephono?

The line is engaged (busy)
La línea está comunicando
La leeneea esta comooneecando.

The number is ...
El número es el ...
El noomero es el ...

Hello, this is ...
Hola, habla ...
Ola, abla ...

Please may I speak to ...?
¿Puedo hablar con ...?
¿Pwedo ablar kon ...?

He/she is not in at the moment. Please can you call back?
No está. ¿Quiere volver a llamar más tarde?
Noh esta. ¿Keyereh bolber a lliamar mas tarrdeh?

SHOPPING

Shops

Librería/Papelería
Leebreree-ah/paplehree-ah
Bookshop/Stationery

Joyería/Regalos
Hoyeree-ah/regalos
Jeweller/Gifts

Zapatería
Thapatos
Shoes

Ferretería
Ferretehree-ah
Hardware

Peluquería (caballeros)/(damas)
Pelookeree-ah(kaballieros)/(damas)
Hairdresser (men's)/(women's)

Panadería
Panaderee-ah
Baker

Supermercado
Soopermerkado
Supermarket

Tienda de fotos
Teeyenda deh fotos
Photo shop

Agencia de viajes
Ahenthya deh byahes
Travel agent

Farmacia
Fahrmatheea
Pharmacy

In the Shops

What time do the shops open/close?
¿A qué hora abren/cierran las tiendas?
¿A kay ora abren/theeyerran las teeyendas?

Where is the nearest market?
¿Dónde está el mercado más próximo?
¿Dondeh kayda el merkado mas proksimo?

Can you show me the one in the window/this one?
¿Quiere enseñarme el del escaparate/este?
¿Keyereh ensehniarmeh el del eskaparateh/esteh?

Can I try this on?
¿Puedo probarme esto?
¿Pwedo probarme esto?

What size is this?
¿Qué talla es esta?
¿Kay tallia es esta?

This is too large/too small/ too expensive. Do you have any others?
Es muy grande/muy pequeño/muy caro. ¿Tienen más?
Es mooy grandeh/mooy pekenio/mooy karo. ¿Teeyenen mas?

My size is ...
Mi número es el ...
Mee noomero es el ...

SPANISH

Where is the changing room/ children's/cosmetic/ladieswear /menswear/food department?
¿Dónde están los probadores/ niños/perfumería/señoras/ caballeros/sección de alimentos?
¿Donde estan los probadores/ neenyos/perfoomereea/senyoras/cab allieros/sectheeon dey alimentos?

I would like a quarter of a kilo/half a kilo/a kilo of bread/ butter/cheese/ham/tomatoes
Quisiera un cuarto de kilo/ medio kilo/un kilo de pan/ mantequilla/queso/jamón/tomates
Keyseeyera oon cwarto dey kilo/ medio kilo/oon kilo dey pan/ mantekillia/keso/hamon/tomates

How much is this?
¿Cuánto es?
¿Cwantoe es?

I'll take this one, thank you
Me llevo éste
Meh llievo esteh

Do you have a carrier (shopping) bag?
¿Me da una bolsa por favor?
¿Meh da oona bolsa por farbor?

Do you have anything cheaper/larger/smaller/ of better quality?
¿Tiene algo más barato/grande/ pequeño/de mejor calidad?
¿Teeyene algo mass baratto/grande/ pekenio/de mehor caleedath?

I would like a film for this camera
Quisiera un rollo para esta cámara
Keyseeyera oon rollio para esta camara

I would like some batteries, the same size as this old one
Quisiera pilas, del mismo tamaño que esta vieja
Keyseeyera peelas, del mismo tamanio kay esta beeha

Would you mind wrapping this for me, please?
¿Le importaría envolvérmelo?
¿Le inportareea enbolbermelo?

Sorry, but you seem to have given me the wrong change
Lo siento, pero no me ha dado la vuelta correcta
Lo seeyento, pero no meh a dado la vwelta correcta

MOTORING

Car Hire (Rental)

I have ordered (rented) a car in the name of ...
Tengo un coche alquilado a nombre de ...
Tengo oon koche alkeyladoe a nombre de ...

How much does it cost to hire (rent) a car for one day/ two days/a week?
¿Cuánto cuesta alquilar un coche por un día/dos días/una semana?
¿Cwantoe cwesta alkeylar oon koche por oon deea/dos deeas/oona semanna?

Is the tank already full of petrol (gas)?
¿Está el depósito de gasolina lleno?

¿Esta el deposeytoe de gasoleena llieno?

Is insurance and tax included? How much is the deposit?
¿Está incluido en el precio los impuestos y el seguro? ¿Cuánto hay que poner de señal?
¿Esta inclooeedoe en el pretheeo los inpwestoes ee el segooro? ¿Cwantoee eye kay poner de senial?

By what time must I return the car?
¿A qué hora debo entregar el coche?
¿A kay ora debo entregar el koche?

I would like a small/large family/sports car with a radio/cassette player
Quisiera un coche pequeño/ grande familiar/deportivo con radio/casete
Keyseeyera oon koche pekenio/ grandeh familiar/deporteevoh con radeeo/caset

Do you have a road map?
¿Tiene un mapa de carreteras?
¿Teeyene oon mapa deh karretehrras?

Parking

How long can I park here?
¿Cuanto tiempo puedo aparcar aquí?
¿Kwanto teeyempo pwedo aparkar akee?

Is there a car park near here?
¿Hay un aparcamiento cerca de aquí?
¿Eye oon aparkameeyento therka deh akee?

At what time does this car park close?
¿A qué hora cierra este aparcamiento?
¿A keh ora thierra esteh aparkameeyento?

Signs and Notices

Sentido único
Senteedo ooneeko.
One way

Prohibido el paso
Proeebeedoh el passoh.
No entry

Prohibido aparcar
Proeebeedo aparcar.
No parking

Desvío
Dehsveeoh
Detour (diversion)

Alto
Alto
Stop

Ceda el paso
Theda el paso
Give way (yield)

Camino resbaladizo
Kameeno resbaladeetho.
Slippery road

Prohibido adelantar
Proybeedo adelantar
No overtaking

¡Peligro!
¡Peleegroh!
¡Danger!

SPANISH

SPANISH

At the Filling Station
(En la gasolinera)

Unleaded (lead-free)/ standard/premium/diesel
Sin plomo/normal/extra/diesel
Seen plohmoh/normall/ekstra/ deezel

Fill the tank please
Me llena el tanque, por favor
Meh lliena el tankeh porr fabor

Do you have a road map?
¿Tiene un mapa de carreteras?
¿Teeyene oon mapa deh karretehrras?

How much is the car wash?
¿Cuánto cuesta el lavado?
¿Kwanto kwesta el labahdo?

Breakdowns

I've had a breakdown at ...
El coche se ha averiado en ...
El cotcheh seh ah aberyado en ...

I am a member of the ... [motoring organisation]
Soy miembro de ...
Soy mee-embroh de ...

I am on the road from ... to ...
Estoy en la carretera de ... a ...
Estoy en la karretehrra deh ... a ...

I can't move the car. Can you send a tow-truck?
El coche no se mueve. ¿Puede enviar una grúa?
El cotcheh noh seh mwehbeh. ¿Pwedeh embeeyar oona groo-ah?

I have a flat tyre
He tenido un pinchazo
Eh tehneedo oom pintchatho

The windscreen (windshield) has smashed/cracked
El parabrisas se ha hecho trizas/se ha agrietado
El parabreesas seh ah etcho treethas/seh ah agree-etahdo

There is something wrong with the engine/brakes/ lights/steering/gearbox/ clutch/exhaust
El motor/los frenos/las luces/la dirección/la caja de cambios/el embrague/el escape no funciona bien
El motor/los frenos/las loothes/la deerekthion/la caha deh cambyos/el embrahge/el escape noh foonthiona bien

It's overheating
Se sobrecalienta
Seh sobrekalienta

It won't start
No arranca
Noh arranka

Where can I get it repaired?
¿Dónde lo pueden arreglar?
¿Dondeh lo pweden arreglar?

Can you take me there?
¿Me puede llevar allí?
¿Meh pwedeh lliebar allyee?

Will it take long to fix?
¿Va a tardar mucho en arreglarlo?
¿Ba a tardahrr mootcho en arreglarlo?

How much will it cost?
¿Cuánto me va a cobrar?
¿Kwanto meh ba a kobrar?

Accidents and Traffic Offences (Violations

Can you help me? There has been an accident
¿Me puede ayudar? Ha habido un accidente
¿Meh pwedeh aiyoodahrr? Ah ahbeedo oon akthidenteh

Please call the police/an ambulance
Llame a la policía/ambulancia
Lliameh a la poleethee-ah/ amboolanthia

Is anyone hurt?
¿Se ha lastimado alguién?
¿Seh ah lasteemado algyen?

I'm sorry, I didn't see the sign
Lo siento, no me fijé en la señal
Lo seeyento, noh meh feeheh en el senyahl

Must I pay a fine? How much?
¿Tengo que pagar una multa? ¿Cuánto?
¿Tengo keh pagar oona moolta? ¿Kwanto?

Enséñeme sus documentos
Ensehniemeh soos dokoomentos
Show me your documents

HEALTH

Pharmacy (Farmacia)

Do you have anything for a stomach ache/headache/sore throat/toothache?
¿Tienen algo para el dolor de estómago/cabeza/garganta/dientes ?
¿Teeyenen algo para el doelor de estoemago/cabeetha/garganta deeyentes?

I need something for diarrhoea/constipation/a cold/a cough/insect bites/ sunburn/travel (motion) sickness
Necesito algo contra la diarrea/ el estreñimiento/el catarro/ la tos/las picaduras de insectos/ la quemadura del sol/el mareo
Netheseeto algo contra la deea-reea/el estrenyiemeeyento/el catar-ro/la tos/las peecadooras de insec-tos/la khemadoora del sol/el mareo

How much/how many do I take?
¿Cuánto/cuántas tengo que tomar?
¿Cwantoe/cwantas tengo kay toemar?

How often do I take it/them?
¿Cada cuánto tiempo tengo que tomarlo/tomarlas?
¿Cada cwantoe teaenpo tengo kay toemarlo/toemarlas?

I am/he is/she is taking this medication
Estoy/está tomando este medicamento
Estoy/esta tomando esteh medeekamento

S P A N I S H

How much does it cost?
¿Cuánto cuesta?
¿Cwantoe cwesta?

Can you recommend a good doctor/dentist?
¿Puede recomendarme un buen médico/dentista?
¿Pwede recomendarmeh oon bwen meddeeco/denteesta?

Is it suitable for children?
¿Es adecuado para niños?
¿Es adecwado para neenios?

Doctor (Médico)

I have a pain here/in my arm/leg/chest/stomach
Tengo dolor aquí/en el brazo/la pierna/el pecho/el estómago
Tengo oon doelor akee/en el bratho/la peeyerna/el pecho/el estomago

Please call a doctor, this is an emergency
Por favor, llamen a un médico, es una emergencia
Por farbor lliamen a oon meddeeco, es oona emerhentheea.

I would like to make an appointment to see the doctor
Quisiera una cita para una consulta
Keyseeyera oona thita para oona consoolta

I am diabetic/pregnant
Soy diabético(a)/estoy embarazada
Soy deeabetteeko/estoy enbarathada

I need a prescription for ...
Necesito una receta para ...
Netheseeto oona rethetta para ...

Can you give me something to ease the pain?
¿Puede darme algo para aliviar el dolor?
¿Pwede darme algo para aleebear el doelor?

I am/he is/she is allergic to penicillin
Soy/es alérgico/alérgica a la penicilina
Soy alerheeko/alerheeka a la peneetheeleena

¿Le duele esto?
¿Leh dweleh esto?
Does this hurt?

Usted/él/ella tiene que ir al hospital
Oosteth/el/ellia teeyene keh eer al ospeetal
You must/he must/she must go to hospital

Tome esto una vez/dos/tres veces al día
Tomeh esto oonah beth/dos/tres bethess al dee-ah
Take these once/twice/three times a day

I am/he is/she is taking this medication
Estoy/está tomando este medicamento
Estoy/esta tomando esteh medeekamento

I have medical insurance
Tengo seguro médico
Tengo sehgooro mehdeeko

Dentist (Dentista)

I have toothache
Tengo dolor de muelas/me duelen las muelas
Tengo dolor de mwelas/mey dwelen las mooeylas

My filling has come out
Se me ha caído un empaste
Se meh a cayeedo oon enpaste

I do/do not want to have an injection first
Quiero/no quiero que me den una inyección
Kiero/no kiero kay meh den oona inyecthion

EMERGENCIES

Help!
¡Socorro!
¡Sawkoro!

Fire!
¡Fuego!
¡Fwegoh!

Stop!
¡Stop!
¡Stop!

Call an ambulance/a doctor/ the police/the fire brigade!
¡Llame a una ambulancia/un médico/la policía/a los bomberos!
¡Lliame a oona anboolanthea/oon meydico/la poletheea/a lohs bombehrohs!

Please may I use a telephone?
¿Puedo usar el teléfono, por favor?
¿Pwehdoh oozahr el telehfonoh, porr fabor?

I have had my traveller's cheques/credit cards/handbag/ rucksack/luggage/wallet/ passport/mobile phone stolen
Me han robado los cheques de viaje/las tarjetas de crédito/el bolso/la mochila/el equipaje/el billetero/el pasaporte/el móvil
Meh an robadoe los chekes dey beahe/las tarhetas dey credeeto/el bolso/la mocheela/el ekeypahe/el bellietero/el pahasporrteh/el mohveel

May I please have a copy of the report for my insurance claim?
¿Podría darme una copia del informe para realizar la reclamación a mi seguro?
¿Podriah dahrmeh oona copeeya del informeh para reahlithar la reclamathiohn a mee seguroh?

Can you help me? I have lost my daughter/son/my companion(s)
¿Puede ayudarme? Se ha extraviado mi hija/mi hijo/mi(s) compañero/a(s)
¿Pwede ajudarme? Sey a extrabeeado mee eekha/mee eekho/mee(s) companyehroh/ah(s)

Please go away/leave me alone
Por favor váyase/déjeme en paz
Por farbor bayase/deheme en path

I'm sorry
Lo siento
Loh see-entoh

I want to contact the British/ American/Canadian/Irish/ Australian/New Zealand/ South African consulate
Quisiera llamar al Consulado Británico/Americano/Canadiense/ Irlandés/de Nueva Zelanda/ Surafricano
Keyseeyera lliamar al Konsoolado Britaneeko/Amehreekano/ Kanadeyenseh/Eerlandess/deh Nweba Theylanda/Surafrikano

I'm/we're/he is/she is/they are/ill/lost/injured
Estoy/estamos/está/están enfermo(s)/perdido(s)/herido(s)
Estoy/estahmohs/estah/estan enfermoh(s)/pehrdeedoh(s)/ ereedoh(s)

TURKISH

INTRODUCTION

Turkish, spoken in Turkey and Northern Cyprus, was brought to the shores of Europe from central-eastern Asia by the invading Ottomans, and is unrelated to other European languages. Although it contains modern words borrowed from English, the main linguistic influence over the centuries has been Arabic.

Turkish uses a Roman alphabet (albeit with a large number of accented characters) which was introduced in the 20th century as part of the modernising reforms which followed on the fall of the Ottoman Empire.

English, German and French are widely spoken in the cosmopolitan and tourist-frequented areas of Istanbul and the Aegean coast, but elsewhere you will need Turkish phrases.

Addresses for Travel and Tourist Information

Australia: *Embassy,* 60 Mugga Way, Red Hill, ACT 2603; tel:(02) 6295 0227/8; fax:(02) 6239 6592.

Canada: *Embassy,* 197 Wurtemburg Street, Ottawa, Ontario K1N 8L9; tel: (613) 789 4044; fax: (613) 789 3442.

UK: *Turkish Tourist Office,* Turkish Embassy, First Floor, 170–173 Piccadilly, London W1J 9EJ; tel: (020) 7629 7771; fax: (020) 7491 0773.

USA: *Turkish Embassy Information Counsellor's Office,* 821 United Nations Plaza, New York, NY 10017; tel: (212) 687 2194/5/6; fax: (212) 599 7568. *Turkish Embassy Information Counsellor's Office,* 2525 Massachusetts Ave, N.W., Washington, DC 20006; tel: (202) 612 6800; fax: (202) 319 7446.

Official tourism websites: www.gototurkey.co.uk (UK); www.tourismturkey.org (USA).

Turkey Facts

CAPITAL: Ankara

CURRENCY: Yeni (New) Turkish Lira (YTL). YTL1 = 100 kuruş *(kurush)* and is the equivalent of 1 million old (pre-2005) lira.

OPENING HOURS: Banks: Mon–Fri 0830–1200, 1330–1700. Shops: Mon–Sat 0900–1900/2000. Some shops also open on Sunday. Museums: Tues–Sun, 0800–1800 (may be closed 1230–1330).

TELEPHONES: To dial in, + 90. Outgoing, 00 plus the country code. Police, 155. Fire, 110. Ambulance, 112.

PUBLIC HOLIDAYS: 1 Jan; 23 Apr; 19 May; 30 Aug; 29 Oct; 1 Nov. Also the religious festivals of the Feats of the Sacrifice and the end of Ramazan, dates variable. A minute's silence is observed on 10 Nov, the date of Ataturk's death.

Technical Language Hints

Turkish pronunciation follows regular rules, but one or two characters can cause confusion. The dotless i, ı, is pronounced like the first letter of 'away', so that e.g. Topkapı is pronounced 'Topkapa'. The letter c has the sound of the English j, not c. The letter ğ is not pronounced at the end of a word, but it lengthens the preceding vowel, so that e.g. dağ (mountain) is pronounced 'daa'.

ESSENTIALS

Alphabet and Pronunciation

	Name	Pronounced
A a	*ah*	**like a in father**
B b	*beh*	**like b in boy**
C c	*jeh*	**like j in jewels**
Ç ç		**like ch in church**
D d	*deh*	**like d in day**
E e	*eh*	**like e in end**
F f	*feh*	**like f in foot**
G g	*geh*	**like g in go**
Ğ ğ		**throaty r, like the French r, with hard vowels, but like y in yacht with soft vowels**
H h	*heh*	**like h in how**
I ı	*ee*	**er sound, as in serve**
İ i		**long ee, like the i in machine or short i as in tip**
J j	*zheh*	**soft zh sound, like the s in pleasure**
K k	*keh*	**like k in kid**
L l	*leh*	**like l in law**
M m	*meh*	**like m in monkey**
N n	*neh*	**like n in no**

O o	*o*	**long aw sound, like the o in for**
Ö ö		**like the vowel sound in fur**
P p	*peh*	**like p in part**
R r	*reh*	**like r in rat**
S s	*she*	**like s in soda**
Ş ş		**like sh in show**
T t	*the*	**like t in tip**
U u	*u*	**like oo in zoo**
Ü ü	*ew*	**like the vowel sound in hewn**
V v	*veh*	**like v in voice**
Y y	*yeh*	**like y in year**
Z z	*zeh*	**like z in zoo**

Basic Words and Phrases

Yes
Evet
Evet

No
Hayır
Hayer

Please
Lütfen
Lewtfen

Thank you
Teşekkür ederim
Teshekkuer ederim

Hello
Merhaba
Merhaba

Goodbye
Hosça kal
Hoshcha kal

Excuse me
Affedersiniz
Af-feh-dehr-see-neez

Sorry
Pardon
Pahr-dohn

How
Nasıl
Nasel

When
Ne zaman
Ne zaman

Why
Neden
Neden

What
Ne
Ne

Who
Kim
Kim

That's O.K.
Bir şey değil
Bir shey deh-il

Perhaps
Belki
Belki

To
e/a
e/a

From
den/dan
dan/den

Here
Burada
Burada

There
Orada
Orada

I don't understand
Anlamıyorum
Anlameyourum

I don't speak Turkish
Türkçe bilmiyorum
Tuerkche bilmiyourum

Do you speak English?
İngilizce biliyor musunuz?
Inghilizh'dje biliyour musunuz?

Can you please write it down?
Lütfen şuraya yazar mısınız?
Lewtfen shuraya yazar me-se-nez?

Please can you speak more slowly?
Lütfen biraz daha yavaş konuşur musunuz?
Lewtfen biraz daha yavash konushur musunuz?

Greetings

Good morning/good afternoon/good evening/ goodnight
Günaydın/merhaba/iyi akşhamlar/iyi geceler
Guenayden/merhaba/iyi akshamlar/iyi gedjeler

Pleased to meet you
Tanıştığımıza memnun oldum
Tanaeshtae'maeza memnun oldum

How are you?
Nasılsınız?
Nasaelsaenaez?

I am well thank you. And you?
Teşekkür ederim, iyiyim. Siz nasılsınız?
Teshekkuer ederim, iyiyim. Siz naselsenez?

My name is ...
Adım ...
Adaem ...

This is my friend/boyfriend/ girlfriend/husband/wife/ brother/sister
Bu benim arkadaşım/erkek arkadaşım/kız arkadaşım/ kocam/karım/erkek kardeşim/kız kardeşim
Bu benim arkadashaem/erkek arkadashaem/kaez arkadashaem/kodjam/karaem/erkek kardeshaem/kaez kardeshaem

Where are you travelling to?
Nereye gidiyorsunuz?
Nereye ghidiyoursunuz?

I am going to ... /We are going to ...
Ben ... e/a gidiyorum/Biz ...e/a gidiyoruz
Ben ... e/a ghidiyourum/Beez ... e/a ghidiyouruz

How long are you travelling for?
Kaç günlük bir geziye çıkıyorsunuz?
Kach guenluek beer gheziye chekeyoursunuz?

Where do you come from?
Neredensiniz?
Neredensiniz?

I am/we are from ... Australia/Britain/Canada/ America
Avustralya/Ingiltere/Kanada/ Amerika' den/'dan
Avustralia/Inghiltere/Kanada/ Amerika' den/dan

We are on holiday.
Tatildeyiz
Tatildeyiz

This is our first visit here
İlk defa buraya geliyoruz
Ilk def'a buraya geliyouruz

How old are you?
Kaç yaşındasınız?
Kahch yashendah-senez?

I am ... years old
... yaşındayım
... yashendayem

I am a business person/ doctor/journalist/manual worker/administrator/ scientist/student/teacher

Ben iş adamı(kadını)yım/doktorum/gazeteciyim/işçiyim/yöneticiyim/bilim adamı(kadını)yım/öğrenciyim/öğretmenim
Ben eesh adame-yem (kadene-yem fem.)/doktoroom/gazete-jee-yeem/eesh-chee-yeem/yoh-netee-jee-yeem/bee-leem adame-yem (kadene-yem fem.)/oh-renjee-yem/oh-retmeen-eem

I am waiting for my husband/wife/boyfriend/girlfriend
Kocamı/eşimi/erkek arkadaşımı/kız arkadaşımı bekliyorum
Kodjame/eshimi/erkek arkadasheme/kez arkadasheme bekliyorum

Would you like a cigarette/may I have a cigarette?
Sigara alır mısınız?/Sigara alabilir miyim?
Sigara aler mesenez?/Sigara alabilir miyim?

Do you mind if I smoke?
Sigara içmem sizi rahatsız eder mi?
Sigara ichmem sizi rahatsaez eder mi?

Do you have a light?
Kibritiniz/Çakmağınız var mı?
Kibritiniz/Chakma'anaez var mae?

Days

Monday
Pazartesi
Pazartesi

Tuesday
Salı
Salae

Wednesday
Çarşamba
Charshamba

Thursday
Perşembe
Pershembe

Friday
Cuma
Djuma

Saturday
Cumartesi
Djumartesi

Sunday
Pazar
Pazar

Morning
Sabah
Sabah

Afternoon
Öğleden sonra
Oe'leden sonra

Evening
Akşam
Aksham

Night
Gece
Ghedje

Yesterday/Today/Tomorrow
Dün/Bugün/Yarın
Duen/Buguen/Yaren

Numbers

Zero
Sıfır
Saephaer

One
Bir
Beer

Two
Iki
Eki

Three
Üç
Uech

Four
Dört
Doert

Five
Beş
Besh

Six
Altı
Alte

Seven
Yedi
Yedi

Eight
Sekiz
Sekiz

Nine
Dokuz
Dokuz

Ten
On
On

Eleven
On bir
On beer

Twelve
On iki
On eki

Thirteen
On üç
On uech

Fourteen
On dört
On doert

Fifteen
On beş
On besh

Sixteen
On altı
On alte

Seventeen
On yedi
On yedi

Eighteen
On sekiz
On sekiz

Nineteen
On dokuz
On dokuz

Twenty
Yirmi
Yirmi

Twenty-one
Yirmi bir
Yirmi beer

Twenty-two
Yirmi iki
Yirmi eki

Thirty
Otuz
Otuz

Forty
Kırk
Kaerk

Fifty
Elli
Elli

Sixty
Altmış
Altmaesh

Seventy
Yetmiş
Yetmish

Eighty
Seksen
Seksen

Ninety
Doksan
Doksan

One hundred
Yüz
Yuez

Five hundred
Beş yüz
Besh yuez

One thousand
Bin
Been

One million
Bir milyon
Beer million

Time

What time is it?
Saat kaç?
Saat kach?

It is ...
Saat ...
Saat ...

9.00
Dokuz
Dokuz

9.05
Dokuzu beş geçiyor
Dokuzu besh gechiyour

9.15
Dokuzu on beş geçiyor
Dokuzu on besh gechiyour

9.20
Dokuzu yirmi geçiyor
Dokuzu yirmi gechiyour

9.30
Dokuz buçuk
Dokuz buchuk

9.35
Ona yirmi beş var
Ona yirmi besh var

9.40
Ona yirmi var
Ona yirmi var

9.45
Ona çeyrek var
Ona cheyrek var

9.50
Ona on var
Ona on var

9.55
Ona beş var
Ona besh var

12.00/Midday/Midnight
On iki/Öğle üzeri/Gece yarısı
Oneki/Oegle uezeri/Ghedje yarese

Money

I would like to change these traveller's cheques/this currency
Bu seyahat çeklerini/bu parayı bozdurmak istiyorum
Bu sey'ahat cheklerini/bu paray bozdurmak istiyourum

How much commission do you charge (what is the service charge)?
Ne kadar komisyon alıyorsunuz?
Ne kadar komision alaeyoursunuz?

Can I obtain money with my Mastercard?
Master kartla para alabilir miyim?
Mastaer cartla para alabilir miyim?

Where is the nearest ATM?
En yakın ATM nerede?
En yaken ATM neredeh?

My name is ... Some money has been wired to here for me to collect
Ben ... Adıma havale edilen parayı teslim almaya geldim
Ben ... Ah-duhmah how-aleh edee-len paraye tesleem almaya gel-deem

ARRIVING AND DEPARTING

Airport

Excuse me, where is the check-in desk for ... airline?
Afedersiniz, ... havayollarının çekin bürosu neresi acaba?
Afedersiniz, ... havayollarenen checkin buerosu ne'resi adjaba?

What is the boarding gate/time for my flight?
Benim uçağımın biniş kapısı neresi/biniş saati kaç acaba?
Benim ucha'emen binish kapese neresi/binish saati kach adjaba?

How long is the delay likely to be?
Uçağın gecikme süresi ne kadar acaba?
Ucha'en gedjikme sueresi ne kadar adjaba?

Where is the duty-free shop?
Gümrüksüz mal satış yeri neresi acaba?
Guemrueksuez mal satesh yeri ne'resi adjaba?

Which way is the luggage reclaim?
Bavulları alma yeri neresi acaba?
Bavullare alma yeri neresi adjaba?

I have lost my luggage. Please can you help?
Bagajım kayboldu. Yardım edebilir misiniz?
Bagajem kayboldoo. Yaardem ede-bee-leer mee-seeneez?

I am flying to ...
... 'e ('a) uçuyorum
... 'e ('a) oocooyoroom

Where is the bus for the city centre (downtown)?
Kentin merkezine otobüs nereden kalkıyor acaba?
Kentin merkezine otobues nereden kalkeyor adjaba?

Trains and Boats

Where is the ticket office/ information desk?
Bilet gişesi nerede?/ Enformasyon masası nerede?
Bilet gishesi nerede?/ Enformasyon masase nerede?

Which platform does the train/speedboat/ferry to ... depart from?
... 'e ('a) giden tren/motor/ vapur nereden kalkıyor?
... 'e ('a) geeden tren/vapoor nereden kalkeyor?

Where is platform ...?
... peronu nerede?
... peronu nerede?

When is the next train/boat to ...?
... 'e ('a) bir sonraki tren/ motor/vapur ne zaman?
... 'e ('a) beer sonrakee tren/vapoor neh zaman?

Is there a later train/boat to ...?
...'e ('a) daha sonra giden bir tren/vapur var mı?
... 'e (or) 'a daha sonra geeden tren/vapoor var meh?

Notices and Signs

Yemekli vagon
Yemekli vagon
Buffet (Dining) car

Otobüs
Otobeus
Bus

İçilir/İçilmez su
Echilir/Echilmez su
Drinking/Non-drinking water

Giriş
Girish
Entrance

Çıkış
Chekesh
Exit

Hastane
Hastaneh
Hospital

Enformasyon
Enformasyon
Information

Emanet
Emanet
Left luggage (Baggage claim)

Bagaj dolapları
Bagadj dolaplare
Luggage lockers

Postane
Postane
Post office

ARRIVING AND DEPARTING

TURKISH

Peron
Peron
Platform

İstasyon
Istasyon
Railway (Railroad) station

Havaalanı
Hava a'lane
Airport

Karakol
Karakol
Police station

Liman
Liman
Port

Restoran
Restoran
Restaurant

Sigara içilir/içilmez
Sigara echilir/echilmez
Smoking/non-smoking

Telefon
Telephon
Telephone

Bilet gişesi
Beelet ghishese
Ticket office

Çekin bürosu
Checkin buerosu
Check-in desk

Tarife
Tarife
Timetable (Schedule)

Tuvaletler
Tuvaletler
Toilets (Restrooms)

Bayanlar/Erkekler
Baianlar/Erkekler
Ladies/Gentlemen

Metro
Metro
Underground (Subway)

Bekleme odası
Bekleme odase
Waiting room

Buying a Ticket

I would like a first-class/second-class/third-class single (one-way)/return (round-trip) ticket to ...
... e/a birinci/ikinci/üçüncü mevki sadece gidiş/gidiş-geliş bileti istiyorum
... e/a beerindji/ekindji/ewchewndjew mevki sadedje ghedish/ghedish-ghelish beelete estiyourum

Is it an express (fast) train/bus?
Ekspres tren/otobüs mü?
Express tren/oh-toh-bewss mew?

Is my rail pass valid on this train/ferry/bus?
Benim tren pasom bu trende/feribotta/otobüste geçer mi?
Benim teren pasom bu terende/feribotta/otobueste gecher mi?

I would like an aisle/window seat
Pencere/koridor/kenarında bir yer istiyorum
Pendjere/koridoor/kenaraenda beer yer estiyourum

No smoking/smoking, please
Sigara içilmez/sigara içilir, lütfen
Sigara icheler/sigara echelmez, leutphen

We would like to sit together
Yan yana oturmak istiyoruz
Yan yana otoormak estiyouruz

I would like to make a seat reservation
Bir yer ayırtmak istiyorum
Bir yer ayertmak istiyourum

I would like to reserve a couchette/sleeper for one person/two people/my family
Kuşetlide/yataklıda bir kişilik/iki kişilik/ailem için yer ayırtmak istiyorun
Coushetleede/yataklaeda beer kishelik/eki kishelik yer ayeaertmak estiyourum

I would like to reserve a cabin
Bir kabin ayırtmak istiyorum
Bir kabin ayertmak istiyourum

Timetables (Schedules)

Varış
Varash
Arrive

. . . da durur
. . . da durur
Calls (Stops) at...

Lokanta
Lokanta
Catering service

. . . da değiştirin
. . . da de'shtirin
Change at...

Bağlantı/Üzerinden
Ba'lantae/Euzerinden
Connection/Via

Günlük
Geunleuk
Daily

Her 40 dakikada bir
Haer kirk dakekada beer
Every 40 minutes

Birinci mevki
Beerindji mevke
First class

Saatte bir
Sa'atte beer
Hourly

Yer ayırtılması tavsiye edilir
Yer ayertelmase tavsiye edilir
Seat reservations are recommended

İkinci mevki
Ekinci mevki
Second class

Ek ücret ödenir
Ek eudjret eadenir
Supplement payable

Luggage

How much will it cost to send (ship) my luggage in advance?
Bagajımı önceden göndermek kaça mal olur?
Baghadjaemae eandjeden geandermek kacha mal oleur?

Where is the left luggage (baggage claim) office?
Emanet nerede?
Emanet nerede?

What time do you open/close?
Ne zaman açıyorsunuz/kapatıyorsunuz?
Ne zaman achaeyoursunuz/kapataeyoursunuz?

Where are the luggage trolleys (carts)?
Bagaj troleyleri nerede?
Badghadj troleylere nerede?

Where are the lockers?
Kilitli dolaplar nerede acaba?
Kilitli dolaplar neresi adjaba?

I have lost my locker key
Dolap anahtarımı kaybettim
Dolap anahtaraeme kaibettim

On Board

Is this seat free?
Bu yer boş mu?
Bu yer bosh mu?

Excuse me, you are sitting in my reserved seat
Pardon, bana ayrılmış yerde oturuyorsunuz
Pardon, bana airaelmaesh yerde oturuyoursunuz

Which station is this?
Bu hangi istasyon?
Bu hange istasion?

What time is this train/bus/ferry/flight due to arrive/depart?
Bu tren/feribot/uçak saat kaçta gelecek/kalkacak?
Bu teren/feribot/uchak sa't kachta gelecek/kalkadjak?

Travelling with Children

Do you have a high chair/babysitting service/cot?
Bebek için sandalye/çocuk bakım servisi/karyola var mı?
Bebek ichin sandalie/chodjuk bakem servisi/kariola var mae?

Where is the nursery/playroom?
Çocuk yuvası/oyun odası nerede?
Chodjuk yuvase/oyun odase nerede?

Where can I warm the baby's bottle?
Biberonu nerede ısıtabilirim?
Beeberonu nerede aesetabilirim?

Customs and Passports

Pasaportlar, lütfen!
Pasaportlar lewtfen!
Passports, please!

I have nothing/wine/spirits (alcohol)/tobacco to declare

Gümrüğe tabi (hiçbir eşyam yok)/şarap/içki/tütün var
Geumreu'e tabe (hichbir eshiam yok)/sharap/eachki/tuetuen var

I shall be staying for ... days/weeks/months
... gün/hafta/ay kalacağım
... guen/hafta/ai kaladja'em

SIGHTSEEING

Asking the Way

Excuse me, do you speak English?
Afedersiniz, İngilizce biliyor musunuz?
Afedersiniz, engilizdje biliyor musunuz?

Excuse me, can you help me please?
Afedersiniz, sizden bir ricada bulunacaktım?
Afedersiniz, sizden bir ridjada bulunadjaktem?

Where is the Tourist Information Office?
Turist enformasyon bürosu nerede?
Tourist enformasion buerosu nerede?

Excuse me, is this the right way to ...?
Afedersiniz, ... 'e/a/ye/ya buradan mı gidilir?
Afedersiniz, ... 'e/a/ye/ya buradan me gidilir?

... the cathedral/the Tourist Information Office/the castle/ the old town
... Katedral/turist enformasyon bürosu/şato/eski şehir
... Cathedral/tourist enformasyon buerosu/shato/eski shehir

Can you tell me the way to the railway station/bus station/taxi rank/city centre (downtown)/beach?
İstasyona/otobüs terminaline/ taksi durağına/şehir merkezine/plaja nasıl gidilir, söyler misiniz?
Estasyona/otobues terminaline/taxi dura'aena/shehir merkezine/paelad-ja nasael ghidilir, soeyler misiniz?

Birinciden/ikinciden sola/sağa/dosdoğru
Beerindjiden/ikinjiden sola/sah'a dosdo'ru
First/second left/right/ straight ahead

Köşede/trafik lambasında
Koh-shede/trafic lambasendah
At the corner/at the traffic lights

Where is the nearest police station/post office?
En yakın polis karakolu/ postane nerede?
En yakaen polis karakolu/postaine neredeh?

Is it near/far?
Yakın/uzak mı?
Yah-kuhn/oo-zahk meh?

Do I need to take a taxi/ catch a bus?
Taksiye mi/otobüse mi binmem gerekli?
Taxiye me/otobuese me binmem gherekle?

Do you have a map?
Haritanız var mı?
Hah-ree-tah var meh?

Can you point to it on my map?
Haritamın üzerinde gösterebilir misiniz?
Haritamaen uezerinde goesterebilir misiniz?

Thank you for your help
Yardımınız için teşekkür ederim
Yardaemaenaez ichin teshekkuer ederim

How do I reach the motorway/main road?
Otobana/ana yola nasıl çıkabilirim?
Autoba'na/ana yola nasel chekabilirim?

I think I have taken the wrong turning
Galiba yanlış yerden/kavşaktan dönüş yaptım
Ga'liba yanlesh yerden/kavshaktan doenuesh yaptem

I am looking for this address
Şu adresi arıyorum
Shu adresi a'reyourum

I am looking for the ... hotel
... oteli/otelini arıyorum
... oteli/otelini a'reyourum

How far is it to ... from here?
Buradan ... 'e/a/ye/ya mesafe/uzaklık ne kadar?
Buradan ... 'e/a/ye/ya mesa'fe/ uzhaklek ne kadar?

Dosdoğru ... kilometre daha gidin/sürün
Dosdo'ru ... kilometre daha ghidin/sueruen
Carry straight on for ... kilometres

Bundan sonraki sapaktan/dönemeçten sağa/sola dönün/sapın
Bundan sonra'ki sapaktan/doene-mechten sa'a/sola doenuen/sa'pen
Take the next turning on the right/left

Bundan sonraki kavşaktan/trafik ışıklarından sağa/sola sapın
Bundan sonra'ki kavshaktan/traffic eshekla'rendan sa'a/sola sapen
Turn right/left at the next crossroads/traffic lights

Ters yönde gidiyorsunuz
Ters yoende ghidiyoursunuz
You are going in the wrong direction

Where is the cathedral/ church/museum/pharmacy?
Katedral/kilise/müze/eczahane nerede?
Catedral/kilise/mueze/ez-aane nerede?

How much is the admission/ entrance charge?
Giriş ücreti ne kadar?
Gherish eudjreti ne kadar?

Is there a discount for children/students/senior citizens?
Çocuklara/ögrencilere/yaşlılara indirim var mı?
Chodjuklara/eurendjilere/yashlaelara endirim var mae?

What time does the next guided tour start (in English)?
Bundan sonraki kılavuzlu tur ne zaman başlıyor (İngilizce)?
Bundan sonraki khaelavuzlu tour ne zaman bashlaeyour (Inghilizh'dje)?

One/two adults/children, please
Bir/iki büyük/çocuk, lütfen
Beer/eki bueyuek/chodjuk, lewtfen

May I take photographs here?
Burada resim çekebilir miyim?
Burada resim chekebilir miyim?

At the Tourist Office

Do you have a map of the town/area?
Bu kentin/bölgenin haritası var mı?
Bu kentin/boelgenin haritasae var mae?

Do you have a list of accommodation?
Kalacak yerlerin bir listesi var mı?
Kaladjak yerlerin bir listesi var me?

Can I reserve accommodation here?
Burada kalacak yer ayırtabilir miyim?
Beurada kaladjak yer ayaertabeler meyem?

ACCOMMODATION

Hotels

I have a reservation in the name of ...
... adına rezervasyon yaptırmıştım
... adaena rezervasyon yaptaermaeshtaem

I wrote to/faxed/telephoned you last month/last week
Geçen ay/geçen hafta size yazmıştım/faks çekmiştim/ telefon etmiştim
Gechen ay/gechen hafta size yazmeshtem/fax chekmishtim/ telephon etmishtim

Do you have any rooms free?
Hiç boş odanız var mı?
Hich bosh odanez var me?

I would like to reserve a single/double room with/ without a bath/shower.
Bir/iki kişilik banyolu/banyosuz duşlu/duşsuz oda ayırtmak istiyorum
Bir/iki kieshielik banyolu/dushlu banyosuz/dushsuz oda ayaertmak istiyourum

I would like bed/breakfast/ (room and) full board
Sadece kahvaltılı/üç öğün yemekli bir oda istiyorum
Sadedje kahvaltaelae/euch oe'oen yemekli oda istiyourum

How much is it per night?
Gecesi kaça?
Ghedjesi kacha?

Is breakfast included?
Kahvaltı dahil mı?
Kahvaltae dahil me?

Do you have any cheaper rooms?
Daha ucuz odalarınız var mı?
Daha oodjuz odalaraenaez var me?

I would like to see/take the room
Odayı görmek/tutmak istiyorum
Odahye gohr-mek ees-tee-yoroom

I would like to stay for ... nights
... gece kalmak istiyorum
... gedje kalmak istiyourum

The shower/light/tap doesn't work
Duş/elektrik/musluk bozuk galiba
Dush/electric/musluk bozuk ga'liba

At what time/where is breakfast served?
Kahvaltı servisi nerede/ne zaman?
Kahvaltee servisi nerede/ne zaman?

What time do I have to check out?
Saat kaçta ayrılmam lazım?
Sa'at kachta ayraelmam lazaem?

Can I have the key to room number ...?
... numaralı odanın anahtarını rica ediyorum
... numarale odanen anakhtarene ridja ediyourum

My room number is ...
Oda numaram ...
Oda numaram ...

My room is not satisfactory/ not clean enough/too noisy. Please can I change rooms?
Odam uygun değil/yeterince temiz değil/çok gürültülü
Odamı değiştirebilir miyim?
O-dam uigoon deh-yeel/yet-ereenjeh temeez deh-yeel/chok gew-rewl-tew-lew. O-dame de-eesh-tee-re-bee-leer-meeyeem?

Where is the bathroom?
Banyo nerede lütfen?
Banyo nehredeh lewt-fen

Do you have a safe for valuables?
Değerli eşya kasanız var mı?
Deh-erlee eshya kasanez var meh?

Is there a laundry/do you wash clothes?
Çamaşırhane var mı/Çamaşır yıkama hizmetiniz var mı?
Chamasherhaneh var meh/Chamasher yikama heezmet-eeneez var meh?

I would like an air-conditioned room
Klimalı bir oda istiyorum
Klee-male beer o-da ees-tee-yoroom

Do you accept traveller's cheques/credit cards?
Seyahat çeki/kredi kartı kabul ediyor musunuz?
Seyahat cheki/kredi karte kabul ediyor musunuz?

May I have the bill please?
Hesap, lütfen?
Hesap, lewtfen?

Excuse me, I think there may be a mistake in this bill
Afedersiniz, bu hesapta bir yanlışlık var galiba
Afedersiniz, bu hesapta bir yanleshlek var ga'liba

Youth Hostels

How much is a dormitory bed per night?
Bir gecelik yatakhane ücreti ne kadar?
Beer ghedjelik yatakhane uedjreti ne kadar?

I am/am not an HI member
Uluslararası Gençlik Hostelleri Birliği üyesiyim/üyesi değilim
Euluslararasae Ghenchlik Hostelleri Beerli'e ueyesiim/ueyesi deelim

May I use my own sleeping bag?
Kendi uyku tulumumu kullanabilir miyim?
Kendi uyku tulumumu kullanabilir miyim?

What time do you lock the doors at night?
Gece kapıları kaçta kilitliyorunuz?
Ghedje kapaelarae kachta kilitliyoursunuz?

Camping

May I camp for the night/ two nights?
Burada bu gece/iki gece kamp yapabilir miyim?
Burada bu ghedje/eki ghedje kamp yapabilir miyim?

Where can I pitch my tent?
Çadırımı nereye kurabilirim?
Chadaeraemae nereye kurabilirim?

How much does it cost for one night/week?
Bir geceliği/bir haftalığı kaça?
Beer ghedjeli'e/beer haftalae'e kacha?

Where are the washing facilities?
Yıkanma yerleri nerede?
Yaekanma yerleri nerede?

Is there a restaurant/ supermarket/swimming pool on site/nearby?
Burada/yakında bir restoran/ çarşı/yüzme havuzu var mı?
Burada/yakaenda bir restoran, charshae/yuezme havuzu var mae?

Do you have a safety deposit box?
Kıymetli eşya için kasanız var mı?
Kaeymetli eshia eachin kasanaez var mae?

EATING AND DRINKING

Cafés and Bars

I would like a cup of/two cups of/another coffee/tea
Bir fincan/iki fincan/bir fincan daha kahve/çay istiyorum
Beer findjan/eki findjan/beer findjan daha kahve/chai istiyourum

With milk/sugar
Sütlü/şekerli
Suetlue/shekerli

Without milk/sugar
Sütsüz/şekersiz
Suetsuez/shekersiz

I would like a bottle/glass/ two glasses of mineral water/ red wine/white wine, please
Bir şişe/bardak/iki şişe maden suyu/kırmızı şarap/beyaz şarap lütfen
Beer shishe/bardak/eki shishe maden suyu/kaermaezae sharap/beyaz sharap lewtfen

I would like a beer/two beers, please
Bir bira/iki bira lütfen
Beer beera/eki beera lewtfen

Please may I have some ice?
Biraz buz alabilir miyim?
Biraz buz alabilir miyim?

Do you have any matches/ cigarettes/cigars?
Kibritiniz/sigaranız/puronuz var mı?
Kibritiniz/sigaranaez/pueronuz var me?

Restaurants

Can you recommend a good/ cheap restaurant in this area?
Bu bölgede iyi/ucuz restoran tavsiye eder misiniz?
Bu boelgede eyi/ujuz restoran tavsiye eder misiniz?

I would like a table for ... people
... kişilik bir masa istiyorum
... kishilik beer masa istiyourum

Do you have a non-smoking area?
Sigara içilmeyen bir yeriniz var mı?
Sighara ichilmeyen bir yeriniz var me?

Waiter/Waitress!
Garson!
Garson!

Excuse me, please may we order?
Afedersiniz, ısmarlamak istiyorum, lütfen
Afedersiniz, asmarlamak istiyourum, lewtfen

Do you have a set menu/ children's menu/wine list ... in English?
İngilizce olarak yemek listesi/ çocuklar için yemek listesi/ şarap listesi var mı?
Eengilizje olarak yemek listesi/ chodjuklar ichin yemek listesi/ sharap listesi var mae?

Do you have any vegetarian dishes?
Etsiz yemekleriniz var mı?
Etsiz yemekleriniz var mae?

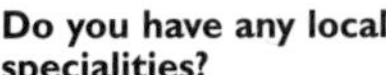

Do you have any local specialities?
Bu bölgeye has yemekler var mı?
Bu boelgheye has yemekler var me?

Are vegetables included?
Garnitür de dahil mi?
Garnituer de dahil mi?

Could I have it well-cooked/medium/rare please?
İyice kızartılmış/normal/az pişmiş olsun lütfen?
Iyidje kezartelmesh/normal/az pishmish olsun lewtfen?

What does this dish consist of?
Bu yemeğin içinde neler var?
Bu yeme'en ichinde neler var?

I am a vegetarian. Does this contain meat?
Ben vejeteryenım. Bu yiyecek et içeriyor mu?
Ben vejeteryen-aem. Boo yee-yecek et ee-cher-ee-yormoo?

I do not eat nuts/dairy products/meat/fish
Fındık-fıstık/süt ürünleri/et/balık yemiyorum
Fendek-festek/sewt ew-rewn-leree/et/balehk yemee-yoroom

Not (very) spicy, please
Lütfen (çok) acılı olmasın
Lewtfen (chok) ajeleh olmasen

I would like the set menu, please
Tabldot lütfen
Tabldot lewtfen

We have not been served yet
Bize hala servis yapılmadı
Bize hala servis yapaelmadae

Please bring a plate/knife/fork
Bir tabak/bıçak/çatal alabilir miyim
Beer tabakh/bechakh/chatal ala-bee-leer-meyeem

Excuse me, this is not what I ordered
Afedersiniz, benim ısmarladığım bu değildi
Afedersiniz, benim esmarlade'em bu de'ildi

May I have some/more bread/water/coffee/tea?
Biraz/biraz daha ekmek/su/kahve/çay verir misiniz?
Beeraz/beeraz daha ekmek/su/kahve/chai verir misiniz?

May I have the bill, please?
Hesap, lütfen?
Hesap, lewtfen?

Does this bill include service?
Servis bu hesaba dahil mi?
Servis bu hesaba dahil mi?

Do you accept traveller's cheques/Mastercard/US dollars?
Seyahat çeki/Mastırkart/Amerikan doları alıyor musunuz?
Seyahat cheki/mastercart/american dolarae alaeyour musunuz?

Can I have a receipt, please?
Bir makbuz rica etsem?
Bir makbuz ridja etsem?

TURKISH

Where is the toilet (restroom), please?
Tuvalet nerede acaba?
Tuvalet nerede adjaba?

On the Menu

Kahvaltı/öğle yemeği/akşam yemeği
Kahvalte/Ew-leh yeme-ee/Aksham yeme-ee
Breakfast/Lunch/Dinner

Aperitifler *Aperitifler* **First courses**	Çorbalar *Chorbalar* **Soups**
Ana yemekler *An'a yemekler* **Main courses**	Balık yemekleri *Balek yemekleri* **Fish dishes**
Et yemekleri *Et yemekleri* **Meat dishes**	Sığır eti *Se-er etee* **Beef**
Bonfile *Bonfeeleh* **Steak**	Domuz eti *Domooz etee* **Pork**
Dana eti *Danah etee* **Veal**	Tavuk *Tavook* **Chicken**
Kuzu *Koozoo* **Lamb**	Jambon *Zhahmbon* **Ham**

Sebze yemekleri
Sebze yemekleri
Vegetarian dishes

Sebze
Sebzeh
Vegetables

Kızarmış patates
Ke-zarmesh patates
Chips (french fries)

Patates haşlaması/sotesi/püresi
Patates hashlamase/sotesee/pew-reh-see
Boiled/sauté/mashed potatoes

Pilav *Peelav* **Rice**	Peynir *Peynir* **Cheese**
Tatlılar *Tatlelar* **Desserts**	Dondurma *Dondurma* **Ice cream**
Kek *Kehk* **Cakes**	Hamur işi *Hamoor eeshee* **Pastries**
Meyve *Meyveh* **Fruit**	Ekmek *Ekmek* **Bread**

Küçük ekmek
Kew-chewk ekmek
Rolls

Tost ekmeği *Tost ekme-ee* **Toast**	Tereyağı *Tere-yahe* **Butter**
Tuz/biber *Tooz/beeber* **Salt/pepper**	Şeker *Sheker* **Sugar**

Buraya özgü yemekler
Buraya oezgue yemekler
Specialities

Yerel yemekler
Yerel yehmek-ler
Local specialities

Fiks mönü
Fix mohnew
Set menu

Şarap listesi
Sharap listesee
Wine list

Kırmızı şaraplar
Kehrmeze sharap-lar
Red wines

Beyaz şaraplar
Behyaz sharap-lar
White wines

Roze şaraplar
Rozeh sharap-lar
Rosé wines

Köpüklü şaraplar
Koh-pewk-lew sharap-lar
Sparkling wines

Bira
Beerra
Beer

Şişede bira/arjantin bira
Sheeshedeh beerra/arjanteen beerra
Bottled beer/draught (draft) beer

Alkolsüz içecekler
Alkol-sews iche-jek-ler
Non-alcoholic drinks

Maden suyu
Mahden sooyoo
Mineral water

Meyve suları
Meyveh soolahre
Fruit juices

Portakal suyu
Portahkal sooyoo
Orange juice

Limonata
Leemonatah
Lemonade

Buz
Booz
Ice

Sütlü kahve/sütsüz kahve/espresso
Sewt-lew kahve/sewt-sewz kahve/espresso
White coffee/black coffee/espresso coffee

Sütlü/limonlu çay
Sewt-lew/leemenloo chai
Tea with milk/with lemon

Kokoa
Cocoa
Chocolate (drink)

Süt
Sewt
Milk

Hafif yiyecekler
Hafeef yeeye-jek-ler
Snacks/Light meals

Salatalar
Salata-lar
Salads

Sandviçler
Sandwich-ler
Sandwiches

Yumurta
Yoomoortah
Eggs

Sosis
Sossiss
Sausage

Katı/sahanda/çırpılmış yumurta
Kahte/sahandah/cherpel-mesh yoomoortah
Boiled/fried/scrambled eggs

TURKISH

Typical Local Dishes

Dügün çorbası
Dewgewn chorbahser
Meat soup with egg yolks

Börek
Ber-rek
Small savoury pastries as appetisers

Çerkes tavuğu
Chehrkesss tahvooyoo
Cold chicken in walnut purée

İmam bayıldı
Eemam bahyerlder
Salad of aubergine with olive oil, tomatoes and onions

Çiğ köfte
Cheey kerfteh
Spicy meatballs

Baklava
Bahklahvah
Flaky pastry stuffed with nuts and honey

GETTING AROUND

Public Transport

Where is the bus stop/coach station/nearest metro (subway) station?
Otobüs durağı/Otobüs terminali/En yakın metro istasyonu nerede?
Otobues dura'ae/Otobues terminali/ En yakaen metro istasionu nerede?

When is the next/last bus to ...?
... e/a bundan sonraki otobüs ne zaman?
... e/a bundan sonrakee otobues ne zaman?

How much is the fare to the city centre (downtown)/ railway (railroad) station/ airport?
Şehir merkezine/Tren istasyonuna/Havaalanına bilet kaça?
Shehir merkezine/Tren istasionuna/ Hava-alanaena bilet kacha?

Will you tell me when to get off?
Ne zaman ineceğimi söyler misiniz?
Ne zaman enedje'emi soeyler misiniz?

Does this bus go to ...?
Bu otobüs ... a/e gidiyor mu?
Bu otobues ... a/e gidiyour mu?

Which number bus goes to ...?
... ya/ye kaç numaralı otobüs gidiyor?
... ye/ya kach numaralae otobues gidiyour?

May I have a single (one-way)/return (round-trip)/day ticket/book of tickets?
Gidiş/gidiş-geliş/günlük/koçan halinde bilet istiyorum?
Gidish/gidish-gelish/guenleuk/kochan halinde bilet istiyourum?

Taxis (Taksi)

I would like to go to ... how much will it cost?
... a/e gitmek istiyorum kaç para tutar?
... a/e ghitmek istiyourum kach para tutar?

Please may I stop here?
Burada durur musunuz?
Burada durur musunuz?

I would like to order a taxi today/tomorrow/at 2pm to go from ... to ...
Bugün/Yarın öğleden sonra saat 2'ye ... den/dan ... e/a taksi ısmarlamak istiyorum
Buguen/Yaraen oe'leden sonra sa'at ikiye ... den/dan ... e/a taxi aesmarlamak istiyourum

Entertainment

Can you recommend a good bar/nightclub?
İyi bir bar/gece kulübü tavsiye edebilir misiniz?
Eyi bir bar/gedje kuluebue tavsiye edebilir misiniz?

Do you know what is on at the cinema (playing at the movies)/theatre at the moment?
Şu anda sinemada/tiyatroda ne oynuyor?
Shu anda sinemada/teyatroda ne oynuyor?

I would like to book (purchase) ... tickets for the matinee/evening performance on Monday
Pazartesi günü öğle seansı/akşam için ... bilet ayırtmak istiyorum
Pazartesi guenue oe'le seansae/aksham ichin ... bilet ayaertmak istiyourum

What time does the film/performance start?
Film/Gösteri kaçta başlıyor?
Film/Goesteri kachta bashley our?

COMMUNICATIONS

Post

How much will it cost to send a letter/postcard/this package to Britain/Ireland/America/Canada/Australia/New Zealand?
İngiltere'ye/İrlanda'ya/Amerika'ya/Kanada'ya/Avustralya'ya/Yeni Zelanda'ya mektup/kartpostal/bu paket kaça gider?
Inghiltere'ye/Erlanda'ya/Amerika'ya/Kanada'ya/Avustralia'ya/Yeni Zelanda'ya mektup/cartpostal/bu paket kacha geder?

I would like one stamp/two stamps
Bir pul/İki pul istiyorum
Bir pul/Eki pul istiyourum

I'd like ... stamps for postcards to send abroad, please
Yurt dışına kartpostal göndermek için ... pul rica ediyorum
Yurt deshena kartpostal goendermek ichin ... pul ridja ediyourum

Phones

I would like to make a telephone call/reverse the charges to (make a collect call to) ...
Telefon etmek/Ödemeli olarak telefon etmek istiyorum
Telephon etmek/Erdemeli olarak telephon etmek istiyourum

Which coins do I need for the telephone?
Telefon için hangi parayı kullanmam lazım?
Telephon ichin hangi parayae kullanmam lazaem?

The line is engaged (busy)
Hat meşgul
Hat meshgul

The number is ...
Numara ...
Numara ...

Hello, this is ...
Alo, ben ...
Alo, ben ...

Please may I speak to ...?
... 'i/ı/yi/yı rica edecektim
... 'i/e/yi/ye ridja ededjektim

He/she is not in at the moment. Can you call back?
Kendisi şimdi burada değil. Daha sonra arar mısınız?
Kendisi shimdi burada de'il. Daha sonra arar mesenez?

SHOPPING

Shops

Kitapçı/Kırtasiyeci
Kitapche/Kertasiyedji
Bookshop/Stationery

Mücevheratçı/Hediyelik eşya
Muedjevheratche/Hediyelik eshya
Jeweller/Gifts

Ayakkabılar/Ayakkabı
Ayakka'belar/Ayakka'be
Shoes

Hırdavat
Herdavat
Hardware

Erkek berberi/Kadın berberi
Erkek berberi/Kaden berberi
Hairdresser (men's)/(women's)

Hamur işleri/Fırın
Hamur ishleri/Feren
Baker

Süpermarket
Suepermarket
Supermarket

Fotoğrafçı
Photo'rafche
Photo shop

Seyahat Acentası
Seyahat Adjenta'se
Travel agent

Eczahane
Ez-aane
Pharmacy

TURKISH

In the Shops

What time do the shops open/close?
Dükkanlar ne zaman açılır/kapanır?
Duekkanlar ne zaman acheler/kapanaer?

Where is the nearest market?
En yakın alışveriş merkezi/pazar neresi?
En yaken aleshverish merkedzi/padzar neresi?

Can you show me the one in the window/this one?
Vitrindekini/Bunu görmek istiyorum?
Vitrindekini/Bunu goermek istiyourum?

Can I try this on?
Bunu prova edebilir miyim?
Bunu prova edebilir miim?

What size is this?
Bunun numarası kaç?
Bunun numarase kach?

This is too large/too small/ too expensive
Bu çok büyük/çok küçük/çok pahalı
Bu chok bueyuek/chok kuechuek/chok paha'le

Do you have any others?
Başka çeşitleriniz de var mı?
Bashka cheshitleriniz de var me?

My size is ...
Benim ölçüm ...
Benim oelchuem ...

Where is the changing room/ children's/cosmetic/ ladieswear/menswear/food department?
Giyinme odaları/çocuk/ kozmetik eşya/bayan giysileri/erkek giysileri/yiyecek bölümü nerede?
Giyinme odalarae/chodjuk/kozmetik eshia/bayan giysileri/erkek giysileri/yiyedjek boeluemue nerede?

I would like a quarter kilo /half a kilo/a kilo of bread/ butter/cheese/ham/tomatoes
Ikiyüzelli gram/yarım kilo/bir kilo ekmek/tereyağ/peynir/ jambon/domates istiyorum
Ekiyuezelli gram/yarem kilo/bir kilo ekmek/tereya' peinir/djambon/ domates estiyourum

How much is this?
Kaça?
Kacha?

I'll take this one, thank you
Bunu alacağım, teşekkür ederim
Bunu aladja'em, teshekkuer ederim

Do you have a carrier (shopping) bag?
Plastik torbanız var mı?
Plastic torbanez var me?

Do you have anything cheaper/larger/smaller/of better quality?
Daha ucuz/büyük/küçük/iyi kalite bir şeyiniz var mı?
Daha eudjuz/bueyuek/kuechuek/eyi kalite bir sheyiniz var mi?

I would like a film for this camera
Bu makineye bir film istiyorum
Bu makineye bir film istiyourum

I would like some batteries, the same size as this old one
Bunlarla aynı büyüklükte yeni pil istiyorum
Bunlarla ayne bueyuekluekte peel istiyourum

Would you mind wrapping this for me, please?
Lütfen bunu sarar mısınız?
Lewtfen bunu sarar mesenez?

Sorry, but you seem to have given me the wrong change
Kusura bakmayın ama paranın üstünü yanlış verdiniz
Kusura baknayen ama paranen uestuenue yanlesh verdiniz

MOTORING

Car Hire (Rental)

I have ordered (rented) a car in the name of ...
... adına araba ısmarladım (kiraladım)
... adaena araba aesmarladaem (kiraladum)

How much does it cost to hire (rent) a car for one day/two days/a week?
Bir günlük/iki günlük/bir haftalık araba kiralama ücreti ne kadar?
Beer guenluek/eki guenluek/beer haftalaek araba kiralama eudjreti ne kadar?

Is the tank already full of petrol (gas)?
Benzin deposu dolu mu?
Benzin deposu dolu mu?

Is insurance and tax included? How much is the deposit?
Sigorta ve vergi dahil mi? Depozit ne kadar?
Sigorta ve verghi dahil me? Depozit ne kadar?

By what time must I return the car?
Arabayı ne zamana kadar geri getirmem lazım?
Arabayae ne zamana kadar geri ghetirmem lazaem?

I would like a small/large family/sports car with a radio/cassette player
Radyolu/teypli küçük bir araba/aile arabası istiyorum
Radiolu/teipli kuechuk beer araba/aile arabasae istiyourum

Do you have a road map of this area?
Sizde bu yörenin yol haritası var mı?
Sizde bu yoerenin yol harita'se var me?

Parking

How long can I park here?
Burada ne kadar süreyle/kaç saat park edebilirim?
Burada ne kadar suereyle/kach sa't park edebilirim?

Is there a car park near here?
Yakınlarda bir otopark var mı?
Yakenlarda bir autopark var me?

At what time does this car park close?
Bu otopark saat kaçta kapanıyor?
Bu autopark sa't kachta kapa'neyor?

Signs and Notices

Tek yön
Tek yoen
One way

Girilmez/Girmek yasaktır
Ghirilmez/Girmek yasakter
No entry

Park yapılmaz/Park etmek yasaktır
Park yapelmaz/Park etmek yasakter
No parking

Zorunlu sapış
Zhorunlu sapesh
Detour (diversion)

Dur!
Dur!
Stop!

Yol ver
Yol ver
Give way (yield)

Kaygan yol
Kayghan yol
Slippery road

Sollama yapılmaz
Sol'lama yapelmez
No overtaking

Tehlike!
Tehlee-ke!
Danger!

At the Filling Station (Benzin istasyonu)

Unleaded (lead-free)/ standard/premium/diesel
Kurşunsuz/normal/süper/dizel
Kurshunsuz/normal/sueper/deezel

Fill the tank please
Depoyu doldurun lütfen
Depoyu doldurun lewtfen

Do you have a road map of this area?
Sizde bu yörenin yol haritası var mı?
Sizde bu yoerenin yol harita'se var me?

How much is the car wash?
Araba kaça yıkanıyor?
Araba kacha yeka'neyor?

Breakdowns

I've had a breakdown at ...
... 'de/da arabam bozuldu
... 'de/da arabam bozhuldu

I am a member of the ... [motoring organisation]
... üyesiyim
... ewye-see-yem

I am on the road from ... to ...
... 'den/dan ... 'e/a/ye/ya giden yol üzerindeyim
... 'den/dan ... 'e/a/ye/ya ghiden yol uezerindeyim

I can't move the car. Can you send a tow-truck?
Arabayı çekemiyorum. Bir çekme aracı gönderebilir misiniz?
Arabaye che'kemiyourum. Bir chekme aradje goenderebilir misiniz?

I have a flat tyre
Lastiğim patladı
Lasti'im patla'de

The windscreen (windshield) has smashed/cracked
Ön cam kırıldı/çatladı
Oen djam ke'relde/chatla'de

There is something wrong with the engine/brakes/ lights/steering/gearbox/ clutch/exhaust
Motorda/frenlerde/ışıklarda/ direksiyonda/vites kutusunda/ debriyajda/egzosta bir arıza var galiba
Motorda/frenlerde/esheklerde/ direxiyonda/vites kutusunda/ debriyazhda/eghzosta bir areza var ga'liba

It's overheating
Motor fazla ısınmış/su kaynatıyor
Motor fazla esenmesh/su kana'teyo

It won't start
Araba çalışmıyor/Marş basmıyor
Araba chaleshmeyor/Marsh bameyo

Where can I get it repaired?
Nerede tamir ettirebilirim?
Ne're'de tamir etti'rebilirim?

Can you take me there?
Beni oraya götürebilir misiniz?
Beni oraya goetuerebilir misiniz?

Will it take long to fix?
Tamiri/takması uzun sürer mi?
Tamiri/takma'se uzhun suerer mi?

How much will it cost?
Kaça çıkar/malolur?
Kacha chekar/malolur?

Please can you pick me up/give me a lift?
Beni alabilir misiniz/götürebilir misiniz?
Benee alabee-leer-mee-seenez/goh-tewre-bee-leer-mee-seenez?

Accidents and Traffic Offences (Violations)

Can you help me? There has been an accident
Bir kaza oldu. Bana yardım edebilir misiniz?
Bir kazha oldu. Bana yardem e'de-bilir misiniz?

Please call the police/an ambulance
Lütfen polisi/bir ambulans çağırın
Lewtfen polisi/bir ambulans cha'eren

Is anyone hurt?
Yaralı var mı?
Yara'le var me?

I'm sorry, I didn't see the sign
Özür dilerim, işareti görmedim
Oezuer dilerim, isha'reti goermedim

Must I pay a fine? How much?
Para cezası mı ödemem gerekiyor? Kaç para?
Para djeza'se me oedemem ghe'rekiyor? Kach para?

Ehliyetinizi/Belgelerinizi gösterin
Ehliyetinizhi/Belghe'lerinizhi goesterin
Show me your documents

HEALTH

Pharmacy (Eczahane)

Do you have anything for a stomach ache/headache/sore throat/toothache?
Mide/baş ağrısı/boğaz ağrısı/diş ağrısı için bir ilacınız var mı?
Mee'de/bash a'raesae/bo'az a'raesae/dish a'raesae ichin bir eladjaenaez var mae?

I need something for diarrhoea/constipation/a cold/a cough/insect bites/sunburn/travel (motion) sickness
İshal/Kabızlık/Soğuk algınlığı/Öksürük/Böcek ısırması/Günes yanığı/Otobüs tutması için bir şey istiyorum
Eshaal/Kabaezlaek/So'uk algaenlae'ae/Oeksueruek/Boedjek aesaermasae/Guenesh yanae'ae/Otobues tutmasae ichin bir shei estiyourum

How much/how many do I take?
Ne kadar/kaç tane alayım?
Ne kadar/Kach tane alayeem?

How often do I take it/them?
Ne kadar aralıklarla alayım?
Ne kadar aralaeklarla alayeem?

I am/he is/she is taking this medication
Ben/o/o bu ilaçları alıyorum/alıyor
Ben/o/o bu ilachla're a'leyourum

How much does it cost?
Kaç para?
Kach para?

Can you recommend a good doctor/dentist?
Iyi bir doktor/dişçi tavsiye edebilir misiniz?
Eyi bir doktor/dishchi tavsiye edebilir misiniz?

Is it suitable for children?
Çocuklara uygun mu?
Chodjuklara uygun mu?

Doctor (Doktor)

I have a pain here/in my arm/leg/chest/stomach
Şuram/Kolum/Ayağım/Göğsüm/Karnım ağırıyor
Shuram/Kolum/Aya'aem/Goe'suem/Karnaem a'raeyour

HEALTH

TURKISH

Please call a doctor, this is an emergency!
Lütfen doktor çağırın, acil bir vak'a!
Lewtfen doktor cha'raen, adjil beer vak'a!

I would like to make an appointment to see the doctor
Doktoru görmek için randevu almak istiyorum
Doctoru goermek ichin randevu almak estiyourum

I am diabetic/pregnant
Şeker hastasıyım/hamileyim
Sheker hastasaeyaem/hamileyim

I need a prescription for ...
... için reçete istiyorum
... ichin rechete estiyourum

Can you give me something to ease the pain?
Ağrıyı azaltacak bir şey verebilir misiniz?
A'raeyae azaltadjak bershey verebilir misiniz?

I am/he is/she is allergic to penicillin
Benim/Onun/Onun penisiline karşı alerjim/alerjisi var
Benim/Onun/Onun penicillin'e karshe allergim/allergisi var

Acıtıyor mu?
Adje'teyor mu?
Does this hurt?

Hastaneye gitmelisiniz/gitmeli
Hasta'neye ghitmelisiniz/ghitmeli
You must/he must/she must go to hospital

Bundan günde bir/iki/üç kere alın
Bundan guende bir/iki/uech ke're a'len
Take these once/twice/three times a day

I am/he is/she is taking this medication
Ben/O/O bu ilaçları alıyorum/alıyor
Ben/O/O bu ilachla're a'leyourum/aleyour

I have medical insurance
Sağlık sigortam var
Sa'lek sighortam var

Dentist (Dişçi)

I have toothache
Dişim ağrıyor
Dishim a'raeyour

My filling has come out
Dolgum düştü
Dolgum dueshtue

I do/do not want to have an injection first
Önceden iğne istiyorum/istemiyorum.
Oendjeden e'ne estiyourum/estemiyourum

EMERGENCIES

Help!
Imdat!/Yardım!
Imdat/Yardaem!

Fire!
Yangın!
Yanghen!

Stop!
Dur!
Door!

Call an ambulance/a doctor/ the police/the fire brigade!
Ambulans/Doktor/Polis/ İtfaiyeyi çağırın!
Ambulance/Doctor/Polees/ Itfaa-ye chaaren!

Please may I use a telephone?
Telefonu kullanabilir miyim?
Telefo-noo kool-lana-bee-leer-mee-yeem?

I have had my traveller's cheques/credit cards/ handbag/rucksack/luggage/ wallet/passport/mobile phone stolen
Seyahat çeklerim/kredi kartlarım/el çantam/ sırt çantam/bagajım/ cüzdanım/pasaportum/ cep telefonum çalındı
Sey'ahat cheklerim/credi cartlarem/ el chantam/saert chantam/ bagadjem/djuezdanem/ passaportoom/jep telefonoom chalendae

May I please have a copy of the report for my insurance claim?
Sigortam için raporun bir kopyasını alabilir miyim lütfen?
Seegore-tam eechen raporoon beer kopyasene ala-bee-leer-meyeem lewtfen?

Can you help me, I have lost my daughter/son/my companion(s)?
Bana yardım eder misiniz, kızımı/oğlumu/arkadaş(lar)ımı kaybettim?
Bana yardem eder misiniz, kezeme/o'lumu/arkadash(lar)ermer kaybetteem?

Please go away/leave me alone
Lütfen gidin/beni yalnız bırakın
Lewtfen ghidin/beni yalnaez baeraken

I'm sorry
Pardon
Pahr-dohn

I want to contact the British/ American/Canadian/Irish/ Australian/New Zealand/ South African consulate
İngiliz/Amerikan/Kanada/ İrlanda/Avustralya/Yeni Zelanda/Güney Afrika konsolosluğuyla görüşmek istiyorum
Inghilizh/Amerikan/Kanada/Irlanda/ Yeni Zhelanda/Gueney Afrika konsoloslu'yla goerueshmek istiyourum

I'm ill/lost/injured
Ben hastayım/kayboldum/ yaralıyım
Ben hastayehm/kayboldoom/ yaraleyem

We're ill/lost/injured
Biz hastayız/kaybolduk/
yaralıyız
Beez hastayez/kayboldook/
yaraleyez

He is/she is ill/lost/injured
O hasta/kayboldu/yaralı
Oh hastah/kayboldoo/yarale

They are ill/lost/injured
Onlar hastalar/kayboldular/
yaralılar
Ohn-lar hastah-lar/kayboldoo-lar/
yarale-lar